Stability, Growth and Sustainability

Stability, Growth and Sustainability

Catalysts for Socio-economic Development in Brunei Darussalam

Edited by

Aris Ananta • Chang-Yau Hoon • Mahani Hamdan

First published in Singapore in 2023 by
ISEAS Publishing
30 Heng Mui Keng Terrace
Singapore 119614

E-mail: publish@iseas.edu.sg
Website: <http://bookshop.iseas.edu.sg>

The responsibility for facts and opinions in this publication rests exclusively with the authors and their interpretations do not necessarily reflect the views or the policy of the publisher or its supporters.

ISEAS Library Cataloguing-in-Publication Data

Name(s): Ananta, Aris, editor. | Hoon, Chang-Yau, editor. | Mahani Hamdan, editor.
Title: Stability, growth and sustainability : catalysts for socio-economic development in Brunei Darussalam / edited by Aris Ananta, Chang-Yau Hoon and Mahani Hamdan.
Description: Singapore : ISEAS-Yusof Ishak Institute, 2023. | Includes index.
Identifiers: ISBN 978-981-5011-68-5 (soft cover) | ISBN 978-981-5011-69-2 (e-book PDF) | 978-981-5011-70-8 (epub)
Subjects: LCSH: Brunei—Economic conditions. | Brunei—Social conditions.
Classification: LCC HC445.85 S77

Cover photo reproduced with kind permission of Liew Chee Shang
Cover design by Lee Meng Hui
Index compiled by Sheryl Sin Bing Peng
Typesetting by International Typesetters Pte Ltd
Printed in Singapore by Mainland Press Ptd Ltd

CONTENTS

PART III:
HUMAN CAPITAL

PART IV:
BUSINESS, ECONOMY AND WELFARE

LIST OF TABLES

LIST OF FIGURES

PREFACE

This book is an attempt to understand socio-economic development in contemporary Brunei Darussalam, which highlights the country's journey in diversification from the dominant oil and gas sectors. The book makes an important contribution to the handful of publications on Brunei and fills in the absence of a comprehensive analysis on socio-economic issues in Brunei.

The publication of this book comes at an important era of the twenty-first century, as Brunei is on its halfway mark towards its Vision 2035. The goal of economic diversification remains vital to Brunei's long-term economic growth but, at the same time, is dramatically shifting toward a more varied structure of production and trade with a view to creating jobs, increasing productivity, and improving the resource efficiency of infrastructure and quality of life.

This is a reference book for students, academics, entrepreneurs, policymakers within and outside Brunei, as well as for general readers who are interested to know about the socio-economic conditions in contemporary Brunei.

The book is a product of the Centre for Advanced Research (CARe), under the leadership of former Director Dr Chang-Yau Hoon; in collaboration with the Institute of Policy Studies, under the leadership of Director Dr Mahani Hamdan; and with the support of colleagues from various faculties at Universiti Brunei Darussalam. As a premier empirical research centre at UBD, CARe has three missions: first is to develop research and data resources that address social issues in Brunei. Second is to be a platform for local and international interdisciplinary research collaboration. And third is to provide professional training to graduate students, university staff and researchers from various sectors. This book is a collective effort to address these missions at CARe.

This book would have never been possible without the strong dedication of the authors and conducive research environment provided by Universiti Brunei Darussalam. We are indebted to the unflagging support of the Vice Chancellor of UBD, Dr Hazri bin Haji Kifle; and the current Director of CARe, Dr Siti Mazidah binti Haji Mohamad. We would like to express our appreciation to the editorial team at ISEAS Publishing for providing us with constructive comments on the draft of the book and their willingness to co-publish it with UBD. Our thanks also go to Pranika Lama, our copy editor, and to Muhammad Amirrudin Ismail, our research assistant, who worked tirelessly in helping us to prepare the manuscript for publication. We are grateful for the grant [UBD/RSCH/1.21.3(b)/2020/1.3.2.3.1(R)] provided by Universiti Brunei Darussalam that has generously funded this book project.

Aris Ananta, Chang-Yau Hoon and Mahani Hamdan
Bandar Seri Begawan
August 2021

ABOUT THE CONTRIBUTORS

Adeline Yuen Sze Goh is a Senior Assistant Professor at Sultan Hassanal Bolkiah Institute of Education, Universiti Brunei Darussalam. She completed her PhD at the Institute of Lifelong Learning, University of Leeds. She was previously appointed as an Honorary Research Fellow at Birkbeck, University of London and was an Associate Research Fellow at Centre on Skills, Knowledge and Organisational Performance (SKOPE), Department of Education, University of Oxford, UK. Her background as an adult educator has entailed engagement with professionals in education, healthcare and other professional sectors. She has been involved in projects such as regional TVET teacher standards for ASEAN, TVET teacher training programmes in the Asia-Pacific region with UNESCO Bangkok and SEAMEO-VOCTECH. She was the lead consultant for the project: Systems Approach for Better Education Results: Workforce Development with the World Bank Organization. Her current research interests focus on workplace learning, such as examining the learning practices of professionals in their workplace.

Aris Ananta is an economist-demographer, currently Professor at the Faculty of Economics and Business, Universitas Indonesia and Visiting Professor at the Centre for Advanced Research (CARe), Universiti Brunei Darussalam. He is also an Adjunct Researcher at the Demographic Institute, Faculty of Economics, Universitas Indonesia. He was President of the Asian Population Association from 2019 through 2021. He spent more than one and a half decades in Singapore as a Senior Fellow at the Department of Economics, National University of Singapore (1999–2000), and Senior Research Fellow at the Institute of Southeast Asian Studies (now ISEAS – Yusof Ishak Institute), 2001–14. He obtained his PhD in economics at Duke University, the United States; his master's degree in socio-economic statistics from George Washington University, the United

States; and his undergraduate degree in economics from Universitas Indonesia. Many of his research projects were published by ISEAS, in addition to articles in international academic journals.

Asiyah az-Zahra Ahmad Kumpoh is an Assistant Professor at the Faculty of Arts and Social Sciences, Universiti Brunei Darussalam. She received First Class BA Honours from Universiti Brunei Darussalam and Master of Arts with Distinction from Australian National University. In 2012, she was awarded PhD from the University of Leicester. She teaches historical methodology, tradition and modernization in Brunei Darussalam and the evolution of philosophy and theories in historical studies. Her current research and publications focus on conversion narratives, the Brunei Dusuns and the historical evolution of religion, culture and ethnic identity in Brunei Darussalam and Southeast Asia. She contributed an annual review on Brunei Darussalam in ISEAS's flagship publication, *Southeast Asian Affairs*, in 2017. She has served as Vice-President (Brunei Darussalam) and council member for the Malaysian Branch of the Royal Asiatic Society since 2017.

Chang-Yau Hoon is an Associate Professor at the Institute of Asian Studies and the former Director of the Centre for Advanced Research, Universiti Brunei Darussalam, and also an Adjunct Research Fellow at the University of Western Australia. Prior to this, he was an Assistant Professor of Asian Studies and Sing Lun Fellow at Singapore Management University, where he was awarded the SMU Teaching Excellence Award in 2012 and SMU Research Excellence Award in 2014. He specializes in the Chinese diaspora, identity politics, multiculturalism, and religious and cultural diversity in contemporary Southeast Asia. He is the author of *Chinese Identity in Post-Suharto Indonesia: Culture, Politics and Media* (2008), and co-editor of *Chinese Indonesians Reassessed: History, Religion and Belonging* (2013), *Catalysts of Change: Ethnic Chinese Business in Asia* (2014), *Contesting Chineseness: Ethnicity, Identity, and Nation in China and Southeast Asia* (2021), *Southeast Asia in China: Historical Entanglements and Contemporary Engagements* (2023), and *Christianity and the Chinese in Indonesia: Ethnicity, Education and Enterprise* (2023).

Evi Nurvidya Arifin is a social statistician-demographer, currently Senior Assistant Professor at the Centre for Advanced Research (CARe), Universiti Brunei Darussalam. She is an Adjunct Researcher at the

Demographic Institute, Faculty of Economics, Universitas Indonesia. She was a Visiting Research Fellow at ISEAS (now ISEAS – Yusof Ishak Institute) and a postdoctoral fellow at the National University of Singapore. She taught at Universitas Indonesia and Universitas Respati Indonesia. She earned her PhD in social statistics from the University of Southampton, her master's degree in population and labour from Universitas Indonesia, and her undergraduate degree in community nutrition from Institut Pertanian Bogor, Indonesia. Her areas of expertise include population and development, population ageing, population mobility, ethnicity, and disability. She mostly works with statistics, enriched with qualitative data.

F. Merlin Franco is an Assistant Professor of Environmental Studies at the Institute of Asian Studies, Universiti Brunei Darussalam. His work deals with the intersection of biodiversity, traditional knowledge and languages (Biocultural Diversity). In the past, he has worked with Curtin Sarawak Research Institute at Curtin University, Malaysia, and Earthwatch Institute – India. He is the co-editor of the journal *Ethnobotany Research and Applications*.

Hamizah Haidi is an Assistant Lecturer at the Institute of Policy Studies, Universiti Brunei Darussalam. She obtained her first degree in Biological Sciences at the Faculty of Science, Universiti Brunei Darussalam; a Master of Teaching at the Sultan Hassanal Bolkiah Institute of Education, Universiti Brunei Darussalam and a PhD at Lucy Cavendish College, University of Cambridge in the field of education, specifically on how the two notions of development and reflectivity coincide and inform one another. She was a recipient of the Annabelle Dixon Prize when she was at Lucy Cavendish College. Her research interests are in the areas of education policy, reflectivity and ethics.

Jérémy Jammes is Professor of Anthropology and Southeast Asian Studies at the Lyon Institute of Political Studies, and a research fellow at the IAO (Institute of East Asian Studies, Lyon). He was Associate Professor at the Centre for Advanced Research (CARe) and Director of the Institute of Asian Studies (2016–18) at Universiti Brunei Darussalam. Between 2010 and 2014, he worked as Deputy Director and Head of Publications of the Research Institute on Contemporary Southeast Asia

(IRASEC) in Bangkok. Among more than sixty publications (books, chapters and articles), he has recently co-edited *Muslim Piety as Economy: Market, Meaning and Morality in Southeast Asia* (2020) and *Fieldwork and the Self: Changing Research Styles in Southeast Asia* (2021).

Ly Slesman is a Senior Assistant Professor and Researcher for the Centre for Advanced Research (CARe) at Universiti Brunei Darussalam. Prior to joining CARe, he was a Senior Lecturer at the School of Business and Economics, Universiti Putra Malaysia (UPM), where he had taught econometrics and economics courses. He obtained his PhD in Economics (with Distinction) from UPM in 2014. His research interests cover linear and nonlinear issues concerning political economy of development processes, foreign capital flows, financial development, socio-economic development, entrepreneurship, resource rents, conflicts and applied econometrics. His research works appear in reputable international refereed journals (indexed by Thomson ISI) including *Economic Modelling, Economic Systems, International Journal of Finance and Economics, Journal of International Development, Quarterly Review of Economics and Finance,* among others.

Mahani Hamdan is an Assistant Professor at UBD School of Business and Economics, and also serves as the Director for the Institute of Policy Studies and Simpur Herbal Café Sdn Bhd in Universiti Brunei Darussalam. She obtained her first degree in Accounting and Financial Management from the University of Sheffield; a master's degree with distinction from the University of Leeds; and a PhD from the Queensland University of Technology in the field of organizational psychology, specifically on how the notion of "fit" or "misfit" between individuals and organizations can lead to positive or negative organizational outcomes. She learned about politics and policies during her postdoctoral period at Goldman School of Public Policy, University of California, Berkeley, through the Independent Leader Scholar Programme. Her current research interests are in the areas of operational excellence, leadership, public finance, governance, public policy and accounting for non-public interest entities. On top of her teaching, research and administrative services in UBD, she is also a member of Brunei Darussalam Accounting Standards Council and Income Tax Board of Review.

Marie-Sybille de Vienne is currently a full Professor of Southeast Asian Studies (economic history and geopolitics) at the French National Institute for Oriental Languages and Civilizations (INALCO, Paris) and a research fellow at the Centre for Southeast Asian Studies (CASE, Paris). She has been elected in October 2021 to the French Academy for Overseas Science (ASOM). She is the editor-in-chief of the ranked academic journal *Péninsule*. She has been INALCO's vice-president for international affairs from 2013 to 2017. A member of the Board of the French Research Institute on Contemporary Southeast Asia (IRASEC, Bangkok), she has been a visiting scholar to Cambodia, Malaysia and Brunei in the 2010s and has been invited to some fifty international conferences and workshops. She has published ten books, such as *Brunei from the Age of Commerce to the 21st Century* (2015) and some fifty-four papers in ranked journals.

Muhammad Anshari is a Senior Assistant Professor at the School of Business and Economics, Universiti Brunei Darussalam (UBDSBE). He received his Bachelor of Management Information Systems (Honours) from International Islamic University Malaysia (IIUM), his Master of IT (E-Business) from James Cook University, Australia, and his PhD from Universiti Brunei Darussalam. His professional experience started when he was an IT Business Analyst at Astra International. He was a research fellow at the National Taiwan University (Jan–Dec 2014) funded by The Government Republic of China (Taiwan). He was also a research fellow at King Saud University, Saudi Arabia (2009). His research profile is internationally competitive and he has collaborated actively with researchers in several other disciplines of Information Systems, particularly digital marketplace, FinTech, big data in business, digital health, ICT & Area Studies, and ICT in Education.

Nik Ani Afiqah Tuah is an Assistant Professor of Public Health at PAPRSB Institute of Health Sciences, Universiti Brunei Darussalam, and appointed as Honorary Research Fellow at Imperial College London, United Kingdom. She graduated with a Bachelor of Science in Nursing from McMaster University in Canada, a Master of Public Health from Melbourne University in Australia and a PhD in Public Health from Imperial College London, United Kingdom. She has undergone postdoctoral trainings at the School of Public Health, University of

Michigan and Bloomberg School of Public Health, Johns Hopkins University, United States. She has been the Coordinator of Master of Public Health (MPH) programme since 2012 in transforming public health education in Brunei Darussalam. She has been serving UBD and the people of Brunei for thirteen years as an educator/academic in the field of medicine and public health. As a local public health expert, she has contributed ideas in a discussion of expert panel to review and develop national policies relevant to non-communicable diseases (NCDs).

Norainie Ahmad is an academic at the Institute of Policy Studies (IPS), Universiti Brunei Darussalam. Her alma mater includes the London School of Economics and Political Science (LSE) where she received her MSc in Public Policy and Administration, and she matriculated at Oxford University in 2009 under the Department of Sociology, while affiliated with the Oxford Institute of Population Ageing. She teaches Gender and Development, Non-Governmental Organizations in Brunei, and Socio-Economic Governance and Globalization. Her research is focused on women and young adults in the population, and their lived experiences in contemporary Brunei. Her recent publications include "Policy Implications for Working Women in Brunei" in *Japan Labor Issues*; "Attitudes Towards Family Formation Among Young Adults in Brunei Darussalam" in *Pakistan Journal of Women's Studies: Alam-e-Niswan*; and a book chapter "The Socioeconomic Context of Fertility Decline and Preference in Brunei" in *Family Demography in Asia: A Comparative Analysis of Fertility Preferences* (2018). She is a member of the Asian Population Association, Asian Association of Women's Studies, and Women in Public Policy Network.

Romeo Pacudan was an Associate Professor in Energy Policy and Management at the Institute of Policy Studies, Universiti Brunei Darussalam. He was the Interim Chief Executive Officer of the policy think tank, Brunei National Energy Research Institute. Prior to this, he worked in various energy research institutions and bilateral cooperation agencies in Denmark, France, Germany and Thailand. He has more than twenty years of work experience in the energy sector and was involved in various energy research studies and projects funded by public and private sectors as well as multilateral and bilateral financing institutions as energy economist, policy, regulatory and planning expert. He has a doctorate in Energy Economics from Université Grenoble-Alpes (France) and a master's degree in Engineering (Energy Technology) from the Asian Institute of Technology (Thailand).

Roslee Baha has been a lecturer in Economics in the School of Business and Economics, Universiti Brunei Darussalam since 2004 after completing his MSc in Economics and Finance. In UBD, he has developed and taught some modules in Economics including managerial economics, public sector economics and labour economics to both postgraduate and undergraduate students. Apart from fulfilling his teaching responsibilities at the Faculty, he has also conducted courses for senior and junior level government officers on topics related to economics. In addition, he has been involved in consultancy projects for different organizations such as Employees Trust Fund (ETF), Narcotic Control Bureau and Department of Agriculture. For the ETF project, he was appointed as the project leader to conduct a study on the adequacy of ETF system in Brunei Darussalam. He has published some research papers and book chapters and has presented in seminars particularly in the area of ageing, social security and poverty.

Siti Fatimahwati Pehin Dato Musa is an Assistant Professor of Economics and Development in UBD School of Business and Economics, Universiti Brunei Darussalam. She obtained her first degree in Education (Economics) from Universiti Brunei Darussalam; a master's degree from Bradford University; and a PhD from Newcastle University, UK in the field of Agricultural Economics and Rural Development. She has presented her papers in several conferences overseas: Qatar, United Kingdom, Phuket and South Korea. She has published several book chapters and journal articles pertaining to issues on youth unemployment, youth in agriculture and agribusiness, food security and sustainability. Her research interest revolves around development economics, agricultural economics—specifically issues on food security and sustainability, youth in agriculture, and issues of youth unemployment and youth occupational aspirations.

PART I

Introduction

1

AN OVERVIEW: DIVERSIFICATION IN THE OIL-DEPENDENT ECONOMY OF BRUNEI DARUSSALAM

Aris Ananta, Chang-Yau Hoon and Mahani Hamdan

WHY DIVERSIFICATION IS NEEDED FOR OIL-DEPENDENT ECONOMIES?

The existence of oil and gas is often seen as a blessing for a country (Fasano 2002; Wright and Czelusta 2004). The revenue from oil and gas can be used to build human capital, including the promotion of entrepreneurship spirit and broadening of the economic base to create sustainable development. However, in most developing countries with abundant natural resources, the paradox of the plenty and resource curse ("Theory of Dutch Disease") from huge reliance on revenue from oil and gas reserves may also distort the resource allocation of a country (including creation of dominance of public sector employment). It therefore jeopardizes future economic growth

3

and stability of the country (Beblawi 1987; Mahdavy 1970). Based on a study on Saudi Arabia, Aljarallah (2021) concluded that the abundance of oil and gas will produce sustainable economic growth only when the country can utilize the current gain from oil and gas to enhance human capital, which eventually replaces oil and gas as the capital of economic growth.

Furthermore, the price volatility of oil and gas and its recent decline in the past decade, as well as the prospect of depletion of hydrocarbon reserves, and the global trend toward climate-neutral economies may endanger the energy future and sustainability of oil and gas exporting economies. Therefore, oil-dependent economies urgently need to diversify, while efficiently developing themselves using the remaining revenue from oil and gas (Alsharif et al. 2017; Callen et al. 2014; Filimonova et al. 2020; Hussein 2020). The COVID-19 pandemic, which caused a decline in global demand for oil and gas, may have resulted in dual shock (i.e., economic and health crises) in oil-dependent countries. This situation further escalates the need for diversification from oil and gas sectors (Azomahou et al. 2021).

Brunei Darussalam (hereafter, Brunei), the least populous and the second richest country in Southeast Asia, is one of the examples of an oil and gas dependent economy (Asiyah az-Zahra 2017; Hamdan and Hoon 2019). Since independence in 1984, this country's national income has heavily relied on hydrocarbon resources, although plans for diversification and investment in renewables have been underway for decades. Progress is being made in several sectors, but overall, action to meet goals for diversification has been slow, not yet advancing at the speed and scale required. A real decade of action and delivery is urgently needed, and this requires a strong voice and participation from all stakeholders (i.e., a whole-of-nation approach).

Currently, Brunei faces challenges of diversification in three broad areas. First is diversification of the source of export and government revenue from oil and gas. Related to this first area, the second diversification is to leverage the role of the private sector, especially businesses, in their contribution to economic growth, employment and welfare of the people. The third area of diversification is to reduce the labour market's overdependence on foreign—both high-skilled and low-skilled—labour.

BRUNEI VISION 2035

In 2007, the government announced the *"Wawasan* Brunei 2035" (Brunei Vision 2035), which aims to provide concrete ways to implement economic diversification. The Economic Blueprint published by the Ministry of Finance and Economy in 2020 outlined six aspirations for Brunei towards a dynamic and sustainable economy (see Ministry of Finance and Economy 2020). First is on "productive and vibrant business", needed to reduce dependence on public sector employment and to make private sector much more economically attractive. Second is "skilled, adaptive, and innovative people", to build marketable human capital to be able to involve in tradeable business for the domestic and global market and non-tradeable business domestically; as well as to change the public mindset away from dependence on government welfare assistance. This is to encourage people to *Bekarih, Bejarih, and Belurih* (or have the strong will to take initiative, work hard to achieve it, and reap the success of the hard work).

The third aspiration is to promote an "open and globally connected economy". With the limited domestic market, Brunei needs to venture into the global market in order to diversify its export from hydrocarbon revenue. Fourth is "sustainable environment", to create a green and blue economy by reducing carbon footprint. This aspiration clearly shows the vision to reduce reliance on the oil and gas sector. The fifth aspiration is to develop "high quality and competitive economic infrastructure", which includes transportation, water, electricity, and digital technology. Last but not least, is to maintain "good governance and public service excellence", to improve efficiency and effectiveness of public sector, which is key to the country's journey toward sustainable development.

With just fifteen years to go, Year 2020 needs to usher in a decade of ambitious action by mobilizing the whole-of-nation to deliver the goals of *Wawasan* Brunei by 2035. *Wawasan* Brunei 2035 aims to transform the country into a nation widely recognized for the accomplishments of its well-educated and highly-skilled people as measured by the highest international standard; quality of life that is among the top ten nations in the world; and dynamic and sustainable economy with income per capita within the top countries in the world. To achieve these goals, several blueprints including strategies, policies and masterplans had been recently released by the

Brunei government to provide guidance for achieving these aspirational targets. They include Digital Economy Master Plan 2025 in June 2020; National Climate Change Policy in July 2020; National Youth Policy and Strategy 2020–2035 in December 2020; Economic Blueprint in January 2021; and Defence White Paper 2021.

In essence, this book explores the current dynamics of socio-economic development and stagnation in Brunei, highlighting its vital part in implementing development programmes and policy initiatives. Particular attention is given to a wide range of issues which have dominated the debate on the combined impacts of COVID-19 and the oil price collapse over the course of 2020: environmental issues, climate changes, energy security, digital society, education and health, welfare, job creation, innovation, international trade and economic cooperation.

SOCIO-ECONOMIC JOURNEY TOWARD BRUNEI VISION 2035

Similar to other oil and gas dependent countries, Brunei faces the challenge of finding other sources of economic growth. Its small population necessitates the country to find other sources of export, away from the dominance of hydrocarbon; and to attract more countries to invest, in addition to the rising foreign direct investment (FDI) from China (Lawrence 2021), to promote economic growth and create productive employment. The supply side is to raise human capital, entrepreneurship and innovation.

The country has intensified its efforts to diversify its sources for socio-economic development as a catalyst for inclusive sustainable development. The priority for action and change matters now more than ever especially in the face of the economic crisis caused by the global pandemic of COVID-19. The global pandemic has given rise to new economic challenges and opportunities for necessary changes and reforms, as well as prospects for the country's stronger economic recovery focusing on growth and sustainable development for all.

The book consists of four parts. Part I is Introduction. Part II examines living and non-living environmental capitals and the emerging digital capital. Part III focuses on changing faces of the population and human capital, and Part IV culminates with analyses on business, economy, employment and welfare.

Part I consists of two chapters. Chapter 1, this current chapter, synthesizes the whole book into one coherent discussion and proposes diversified alternatives to Brunei 2035 outlook. The second chapter elaborates on the history of twentieth-century Brunei, concentrating on the establishment of Brunei as an Islamic country, with *Melayu Islam Beraja* (MIB—Malay Islamic Monarchy) as its national philosophy. It discusses the introduction of modern government in Brunei, its socio-economic progress and its geopolitical position within Southeast Asia and the world. This chapter examines the history of the country's economic reliance on oil and gas, which has helped Brunei to transform from a dying state in the early twentieth century to a prosperous country by the end of the twentieth century. The revenue from oil and gas has been contributing to its economic development and enhancing the well-being of the population, including providing generous social protection.

The chapter focuses on the role of the British Residence in Brunei since 1906, which laid the basis for Brunei's modern institutions as well as the investment in health and education that were needed to promote economic growth. In the regional and global context, this chapter also discusses how the country has navigated its integration into the Association of Southeast Asian Nations (ASEAN), United Nations (UN), and Organisation of Islamic Cooperation (OIC) since its independence in 1984. In particular, it discusses the rising importance of China as an economic and strategic partner of Brunei in strengthening and diversifying its oil-based economy and in preserving peace and stability in the Asia-Pacific region. Under the Belt and Road Initiative, China has been involved in large joint venture projects in Brunei including a petrochemical refinery plant built and managed by the Hengyi Industries Sdn. Bhd.

Part II focuses on living and non-living environmental capitals along with the emerging digital capital in four chapters. Chapter 3 discusses the importance of natural and living resources in Brunei's sustainable development. Historically, Bruneians relied on ecosystems for their livelihood, and over time, with the emergence of non-living capital in the economy such as oil, people have come to rely less on ecosystems for goods and services they produce for themselves and rely more on market-produced and imported goods and services.

But today, the situation has changed. The crisis in the oil industry and slow economic growth in the event of the COVID-19 outbreak is putting pressure on the flexibility and diversity of Brunei's economy, which may result in shifting or transitioning the country to increase its reliance on ecosystems. Therefore, Brunei's Economic Blueprint enforces the need for economic growth to be compatible with natural resource conservation. The blueprint rightly emphasizes on a model that gives back to the environment, rather than depletes it.

Chapter 3 also provides an overview of the current state of natural resource management in Brunei and the challenges faced by the government, local communities and industries in the conservation of natural resources, and management of the ecosystem services.

Both Chapters 4 and 5 focus on fossil fuel energy and climate change. Chapter 4 puts forward the discussion of fossil fuel-based energy in Brunei in the context of ASEAN and strategy to divert from the dependence on fossil fuel-based energy to investing in renewables. Brunei's targets set in 2020 regarding climate change is consistent with the targets to be achieved by 2035 in the ASEAN Plan of Action for Energy Cooperation (APAEC). Yet, there are still insurmountable challenges faced by Brunei in attempting to reach the targets, including delays caused by the policy of carbon-trading.

Chapter 4 also reveals opportunities from the government's environmental campaign through the new *Protokol Hijau* (Green Protocol) such as segregating, reducing and reusing wastes; promoting LED light bulbs; energy saving campaigns; and tree planting. If these protocols are implemented successfully, by 2040, Brunei might well be the most committed country in ASEAN to green environment.

In Chapter 5, Brunei's first national climate change policy is highlighted to facilitate the voluntary transition from fossil fuel dependency to a low-carbon economy by 2035. Following a whole-of-nation approach, the policy consists of ten strategies that aim to reduce greenhouse gas emissions up to 50 per cent in 2035.

The chapter provides historical trajectories and long-term forecast scenarios of energy supply and greenhouse gas emissions in Brunei. It shows that the oil and gas sector remains to be an important component of the economy. The government expects the contribution of the oil and gas sector to gross domestic product to increase from B\$10 billion in 2010 to B\$42 billion in 2035, but what is more concerning is the prospect of a rising economy and growing population that will keep the demand for fossil fuel-based energy to soar. The abundance of fossil fuel-based energy has resulted in the domestic price of petroleum products to be below the international market prices. Even the domestic price of electricity is below the long-run marginal cost of production. The heavy subsidy on domestic energy consumption results in Brunei having the highest energy consumption per capita in the Asia-Pacific Region. Furthermore, the heavily subsidized energy price has resulted in more energy-intensive industries, which can lead to inefficient utilization of electricity. The cheap price of fossil fuel-based energy may discourage both investment and utilization of renewable resources of energy.

The rising economic trend is to promote foreign and private investment in energy-intensive downstream industries, including methanol production, fertilizer manufacturing, and facilities for refinery and aromatics cracker production to diversify sources of energy. However, these industries are generally associated with high carbon emission and air pollutants relative to the gross domestic product. Therefore, in diversifying the sources of energy, Brunei must also work simultaneously to mitigate climate change by absorbing the hydro-carbon emission through the utilization of its diverse and complex forest ecosystem as a carbon sink.

Chapter 6 examines the emerging digital technology, a new capital pursued all over the world. Globally, the digital revolution started in the early 2000s and has been accentuated by the COVID-19 pandemic, accompanied by rapid changes in personal behaviour, population mobility, social norms, business conduct and government policies. Brunei is not spared from this revolution. In its vision to become a smart nation through digital transformation as highlighted in the Digital Economy Masterplan 2025 to support *Wawasan* Brunei 2035, the government has launched projects on national information hub, digital ID and digital payment hub to speed up the digitalization transition.

The chapter evaluates recent progress of the use of digital technology as a new capital needed by Brunei to stay globally competitive and relevant, especially during the COVID-19 pandemic. It examines the challenges on the road to digital transition and proposes solutions and several recommendations for future actions. It also gives an overview of Brunei's national strategic direction to lead digital transformation and enhance stakeholder engagement towards becoming a modern and digital society.

The chapter shows that people in Brunei are high-degree digitalization adopters, and are ready to go through a journey of digital transformation. Progress has been made in several sectors such as governance and public services (through e-Darussalam), healthcare (through BruHIMS), business and economy (through digital economy council), and agriculture (through smart agriculture). Other sectors are also expected to follow.

Furthermore, digitalization is a necessary step in the economic diversification initiative as it creates potentials to enhance productivity, income and social well-being by creating new job opportunities other than the oil and gas sector. In the digital economy, "data" has emerged as a new capital, and has the potential to replace oil and gas. Data may probably be seen as "the new oil" in Brunei's digital economy because it can generate value and improve people's lives. Yet, it also requires a stronger data privacy and security system or programme. Building resilient digital security is therefore critical for strengthening the country's cybersecurity landscape, together with the growth of digital usage that calls for the protection of data, infrastructure, and networks against growing cyber threats.

Part III concentrates on a crucial element in the increasingly global competitive market—the changing face of population and dynamics of human capital with respect to education and health in Brunei. This part contains three chapters. Chapter 7 examines the changing faces of population, as both producers and consumers, and how changes in the demographic structure of Brunei's society affect the socio-cultural and economic development, political, environmental factors and other external influences.

The chapter presents the changing geographical population distribution in Brunei. Brunei has four districts. Brunei-Muara district, where the capital is located, is the most densely populated district, with more than half of the total Brunei population living here. The percentage may keep rising because of the high concentration of socio-economic activities and the historic and political role of the district. However, Brunei-Muara is not the only district with fast population growth. The district of Temburong's population has recently been rising too. The newly opened Temburong bridge and the plan to develop Temburong as an eco-friendly district may change the population distribution in Brunei. The heavy flow of migration has also changed the sex ratio of the Brunei population. As the migrants to Brunei are mostly male, the ratio of male to female population has been rising. Among its local population, there are more males than females, implying different market needs and sources of labour supply. The heavy inflow of migrants has differed from the process of ageing population, but the diversification away from foreign dependence in the labour market will accentuate the process of ageing population. This ageing process among the local population (citizens and permanent residents) and the young population among the non-local migrant workers may have ramifications on the domestic economy. Thus, Brunei's labour market practices and policies must be considered in an integrated manner: how the country wants to address the rising source of older persons and female participation in the labour market as an important source of labour supply and consumers as well as an indicator of economic empowerment.

Chapter 7 also provides analyses on the country's racial composition, encompassing the state-defined racial categories: Malay, Chinese, and Others; with Malay as the majority, and the Chinese as the largest minority. In the Brunei-Muara district, the race composition has been relatively stable. In contrast, the race composition in the Belait district has changed over the years as a result of external migration. There is a rapid decline in the percentage of the Chinese and an increase in the percentage of the Malays in the district, partly contributed by the rising out-migration of the Chinese Bruneians to Australia and Canada after Independence. Internal migration, which can be observed from the increasing percentage of the Chinese community in Temburong and Tutong districts, has also made the social energies for sustainable urban development challenging. As an Islamic country, the growth in Muslim population is increasing primarily due to high fertility rates combined with the rate of non-Muslim's conversion to Islam.

Chapter 8 focuses on education with specific reference to TVET (technical and vocational education and training) as one important factor in the diversification process. However, as seen elsewhere in the world, there are at least two challenges to improve TVET. First is the uncertain future, which makes relevant jobs and skills unpredictable. Many future jobs have not existed and the currently available jobs may no longer exist in the future. Second, in the era of digitalization, vocational skills may depreciate sooner, and therefore, there is a need to keep learning, unlearning and relearning throughout one's life.

The chapter shows how TVET can produce a resilient, adaptable and agile source of labour, within the context of the global economy and rapid digitalization. The question is how to do it. Two particular challenges in the field of TVET in Brunei are identified. One is on the mismatch between the skills acquired by the graduates and those that are needed by industries and career fields. Second is the limited industrial experience among teachers. Vocational training institutions need to design programmes for teachers' placement in various industries. During 2014–16, there had been a decline in TVET graduates working in the public sector because of limited public employment opportunities. As a result, many of them started their own businesses or joined the private sector.

This chapter argues that understanding the digitalization era will provide important insights on what skills are needed in the future. It will therefore create opportunities to achieve Brunei's Vision 2035, including diversification from oil and gas sectors. The success depends on cooperation by all stakeholders (including TVET) to continuously re-examine and re-create relevant curriculums as well as offer opportunities for lifelong learning through flexible TVET and policies in the labour market which shape employment systems.

Chapter 9 focuses on the health of the people, an important factor of the nation's capability and welfare. It emphasizes health as a crucial element in people's capability, productivity and performance in Brunei's journey toward Vision 2035. It examines the health transition, with respect to Brunei's trajectory toward an ageing population. It analyses mortality, morbidity (diseases), disability as well as public health infrastructure and system in the country. The chapter also investigates the impact of the COVID-19 pandemic on Brunei and the new normal in all aspects of life.

Though the country has been successful in running its national health programmes as indicated in the Sustainable Development Goals (SDGs) 2030 (goal number 3), there are still some challenges in managing public health. Non-communicable diseases (including mental health) remain to be addressed, with obesity and smoking being identified as two key factors affecting the health of Bruneians. These are attributable to daily behaviour, such as sedentary lifestyle and consumption of unhealthy foods. At the same time, non-communicable diseases may also re-emerge. This public health challenge is accentuated by an ageing population. Although the country has successfully managed the COVID-19 pandemic, further studies need to be conducted on how the pandemic may affect the health of the population, including its impact on mental health.

With the issues, challenges and opportunities discussed in the first three parts, the last part (Part IV) of the book focuses on business, economy, employment and welfare of the people. It contains three chapters. Chapter 10 is about entrepreneurship and innovation in Brunei, with a focus on its changing business landscape. It contributes to the understanding of the readiness of Bruneians to participate in the private economy and be less dependent on the state for production, employment and welfare.

This chapter sees entrepreneurship development in the Bruneian context as individual and community transformation. High-quality education, changing mindset, enterprising attitudes and marketable skills as well as a commitment to building entrepreneurship and innovation are direly needed for such development to occur.

Globalization, emerging digital era, and global pandemic have changed the way businesses behave, the perception of the locals on doing business, and job opportunities—including a mismatch between available skills and skills needed by the economy—for people who are displaced by COVID-19. The government alone cannot do this job. It needs the cooperation and commitment of the whole society—the individuals, community, and business sectors—to advance and bridge entrepreneurship and innovation as well as to build strong business communities optimizing the use of digital technology.

The chapter covers three areas. First is the government's main initiatives and programmes that support entrepreneurial culture and innovation to address socio-economic challenges and promote full participation in society. Second is the achievements and progress the country has made so far such as improving regulatory practices and the local business climate. Third is challenges and opportunities to create value for society as a whole through nurturing the entrepreneurial spirit and innovation, as well as the need for strong cooperation from all stakeholders especially during the global COVID-19 pandemic along with recommendations.

Chapter 11 provides an overview of the progress in Bruneian economic development from a perspective of oil and gas dependency, by giving emphasis to the development of economic diversification, roles of state and private sectors in the economy, contribution of global market/investment, and its prospect to achieve sustainable development goals.

The revenue from oil and gas has many important ramifications for the overall economy of Brunei. Most large-scale private investments, including joint-venture projects with foreign investors, are started by the government, funded mainly by revenues from oil and gas. The welfare system that encompasses subsidies on petrol, electricity, staple food, education, health, government housing, and land purchase also relies on such revenue. However, the declining price of oil and gas in the decade between 2010 and 2020 has resulted in a declining share of resource revenue to the GDP or a rise in the share of non-oil and gas sectors. The contribution gross domestic product (GDP) of non-oil and gas sectors to the overall economy is still small (below 30 per cent of the GDP), and these sectors are dominated by micro, small and medium enterprises (MSMEs), largely in the service industry.

As in other oil dependent economies, this chapter also provides empirical evidence that the abundance of natural resources was not detrimental to economic growth in Brunei, at least until 2018, the latest data used in this chapter. While the chapter highlighted that institutional factors are key determinants of economic growth and care spending, the question remains on how the natural resources abundance will contribute to long-run economic development and welfare over time if income is derived from the depletion of the natural resources. Hence, the chapter accentuates that the country must wean itself from oil and gas dependence.

The final chapter of the book touches on employment and welfare. The chapter starts with a discussion on four sources of financial support for Brunei citizens. First is the government's generous welfare system, including various programmes to assist the low-income groups. Second is community mutual aid with its *gotong-royong* (mutual and reciprocal assistance), philanthropy acts, and volunteerism. Third is family, especially the extended family system and its living arrangement. Fourth is the individuals themselves, with income originating from employment, interest, rent and profit. The last three are referred to as the so-called passive income.

There has been only a slight shift from public to private sector employment during 2014–18 perhaps due to the declining oil price. Policy on stopping wage increase and recruitment in public sector employment may have also contributed to this shift.[1] However, more incentives for private innovation, opportunities and active participation from the private sector is still much needed to reduce the labour market's reliance on public sector employment.

The chapter also shows the alarming rise in youth unemployment rate (aged 15 to 24), reaching 21.3 per cent in 2019. This shows how difficult it will be to reduce unemployment and achieve sustainable economic growth by 2035. The chapter further points to the occurrence of mismatch (incompatibility) between the high aspiration of the potential young workers and the demand for young workers. First, at the prevailing wage, the economy demands to have a smaller number of young workers than the number of young workers who are willing to work. The youth may need more problem-solving and practical skills as well as stronger motivation to work. Second, the youth can afford to be unemployed possibly because they are still single and/ or are financially supported by their families. Third, the youth may believe that the state will help them.

Foreign workers in Brunei serve to overcome the labour shortage particularly in primary industries like fishing, agriculture and construction: they are contributing to economic growth. But overdependence on the foreign workers and the negative impacts can become a serious social problem. The locals lose out in the competition with foreign workers for jobs.

In 2019, the non-locals constituted 33.5 per cent of total employment. To reduce the over-reliance on high-skilled foreign workers, there should be a strong effort to develop the local human capital, especially in education and health. To reduce the reliance on low-skilled foreign workers, machination (including robotic and AI technology) can be introduced. Raising the retirement age may be a recommendable solution to reduce reliance on foreign workers, but more importantly, employers in both public and private sectors must find new ways to develop a skilled but flexible local workforce that accepts the need for continuous and lifelong learning.

DIVERSIFIED ALTERNATIVES TO BRUNEI 2035 OUTLOOK

Overall, the chapters in this book recommend that Brunei's diversification process is targeted at three specific areas. First is to increase the sources of export and government revenue from non-oil and gas sectors, promote FDI and diversify the source of countries.

Second is to boost the economic growth in the private sector via active community participation in entrepreneurship and innovation. Third is to increase the number of local employment in the labour market. To achieve all these, a necessary step must be undertaken to change the mindset and attitude of Bruneians and increase their capacity in both skills and knowledge, and embrace digital technology that offers benefits, opportunities and flexibilities towards achieving the goals of Brunei Vision 2035.

This book has drawn together the key themes in Brunei's diversification process and provided analyses on the intersection of both social and economic dimensions. In order to improve and strengthen the country's 2035 outlook for future research and policy-making, this chapter offers the following recommendations as diversified alternatives for Brunei.

Diversifying Brunei's Risk Investment Portfolio

The global price of oil and gas will remain volatile with a declining trend. This is especially so with the increasing awareness on the move toward more sustainable sources of energy. At the same time, the source of fossil-fuel energy will soon be depleted. Therefore, it is crucial for the country to increase export and government revenue from the non-oil and gas sector. Given that Brunei has a small domestic market, diversification of export and government revenue implies that the country's economic activities need to be more integrated into regional and global markets. With the ongoing era of digitalization, a global-oriented mindset and "long-term thinking (visionaries)" are essential for Brunei to succeed in regional and global integration.

Diversification of Brunei's FDI means prioritizing investments in areas which do not depend on fossil fuel energy, to control energy crisis in the country. The formulation of sustainable energy policies must contribute toward other societal and economic development objectives. The government should look across policies to maximize positive synergies where they exist and avoid creating cost-cutting incentives. To a significant extent, the diversification from the oil and gas sector may be aligned with the goal of reducing greenhouse gas emissions and mitigating global climate change. For example, by maintaining carbon sink from Brunei's forest ecosystem and non-forest plantations.

There have been many initiatives and public involvement from NGOs, volunteers and social enterprises to build a clean and safe green environment. Going green is not just about compliance and competitiveness but having a strong environmental awareness and sense of environmental responsibility. The remaining challenge of going green in Brunei lies with weak enforcement and effective incentive mechanisms. Thus, mitigation policies need to be continually reviewed and enforcement can be improved by educating the public on environmental liabilities (fines) and benefits they would gain or receive from conducting environmental protection activities.

While some of the current FDIs have begun to drive the establishment of downstream oil and gas as well as non-energy sectors, it is still unclear when and if substantial technology and knowledge transfer will take place for the purpose of developing a sustained and diversified economy (Lawrence 2021).

Leveraging MSME Performance of Sustainability

To leveraging MSMEs' performance of sustainability, attention and support should be directed towards increasing business activities and expanding human capital in the tertiary or service industry—particularly in IT, engineering, finance and creative industries—at both local and international markets. While the country sees downstream oil and gas industry as good news that can help to accelerate economic growth, there is a question of sustainability if local capacity-building and skills and knowledge transfer fail to take place.

Brunei government must therefore ensure two goals. First is to ensure that all its investment and contractual agreements with foreign investors or companies clearly outline the sustainability of the industry and the terms and conditions meet the national interests and strategies of Vision 2035. Second is to improve and strengthen the board of governance and board effectiveness. The board practises transparency of selection of members and committees, and provides careful and dynamic scrutiny in their evaluations to ensure both national and private projects, activities and programmes in the country meet the national needs and society's expectations, such as job security and employment for the locals and evidence transfer of skills and knowledge.

The Role of Restructuring

Restructuring financial, legal, operational, business and education dimensions in a challenging landscape is needed in order for the private sector to survive. The reduction in heavy dependence on export and government revenue from oil and gas sector means a reduction in the reliance on public sector employment and a smaller financial outflow for Brunei's generous welfare system. The business spectrum in Brunei must change from having pure monopoly and oligopoly market structures to monopolistic competition. Monopolistic competition[2] does not only allow new businesses to venture into most desired industries, but also permits more companies to coexist and offer similar products or maybe different products serving the same need and purpose. Local enterprises can take full advantage of Information Technology (IT) and digital features to achieve product differentiation and promote healthy competition. However, in order to achieve sustainability of local business development projects, which are commercially viable, the future lies in integrating creativity, innovation and entrepreneurship.

Developing and promoting entrepreneurship education has been one of the key national educational policy objectives implemented by many higher education institutions in the country. The promotion of relevant technical and vocational education and training including lifelong learning is a pressing priority so that the nation can adapt to the rapidly changing future. Although the drive towards digitalization will help keep Brunei globally competitive, resilient and innovative, it requires the transition of human resources into human capital and transformational leadership. Few organizations in Brunei's public sector have incorporated talent management in their strategic plans to provide all the necessary information about the employees in order to anticipate the need for human capital, create a plan to achieve it, and meet the specific talent management needs. But the implementation of these activities has been very slow. Moreover, organizations must consider the future and the technological implications of new roles and account for the fact that the culture of the organization may shift during change.

Developing a Fully Integrated Healthcare Ecosystem

Health spending is key to an individual's welfare and standard of living, on the grounds that it has a direct effect on human well-being and happiness. Healthy lifestyle remains a national priority as Brunei is facing the double burden of rising non-contagious and degenerative diseases, including mental health and disability, and the re-emergence of contagious diseases such as the COVID-19 pandemic. Inevitably, the provision of health often requires a large element of involvement by the government. To create a sustainable healthcare system, social enterprises and non-profit organizations can play an important role in addressing health challenges and help promote health and well-being of the population through wellness programmes. They are increasingly viewed as a vehicle to promote public health, but the impact of this is magnified considering the unfolding challenge of population ageing that might be associated with increases in healthcare costs and pension costs. Hence, in order to develop a fully integrated healthcare ecosystem through sustainable development practices, administrative bureaucracy, lack of legal frameworks, financial support options and economic difficulties that many local social entrepreneurs experience within the country must first be overcome.

Job Creation at the Core of Development

Private sector development interventions alone will not automatically create the better quality jobs needed for locals in Brunei. A balance must be found between a focus on reducing unemployment and tackling underemployment in labour-intensive sectors such as agriculture, fishing and construction, and creating better quality jobs in high-potential and larger firms for national economic growth. Innovative policies are needed to make private sector employment sufficiently attractive for Bruneians. The public must recognize that the reputation of working in the private sector can be at par with public sector employment in terms of salary offered, perks, financial benefits and entitlements. Perhaps it is time for the government to consider setting up a minimum wage for employees in the private sector to protect the interests of local employees. The country also needs both public and private sectors to have a job lens and build job strategies which entail identified sectors that can be competitive and offer major potential for increasing employment. For example, Temburong district, as the least densely populated and previously almost unconnected district, could potentially change the country's economic viability.

Job creation in larger firms (mainly by encouraging investments and an enabling business environment) can generally provide higher wages and better and more sustainable jobs. Though investments in capital-abundant sectors can generate transformational effects spurring labour market dynamics through job creation, the indirect and induced effects of the country's FDI may be harder to estimate. An information asymmetry would have also affected the quality of domestic goods and services and the national labour market.

Thus, the country's income level, demographic structure such as age, gender, education and geographical distribution, and phase of economic transformation to develop more targeted approaches must be considered, as well as interactions between productivity, business performance and employment outcomes.

Active Ageing Population as Opportunity

One of the new faces of the Brunei population is the rising number and percentage of older persons, especially if foreigners are not counted. Until 2021, foreign workers have increased the number and percentage of the nation's young population. However, this should not always be the case. To avoid the rising number and percentage of older persons as an economic burden, life-course oriented policies should be made to create future smart older persons. Therefore, an ageing population in the country may be seen as an opportunity because older persons who are healthy, independent and active, equipped with marketable skills and capability in IT would still be able to work and do not depend much on families, communities and the government.

Though an ageing population may provide opportunities for employment generation and services development, it requires policy actions to speed up the transformation of the pattern of growth, coupled with labour market reforms and improved human capital to foster labour productivity. The policy actions must fuel the silver economy, meet caregiving needs, advance women's equality, and ensure that societies remain prosperous, healthy and vibrant as they age. Moreover, the country should redesign work to address the needs of an ageing workforce, and create economic pathways to women's empowerment and active citizenship, as these will help to advance the lifelong well-being of Bruneians of all ages.

To support productive ageing across the working life, higher public expenditure to finance the growing needs of the elderly, including pensions, is needed, and interventions and strategies such as buying life insurance at a young age may be explored.

Foreign Labour to Support Economic Growth

Brunei faces serious challenges to reducing its reliance on both high and low skilled foreign workers, an inevitable effect of its small and ageing population as well as its growing economy. The country will still need these workers in sectors such as construction and plumbing, given the small domestic population and the unwillingness of the locals to take up such jobs. Reduction in cheap, low skilled foreign workers may have an undesirable impact, reflecting in higher production costs and therefore higher prices of consumer goods.

Given the country's limited workforce, Brunei would not be able to stay competitive in certain sectors if not for migrant workers to take on many lower-end jobs. Yet, the government and Bruneians must still carefully consider stricter policies to deal with foreign worker issues while highlighting the value of foreign labour in different areas, such as in the manufacturing and construction industries.

The recent global outbreak of COVID-19 may have provided an important lesson not to depend heavily on foreign workers as it is very costly to import them during the pandemic. At the same time, it has also seen calls for Brunei to rethink its reliance on such labour. Can Brunei rely less on foreign labour? To answer the question of whether to control the number of foreign workers or reduce the country's reliance on foreign workers, finding the right balance on the proportion of foreign workers needed to keep the economy running smoothly is the key. To restructure the economy and society for a more sustainable and resilient future, there are labour policies which could help reduce heavy dependency on these foreign workers. First is to enhance human capital, covering education, health, and the ability to move geographically within Brunei. Second is utilizing more mechanization, including robotic and artificial intelligence technology. Third is creating future smart local older persons. Fourth is continuing to bring more women to the labour market, and fifth is to raise the job profiling and employee recognition on jobs usually performed by foreign workers, and locals are to be rewarded for taking these jobs.

Public Sector Reform

With the decline of revenue from oil and gas, the government certainly needs to find other sources for the budget. Policymakers may posit to expand the tax base to increase tax revenues, but an increase in tax rate can reduce the incentive for FDI and limit knowledge spillovers. Alternatively, greater attention should be directed to strategies which remain critical for the country's long-term goals. These strategies can help to eliminate constraints in productivity, increase the country's revenues from export and FDI activities, and reduce the subsidy, especially on petrol and utilities.

The government has been very active in privatization and corporatization as a more appropriate reform strategy which could serve the purposes of limiting excessive autonomy and retaining political controls for promoting the public interest. Indeed, the government is already making progress in reforms such as in the telecommunication industry, ports operations and postal services. Nevertheless, further reforms to reduce spending and balance the budget are still highly required in three areas: public financial management, revenue administration and transparency.

Transparency provides the required level of openness to government operations, and it can shed light on public expenditures that state enterprises make on behalf of the state and enhance the enterprises' efficiency to increase revenues. The business activities of state enterprises could become much more competitive and accountable if rules governing the financial relationship between state enterprises and the government are clarified and they would also be able to significantly contribute to the national budget.

The use of social media and related tools can offer a platform for elevating the level of transparency in governance. In the age of digital communication and transformation, the use of the internet and social media play an increasingly important role in promoting sustainable development and preventing or resolving ecological crises. Brunei has a high internet penetration rate and the people are quick to adopt digital technology. But the progress to achieve all the targets in each goal of Brunei Vision 2035 has been slow due to a lack of socialization and participation from everyone at all levels. "Social media-enabled governance" can therefore be used to facilitate collaborative practices in policymaking. The government has started to use social media to raise awareness of certain issues, build credibility with specific stakeholder groups, and engage local representatives in policy consultation and development. A number of new policies have been introduced in the past several years that address climate change, education, digitalization and social security in line with sustainable development goals by the United Nations. E-commerce has also been widely practised in the private sector since the enactment of the Electronic Transactions Act in 2000 to increase their business activities and improve performance.

Certainly, the use of social media in both public and private affairs comes with risk, which leads to the urgent need to develop a social media policy and prepare risk mitigation strategies. The policy should provide a comprehensive guideline for public and private users, and the significance of social media for checks and balances. Transparency is largely affected by emerging technology trends and would also depend on institutional and design factors.

THE WAY FORWARD

Finally, in a context of nature-society imbalances which can threaten economic and social stability, economic diversification is the heart of many kinds of development-oriented responses to concerns about the abundance of hydrocarbon resources, changing faces of population, human capital and entrepreneurship. Brunei, as a small oil and gas producing nation, strives to achieve sustainable development goals through innovation and collaboration for the wealth creation and welfare of the nation. The diversified alternatives described above are expected to create a new Brunei's economy with new different faces—a digitized globally competitive economy with a sustainable environment, transforming the country into a smart nation (a digital and future-ready society), rising private sector and greater contribution of the local in Brunei's labour market.

In essence, the key to understanding Brunei's new economy lies primarily in the changing local and global patterns of ecosystem structure and dynamics of socio-economic interactions that shape policy choices about education, medical care, welfare, employment and more. The country's national budget may currently limit these choices but the prospect of revenue-driven lead generation can help cushion the adverse impacts on the community or society, environment and development.

NOTES

1. See Wardi (2019) for a discussion on the policy.
2. Monopolistic competition is a market structure with a relatively large number of firms and consumers, free entry and exit of market, and slightly differentiated commodities sold.

REFERENCES

Asiyah az-Zahra Ahmad Kumpoh. 2017. "Brunei Darussalam in 2016: Adjusting to Economic Challenges". In *Southeast Asian Affairs 2017*, edited by Daljit Singh, and Malcolm Cook, pp. 117–30. Singapore: ISEAS – Yusof Ishak Institute.

Aljarallah, Rub A. 2021. "An Assessment of the Economic Impact of Natural Resource Rents in Kingdom of Saudi Arabia". *Resources Policy* 72: 102070.

Alsharif, Nouf, Sambit Bhattarcharyya, and Maurizio Intartaglia. 2017. "Economic Diversification in Resource Rich Countries: History, State of Knowledge, and Research Agenda". *Resource Policy* 52: 154–64.

Azomahou, Theophile, Njuguna Ndhung'u, and Mahamady Oueraogo. 2021. "Coping with a Dual Shock: The Economic Effects of COVID-19 and Oil Price Crises on African Economies". *Resource Policy* 72: 102093.

Beblawi, Hazem. 1987. "The Rentier State in the Arab World". In *The Rentier State*, edited by Hazem Beblawi, and Giacomo Luciani, pp. 49–62. London: Croom Helm.

Callen, Tim, Reda Cherif, Fuad Hasanov, Amgad Hegazy, and Padamja Khandelwal. 2014. "Economic Diversification in the GCC: Past, Present, and Future". Washington, D.C.: IMF Discussion Note.

Fasano, Ugo. 2002. "With Open Economy and Sound Policies, U.A.E. Has Turned Oil 'Curse' into a Blessing". *IMF Survey* 31, no. 19: 330–32.

Filimonova, I.V., D.M. Cherepanova, I.V. Provornaya, V.D. Kozhevin, and V.Y. Nemov. 2020. "The Dependence of Sustainable Economic Growth on the Complex of Factors in Hydrocarbons-Exporting Countries". *Energy Reports* 6: 68–73.

Hamdan, Mahani, and Chang-Yau Hoon. 2019. "Brunei Darussalam: Making Strides with a Renewed Focus on the Future". *Southeast Asian Affairs 2019*. Singapore: ISEAS – Yusof Ishak Institute.

Hussein, Bina. 2020. *Energy Sector Diversification: Meeting Demographic Challenges in the MENA Region*. Washington, D.C.: Atlantic Council.

Lawrence, Ithrana. 2021. "Brunei's Response to China's Belt and Road Initiative: Embracing Asymmetry, Enhancing Authority". *Asian Perspective* 45, no. 2: 397–420.

Mahdavy, Hossein. 1970. "Patterns and Problems of Economic Development in Rentier States: The Case of Iran". In *Studies in Economic History of the Middle East from the Rise of Islam to the Present Day*, edited by M.A. Cook, pp. 428–67. Oxford: Oxford University Press.

Ministry of Finance and Economy. 2020. *Towards a Dynamic and Sustainable Economy: Economic Blueprint for Brunei Darussalam*. Brunei Darussalam: Ministry of Finance and Economy. http://www.deps.gov.bn/DEPD%20 Documents%20Library/NDP/BDEB/Econ_Blueprint.pdf.

Wardi, Wasil. 2019. "LegCo Members Urge Gov't Open Up Jobs in the Public Sector". *The Scoop*, 13 March 2019.

Wright, Gavin, and Jesse Czelusta. 2004. "Why Economies Slow: The Myth of the Resource Curse". *Challenge* 47, no. 2: 6–38.

2

BRUNEI IN HISTORICAL CONTEXT: GOVERNANCE, GEOPOLITICS AND SOCIO-ECONOMIC DEVELOPMENT

Asiyah az-Zahra Ahmad Kumpoh and Chang-Yau Hoon

INTRODUCTION

Brunei is a predominantly Muslim country with a population of 459,500 in 2019 (Department of Economic Planning and Statistics 2019). As one of the oldest monarchies in the world, the sultanate of Brunei began in the fourteenth century when Awang Alak Betatar converted to Islam and married a Johore princess. He was coronated as the first Sultan of Brunei in 1368 and became Sultan Muhammad Shah. Despite political turbulences, foreign interference, economic instability and substantial territorial loss at the end of the nineteenth century, the monarchical system remains intact until the present day.

There are many factors that contributed to the continued existence of Brunei's monarchical system. Hamzah (1989) considered the skilful tact, diplomacy and political experience of the Brunei Sultans in dealing with external pressures as the main factor that overcame the political deficiency that could jeopardize the integrity of the monarchical system. Whereas Talib (2013) emphasized "the traditional and religious sources of legitimacy" from which the Brunei monarchy draws its strength as fundamental to the country's survival.

In the present day, Brunei's monarchy implements a unique governance model that strikes a balance between tradition and modernity. The traditional components are solely implemented in the royal court whereas the modern elements of governance shape the present-day state administration (Asiyah az-Zahra, Siti Norkhalbi and Noor Azam 2017, pp. 4–5). As will be discussed later, this unique model shapes what Talib (2013) regarded Brunei as a neo-traditional polity that enables the country to respond well to the changing needs of the modern globalized world.

THE BRITISH RESIDENCY (1906–59)

Before the turn of the twentieth century, Brunei was in a deep political crisis, following a substantial territorial loss to the Brookes in Sarawak and the British North Borneo Chartered Company in the present-day Sabah. By the turn of the century, Brunei was truly desperate to retain and ready to fight for what was left of its sovereignty. After several pleas made by Sultan Hashim (r. 1885–1906), the British agreed to the establishment of the British Residency in Brunei. With the signing of the Supplementary Agreement between Brunei and Britain in 1905/1906, Malcolm McArthur was appointed as the first British Resident.

Most literature holds that the supreme power of Brunei Sultan during the Residential period was practically non-existent as the executive authority in the government lay in the hands of the British Resident (Muhammad Hadi 2010; Ranjit Singh 1984; Sidhu 1995). One of the frequently-mentioned examples of this is taken from the incident which involved Sultan Muhammad Jamalul Alam II (1906–24) who was given an ultimatum by the British Resident for initially refusing to accept the Land Code in 1909, following the abolition of the traditional land system (Hussainmiya 1995, p. 18).

At the same time, it was the abolition of the land system that ironically allowed the British Resident to effectively protect the sovereignty of the Sultan. The nobilities (*wazirs*) could no longer bequeath their private hereditary lands (*tulin*) as well as the lands they held as ex-officio ministers (*kuripan*) to either Sarawak or North Borneo or any interested foreign powers. This also means that the damaging political conflicts among the nobilities which almost destroyed the integrity of the Sultanate in the second half of the nineteenth century gradually disappeared. There were also no more signs of popular rebellions against the Sultan and this eliminated potential disputes between the people and the government. This positive change gradually became the contributing condition for political stability in the country, making it much easier for the British Resident to introduce and initiate fundamental socio-economic transformations.

The initial plan to rejuvenate Brunei was to provide the state "with a 'proper' administration" (Horton 1986, p. 360). As the state was at the brink of economic unviability, McArthur made a loan of $200,000 from the Federated Malay States in 1906 to support the plan. Gradually, a modern, albeit limited, administration was introduced with the establishment of several departments that provided essential services such as Medical, Forestry and Agricultural Departments, headed by foreign officers seconded from Malaya (Horton 1984, pp. 29–30). Currency Enactment was passed in 1906 to regulate the use of the Straits Dollar, a new currency, which replaced the legal tender of the British and Mexican Dollar in circulation.

However, it was education and health which were the primary concerns of the British Resident in the early years of its establishment. As there were only a few locals who were literate in the Roman alphabet, the new administration found it challenging to employ suitable and qualified locals. Hence, the British Resident introduced rudimentary vernacular education to teach the locals the Rumi script (the Roman alphabet) in order to improve the literacy rate of the population as well as their prospect of employability (Awang Asbol 2006, p. 22; Chevallier 1913, p. 10). Thus, in 1914, a Malay school in Brunei Town was opened with a humble attendance of less than forty pupils. The opening of this Malay school marked the beginning of formal education in the country.

However, the lacklustre response from parents towards the formal education significantly hampered the British Resident's initial effort. It was not until the passing of the School Attendance Enactment in 1929 that the number of children attending formal education increased drastically. Department of Education was also formed in

1932 to oversee and administer formal education which at that time was solely focused on primary education. Before the outbreak of the Second World War, there were 21 Malay schools to accommodate 1,810 pupils, out of which 189 were female (Sidhu 1995, p. 88). Such drastic expansion of enrolment in Malay schools led to an increased demand for qualified teachers. The government began to send teacher trainees to Malaya including the sending of six female teacher trainees to Malay Women Training College in Durian Daun, Malacca in 1937 (Mohsin 2008).

The introduction of rudimentary literacy among the population complemented the establishment of modern health services initiated by the British Resident. Prior to the Residential period, the locals resorted to traditional healing practices. It was reported in 1906 that no organized medical care or sanitary measures had ever been introduced in the state (McArthur 1906, p. 19). Even if there was such provision of healthcare available, it would never be understood or appreciated due to the people's uncompromising insistence on traditional healing practices at that time. Nevertheless, a government dispensary was opened in 1911 and it was maintained by a postmaster who was also served as a dresser (Chevallier 1913, p. 10). The government also conducted outstation visits and introduced vaccination against epidemics such as smallpox. G.E. Cator, the British Resident, reported that in 1919, there was a "sudden popularity of vaccination" among the people, following the steps of Sultan Muhammad Jamalul Alam II (r. 1906–24) who ordered the royal household to be vaccinated (Cator 1920, p. 6). This, according to the Resident, was "the most satisfactory feature of the year…" (ibid.).

The state health facilities expanded greatly with the opening of government hospitals in all four districts in the first five years of the discovery of oil in 1929. The Medical and Health Department was reorganized in 1930, following the employment of a full-time European medical professional to administer the daily operation of the department (McKerron 1931, p. 18). Vaccination programmes were introduced and carried out to prevent epidemic outbreaks and transmissible diseases. The expansion and distribution of health facilities were immediately accompanied by the recruitment of foreign medical workforce to address the inadequacy of health personnel. This enabled the government to conduct routine health screenings at vernacular schools in Brunei Town as there were reports of prevalent roundworm infection among school children (McKerron 1930, p. 19). A subject on personal hygiene and diseases was also introduced and incorporated in the school curriculum.

In 1933, the maternity clinic engaged a midwife, the first to be appointed in the state, to address the high mortality rate among infants. Ten years later, the government made substantial efforts to engage more foreign nurses and assistant nurses including local midwives to support and sustain the government's new mother and child health intervention programme (Sidhu 1995, p. 76).

Although the Second World War interregnum caused massive destruction on health facilities, due to the oil boom and the firm leadership shown by the newly coronated Sultan Omar Ali Saifuddien III (r. 1950–67), the rebuilding of the health infrastructure was done in a coordinated and swift manner. In 1952, a new hospital with modern facilities in Brunei Town was opened, followed by several health centres in areas with high demographic density such as Sengkurong, Muara, Serasa, Berakas and one in Tanjung Maya in Tutong district (Sidhu 1995, p. 78). To complement the rapid expansion of health infrastructure, health officers were sent to Kuching, Singapore, Kuala Lumpur and Penang for training programmes. With the construction of roads particularly in remote areas, more people benefitted from the rapid proliferation of health facilities.

Overall, formal education had significantly brought about the awareness and attractiveness of modern medical care and this gradually fuelled the growing demand for healthcare in the country. Education opened up employment prospects for the population, and as the education provision continued to expand in the country, the number of locals with competency and skills was proportionately increased. In particular, those with qualifications in vocational education had almost immediate relevance to the labour market in the oil industry, a key enabler in the socio-economic development of twentieth-century Brunei.

OIL DISCOVERY AND ECONOMIC TRANSFORMATION

In the midst of the plummeting price of rubber, the then economic backbone of Brunei, oil was discovered in Seria in the Belait district by the British Malayan Petroleum Company (BMPC) in April 1929. This discovery could not be made at a better time. For a state that was once almost on the brink of extinction and facing a crippling economy, the black gold could only mean one thing to Brunei: it brought real hope for survival for the tiny state and the livelihood of the people. Evidently, after Brunei successfully made the first oil export in 1932, the stage was set for an entirely different economic growth trajectory which brought about rapid and remarkable socio-economic transformations. Without doubt, oil has been the main impetus of the substantial prosperity enjoyed by the population since the first half of the twentieth century.

The effects of the oil industry on Brunei were remarkable. Hamzah (1991) defined "the political history of Brunei in the twentieth century has been a story of oil imperialism" (p. 11). This is undoubtedly true, particularly when one considers the statement in the context of the Brunei-Britain relationship. Hamzah (1991) further argued that the British "has the power to cut the colonial knot [and in fact] Great Britain could have granted Brunei independence in 1959, 1962, 1971 or 1979; instead on each occasion, its presence was negotiated and renewed" (p. 15).

In less than two decades after the first export, the state's income improved tremendously that by 1938, Brunei was the third largest oil producer in the Commonwealth. The state was also able to pay the loan it sought from the Federated Malay States four years after the first oil export. In 1947, the payment of the oil royalties alone amounted to $548,701, higher than the government expenditure of $379,000 in 1930 (Jamit 2010, p. 133) whereas the revenue surplus in 1950 was around $9 million (Hussainmiya 1995, p. 50). Unemployment was practically non-existent at the time as there was an increasing demand for manpower to fill in the different rungs of oilfield employment (Sidhu 1995, pp. 36–37). As a result, a growing immigrant population consisting of the Europeans, Chinese and Indians began to emerge in Kuala Belait and formed their own community area with sufficient housing provision, medical and educational services, transport and leisure facilities and other necessary infrastructures provided by the BMPC (Saunders 2002, p. 119).

Retrospectively, the British Residency and oil were critical to the socio-economic transformations of Brunei in the twentieth century. From the above discussion, it is clear that they were the enablers that created the platform that was needed for the initial phase of the state's development. The British Resident provided the necessary administration and developed appropriate infrastructures in order to facilitate access to fundamental services such as education and health. More government departments were formed to provide better provisions such as in forestry and agriculture. This became the foundation of the establishment of the state public service. On the other hand, the discovery of oil created and increased opportunities for development and employment later made Brunei an attractive destination for foreign workers (Ullah and Asiyah az-Zahra 2019, p. 16).

As the British Residency and oil continued to create enabling conditions for growth and transformation, the second half of the twentieth century witnessed the emergence of strong monarchical leadership in the form of Sultan Omar Ali Saifuddien III (SOAS III) who ascended to the throne in 1950 and became the 28th Sultan of Brunei. As discussed below, SOAS III proved to be a robust political strength that when combined with the two enablers, collectively underpinned Brunei's transformative capacity and accelerated further socio-economic and political developments, as drawn by the constitutional provisions and the national development plans.

FORMULATION OF CONSTITUTION AND NATIONAL DEVELOPMENT PLANS

SOAS III's strong leadership in politics and his insistence on developing the country for the benefit of the people led to the formulation of two impactful policy directives that transformed the state's political and socio-economic landscapes. One of the policy directives was the enactment of the written constitution which SOAS III had already envisaged to achieve ever since he ascended to the throne. This went hand in hand with his other comprehensive and strategic plan to modernize Brunei and provide the people with the necessary tools and skills to improve their livelihood. However, SOAS III was also aware of the deteriorating relationship and growing political tension between the previous Sultans and the British Residents as the latter had become more powerful and patronizing at times (Hussainmiya 1995; Mohamad Yusop 2013). Thus, in order to retrieve the state sovereignty and executive power to govern Brunei, SOAS III drafted and promulgated a constitution which was successfully enacted in September 1959.

Under the Constitution, the British Residency was abolished and replaced by the British High Commissioner who was vested with lesser authority and advisory role than that of the British Resident. This allowed an effective retrieval and protection of the Sultan's sovereignty which subsequently contributed to the preservation and strengthening of the monarchical system during the reign of SOAS III. In exercising his executive authority and duties, the Sultan was assisted by several councils including the Privy Council, the Executive Council, the Legislative Council, and the Council of Ministers (*Perlembagaan Negeri Brunei 1959*, n.d.). The Constitution also declared Islam and Bahasa Melayu as the official religion and language of Brunei. Together with the consolidation of the monarchical system, these later formed the integral elements that underpinned the formulation of the national philosophy.

With the retrieval of the state's internal independence, SOAS III proceeded in real earnest to develop and modernize Brunei through the launching and implementation of the national development plans that aimed to develop human and relevant capacities. Even before the promulgation of the written constitution, the monarch had already launched the First National Development Plan in 1953 (which ran until 1958) with an allocated budget of B$100 million. SOAS III made it clear that one of the targets of the Plan was to expand the education provision, particularly the building of English schools with an aim of preparing the population for higher learning and skilled employment (Hussainmiya 1995, p. 121). Brunei's first educational policy was passed in 1954 which offered opportunities for children from the age of six years old to twelve years old to attend Malay education. Those who successfully passed the preparatory examination to attend English school would be given a further pathway to attend secondary education. Those who were able to progress and complete secondary education were given a further opportunity to continue their studies overseas (Padmore 1954).

As prioritized by SOAS III, the government provided a greater provision for English education. In the 1950s alone, English schools were built including the opening of Sultan Omar Ali Saifuddien College and Anthony Abell College in Brunei Town and Seria respectively. Recognizing parents' hesitation in sending their daughters to attend schools which were dominated by male students, the government opened Raja Isteri Girls High School which was, and remains as, an all-female secondary school.

With a solid foundation of the initial education system laid out by the First National Development Plan, the subsequent second (1962–66), third (1975–79) and fourth NDP (1980–84) continued to target on diversifying the existing education provision by introducing vocational education in 1966 and the revival of the Arabic secondary education in the same year (Awang Asbol 2006). The National Educational Policy of 1962 and 1972 were passed in their respective years and both aimed at streamlining the existing education system and enabled it to become the driving force for the growth of human capital (Awang Asbol 2014). However, once again, there was a severe inadequacy of qualified teachers to support the expansion of education provision. This shortcoming not only affected the full implementation of the national development plan but also became one of the root reasons for the failure of the two education policies. The serious lack of teachers led to the establishment of Sultan Hassanal Bolkiah Teachers College (SHBTC) in 1972 to provide pre-service teacher education, particularly for Malay and English teachers. By 1975, 613 teacher trainees had attended the teaching courses at the college (Sofiah 2014, p. 132). Following the rapid expansion of the education system and school provision which led to a consistent increase of teacher population, SHBTC was upgraded to become an institute of education, known as Sultan Hassanal Bolkiah Institute of Education (SHBIE) in 1984, which later merged with Universiti Brunei Darussalam (UBD) in 1988.

The government also paid equal attention to the teacher training for religious education. In 1972, the Seri Begawan Teachers' College (SBTC) was established to offer three-year training courses. In 2007, similar to the development of SHBTC, SBTC was upgraded to a university college known as the Seri Begawan Islamic Teachers University College. Qualified religious teachers were given the opportunity to further their studies at postgraduate level when Universiti Islam Sultan Sharif Ali was established in 2007.

The four NDP after Brunei gained independence (the fifth NDP 1986–90; the sixth NDP 1991–95; the seventh NDP 1996–2000; and the eight NDP 2001–5) were predominantly economic that aimed to fulfil long-term objectives, among others, to develop non-oil sectors, to foster human capital and employment growth and to generate an independent and self-sufficient population. At the same time, with the total allocation of B$25.9 billion for the four NDP, the government equally prioritized the continued improvement of the living quality of the population through extensive welfare assistance programmes

(Department of Economic Planning and Statistics 2020). Hence, free education and healthcare continue to be made available to the population. Government scholarships are available for tertiary education and recently, vocational education. The government does not impose personal income tax, and government pension scheme had been put in place to ensure quality livelihood for government retirees (Sainah 2010). The pension scheme was later replaced by the establishment of Employee Trust Fund in 1992. Resettlement schemes introduced during the British Residency period were later restructured and upgraded to become National Housing Schemes under the National Development Plans (Hassan 2017). The schemes which are heavily subsidized by the government are primarily for landless and low-income citizens. Interest-free government loans are available for potential homeowners. In addition, monthly welfare assistance schemes have also been put forth to alleviate the financial burden of welfare recipients including single mothers, orphans, special needs population and underprivileged individuals (Sainah 2010).

Because of the extensive welfare assistance, Brunei has been known and described as a welfare state (Blomqvist 1993; Hassan 2017; Somjee and Somjee 1995). While these welfare schemes have tremendously improved the literacy rate, education level, quality of health and social care of the population and address the poverty concerns in the country, the beneficiaries have become less proactive, inevitably fostering "a dependency syndrome among the local population" (Lawrey 2010, p. 17). There are also growing challenges of adequacy and sustainability in the country's generous welfare provision, particularly in light of the recent dips in oil prices.

TOWARDS FULL INDEPENDENCE AND PROCLAMATION OF NATIONAL PHILOSOPHY

Brunei proclaimed its full independence on 1 January 1984. His Majesty Sultan Haji Hassanal Bolkiah Mu'izzaddin Waddaulah Sultan and Yang Di-Pertuan of Brunei Darussalam declared Brunei as "a sovereign, democratic and independent Malay Muslim Monarchy..." (*Proclamation of Independence Brunei Darussalam* 1984). While preserving its political, cultural and religious values, Brunei also showed a real capacity to blend modernity and innovation in its political priorities through the creation of a ministerial form of government immediately after the independence. His Majesty the Sultan assumed the paramount leadership role as the Prime Minister, Home Minister and Finance Minister (Pelita Brunei 1984, p. 1). In the first decade of its formation, a considerable number of ministerial offices were held by royal family members and traditional elites. Over time, however, a group of educated elites were appointed to hold important ministerial and deputy ministerial positions in the government.

Another important announcement during the declaration of Brunei's independence was the promulgation of *Melayu Islam Beraja* (MIB) or Malay Islamic Monarchy as the national philosophy. To define the national philosophy in a broad sense of its meaning, MIB is driven and strengthened by the Islamic principles and values based on the teaching of Al-Quran and the Sunnah as well as the hadith of Prophet Muhammad (peace be upon him). The Malay component of the national philosophy maintains the Malay identity of the country which establishes the preservation of the cultural and traditional values of the Malays. It is worthwhile to mention that, according to the 1959 Constitution and 1961 Nationality Act of Brunei, the definition of "Malay" encompasses the seven ethnic groups namely Brunei Malay, Kedayan, Tutong, Belait, Dusun, Bisaya and Murut. The monarchy, which constitutes the Head of State and government, holds the highest executive authority, as defined by the country's 1959 Constitution. The Constitution also outlines the main responsibility of the monarch in ensuring the people's welfare, well-being and general social progress (*Perlembagaan Negeri Brunei 1959*, n.d.).

The promulgation of MIB as the national philosophy was decisive in the nation-building process during the post-independence period. MIB was incorporated extensively in government planning and policy agenda and became one of the influential forces that transformed the education system, teachers' training programme and financial institutions. In other words, the government considered modern and western input in its national policy planning to meet the national interests according to distinctive MIB criteria. The all-encompassing institutionalization of MIB in the country witnessed unprecedented socio-cultural transformations. Regardless of their religious, ethnic and cultural background, the people generally demonstrate a strong sense of familiarity with Malay culture and Islamic tenets as well as deep respect towards the monarch. This in many ways illustrates the fact that MIB has also delivered its key role in building the sense of

Bruneian identity among the people (Asiyah az-Zahra, Siti Norkhalbi and Noor Azam 2017, p. 17). Furthermore, many have argued that the peace and prosperity that Brunei is known for is primarily due to the implementation of MIB (Abdul Latif 2003; Sulaiman 2016), illustrating the fact that MIB has indeed carried out successfully its function as the country's national adhesive.

It is noteworthy that MIB also profoundly intersects with *Wawasan Brunei 2035* (WB2035) or Brunei Vision 2035. In this national vision, Brunei aims, firstly, to produce quality population who are well-educated and highly skilled; secondly, to achieve high quality of life for the people; and thirdly, to ensure the creation of a national economy which is dynamic and sustainable. To achieve these aims, WB2035 adopts the homogenization and guiding role of MIB to ensure that the population is in unison behind the aims through their loyalty to the monarch and the country. In addition, both WB2035 and MIB promote the people's adherence to Islamic values in the spirit of tolerance and social harmony. A number of reforms and policies were introduced in this direction including the re-enactment of the Legislative Council in 2005 and the effective implementation of the Syariah Penal Code in 2019. The current monarch, His Majesty the Sultan and Yang Di-Pertuan of Brunei Darussalam, in his *titah* (royal speech) for the National Day in 2018, urged for the strengthening of the *Maqasid Syariah* (the objectives of the Islamic law) as the precondition for the country's success, prosperity and security (Bandial and Rasidah 2018).

BRUNEI'S FOREIGN RELATIONS SINCE INDEPENDENCE

With the declaration of independence, Brunei took back the responsibility of its international affairs after being a British protectorate for ninety-four years. As a new independent sovereign state, its foremost priority was to establish international legitimacy. The importance of Brunei accorded to its neighbouring countries was demonstrated in its immediate move to join the Association of Southeast Asian Nations (ASEAN) after independence. The country expanded its international relations by joining international bodies such as the Commonwealth, Organisation of the Islamic Conference (now Organisation of Islamic Cooperation, OIC) and the United Nations to amplify its voice on the world stage (Mulliner 1985). The primary objective of Brunei's foreign policy has been to promote and maintain regional and global peace, security, prosperity and stability. As His Majesty remarked in his speech at the United Nations General Assembly in 1984, "For small countries like ours, peace is a necessary precondition for our economic and political survival" (Bolkiah 2016, p. 276).

Since Brunei's economy largely depends on hydrocarbon exports and overseas investments, to maintain good relations with its trading partners the country has traditionally adopted a "low diplomatic posture" in its foreign policy (Case 1996, p. 132). Menon observed that Brunei has "developed and employed the weapon of diplomacy as an instrument of international behaviour" (1987, p. 100). This is further elucidated in a speech delivered in 2011 by Prince Mohamed Bolkiah, who was Brunei's Foreign Minister from 1984 to 2015. In his speech, the Prince argued that Brunei practises "Defence Diplomacy", which he referred to as "defence designed by diplomacy and diplomacy shaped by defence" (Bolkiah 2016, pp. 276 and 278), and further contended that it is strategic to put diplomacy at the front line of Brunei's defence and use international relations to build friendship and cooperation with its partners (Bolkiah 2016).

Brunei regards ASEAN as the foundation and cornerstone of its foreign policy (Kling 1990). Since joining the organization, Brunei has regularly hosted ASEAN-based meetings. The non-intervention policy of ASEAN is a strong factor that encouraged Brunei to participate actively in the bloc. Brunei has played a low-profile but influential role in ASEAN while maintaining its "quiet diplomacy" in approaching sensitive topics such as the South China Sea disputes (Thambipillai 2018). During the Asian Financial Crisis, Brunei helped its neighbours to weather the storm by pledging funds to support regional currencies and economic stabilization or by investing in infrastructural projects in order to contain the economic recession in the region (Cleary and Francis 1999; Mohamad Yusop 2000).

Brunei has also contributed to the development in trade with ASEAN members including the establishment of the ASEAN Free Trade Area (AFTA) in 1992. About half of the imports into Brunei came from ASEAN nations, which include manufactured and agricultural goods. As of mid-2016, 99.2 per cent of all intra-ASEAN tariffs in Brunei, Indonesia, Malaysia, the Philippines, Singapore and Thailand had been eliminated. This had allowed Brunei to import raw materials at a lower price and improve the cost competitiveness of Brunei exports (Siti Fatimahwati 2019). The integration of ASEAN into the regional economy was enhanced by the subsequent establishment of free trade areas with Australia, New Zealand, China, India, Japan and South Korea. In November 2020, this multilateralism was further solidified with the signing of the world's largest free trade pact—the Regional Comprehensive Economic Partnership (RCEP)—between the ten-member countries in ASEAN and their trade partners: China, Japan, South Korea, Australia and New Zealand.

Another important sub-regional initiative of which Brunei is an active and committed partner since signing an agreement in Davao in 1994 is the four-party Brunei-Indonesia-Malaysia-Philippines East ASEAN Growth Area (BIMP-EAGA). Covering key industry sectors such as agriculture, fisheries, tourism, transport and energy, the EAGA aims to make use of the economic complementation, infrastructure and natural resources of the sub-region to facilitate the free movement of people, goods and services. The sub-regional grouping has allowed Brunei to cooperate more closely with its immediate neighbours like the Malaysian states of Sabah and Sarawak, as well as several provinces in Kalimantan Indonesia, in initiatives such as the Heart of Borneo tropical forest protection and management programme (Thambipillai 2010).

Brunei has maintained a special security relationship with the United Kingdom, which continues to contribute to Brunei's external defence. This is signified most ostensibly by the ongoing deployment of a battalion of Gurkha troops (Doshi 1991). Within ASEAN, Brunei has historically shared a very special relationship of cooperation and a deep-rooted bilateral tie with Singapore. This is hallmarked by the Currency Interchangeability Agreement of 1967, which has enabled the Brunei Dollar and Singapore Dollar to be customary tender in both countries. The Brunei-Singapore bilateral relations also encompass extensive cooperation in defence and security, and cooperation in trade, education and research (Rasidah 2019). Brunei's direct involvement in ASEAN Defence Industry Collaboration (ADIC) further demonstrates the country's commitment to promoting regional defence cooperation for a dynamic ASEAN community.

Nonetheless, Brunei's military, diplomatic and trade relations have developed beyond ASEAN, the OIC and the Commonwealth. In recent years, China has become one of the most important partners of Brunei in strengthening and diversifying its oil-based economy and in preserving peace and stability in the Asia-Pacific region (Hamdan and Hoon 2019). Since the first state visit by Chinese President Jiang Zemin to the sultanate in 2000, economic relations between Brunei and China have been steadily increasing. Subsequent state visits by President Hu Jintao in 2005 and more recently, President Xi Jinping in 2018 had further enhanced the bilateral relations between the two countries. On the other hand, the Sultan has made a dozen trips to China since his first state visit in 1993. These include his 2017 trip to officiate the China-ASEAN Expo (CAEXPO) in Nanning where Brunei was accorded the "Country of Honour", and his 2019 trip to attend the Second Belt and Road Forum for International Cooperation in Beijing.

China is now the largest source of foreign investment in Brunei (Storey 2018). Under the Belt and Road Initiative, China is involved in two large joint venture infrastructure projects in Brunei: the Muara Port Company and a petrochemical refinery plant built and managed by the Hengyi Industries. As a joint venture between the Brunei government and the Guangxi Beibu Gulf Group, the Muara Port Company is a major outcome of the Brunei-Guangxi Economic Corridor (BGEC) established in 2014 between Brunei and Guangxi Zhuang Autonomous Region in China. Other areas of cooperation under the BGEC include agriculture, fisheries, halal food processing, tourism, transportation and logistics (Pan and Hoon 2018). On the other hand, the Hengyi Oil Refinery and Aromatics Complex located in Pulau Muara Besar is the most economically significant Chinese investment project in Brunei. This joint venture development is the largest bilateral collaboration between the two countries and the largest single Foreign Direct Investment project in Brunei in recent years. Construction on the two-phase project began in 2015 with a total investment of US$17 billion. The first phase began operation in late 2019 and the construction of the second phase expansion is expected to begin soon. Upon completion of phase two, the oil refinery and petrochemical project is expected to contribute significantly to Brunei's gross domestic product (Bandial 2020).

CHARTING A WAY FORWARD FOR *WAWASAN* BRUNEI 2035 (WB2035)

As mentioned earlier, WB2035 focuses on developing human capital and the national economy through its overarching aims to produce a well-educated and skilled population with high quality of life and to create a dynamic and sustainable national economy. Since the launching of WB2035 in 2007, the government has taken a whole-of-nation approach and developed a comprehensive national plan designed to achieve the aims of the *Wawasan*. There are twelve key strategies emphasized by the plan, among which are the implementation of an education strategy that will equip the young generation with essential skills for employment and to ensure their integration into an increasingly competitive world. In addition, the government has also formulated an economic strategy that provides better business and employment opportunities for the locals through domestic and foreign investments, both within as well as beyond the oil sector (Wawasan Brunei 2035, 2016). These key strategies have also been incorporated into the objectives of the ninth (2007–12), the tenth (2012–18) and the eleventh (2018–23) NDP such as the development of value-added industries and the enhancement of skills and competency of the labour force through quality education (Department of Economic Planning and Statistics 2020).

Consequently, in the field of education, Brunei has successfully implemented *Sistem Pendidikan Negara Abad ke-21* (SPN21) or Brunei's National Education System for the 21st Century. SPN21 was launched in 2009 and it moved the national education system significantly towards the teaching and inculcation of the twenty-first-century learning skills in order "to raise the quality of education in line with current/contemporary needs and the anticipated needs in the future years" (Ministry of Education 2013, pp. 19–20). The current strategic plan of Ministry of Education (2018–22) has also bolstered further the implementation of SPN21 through its commitment to championing equitable access to high quality education (Ministry of Education 2019, p. 14). The Ministry has also introduced its flagship programme, the Literacy and Numeracy Coaching Programme, which aims at producing high quality English and Mathematics teachers. The programme which has successfully produced more than 170 teachers in 2019 is currently in its sustainability phase (Othman 2019).

Polytechnic and tertiary education institutions have also shown their firm commitment towards the achievement of WB2035. They have undergone strategic reforms to prepare their graduates with relevant employability skills, competency and resilience to meet competitive job markets. Technical and vocational education institutions, both private and public establishments, have revitalized their programmes to synchronize with the demands for human resources talents in business sectors such as finance, hospitality and tourism as well as service sectors in transport and logistics (Ministry of Education 2020, p. 3). Cooperation with stakeholders has also been forged more frequently in recent times. Despite the challenges such as limited industries, there is no question about the importance of such cooperation in increasing the employability of graduates and as a potential catalyst in improving the socio-economic standards and social welfare of the population (Ministry of Education 2020, p. 85)

This positive development without doubt allows the country to reduce the dependency on the government as the traditional job provider for the population. It also addresses the burgeoning strains placed on the government due to its responsibility as the main social service and welfare provider for the country. Since about ten years ago, the government has taken serious steps to reduce such dependency in light of the rising costs of social services which could erode the country's fiscal capacity to deliver adequate welfare to the population (Talib 2013, p. 6).

One of these significant steps is to formulate effective strategies to diversify the economy. Fiscal and structural policy reforms have been introduced since 2016 including the formation of a Foreign Direct Investment and Downstream Industry Committee and the establishment of a Small and Medium Enterprise Centre, both of which aim at fostering a conducive business environment for local businesses and foreign investment (Asiyah az-Zahra 2017, pp. 117–18). The reforms were followed by increased investments in infrastructures and production facilities including the construction of Pulau Muara Besar Bridge, completed in 2018, which connects the mainland and Hengyi Industries' oil refinery and petrochemical plant, an emerging source of direct and indirect job opportunities in the country. The construction of B$1.4 billion Sultan Haji Omar Ali Saifuddien Bridge which links the mainland and Temburong district was also completed and officially opened in March 2020. The opening of the bridge has led to the opening of the once isolated part of the country to domestic tourism. Combined with the travel restrictions due to the COVID-19 pandemic situation, the district has increasingly positioned itself as an emerging tourist destination with a great potential of generating employment and business opportunities for the locals (Azahari 2020; Kon 2020).

In other areas of development, the country has also been making a steady stride in accelerating the development of cultural and creative industries through the strengthening of cooperation between public and private sectors to create more entrepreneurial and job opportunities for the youth (Lopes and Mohammed Rahiman 2019). Brunei's halal industry is also demonstrating strong growth potential which could boost job creation and investment opportunities. In 2019, Brunei was recognized and ranked 11th in the Global Islamic Economy Indicator Score with a reputable top ten ranking in halal food sector (Dinar Standard 2019). Moreover, with the effective implementation of strategic priorities and policy directions, as outlined by the recent Economic Blueprint for Brunei Darussalam (Ministry of Finance and Economy 2021), Brunei will definitely be inching closer to achieving economic stability and sustainability by the year 2035.

CONCLUSION

Twentieth-century Brunei was the beginning of the major transformative period for the country. With two key enablers—the British Residency and the oil sector—that underpinned the socio-economic recovery and development of the country, Brunei had steadily transformed from a state that "had no government in the usual sense of the term..." (McArthur 1987, p. 25) to a state that was "able to sit back and watch the oil flow and the money flow in" (*CO 825/76*, quoted in Horton 1985, p. 380). In addition, the role of the local factor in the form of strong political leadership, as demonstrated by SOAS III and the current monarch, has significantly delivered effective governance which is an equally prime necessity for robust socio-economic development. Unquestionably, barriers and challenges are inevitable. Brunei is a small country with non-renewable natural resources. It has limited industries, is currently experiencing slow economic growth and facing high unemployment rate. However, with WB2035 as a comprehensive national roadmap that guides the country's initiatives for the next fourteen years, the country's prospects for further socio-economic progress should become clearer and more certain. As will be dealt more fully by the subsequent chapters of this book, there are tangible ways to deal with the challenges, as the government puts all its weight behind the effort to protect Brunei's survival and sovereignty in the face of the prevailing socio-economic realities.

REFERENCES

Abdul Latif Ibrahim, Haji. 2003. *Melayu Islam Beraja: Pengantar Huraian* [Malay Islamic Monarchy: An Introductory Description]. Bandar Seri Begawan: Universiti Brunei Darussalam, Akademi Pengajian Brunei.

Asiyah az-Zahra Ahmad Kumpoh. 2017. "Brunei Darussalam in 2016: Adjusting to Economic Challenges". In *Southeast Asian Affairs 2017*, edited by Daljit Singh, and Malcolm Cook, pp. 117–30. Singapore: ISEAS – Yusof Ishak Institute.

Asiyah az-Zahra Ahmad Kumpoh, Siti Norkhalbi Haji Wahsalfelah, and Noor Azam Hj-Othman. 2017. "Socio-Cultural Dynamics in Bruneian Society". In *Comparative Studies in ASEAN Cultures and Societies*, pp. 1–44. Bangkok: Semadhma Publishing House.

Awang Asbol bin Haji Mail, Haji. 2006. *Sejarah Perkembangan Pendidikan Brunei 1950–1985* [The History of the Development of Education in Brunei 1950–1985]. Bandar Seri Begawan: Pusat Sejarah Brunei.

————. 2014. "Dasar-Dasar Pendidikan Negara Brunei Darussalam (1950–2000): Kemunculannya dan Hubungannya dengan Falsafah Melayu Islam Beraja" [Educational Policies of Negara Brunei Darussalam (1950–2000): Their Emergence and Connection with the State Philosophy Malay Islamic Monarchy]. In *Tradisi dan Reformasi Pendidikan, Merista Jasa Sultan Haji Omar 'Ali Saifuddien Sa'adul Khairi Waddien* [Tradition and Reformation in Education, Reminiscing Sultan Haji Omar 'Ali Saifuddien Sa'adul Khairi Waddien's Contributions], Vol. II, edited by Ampuan Dr Haji Brahim bin Ampuan Haji Tengah, pp. 47–63. Bandar Seri Begawan: Akademi Pengajian Brunei, UBD and Yayasan Sultan Haji Hassanal Bolkiah.

Azahari, Izah. 2020. "SHOAS Bridge a Game-Changer for Temburong's Progress". *Borneo Bulletin*, 10 December 2020. https://borneobulletin.com. bn/2020/12/shoas-bridge-a-game-changer-for-temburongs-progress-2/ (accessed 2 January 2021).

Bandial, Ain. 2020. "MoFE: Expansion of Hengyi Complex Will Be 'Significant' Boost to Brunei Economy". *The Scoop*, 29 September 2020. https://thescoop. co/2020/09/29/mofe-expansion-of-hengyi-complex-will-be-significant-boost-to-brunei-economy/ (accessed 28 December 2020).

Bandial, Ain, and Rasidah Hj Abu Bakar. 2018. "Youth Must Dare to Lead Brunei's Development, Says HM". *The Scoop*, 22 February 2018. https:// thescoop.co/2018/02/22/youth-must-dare-lead-bruneis-development-says-hm/ (accessed 3 January 2021).

Blomqvist, Hans C. 1993. "Brunei's Strategic Dilemmas". *The Pacific Review* 6, no. 2: 171–75.

Bolkiah, Mohamed. 2016. *Sana'a to San Jose, 1984–2015*. Bandar Seri Begawan: Brunei Press.

Case, William. 1996. "Brunei Darussalam in 1995: New Party Politics and Diplomatic Presence". *Asian Survey* 36, no. 2: 130–34.

Cator, G.E. 1920. *Annual Report on the State of Brunei 1919*. Kuala Lumpur: The Federated Malay States Government Printing Office.

Chevallier, H. 1913. *Annual Report on the State of Brunei 1911*. Singapore: Government Printing Office.

Cleary, Mark, and Simon Francis. 1999. "Brunei Darussalam: The Outside World Intrudes". In *Southeast Asian Affairs 1999*, edited by Daljit Singh and John Funston, pp. 75–84. Singapore: ISEAS – Yusof Ishak Institute.

CO 825/76. Report by L.S. Greening, 12 April 1949. Quoted in A.V.M. Horton, "The Development of Brunei during the British Residential Era, 1906–1959: A Sultanate Regenerated". PhD dissertation, University of Hull, 1985.

Department of Economic Planning and Statistics. 2019. *Brunei Darussalam Statistical Yearbook 2019*. Bandar Seri Begawan: Ministry of Finance and Economy.

———. 2020. "RKN Journey". http://www.deps.gov.bn/SitePages/RKN%20 Journey.aspx (accessed 9 January 2021).

Doshi, Tilak. 1991. "Brunei: The Steady State". In *Southeast Asian Affairs 1991*, edited by Sharon Siddique and Ng Chee Yuen, pp. 71–80. Singapore: ISEAS – Yusof Ishak Institute.

Hamdan, Mahani, and Chang-Yau Hoon. 2019. "Brunei Darussalam: Making Strides with a Renewed Focus on the Future". In *Southeast Asian Affairs 2019*, edited by Daljit Singh and Malcolm Cook, pp. 85–102. Singapore: ISEAS – Yusof Ishak Institute.

Hamzah, Abu Bakar. 1989. "Brunei Darussalam: Continuity and Tradition". In *Southeast Asian Affairs 1989*, edited by Ng Chee Yuen, pp. 91–104. Singapore: ISEAS – Yusof Ishak Institute.

Hamzah, B.A. 1991. *The Oil Sultanate: Political History of Oil in Brunei Darussalam*. Kuala Lumpur: Mawaddah Enterprise Sdn. Bhd.

Horton, A.V.M. 1984. *The British Residency in Brunei, 1906–1959*. Centre for South-East Asian Studies Occasional Paper, no. 6. Hull: University of Hull.

———. 1986. "British Administration in Brunei 1906–1959". *Modern Asian Studies* 20, no. 2: 353–74.

Hussainmiya, Bachamiya Abdul. 1995. *Sultan Omar Ali Saifuddin III and Britain: The Making of Brunei Darussalam*. Oxford; Singapore; New York: Oxford University Press.

Jamit, Jiram. 2010. "Perkembangan Pentadbiran Kewangan Brunei di bawah Sistem Residen" [The Development of Financial Administration of Brunei under the Residential System]. In *100 Tahun Hubungan Brunei-British 1906–2000* [100 Years of Brunei-British Relations 1906–2000], edited by Haji Rosli bin Haji Ampal and Salina binti Haji Jaafar, pp. 124–44. Bandar Seri Begawan: Pusat Sejarah Brunei.

Kling, Zainal. 1990. "The Changing International Image of Brunei". In *Southeast Asian Affairs 1990*, edited by Ng Chee Yuen and Chandran Jeshurun, pp. 89–100. Singapore: ISEAS – Yusof Ishak Institute.

Lawrey, Roger Neil. 2010. "An Economist's Perspective on Economic Diversification in Brunei Darussalam". *CSPS Strategy and Policy Journal* 1 (July): 13–28.

Lopes, Rui Oliveira, and Mohammed Rahiman Aliudin. 2019. "The Cultural and Creative Industries as a New Road to Economic Diversification in Brunei Darussalam". *Southeast Asia: A Multidisciplinary Journal* 19: 64–77.

McArthur, M.S.H. 1906. *Report on the State of Brunei for 1906*. No publisher.

———. 1987. *Report on Brunei in 1904 by M. S. H. McArthur*, edited and annotated by A.V.M. Horton. Monographs in International Studies, Southeast Asia Series, no. 74. Athens: Center for International Studies, Ohio University.

McKerron, P.A.B. 1930. *Annual Report on the State of Brunei 1929*. Singapore: Government Printing Office.

———. 1931. *Annual Report on the State of Brunei 1930*. Singapore: Government Printing Office.

Menon, K.U. 1987. "Brunei Darussalam in 1986: In Search of the Political Kingdom". In *Southeast Asian Affairs 1987*, edited by M. Ayoob, pp. 85–101. Singapore: ISEAS – Yusof Ishak Institute.

Ministry of Education. 2013. *The National Education System for the 21st Century SPN21*. Bandar Seri Begawan: Ministry of Education, Brunei Darussalam.

———. 2019. *Ministry of Education Strategic Plan 2018–2022*. Bandar Seri Begawan: Strategic Enterprise Performance and Delivery Unit (SEPaDU).

———. 2020. *Brunei Darussalam TVET Report 2019*. Bandar Seri Begawan: Ministry of Education.

Ministry of Finance and Economy. 2021. *Towards a Dynamic and Sustainable Economy: Economic Blueprint for Brunei Darussalam*. Brunei Darussalam: Ministry of Finance and Economy.

Mohamad Yusop bin Awang Damit. 2000. "Brunei Darussalam: Weathering the Storm". In *Southeast Asian Affairs 2000*, edited by Daljit Singh, pp. 87–97. Singapore: ISEAS – Yusof Ishak Institute.

———. 2013. "Pembentukan Perlembagaan Negeri Brunei 1959: Dasar British dan Respons Brunei" [The Formulation of the 1959 Brunei Constitution: British Policy and Brunei Response]. In *Survival Negara Bangsa: Himpunan Kertas Kerja Seminar Serantau* [The Survival of Nation-State: A Compilation of Papers for the Regional Seminar], edited by Haji Rosli bin Haji Ampal and Yus Sa'bariah binti Haji Adanan, pp. 87–112. Bandar Seri Begawan: Pusat Sejarah Brunei.

Mohsin Abu Bakar, Haji. 2008. *Perguruan Melayu dan Inggeris di Brunei 1914– 1983: Sejarah, Sumbangan dan Cabaran* [Malay and English Teacher Training in Brunei 1914–1983: History, Contribution and Challenges]. Bandar Seri Begawan: Universiti Brunei Darussalam.

Muhammad Hadi Muhammad Melayong. 2010. "Hubungan Brunei-British" [Brunei-British Relations]. In *100 Tahun Hubungan Brunei-British 1906–2000* [100 Years of Brunei-British Relations 1906–2000], edited by Haji Rosli bin Haji Ampal and Salina binti Haji Jaafar, pp. 23–58. Bandar Seri Begawan: Pusat Sejarah Brunei.

Mulliner, K. 1985. "Brunei in 1984: Business as Usual after the Gala". *Asian Survey* 25, no. 2: 214–19.

Noor Hasharina Hassan. 2017. "Housing Matters: The Value of Home Ownership in Brunei Darussalam". *Working Paper*, no. 36. Brunei: Institute of Asian Studies, Universiti Brunei Darussalam.

Othman, Azlan. 2019. "206 Receive LNCP Certificates". *Borneo Bulletin*, 3 November 2019. https://borneobulletin.com.bn/2019/11/206-receive-lncp-certificates/ (accessed 2 January 2021).

Padmore, H.J. 1954. *Proposed Development Plan for Education Department 1954–1960*. Kuala Belait: The Brunei Press.

Pan, Yanqin, and Chang-Yau Hoon. 2018. "Fruitful Cooperation between China and Brunei Darussalam". *China Report ASEAN* 3, no. 11: 16–18.

Perlembagaan Negeri Brunei 1959 [1959 Brunei Constitution]. n.d. Brunei: Jabatan Perchetakan Kerajaan.

Proclamation of Independence Brunei Darussalam. 1984.

Ranjit Singh, D.S. 1984. *Brunei, 1839–1983: The Problems of Political Survival*. Singapore: Oxford University Press.

Rasidah Hj Abu Bakar. 2019. "Singapore: Build on Currency Peg to Boost Cooperation". *The Scoop*, 3 October 2019. https://thescoop.co/2019/10/03/singapore-build-on-currency-peg-to-boost-cooperation/ (accessed 28 December 2020).

Sainah binti Haji Saim, Hajah. 2010. "Social Protection in Brunei Darussalam: Current State and Challenges". In *Social Protection in East Asia: Current State and Challenges*, edited by Mukul G. Asher, Sothea Oum and Friska Parulian, pp. 124–56. ERIA Research Project Report. Jakarta: Economic Research Institute for ASEAN and East Asia.

Saunders, Graham. 2002. *A History of Brunei*, 2nd ed. London and New York: RoutledgeCurzon.

Sidhu, Jatswan S. 1995. *Sejarah Sosioekonomi Brunei 1906–1959* [The Socio-Economic History of Brunei 1906–1959]. Kuala Lumpur: Dewan Bahasa dan Pustaka, Kementerian Pendidikan Malaysia.

Siti Fatimahwati Pehin Dato Musa. 2019. "Brunei Darussalam, a Country Profile". In *Southeast Asia and the ASEAN Economic Community*, edited by Roderick Macdonald, pp. 295–311. Cham: Palgrave Macmillan.

Sofiah A. Haji Serudin, Hajah. 2014. "A Decade of Institutional Changes from Sultan Hassanal Bolkiah Teachers College to Universiti Brunei Darussalam". In *Tradisi dan Reformasi Pendidikan, Merista Jasa Sultan Haji Omar 'Ali Saifuddien Sa'adul Khairi Waddien* [Tradition and Reformation in Education, Reminiscing Sultan Haji Omar 'Ali Saifuddien Sa'adul Khairi Waddien's Contributions], Vol. II, edited by Ampuan Dr Haji Brahim bin Ampuan Haji Tengah, pp. 131–39. Bandar Seri Begawan: Akademi Pengajian Brunei, UBD and Yayasan Sultan Haji Hassanal Bolkiah.

Somjee, A.H., and Geeta Somjee. 1995. *Development Success in Asia Pacific: An Exercise in Normative-Pragmatic Balance*. London: Palgrave Macmillan.

Storey, Ian. 2018. "President Xi Jinping's Visit to Brunei Highlights Progress and Problems in Bilateral Relations". *ISEAS Perspective*, no. 2018/83, 28 December 2018.

Sulaiman Haji Duraman, Haji. 2016. *Melayu Islam Beraja: Satu Interpretasi* [Malay Islamic Monarchy: An Interpretation]. Bandar Seri Begawan: Dewan Bahasa dan Pustaka.

Talib, Naimah S. 2013. "Brunei Darussalam: Royal Absolutism and the Modern State". *Kyoto Review of Southeast Asia* 13 (March): 1–8.

Thambipillai, Pushpa. 2010. "Brunei Darussalam in 2009: Addressing the Multiple Challenges". In *Southeast Asian Affairs 2010*, edited by Daljit Singh, pp. 71–82. Singapore: ISEAS – Yusof Ishak Institute.

———. 2018. "Brunei Darussalam: The 'Feel-Good Year' Despite Economic Woes". In *Southeast Asian Affairs 2018*, edited by Malcolm Cook and Daljit Singh, pp. 77–94. Singapore: ISEAS – Yusof Ishak Institute.

Ullah, A.K.M., and Asiyah az-Zahra Ahmad Kumpoh. 2019. "Diaspora Community in Brunei: Culture, Ethnicity and Integration". *Diaspora Studies* 12, no. 1: 14–33. doi:10.1080/09739572.2018.1538686.

Wawasan Brunei 2035. 2016. "Wawasan Brunei 2035". http://wawasanbrunei.gov.bn/SitePages/Our%20Strategy.aspx (accessed 2 January 2021).

PART II

Environment, Energy and Technology

3

NATURAL ECOSYSTEMS AND THEIR MANAGEMENT IN BRUNEI DARUSSALAM

F. Merlin Franco

INTRODUCTION

Brunei is one of the smallest countries in the world. Yet, it boasts one of the highest percentages of forest cover in the world. The monarchy is endowed with a coastline of 161 km and 11 ecosystems that are home to around 15,000 vascular plant species, including 2,000 tree species. The major mountainous peak, Bukit Pagon on the eastern part of Brunei rises to 1,850 m (Ranjith and De Silva 1998; SCBD, n.d.). Brunei's economy today is largely driven by oil and gas. Yet, local communities and industries have also actively been using the ecosystems and the various tangible and intangible benefits they provide (ecosystem services). In this chapter, I provide an overview of the changing dependencies on Brunei's ecosystems and their current state. Following that, I explore the challenges faced by the government and local communities in the conservation and management of ecosystems.

CHANGING DEPENDENCIES ON THE ECOSYSTEMS

Brunei is a natural resource dependent state. However, the nature of dependence and the resources that sustained its economy has changed over time. Although oil fields were discovered in 1929, the economy transitioned into an oil and gas dependent only in the 1970s (Hussainmiya 2014; Mukoyama 2020; Schelander 1998). Prior to that, it depended on forest produces (camphor from *Dryobalanops aromatica* Gaertn.f., rattans, resins, pepper etc.), agriculture, minerals and coal during various points on the historical timescale (Schelander 1998). Cutch emerged as a major forest produce only towards the end of the nineteenth century. Cutch is a khaki dye obtained from mangroves for tanning of leather and treatment of fishing nets (Horton 1985). A cutch factory operated between 1901 and 1904 provided job opportunities to around 300 men from Kampong Ayer (Hussainmiya 2006, pp. xi, 22, 34). From 1906 to 1922, and in 1931, export of cutch made the largest contribution to the exchequer. As a consequence of the boom, mangroves around Brunei Town were overexploited to such an extent that by 1920, most of the mangrove bark that forms the raw material for cutch production was imported (Horton 1985).

During the early part of the twentieth century, Brunei also experimented with plantations. Rubber plantations were introduced first in Temburong and Brunei Town in 1908, and the first rubber export is recorded to have happened in 1914 (Horton 1985, p. 128; Hussainmiya 2006, p. xii). Yet in 1915, cutch continued to be the major export, while sago primarily produced on the banks of Belait, Tutong and Temburong Rivers was also exported to a smaller extent. From 1914–20s, smallholder cultivation of rubber increased, and there was a boom in rubber exports during 1925–30. It began declining thereafter, though there was a spike during 1933–34. Its contribution to the national exchequer had declined from 55–59 per cent in 1928–29 to 19.5 per cent in 1934 (Horton 1985, 2005). Jelutong, a wild rubber possibly obtained from *Dyera costulata* (Miq.) Hook.f. was also exported along with rubber during the rubber boom (Horton 1985). The first non-renewable resource to be exploited by Brunei on an industrial scale was coal. Coal mined from the Brooketon mines (Muara Damit) and Buang Tawar were exported during 1888–1924. They formed a major export during 1918 and 1921. However, coal mining ended at

Brooketon in 1924, followed by the termination of its exports (Horton 1985; Hussainmiya 2006).

On the agricultural side, swidden agriculture involving dryland cultivars and foraging of forest produces was the norm to begin with, prior to Brunei's colonization (Walker 2010). This practice was alive in the Temburong region even in 2002, with a short fallow period of 5–10 years (Lim et al. 2002). The Dusun (Sang Jati Dusun), Kedayan and Ibans were all known for their agricultural practices, especially the swidden farming (Binchin 2010; Franco and Minggu 2019; Horton 1985; Walker 2010). During the Japanese invasion, the Kedayan had established new swidden rice fields by clearing forests in Kampong Pyasaw-pyasaw (Horton 1985; Maxwell 1996). The Kedayan community in Kampong Ayer also prospected non-agricultural alternate food resources such as sago and gula anau, a raw sugar obtained from Nipah palm. In addition, they had also cultivated cassava as a famine food (Franco and Bakar 2020).

Since the advent of the oil and gas economy, Brunei's dependence on other natural resources had declined. Contrary to the beginning of the twentieth century, only 1 per cent of gross domestic product (GDP) came from agriculture, forestry and fishery sector in 2008 (Yakub 2012). A positive outcome of this is the reduced pressure on natural ecosystems which explains their better state when compared to Malaysian and Indonesian Borneo. However, realizing that oil and gas are not perpetual resources, the Brunei government has been devising strategies to diversify the economy. As a part of this, the country has begun relying on its natural resources once more. More than one hundred years since the boom of cutch production, natural resources are being prospected again (Christopher 2011). As before, the major challenge is to ensure that economic growth happens without depletion of ecosystems and their services. Following a *titah* (royal decree) from His Majesty Sultan Haji Hassanal Bolkiah where he emphasized on economic diversification, the Ministry of Finance and Economy (MoFE) has developed a blueprint for Brunei's economy that emphasizes on balancing economic growth and environmental sustainability. The blueprint aspires to achieve sustainable development through green and blue economy. It strives for sustainable businesses and technology that would increase productivity while at the same time also foster environmental conservation (Kementerian Kewangan dan Ekonomi Brunei Darussalam 2020). Thus, the new economic model envisages a change in the human-ecosystem dependency, from the usual model that exploits ecosystems to a model that prophesies utilization of technology to give back to ecosystems.

NATURAL ECOSYSTEMS OF BRUNEI

Brunei's National Biological Resources (Biodiversity) Policy and Strategic Plan of Action lists eleven ecosystems: agro ecosystems, beach forests, coastal and marine ecosystems, freshwater forest wetlands, heath forests, mangrove forests, mixed dipterocarp forests, montane forests, peat swamp forests, secondary forests and urban forests (Biodiversity Research and Innovation Centre, n.d.). For administrative purposes, the forests are classified into gazetted forest reserves and state land forests; gazetted forests occupy around 40 per cent of the total land area (FAO 2000). I provide a brief overview of these ecosystems in the following sections.

Agro Ecosystems

Agro ecosystems of Brunei are not mere food production centres. The National Biological Resources (Biodiversity) Policy and Strategic Plan of Action recognizes the ability of these ecosystems to provide watershed functions, harbour avian and pollinator biodiversity, sequester atmospheric carbon, etc., in addition to the core function of food production. Grealish, Ringrose-Voase and Fitzpatrick (2010) identified twenty-four soil types from Brunei; such a diversity calls for an equivalent diversity in cultivation methods and crops. Vegetables are grown on peat soil supplemented with mineral fertilizers, poultry manure and lime (Williams 1978). Organic farming has also been introduced, with the aquaculture sector being the pioneer. Aquaculture output has grown at a rate of 14.3 per cent per annum since 1998 onwards from B$2 million in 1998 to B$22 million in 2017 (*Borneo Bulletin Yearbook 2020*). As of 2015, there were 29 hectares of organic aquaculture fields in Brunei (Lernoud and Willer 2017).

Perdayan (Temburong district), Lamunin (Tutong district), Lot Sengkuang (Belait district) and Wasan (Brunei-Muara) are some of the most important wetland rice ecosystems in Brunei (Yakub 2012). Of these, Wasan paddy field is the oldest commercial wetland rice farm in the country. Between 1979 and 1982, the area in Wasan under rice cultivation increased from 130 ha to 280 ha. However, it declined thereafter to just 80 ha in the 1990s owing to a lack of competencies and financial capital (Yakub 2012). In 1997, about 97 per cent of rice consumed in the country was imported (Galawat and Yabe 2012). However, the area under cultivation in Wasan had increased again in 2019 to around 286 ha due to renewed thrust from the government and entrepreneurs of Koperasi Setia Kawan (KOSEKA) (A. Wong 2019). The government has been working towards a substantial increase in rice production within the country (Shams et al. 2015). A new commercial rice field was launched recently in Kandol of Belait district with an acreage of around 500 ha. By 2025, it is expected to reach an optimal yield of 6,000–8,000 tonnes of paddy per annum (*Borneo Bulletin Yearbook 2020*).

A major challenge in Brunei's rice ecosystems is the acidity of wetland soil which has to be managed by adding lime in the industrial rice farms. Local entrepreneurs who do not conform to the industrial agricultural style have successfully adopted local knowledge from elsewhere to holistically overcome this challenge. An example is the Chinampa farm at "The Living Earth" organic farm at Pengkalan Batu. The farm has been running a pilot Chinampa farm where leafy vegetables such as ladies' finger, brinjal and moringa are grown on raised beds in swamp land (see Figure 3.1). Food and agricultural waste from the farm are added to the water channel which raised the pH to 7 (Jeff Ong, personal communication). Chinampa is a cultivation system that was pioneered in Mesoamerica by the Aztecs where crops are cultivated in soil beds raised as islands in shallow water bodies (Ebel 2020). The cultivation technique is believed to be the secret behind the flourishing of Aztec civilization, and could be an excellent fit for Brunei's swamps, if adapted suitably.

Beach Forests

Beach forests appear on coastal sandy soils beyond the influence of high tides. They are found on the coasts in Muara and Tutong, and Kuala Belait (Forestry Department 2020a). At least twenty-five tree species have been recorded to occur in the beach forests of Brunei (Ashton, Kamariah and Md. Said 2003). Typical plant species of this ecosystem includes *Hibiscus tiliaceus* L., *Casuarina equisetifolia* L., *Barringtonia asiatica*

FIGURE 3.1
The pilot Chinampa farm at "The Living Earth" farm, Pengkalan Batu

Source: Photograph © F. Merlin Franco

(L.) Kurz, *Planchonella obovata* (R.Br.) Pierre, and *Thespesia* spp. (Forestry Department 2020a; Sandal 1996). The beach forests are easily influenced by even the slightest changes in the ecosystem (Scialabba 1998), which makes their conservation challenging. Their survival is important for the nesting of marine turtles and the prevention of siltation of rivers and lagoons. Besides, they also form a natural barrier that prevents the sand dunes from advancing landwards.

Coastal and Marine Ecosystems

With 161 km of coastline, the small country is in essence a coastal state (MoFE 2020; Ranjith and De Silva 1998). Brunei has around 50 sq. km of coral cover that harbours 711 species of fish and 410 reef-building coral species (Department of Fisheries 2014). Coral reefs in Brunei are generally considered to be in good condition. The capture fisheries industries are estimated to have contributed around B$112 million to Brunei's GDP in 2003 (Department of Fisheries 2020). Brunei's Integrated Coastal Zone Management Plan is hailed as a progressive one in the region. The setting up of National

Committee on the Environment (NCE) in 1993, devising of a National Oil Spill Contingency Plan, the Red Tide Action Plan, and artificial reef development involving defunct oil rigs are all worth emulating (Ranjith and De Silva 1998).

Freshwater Forest Wetlands

Freshwater swamp forests cover around 12,668 ha of Brunei's surface area, accounting for about 3 per cent of Brunei's total forests (Yussof 2005). They mostly occur on the banks of the Belait River, Tasek Merimbun and Sungai Medit. Characteristic plant species of these forests include *Shorea macrophylla* (de Vriese) P.S.Ashton, *Shorea seminis* (de Vriese) Slooten, *Eusideroxylon zwageri* Teijsm. & Binn., *Dryobalanops rappa* Becc., and *Intsia palembanica* Miq. (Forestry Department 2020b; Yamada and Suzuki 2004). Of these, *E. zwageri*, *D. rappa* and *I. palembanica* are economically valuable timber species. The *empran* sub-type of freshwater swamp forests house around 600 tree species, of which 25 are endemic to Borneo (Ashton, Kamariah and Md. Said 2003). The freshwater swamp forests in Tasek Merimbun are protected as habitat in an ASEAN Heritage Park, as well as an Important Bird Area (BirdLife International 2020b; M. Wong 2006).

Heath Forests (Kerangas)

Heath forests of Borneo are known by the Iban term *kerangas*. They occur on well-drained, nutrient-poor, sandy soils. The area under heath forests in Brunei is around 3,000 ha. Thus, it accounts for just around 1 per cent of Brunei's forest cover (Suhaili, Tennakoon and Sukri 2015; K.M. Wong et al. 2015). They are known to have relatively lesser species richness when compared to mixed dipterocarp forests (Davies and Becker 1996). Yet, these forests are of immense ecological significance owing to their unique habitat and species composition. Estimates suggest that the heath forests of Brunei harbour only around 300 tree species. But these forests are rich in endemic species and species of economic importance (Ashton 2010; Hazimah, Metali and Sukri 2015). Biologists recognize two types of *kerangas* in Brunei: a type that is comprised of trees up to 40 m tall, found on white sand terraces, and a second type occurring on shallow white sand soils (Ashton, Kamariah and Md. Said 2003). Heath forests of

Brunei and the larger Borneo are threatened by frequent forests fires. Forest fires alter soil properties, reduce the diversity of native tree species, and offer conducive conditions such as an open canopy for the establishment of populations of invasive *Acacia mangium* Willd. (Wardah et al. 2020; Yusoff et al. 2019). In addition, *Acacia* is able to fix nitrogen, which imparts a competitive edge in the nutrient-deficient podzolized soil, especially when the forest is disturbed (Osunkoya, Othman and Kahar 2005; Suhaili, Tennakoon and Sukri 2015). The most cost-effective and efficient way of preventing the conversion of heath forests into *Acacia* stands is to prevent forest fires; *Acacia* is a poor competitor against native species under the shady conditions provided by intact forest covers (Jambul et al. 2020).

Mangrove Forests

Mangrove forests are found on saline soils influenced by tidal cycles. In Brunei, they cover approximately 18,418 ha of the surface area (Duratul Ain and Iskandar 2020). There are thirty-three trees species known to occur in the mangrove forests of Brunei (Ashton, Kamariah and Md. Said 2003). Generally, mangroves of Southeast Asia are known to exhibit zonation (Ng and Sivasothi 2001). Zone 1 on the seaward edge is usually dominated by *Avicennia* spp. and *Sonneratia* spp., zone 2 is dominated by *Rhizophora* spp., and zone 3 by *Bruguiera* spp., *Ceriops* spp., *Xylocarpus* spp. and *Heritiera* spp. Mangroves of Brunei occur as mixed communities dominated by a few species, or as pure stands. One of the largest tracts of relatively undisturbed mangroves is found in the Brunei Bay that is shared between Brunei and Sarawak. The vegetation here is dominated by *Sonneratia caseolaris* (L.) Engl., *Sonneratia alba* Sm., *Rhizophora apiculata* Blume, *Nypa fruticans* Wurmb and *Xylocarpus granatum* J.Koenig (Satyanarayana et al. 2018). These mangroves support populations of charismatic animals such as proboscis monkey (*Nasalis larvatus*), silver leaf monkeys (*Trachypithecus cristatus*), crab-eating macaque (*Macaca fascicularis*), Müller's Bornean gibbon (*Hylobates muelleri*) and flat-headed cat (*Prionailurus planiceps*), and the endangered birds Storm's Stork (*Ciconia stormi*) and Spotted Greenshank (*Tringa guttifer*) (BirdLife International 2020a; Nowak 2012). A pure stand of *Avicennia marina* (Forssk.) Vierh. occurs in Sungei Pemburonguna (Choy and Booth 1994).

Between 2002 and 2017, Brunei lost around 1,039 ha of mangroves to deforestation, emitting around 459,640 to 1,838,560 total carbon dioxide into the atmosphere (Jakovac et al. 2020). Mangroves of Southeast Asia are the foremost line of defence in mitigating climate change, and there is a renewed thrust on regenerating them. However, an analysis using hydrodynamic, geomorphological, climatic and socio-economic parameters found Brunei as one of the least feasible countries for future mangrove afforestation programmes (Syahid et al. 2020). Hence, it is important to conserve the existing mangroves of Brunei from degradation. Brunei has initiated conservation of mangrove ecosystem by zoning them according to land use categories. Accordingly, protected areas such as the Silirong Forest Reserve and Labu Forest Reserve were created (Laila 2000). There is an urgent need for the creation of more of such protected areas, and effective implementation of sound mangrove management processes to arrest further deforestation of mangroves.

Mixed Dipterocarp Forests (MDF)

Mixed Dipterocarp Forests form the largest percentage of lowland forest cover in Borneo (Davies and Becker 1996). They are popular for their exceptionally tall trees growing up to 40–60 m (Davies and Becker 1996; Yussof 2005). Although they are named as Mixed Dipterocarp Forests (MDF), families other than Dipterocarpaceae are also known to dominate tracts considered as MDF (Small et al. 2004). MDFs account for the largest percentage of forest cover in Brunei (41 per cent) (Forestry Department 2020c). These forests are found up to an altitude of over 800 metres above sea level. In Brunei, between 500 and 1,000 metres asl, they transition into hill dipterocarp forests (Orr 2006; Pendry and Proctor 1997). The MDFs of Andulau forest reserve has the highest floristic species richness in the entire Borneo (Ashton 2010; Das 1994). Davies and Becker (1996) had recorded 716 tree species from 4 ha of Andulau forests alone which highlights the tremendous tree diversity harboured by these forests. MDFs of Brunei support a diverse range of bat species. Struebig et al. (2012) recorded thirty-five bat species, which is believed to represent the total bat diversity of Borneo. The primary MDFs are the richest in odonate diversity and endemicity of all the forest types in Brunei (Orr 2006). In Brunei, the area under MDF has remained constant at 223,754 ha between 1979 and 1996. However, MDF that could be considered as primary forests declined in area cover from 192,575 ha to 164,775 ha (Yussof 2005).

Montane Forests

Montane forests are found from an altitude of 700 m onwards, in Temburong district. Their altitudinal range often overlaps with that of hill dipterocarp forests (Ashton, Kamariah and Md. Said 2003). The trees here are stunted. *Lithocarpus* spp., *Quercus* spp., *Madhuca* spp., *Palaquium* spp., *Payena* spp., *Podocarpus neriifolius*, *Agathis endertii* and *Shorea coriacea* are the major species of the lower montane forests, while the upper montane forests (1,200 m onwards) are characterized by the presence of *Dacrydium beccarii, Phyllocladus hypophyllus, Syzygium bankase, and Calophyllum nodosum* (Forestry Department 2020d). The lower and upper montane forests of Brunei together are home to around 600 tree species, of which 95 are Bornean endemics (Ashton, Kamariah and Md. Said 2003). In Bukit Belalong, as we move up from the lowland forests, the temperature decreases progressively, which leads to changes in forest structure and species composition (Pendry and Proctor 1996). From 850 m onwards, species diversity of the families Lauraceae, Myrtaceae, Euphorbiaceae and Clusiaceae increases unlike the Dipterocarp dominated lowland forests. Maximum tree height also decreases from 60 m at 200 m to 33 m at 850 m (Pendry and Proctor 1997). In 1979, montane forests occupied an area of approximately 7,196 ha, accounting for 1.5 per cent of the country's total forest cover. The area has remained constant since then (Yussof 2005).

Peat Swamp Forests

True to its name, peat swamp forests occur on waterlogged peatlands (Posa, Wijedasa and Corlett 2011). Much of Brunei's peatlands are concentrated in the Belait district. A noteworthy feature is that plant families such as Dipterocarpaceae, Anacardiaceae, Annonaceae, Euphorbiaceae, Guttiferae, Lauraceae, leguminosae, Myrtaceae, Rubiaceae and Sapotaceae that are known to dominate lowland mixed dipterocarp forests also dominate peat swamp forests (Anderson 1963). Peat swamp forests of Brunei harbour around 200 tree species, of which 25 are endemic to Borneo (Ashton, Kamariah and Md. Said

2003). Generally in Southeast Asia, primates reported to depend on mangroves also depend on peat forests. Peat forests offer them more food options, while mangroves offer them refuge from predators (Nowak 2012).

Since peat is partially decayed organic matter, peatlands together with their forests are repositories of carbon. Brunei's peat swamp forests have been shown to store up to 1,700 Ct/ha/m of carbon (Kobayashi 2016). Of the total 1,040 sq. km of peat swamp forest that Brunei once had, 16.1 per cent was lost by 2011 to logging, forest fires and land use changes. An estimated 873 sq. km of peat swamp forests remain today (Posa, Wijedasa and Corlett 2011). Forest fires and both legal and illegal logging are major threats to the peat swamp forests of Brunei. During the El Nino drought of 1997–98, forest fires had burnt down a considerable extent of peat swamp forests in Anduki (Hazimah et al. 2018). Commercially valuable species such as *Shorea albida* Symington form continuous pure stands, and harvesting them is similar to clear felling. *S. albida* is slow to regenerate naturally, resulting in a secondary forest with very few individuals of *S. albida* (Kobayashi 2000). Likewise, *Dryobalanops rappa* Becc. populations are threatened by illegal logging (Hazimah et al. 2018).

Secondary Forests

These are young forests less than fifty years of age, resulting from either secondary succession after deforestation events or through afforestation efforts; Forest Act considers secondary forests that are more than fifty years of age as "old forest" (CommonLII, n.d.; Duratul Ain and Iskandar 2020). As they are yet to reach the climax stage, their canopy is not closed, permitting more light to reach the forest floor. Consequently, forest floors of secondary forests are relatively rich in vegetation when compared to primary forests (Safwana, El-Said and Shams 2017). Primary forests subjected to disturbances such as controlled logging are also considered secondary forests (Kobayashi 1994). Although not officially considered as secondary forests, the homegardens and orchards of the Kedayan, Dusun and Iban communities are known to harbour rich tree diversity and offer great scope for conserving native economically valuable tree species (Ashton, Kamariah and Md. Said 2003; Franco and Minggu 2019). The Dusun, Kedayan and Ibans were all once known to practise swidden farming in Brunei (Binchin 2010; Franco and Minggu 2019; Horton 1985; Walker 2010). Since the abandonment of swidden farming, these farms have gone through succession and are now classified as old forests. Thus, a considerable portion of Brunei's old forests has been culturally influenced by the local communities in the recent past.

Urban Forests

Urban forests are fondly called as green lungs of urban ecosystems. They provide opportunities for residents to stay in touch with nature. They play an important role in reducing pollution levels while also serve as recreational avenues (Chen and Jim 2008). In addition to these, Brunei's National Biological Resources (Biodiversity) Policy and Strategic Plan of Action also recognizes urban forests as useful in mitigating flooding, cycle nutrients, conserve biodiversity and also serve as ecological corridors connecting green spaces (Biodiversity Research and Innovation Centre, n.d.). Brunei's urban forests include Tasek Lama Recreational Park, Bukit Shahbandar Forest Recreational Park and Berakas Forest Reserve Recreational Park. In addition, there are also many other forested areas that are not designated as parks. A major threat facing Brunei's urban forests is the increasing fragmentation which I discuss under the "challenges in ecosystem management" section.

CHALLENGES IN ECOSYSTEM MANAGEMENT

Balancing Urbanization and Ecosystem Conservation

Among the ASEAN countries, economic growth and increase in carbon emissions have gone hand in hand. However, an analysis by Le (2019) indicated the existence of Environmental Kuznets Curve in the case of Singapore and Brunei, where there is an inverse relationship between economic growth and per capita carbon emissions. Environmental Kuznets Curve predicts that economic growth leads to environmental degradation in the initial phases. However, as per capita incomes grow, countries will begin investing in environmental conservation, leading to better environmental quality (Dinda 2004). As per an analysis undertaken by Bryan et al. (2013), 54 per cent of Brunei's land surface in 2009 was covered by unlogged forests. A subsequent analysis pegs the figure at 56.9 per cent for the year 2010; Brunei also experienced the lowest loss of forest cover in Borneo during 1973–2010 (Gaveau et al. 2014). Thus, Brunei's forests are a major carbon sink for Borneo. However, the relatively smaller expanse of forest tracts is a major challenge for their long-term sustainability. Forest tracts, especially of the *kerangas* have been subjected to fragmentation leading to change in species composition and dynamics (Charles and Ang 2010).

Bandar Seri Begawan (BSB), Brunei's capital, is one of the notable cities of the world with proportionately large tracts of forest cover. However, BSB and the larger Brunei-Muara district is where much of the urbanization and population growth is accumulated. During 1981–2011, Brunei-Muara district lost around 64.5 per cent of vegetation cover comprising of grasslands and rainforests to urbanization; the proportion of built-up area in the district increased from 13.5 per cent to 31 per cent during the same period. Today, the remaining vegetation cover is fragmented into disjointed green spaces by roads and built environment (Ng, Shabrina and Buyuklieva 2019). Tasek Lama Recreational Park, Berakas Forest Reserve Recreational Park and Bukit Shahbandar Forest Recreation Park, the three major urban forests of Brunei-Muara are separated by a growing built environment (see Figure 3.2). Fragmentation renders forests vulnerable to degradation while also leading to disruption of animal movement. Animal crossings and road kills of endangered animals such as the critically endangered Sunda Pangolin are often encountered on Brunei roads (Fletcher 2016). Although fragmentation is an inevitable fallout of urbanization, green corridors could mitigate the negative impact by connecting urban green spaces (Peng, Zhao and Liu 2017; Rudd, Vala and Schaefer 2002). Brunei aims to connect existing forest patches within the Heart of Borneo region (HoB) through ecological corridors (Biodiversity Research and Innovation Centre, n.d.). Ideally, such corridors should also be established in the Brunei-Muara district to link the various forest fragments. In this context, Brunei could also look inward into its traditional land use pattern which is a matrix landscape comprising of inter-connected spatial units of mixed land use. Such landscapes prevail even today in the hinterland of Brunei where residential dwellings co-exist with farms, orchards and forests. The revival of such landscape units in urban landscapes are possible, as understood from the experience of Japan with Satoyama landscapes (Takeuchi 2010).

FIGURE 3.2
Map showing the disjoint Tasek Lama Recreational Park,
Berakas Forest Reserve Recreational Park and Bukit Shahbandar
Forest Recreation Park in Brunei-Muara district

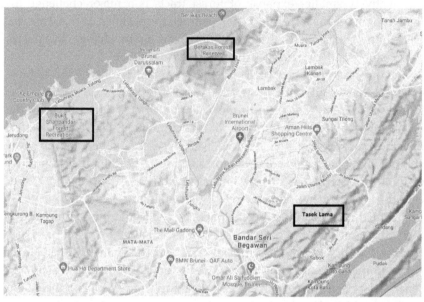

Source: Google (n.d.)

Loss of Local Knowledge

Much of Brunei's forests were once culturally managed by the local
communities through cultural practices such as hunting and gathering.
In fact, patches that were once under swidden cultivation have now
grown into forest patches that are virtually indistinguishable from
primary forests. These forests are often branded as pristine, ignoring
the cultural inputs from local communities (Voeks and Nyawa 2006).
Acculturation and the rise of an oil and gas based economy have led
to local communities distancing themselves from the forest, leaving
the forests as islands conserved through formal measures (Ellen and
Bernstein 1994). In this context, it is important to bring the local
communities emotionally closer to the ecosystems, by building upon
their local ecological knowledge. A valuable component of local
knowledge is the local ecological calendar (Franco 2015). These calendars

are not only repositories of knowledge on the ecosystems, but also tools to manage them. They are also known to significantly boost our capacity to mitigate climate change. However, except for the Dusun and Kedayan calendars, local ecological calendars in Brunei are yet to be documented. The local knowledge of Brunei's communities on ecosystem management could be a valuable tool in developing locally relevant and culturally appropriate management measures for Brunei's ecosystems (Ulluwishewa et al. 2008).

Forest Fires and Invasive Species

Incidences of forest fires in Brunei peak during the months of February to April. Lesser precipitation rates, coupled with high temperatures during this period, make the situation conducive for fire breakouts. Interestingly, much of the forest fire incidents are reported from the densely populated Brunei-Muara district. Likewise, the percentage of fire-affected areas is also reported to be higher in the Brunei-Muara district (55 per cent) (Shams et al. 2019). Belait district ranks second in incidences of forest fire. The district is prone to forest fires due to the presence of peatlands that become vulnerable when the groundwater table goes down either naturally or drained by humans. Similar to Brunei-Muara district, forest fire incidences in Belait too are frequent in areas with high residential density (El-Said, Shams and Safwanah 2020). These observations show that forest fires in Brunei are largely anthropogenic in nature.

Forest fires occurring in heath and peat forests emit large amounts of carbon, degrade the quality of forests, reduce the population of economically valuable species and render them vulnerable to colonization by invasive species such as *Acacia mangium* Willd. (Hazimah et al. 2018; Lupascu et al. 2020; Wardah et al. 2020; Yusoff et al. 2019). They are also the major drivers of haze and deterioration of air quality (Radojevic 2003). Brunei's fire management approach emphasizes on prevention of fire incidents by deterring open burning, attending to forest fires swiftly and penalizing offenders (A Bakar 1999). Section 277A of the Emergency Order (Penal Code Amendment 1998) provides the law enforcers with a new provision to tackle fire incidents. Accordingly, offenders could be fined up to B$100,000. The penalty would also exceed this sum along with imprisonment for up to five years in cases where such offences lead to pollution or damage to human life and property (Ganz 2002). However, incidents of forest fires have been increasing in Brunei, posing a serious challenge to human well-being and ecosystem health (Safwana, El-Said and Shams 2017). Given the anthropogenic origin of most fires, it is imperative to create more awareness among the general public on the hazards of fire, and also invest in modern forest fire detection systems (Alkhatib 2014).

Climate Change

The paltry contribution of the agriculture, forestry and fishery sector (Yakub 2012) to Brunei's economy has been changing. Renewed thrust on agriculture has led to a considerable increase in agricultural output. However, climate change is projected to hamper agricultural productivity. Brunei's mean annual rainfall and temperature have been increasing since 1978, while dry days per year have been decreasing at the rate of 1.79 days per year (Ratnayake 2014). To meet the challenges of climate change, Brunei will have to invest in upgrading the farming skills and experience of farmers, especially the younger generation (Shams et al. 2015). While striving to improve productivity and flow of ecosystem services from agricultural lands, Brunei should also pay attention to the potential of climate-friendly native fruits such as *tarap* (*Artocarpus odoratissimus* Blanco) that grow both in the wild as well as cultivated conditions (Tang, Linda and Franz 2013).

Pollution

Grealish, Ringrose-Voase and Fitzpatrick (2010) identified soil conditions that limit the cultivation of vegetables, grasses, rice and fruit trees in Brunei. Water logging, soil erosion from hill slopes, acid sulfate soils, application of too much or insufficient fertilizers are all identified as limiting factors. These limiting factors underline the need for prudent management of agro ecosystems for maintaining their productivity and ecosystem services. The application of fertilizers especially has to be fine-tuned according to the local requirements to avoid heavy metal pollution (Zunaidi, Lim and Metali 2020). More than 85 per cent of Brunei population reside on the coast (Ranjith and De Silva 1998), an area that would receive pollutants from the inland. In the Brunei Bay area, lead pollution is steadily climbing due to anthropogenic influences on the draining rivers (Adiana et al. 2017). Although Brunei has little control over anthropogenic pollutants arising from beyond its borders, as a stakeholder, it is bound to be affected by the pollution of Brunei Bay.

Declining Fisheries Yield

Fish density has declined by 79 per cent, with the decline more pronounced in the coastal waters of depth up to 50 m. In order to maintain fishing within sustainable levels, steps such as limiting new fishing licenses, construction of artificial reefs, stemming Illegal, Unreported and Unregulated (IUU) fishing, establishment of marine protected areas, etc. have been introduced over time. In addition, aquaculture projects such as freshwater fish and prawn farming, marine fish farming in floating cages, offshore fish culture, etc. have also been promoted to lessen the pressure on the natural fish population (Department of Fisheries 2020). A strength and weakness analysis undertaken in 2010 showed that Brunei's existing legislation related to fisheries did not explicitly emphasize ecosystem-based fisheries management among various other weaknesses. However, the legislative framework has its strengths in providing for optimal utilization of fishery resources, implementation of sound scientific management policies, creation of marine protected reserves, listing of protected marine species and banning of destructive fishing technologies (Edeson et al. 2010). Brunei has been imparting training to its stakeholders on the Electronic ASEAN Catch Documentation System (eACDS) that helps in tracing the journey of fish and fishery products from the fishing process to the table. It is noteworthy that the system was first pilot-tested in Brunei in 2016 (SEAFDEC Secretariat 2018). When implemented, the eACDS system will help Brunei to prevent outputs of IUU fishing from entering the food supply chain.

HEALTHY ECOSYSTEMS FOSTER SOCIO-ECONOMIC DEVELOPMENT

Healthy ecosystems provide various goods and services to humankind. Collectively termed as ecosystem services (Fisher, Turner and Morling 2009), their contribution to a country's socio-economic progress is often undervalued, as existing GDP measures emphasize benefits from the built environment rather than natural ecosystems (Costanza et al. 2014). An estimate from Kubiszewski et al. (2016) showed that the services provided by Brunei's terrestrial ecosystems alone in 2011 were around US\$7,381 million. This figure would be much higher if we take into consideration the services provided by coastal and marine ecosystems. A major challenge in understanding the contribution of Brunei's ecosystems to human well-being is the absence of a comprehensive assessment of ecosystem services. Therefore, researchers and policymakers should prioritize the assessment and quantification of ecosystem services provided by the eleven ecosystems of Brunei. Emphasis should be given to understanding the role of local knowledge in accessing these ecosystem services sustainably. This would help Brunei leverage the full potential of its ecosystem for sustainable economic growth, and human well-being.

Similar to natural ecosystems, the health status of agro ecosystems that are actively managed by humans is also important. A healthy agro ecosystem could provide services such as pollination, pest control, genetic diversity, topsoil retention, maintenance of soil fertility, and nutrient and water cycling (Power 2010), besides food. Unhealthy agro ecosystems could emerge as a fertile ground for epidemic diseases. As Brunei aims to increase the acreage under wetland agriculture, it would also have to implement integrated vector management approaches including alternate wet and dry irrigation and cultivation of fishes in agricultural fields (Keiser et al. 2005). The 300-hectare rice field at Sengkuang of Belait is reported to be near-abandoned due to loss of productivity resulting from deprivation of flood waters from the nearby river (A. Wong 2019). The government is exploring measures such as the exploitation of groundwater to revive the field (Wasil 2018). In this scenario, local adaptations of solutions such as the chinampa system of cultivation could help in maintaining a healthy agro ecosystem while also providing rich yield.

CONCLUSION

Thanks to an oil and gas based economy, contemporary Brunei has been successful in allocating a large proportion of its land surface area for the conservation of forests. However, realizing that oil and gas reserves are not perpetually available, Brunei has developed a new economic blueprint that emphasizes on economic growth that goes hand in hand with ecosystem conservation. The eleven ecosystems of Brunei when maintained in healthy condition, could provide significant ecosystem services that could, in turn, help Brunei realize this goal. However, the expansion of urban areas that fragments the forest cover, loss of local knowledge, forest fires, climate change, pollution and declining yield from the fisheries sector emerge as major challenges faced by the ecosystems today. Mitigating these challenges through culturally appropriate and locally relevant measures that build upon Brunei's local knowledge would help Brunei reach its goal of an environmentally sound diversified economy comfortably.

REFERENCES

A Bakar bin Jaafar, Dato Dr. 1999. "Review of Government Environmental & Health Policies, Legislation and Emergency Response Mechanisms". In *Health Guidelines for Vegetation Fire Events, Lima, Peru, 6–9 October 1998*. WHO. https://www.who.int/docstore/peh/Vegetation_fires/Backgroundpapers/BackgrPap14.pdf (accessed 15 April 2021).

Adiana, Ghazali, Hafizan Juahir, Bidai Joseph, and Noor Azhar Mohamed Shazili. 2017. "Tracing the Sources of Lead (Pb) in Brunei Bay, Borneo by Using Integrated Spectrometry ICP-MS and Chemometric Techniques". *Marine Pollution Bulletin* 123, no. 1–2: 232–40. https://doi.org/10.1016/j.marpolbul.2017.08.055.

Alkhatib, Ahmad A.A. 2014. "A Review on Forest Fire Detection Techniques". *International Journal of Distributed Sensor Networks* 10, no. 3: 597368. https://doi.org/10.1155/2014/597368.

Anderson, J.A.R. 1963. "The Flora of the Peat Swamp Forests of Sarawak and Brunei, Including a Catalogue of All Recorded Species of Flowering Plants, Ferns, and Fern Allies". *The Gardens' Bulletin, Singapore* 20, no. 2: 131–228.

Ashton, Peter S. 2010. "Conservation of Borneo Biodiversity: Do Small Lowland Parks Have a Role, or Are Big Inland Sanctuaries Sufficient? Brunei as an Example". *Biodiversity and Conservation* 19, no. 2: 343–56. https://doi.org/10.1007/s10531-009-9717-0.

Ashton, Peter S., A.S. Kamariah, and Idris Md. Said, eds. 2003. *A Field Guide to the Forest Trees of Brunei Darussalam and the Northwest Borneo Hot-Spot*, Vol. 1. Brunei Darussalam: Universiti Brunei Darussalam.

Binchin, Pudarno. 2010. "Temarok Belief, Siram-Songs, and the Repertoire of Epic Tales of Derato". In *ICH Courier*, August 2010. https://ichcourier.unesco-ichcap.org/temarok-belief-siram-songs-and-the-repertoire-of-epic-tales-of-derato/ (accessed 15 April 2021).

Biodiversity Research and Innovation Centre. n.d. "National Biological Resources (Biodiversity) Policy and Strategic Plan of Action". Brunei Darussalam: Biodiversity Research and Innovation Centre, Ministry of Industry and Primary Resources.

BirdLife International. 2020a. "Important Bird Areas Factsheet: Brunei Bay". https://www.datazone.birdlife.org/site/factsheet/brunei-bay-iba-brunei (accessed 15 April 2021).

———. 2020b. "Important Bird Areas Factsheet: Tasek Merimbun". http://www.birdlife.org (accessed 15 April 2021).

Borneo Bulletin Yearbook 2020: The Guide to Brunei Darussalam. 2020. Bandar Seri Begawan: Brunei Press Commercial Printing Services. https://borneobulletinyearbook.com.bn/2020 (accessed 15 April 2021).

Bryan, Jane E., Philip L. Shearman, Gregory P. Asner, David E. Knapp, Geraldine Aoro, and Barbara Lokes. 2013. "Extreme Differences in Forest Degradation in Borneo: Comparing Practices in Sarawak, Sabah, and Brunei". *PLoS ONE* 8, no. 7: e69679. https://doi.org/10.1371/journal.pone.0069679.

Charles, Joseph K., and Bee Biaw Ang. 2010. "Non-Volant Small Mammal Community Responses to Fragmentation of Kerangas Forests in Brunei Darussalam". *Biodiversity and Conservation* 19, no. 2: 543–61. https://doi.org/10.1007/s10531-009-9691-6.

Chen, Wendy Y., and C.Y. Jim. 2008. "Assessment and Valuation of the Ecosystem Services Provided by Urban Forests". In *Ecology, Planning, and Management of Urban Forests*, edited by Margaret M. Carreiro, Yong-Chang Song, and Jianguo Wu, pp. 53–83. New York, NY: Springer. https://doi.org/10.1007/978-0-387-71425-7_5.

Choy, Satish C., and Webber E. Booth. 1994. "Prolonged Inundation and Ecological Changes in an Avicennia Mangrove: Implications for Conservation and Management". *Hydrobiologia* 285: 237–47.

Christopher, Roberts. 2011. "Brunei Darussalam: Consolidating the Foundations of Its Future?". In *Southeast Asian Affairs 2011*, edited by Daljit Singh, pp. 35–50. Singapore: ISEAS – Yusof Ishak Institute.

Commonwealth Legal Information Institute (CommonLII). n.d. "Forest Act (Chapter 46) Forest Rules". http://www.commonlii.org/bn/legis/fa46fr309/ (accessed 15 April 2021).

Costanza, Robert, Rudolf de Groot, Paul Sutton, Sander van der Ploeg, Sharolyn J. Anderson, Ida Kubiszewski, Stephen Farber, and R. Kerry Turner. 2014. "Changes in the Global Value of Ecosystem Services". *Global Environmental Change* 26 (May): 152–58. https://doi.org/10.1016/j.gloenvcha.2014.04.002.

Das, Indraneil. 1994. "Evaluating Biodiversity: The Batu Apoi Experience". *Ambio* 23, no. 4–5: 238–42.

Davies, Stuart J., and Peter Becker. 1996. "Floristic Composition and Stand Structure of Mixed Dipterocarp and Heath Forests in Brunei Darussalam". *Journal of Tropical Forest Science* 8, no. 4: 542–69.

Department of Fisheries. 2014. "Coral Conservation, Awareness, Rehabilitation & Enrichment Programme". Brunei Darussalam: Department of Fisheries, Ministry of Primary Resources and Tourism. http://www.mprt.gov.bn/ SiteCollectionDocuments/Newsletter/coralcare.pdf (accessed 15 April 2021).

_____. 2020. "Programmes and Focus". http://www.fisheries.gov.bn (accessed 15 April 2021).

Dinda, Soumyananda. 2004. "Environmental Kuznets Curve Hypothesis: A Survey". *Ecological Economics* 49, no. 4: 431–55. https://doi.org/10.1016/j. ecolecon.2004.02.011.

Duratul Ain Haji Durani, and Iskandar. 2020. "Global Forest Resources Assessment 2020 Report: Brunei Darussalam". Rome. http://www.fao. org/3/ca9977en/ca9977en.pdf (accessed 15 April 2021).

Ebel, Roland. 2020. "Chinampas: An Urban Farming Model of the Aztecs and a Potential Solution for Modern Megalopolis". *HortTechnology* 30, no. 1: 13–19. https://doi.org/10.21273/HORTTECH04310-19.

Edeson, William, Martin Tsamenyi, Mary Ann Palma, and Jo-Anne McCrea. 2010. "Framework Study for Model Fisheries Legislation in South East Asia: Report on Legislation of Brunei Darussalam". Wollongong. https://apip- apec.maff.go.jp/au/good-practices/files/37d230b932323ba22c2d2d5afc17378f. pdf (accessed 15 April 2021).

Ellen, Roy, and Jay Bernstein. 1994. "Urbs in Rure: Cultural Transformations of the Rainforest in Modern Brunei". *Anthropology Today* 10, no. 4: 16. https://doi.org/10.2307/2783436.

El-Said Mamdouh Mahmoud Zahran, Shahriar Shams, and Safwanah Ni'matullah Mohd Said. 2020. "Validation of Forest Fire Hotspot Analysis in GIS Using Forest Fire Contributory Factors". *Systematic Reviews in Pharmacy* 11, no. 12: 249–55.

Fisher, Brendan, R. Kerry Turner, and Paul Morling. 2009. "Defining and Classifying Ecosystem Services for Decision Making". *Ecological Economics* 68, no. 3: 643–53. https://doi.org/10.1016/j.ecolecon.2008.09.014.

Fletcher, Louise. 2016. "Developing a Strategy for Pangolin Conservation in Brunei: Refining Guidelines for the Release of Confiscated Animals and Gathering Baseline Data". https://sundapangolin.files.wordpress. com/2016/01/a-strategy-for-pangolin-conservation-in-brunei.pdf (accessed 14 April 2021).

Food and Agriculture Organization (FAO). 2000. *Asia and the Pacific National Forestry Programmes: Update 34*. Bangkok: Food and Agriculture Organization Regional Office for Asia and the Pacific.

Forestry Department. 2020a. "Beach Type". http://www.forestry.gov.bn/
SitePages/Beach Type.aspx (accessed 22 December 2020).
———. 2020b. "Freshwater Swamp". http://www.forestry.gov.bn/SitePages/
Freshwater Swamp.aspx (accessed 28 December 2020).
———. 2020c. "Mixed Dipterocarp". http://www.forestry.gov.bn/SitePages/
Mixed Dipterocarp.aspx (accessed 28 December 2020).
———. 2020d. "Montane". http://www.forestry.gov.bn/SitePages/Montane.
aspx (accessed 28 December 2020).
Franco, F. Merlin. 2015. "Calendars and Ecosystem Management: Some
Observations". *Human Ecology* 43, no. 2. https://doi.org/10.1007/s10745-
015-9740-6.
Franco, F. Merlin, and Misa Juliana Minggu. 2019. "When the Seeds Sprout,
the Hornbills Hatch: Understanding the Traditional Ecological Knowledge
of the Ibans of Brunei Darussalam on Hornbills". *Journal of Ethnobiology
and Ethnomedicine* 15, no. 1: 46. https://doi.org/10.1186/s13002-019-0325-0.
Franco, F. Merlin, and Nurzahidah Bakar. 2020. "Persistence of the Salty-Sweet
Nipah Sugar in the Popular Foodways of Brunei Darussalam". *Journal of
Ethnobiology* 40, no. 3. https://doi.org/10.2993/0278-0771-40.3.368.
Galawat, Fadil, and Mitsuyasu Yabe. 2012. "Profit Efficiency in Rice Production
in Brunei Darussalam: A Stochastic Frontier Approach". *Journal of ISSAAS*
18, no. 1: 100–12.
Ganz, David. 2002. *Framing Fires: A Country-by-Country Analysis of Forest and
Landfires in the ASEAN Nations*. Jakarta: Project FireFight South East Asia.
Gaveau, David L.A., Sean Sloan, Elis Molidena, Husna Yaen, Doug Sheil,
Nicola K. Abram, Marc Ancrenaz, Robert Nasi, Marcela Quinones, Niels
Wielaard, and Erik Meijaard. 2014. "Four Decades of Forest Persistence,
Clearance and Logging on Borneo". *PLoS ONE* 9, no. 7: e101654. https://
doi.org/10.1371/journal.pone.0101654.
Google. n.d. "Berakas Forest Reserve". https://www.google.com/
maps/@4.9371479,114.891757,13z/data=!5m1!1e4 (accessed 24 July 2021).
Grealish, Gerard, Anthony Ringrose-Voase, and Rob Fitzpatrick. 2010. "Soil
Fertility Evaluation in Negara Brunei Darussalam". In *19th World Congress
of Soil Science, Soil Solutions for a Changing World, Brisbane, 1–6 August 2010*,
edited by R.J. Gilkes, and N. Prakongkep, pp. 121–24. https://www.iuss.
org/19th WCSS/Symposium/pdf/2139.pdf.
Hazimah Haji Mohd Din, Faizah Metali, and Rahayu Sukmaria Sukri. 2015.
"Tree Diversity and Community Composition of the Tutong White Sands,
Brunei Darussalam: A Rare Tropical Heath Forest Ecosystem". *International
Journal of Ecology* 2015: 1–10. https://doi.org/10.1155/2015/807876.
Hazimah Haji Mohd Din, Nor Basirah Bakiri, Rahayu Sukmaria Sukri, and Faizah
Metali. 2018. "Assessment of Seedling Abundance, Survival and Growth of

Two Dipterocarp Species in Peat Swamp Forests of Brunei Darussalam". *Biotropia* 25, no. 2: 148–54. https://doi.org/10.11598/btb.2018.25.2.805.

Horton, Anthony Vincent Michael. 1985. "The Development of Brunei during the British Residential Era 1906–1959: A Sultanate Regenerated". PhD dissertation, University of Hull.

_____. 2005. "Colonial Office Correspondence Relating to Brunei 'Destroyed under Statute' 1906–1934". *IJAPS* 1: 1–43.

Hussainmiya, B.A. 2006. *Brunei Revival of 1906*. Bandar Seri Begawan: Brunei Press Sdn. Bhd.

_____. 2014. "Malcolm MacDonald and Brunei: Diplomacy with Intimacy". *Journal of Southeast Asian Studies* 45, no. 3: 393–418. https://doi.org/10.1017/S0022463414000344.

Jakovac, Catarina C., Agnieszka Ewa Latawiec, Eduardo Lacerda, Isabella Leite Lucas, Katarzyna Anna Korys, Alvaro Iribarrem, Gustavo Abreu Malaguti, R. Kerry Turner, Tiziana Luisetti, and Bernardo Baeta Neves Strassburg. 2020. "Costs and Carbon Benefits of Mangrove Conservation and Restoration: A Global Analysis". *Ecological Economics* 176 (October): 106758. https://doi.org/10.1016/j.ecolecon.2020.106758.

Jambul, Rafi'ah, Army Limin, Adibah Nabilah Ali, and Ferry Slik. 2020. "Invasive Acacia Mangium Dominance as an Indicator for Heath Forest Disturbance". *Environmental and Sustainability Indicators* 8 (December): 100059. https://doi.org/10.1016/j.indic.2020.100059.

Keiser, Jennifer, Michael F. Maltese, Tobias E. Erlanger, Robert Bos, Marcel Tanner, Burton H. Singer, and Jürg Utzinger. 2005. "Effect of Irrigated Rice Agriculture on Japanese Encephalitis, Including Challenges and Opportunities for Integrated Vector Management". *Acta Tropica* 95, no. 1: 40–57. https://doi.org/10.1016/j.actatropica.2005.04.012.

Kementerian Kewangan dan Ekonomi Brunei Darussalam. 2020. *Towards a Dynamic and Sustainable Economy: Economic Blueprint for Brunei Darussalam*. Bandar Seri Begawan: Ministry of Finance and Economy, Brunei Darussalam.

Kobayashi, Shigeo. 1994. "Effects of Harvesting Impacts and Rehabilitation of Tropical Rain Forest". *Journal of Plant Research* 107, no. 1: 99–106. https://doi.org/10.1007/BF02344536.

_____. 2000. "Initial Phase of Secondary Succession in the Exploited Peat Swamp Forest (Shorea Albida) at Sungai Damit, Belait in Brunei Darussalam". In *Proceedings of the International Symposium on TROPICAL PEATLANDS*, pp. 205–14. Bogor: Hokkaido University and Indonesian Institute of Sciences.

_____. 2016. "Peatland and Peatland Forest in Brunei Darussalam". In *Tropical Peatland Ecosystems*, edited by Mitsuru Osaki, and Nobuyuki Tsuji, pp. 75–89. Tokyo: Springer Japan. https://doi.org/10.1007/978-4-431-55681-7_5.

Kubiszewski, Ida, Sharolyn J. Anderson, Robert Costanza, and Paul C. Sutton. 2016. "The Future of Ecosystem Services in Asia and the Pacific". *Asia & the Pacific Policy Studies* 3, no. 3: 389–404. https://doi.org/10.1002/app5.147.

Laila Haji Abdul Hamid, Hajah. 2000. "Brunei Darussalam: Mangrove-Friendly Aquaculture". In *Mangrove-Friendly Aquaculture: Proceedings of the Workshop on Mangrove-Friendly Aquaculture Organized by the SEAFDEC Aquaculture Department, Iloilo City, Philippines, 11–15 January 1999*, edited by Jurgenne H. Primavera, Luis Ma. B. Garcia, Milagros T. Castaños, and Marilyn B. Surtida, pp. 95–103. Tigbauan, Philippines: Southeast Asian Fisheries Development Center, Aquaculture Department.

Le, Duc Nha. 2019. "Environmental Degradation and Economic Growth in ASEAN-10: The Perspective of EKC Hypothesis". *Malaysian Journal of Economic Studies* 56, no. 1: 43–62. https://doi.org/10.22452/MJES.vol56no1.3.

Lernoud, Julia, and Helga Willer. 2017. "Current Statistics on Organic Agriculture Worldwide: Area, Operators, and Market". In *The World of Organic Agriculture Statistics and Emerging Trends 2017*, edited by Helga Willer, and Julia Lernoud, pp. 36–75. Rheinbreitbach: Research Institute of Organic Agriculture (FiBL), Frick, and IFOAM – Organics International, Bonn.

Lim Jong En, Angie, Idzuan bin Pedian, Janis Wong Chwang Ing, Jeli anak Chuat, Lydia Wong Chwang Yuh, Norazirawandi Haji Ismail, Norhazemah Kalong, and Wedy Arweanddy Luon. 2002. Report on "Shifting Cultivation in the Temburong: An Investigation into the Impact of Human Activity on Secondary Forests". Temburong: SM Sultan Hassan, Bangar.

Lupascu, Massimo, Hasan Akhtar, Thomas E.L. Smith, and Rahayu Sukmaria Sukri. 2020. "Post-fire Carbon Dynamics in the Tropical Peat Swamp Forests of Brunei Reveal Long-term Elevated CH_4 Flux". *Global Change Biology* 26, no. 9: 5125–45. https://doi.org/10.1111/gcb.15195.

Maxwell, Allen R. 1996. "The Place of the Kadayan in Traditional Brunei Society". *South East Asia Research* 4, no. 2: 157–96. www.jstor.org/stable/23746966.

Ministry of Finance and Economy (MoFE). 2020. *United Nations High-Level Political Forum for Sustainable Development: Voluntary National Review Report of Brunei Darussalam*. Bandar Seri Begawan: Ministry of Finance and Economy, Brunei Darussalam. https://landportal.org/library/resources/2020-united-nations-high-level-political-forum-sustainable-development-voluntary (accessed 14 April 2021).

Mukoyama, Naosuke. 2020. "Colonial Origins of the Resource Curse: Endogenous Sovereignty and Authoritarianism in Brunei". *Democratization* 27, no. 2: 224–42. https://doi.org/10.1080/13510347.2019.1678591.

Ng, Matthew, Zahratu Shabrina, and Boyana Buyuklieva. 2019. "Characterising Land Cover Change in Brunei Darussalam's Capital District". https://eartharxiv.org/repository/view/856/ (accessed 15 April 2021).

Ng, Peter K.L., and N. Sivasothi, eds. 2001. *A Guide to Mangroves of Singapore.* Singapore: Raffles Museum of Biodiversity Research, The National University of Singapore and The Singapore Science Centre.

Nowak, Katarzyna. 2012. "Mangrove and Peat Swamp Forests: Refuge Habitats for Primates and Felids". *Folia Primatologica* 83, no. 3–6: 361–76. https://doi.org/10.1159/000339810.

Orr, A.G. 2006. "Odonata in Bornean Tropical Rain Forest Formations: Diversity, Endemicity and Implications for Conservation Management". In *Forests and Dragonflies. Fourth WDA International Symposium of Odonatology, Pontevedra (Spain), July 2005*, edited by Adolfo Cordero Rivera, pp. 51–78. Moscow: Pensoft Publishers.

Osunkoya, Olusegun O., Farah E. Othman, and Rafhiah S. Kahar. 2005. "Growth and Competition between Seedlings of an Invasive Plantation Tree, *Acacia Mangium*, and Those of a Native Borneo Heath-Forest Species, *Melastoma Beccarianum*". *Ecological Research* 20, no. 2: 205–14. https://doi.org/10.1007/s11284-004-0027-4.

Pendry, Colin A., and John Proctor. 1996. "The Causes of Altitudinal Zonation of Rain Forests on Bukit Belalong, Brunei". *The Journal of Ecology* 84, no. 3: 407. https://doi.org/10.2307/2261202.

————. 1997. "Altitudinal Zonation of Rain Forest on Bukit Belalong, Brunei: Soils, Forest Structure and Floristics". *Journal of Tropical Ecology* 13, no. 2: 221–41. https://doi.org/10.1017/S0266467400010427.

Peng, Jian, Huijuan Zhao, and Yanxu Liu. 2017. "Urban Ecological Corridors Construction: A Review". *Acta Ecologica Sinica* 37, no. 1: 23–30. https://doi.org/10.1016/j.chnaes.2016.12.002.

Posa, Mary Rose C., Lahiru S. Wijedasa, and Richard T. Corlett. 2011. "Biodiversity and Conservation of Tropical Peat Swamp Forests". *BioScience* 61, no. 1: 49–57. https://doi.org/10.1525/bio.2011.61.1.10.

Power, Alison G. 2010. "Ecosystem Services and Agriculture: Tradeoffs and Synergies". *Philosophical Transactions of the Royal Society B: Biological Sciences* 365, no. 1554: 2959–71. https://doi.org/10.1098/rstb.2010.0143.

Radojevic, Miroslav. 2003. "Haze Research in Brunei Darussalam During the 1998 Episode". In *Air Quality (Pageoph Topical Volumes)*, edited by Gandikota V. Rao, Sethu Raman, and M.P. Singh, pp. 251–64. Basel: Birkhäuser Basel. https://doi.org/10.1007/978-3-0348-7970-5_15.

Ranjith, M.W., and N. De Silva. 1998. "The Coastal Resources Management Program in Brunei Darussalam". *Ocean & Coastal Management* 38, no. 2: 147–60. https://doi.org/10.1016/S0964-5691(97)00070-7.

Ratnayake, Uditha. 2014. "Rainfall Trends of Brunei Darussalam". In *5th Brunei International Conference on Engineering and Technology (BICET 2014), Bandar Seri Begawan, Brunei, 1–3 November 2014*, pp. 1–5. Institution of Engineering and Technology. https://doi.org/10.1049/cp.2014.1064.

Rudd, Hillary, Jamie Vala, and Valentin Schaefer. 2002. "Importance of Backyard Habitat in a Comprehensive Biodiversity Conservation Strategy: A Connectivity Analysis of Urban Green Spaces". *Restoration Ecology* 10, no. 2: 368–75. https://doi.org/10.1046/j.1526-100X.2002.02041.x.

Safwanah Ni'matullah Binti Mohd Said, El-Said Mamdouh Mahmoud Zahran, and Shahriar Shams. 2017. "Forest Fire Risk Assessment Using Hotspot Analysis in GIS". *The Open Civil Engineering Journal* 11, no. 1: 786–801. https://doi.org/10.2174/1874149501711010786.

Sandal, S.T., ed. 1996. *The Geology and Hydrocarbon Resources of Negara Brunei Darussalam*, 2nd ed. Seria: Brunei Shell Petroleum Company Sendirian Berhad. https://www.bsp.com.bn/panagaclub/pnhs_old/geology/web/WEB0.HTM (accessed 15 April 2021).

Satyanarayana, Behara, Aidy M. Muslim, Nurul Amira Izzaty Horsali, Nurul Ashikin Mat Zauki, Viviana Otero, Muhammad Izuan Nadzri, Sulong Ibrahim, Mohd-Lokman Husain, and Farid Dahdouh-Guebas. 2018. "Status of the Undisturbed Mangroves at Brunei Bay, East Malaysia: A Preliminary Assessment Based on Remote Sensing and Ground-Truth Observations". *PeerJ* 6 (February): e4397. https://doi.org/10.7717/peerj.4397.

Schelander, Bjorn. 1998. *Brunei: Abode of Peace*. Hawai'i: Center for Southeast Asian Studies, University of Hawai'i.

Scialabba, Nadia, ed. 1998. *Integrated Coastal Area Management and Agriculture, Forestry and Fisheries. FAO Guidelines*. Rome: Environment and Natural Resources Service, FAO. http://www.fao.org/3/W8440E01.htm#P0_0 (accessed 15 April 2021).

SEAFDEC Secretariat. 2018. "Regional Initiatives/Programs and Capacity Building to Support the Implementation of General Assembly Resolution 71/257". https://www.un.org/depts/los/general_assembly/contributions_2017/2/SEAFDEC.pdf (accessed 15 April 2021).

Secretariat of the Convention on Biological Diversity (SCBD). n.d. "Brunei Darussalam: Main Details". https://www.cbd.int/countries/profile/?country=bn (accessed 28 December 2020).

Shams, Shahriar, El-Said Mamdouh Mahmoud Zahran, Safwanah Ni'matullah Binti Mohd Said, Kho J. Hui, Naderah N.D.H.M.F. Lee, and Hasim N.H.H. 2019. "Risk Assessment for Forest Fire in Brunei Darussalam". *MATEC Web of Conferences* 258: 05033.

Shams, Shahriar, K.B.M. Hj Shafiuddin, Asmaal Muizz Sallehhin Bin Hj Moham Sultan, and Rozeana Binti Hj Md. Juani. 2015. "Agriculture Adaptation to Climate Change in Brunei Darussalam". *Environment and Urbanization ASIA* 6, no. 1: 59–70. https://doi.org/10.1177/0975425315585193.

Small, Andrew, Tara G. Martin, Roger L. Kitching, and Khoon Meng Wong. 2004. "Contribution of Tree Species to the Biodiversity of a 1ha Old World

Rainforest in Brunei, Borneo". *Biodiversity and Conservation* 13, no. 11: 2067–88. https://doi.org/10.1023/B:BIOC.0000040001.72686.e8.

Struebig, Matthew J., Monika Bożek, Jan Hildebrand, Stephen J. Rossiter, and David J.W. Lane. 2012. "Bat Diversity in the Lowland Forests of the Heart of Borneo". *Biodiversity and Conservation* 21, no. 14: 3711–27. https://doi.org/10.1007/s10531-012-0393-0.

Suhaili, Adrian Lee Rahman, Kushan Tennakoon, and Rahayu Sukmaria Sukri. 2015. "Soil Seed Bank of an Exotic *Acacia* Sp. Plantation and an Adjacent Tropical Heath Forest in Brunei Darussalam". *Bioptropia* 22, no. 2: 140–50. https://doi.org/10.11598/btb.2015.22.2.487.

Syahid, Luri Nurlaila, Anjar Dimara Sakti, Riantini Virtriana, Ketut Wikantika, Wiwin Windupranata, Satoshi Tsuyuki, Rezzy Eko Caraka, and Rudhi Pribadi. 2020. "Determining Optimal Location for Mangrove Planting Using Remote Sensing and Climate Model Projection in Southeast Asia". *Remote Sensing* 12, no. 22: 3734. https://doi.org/10.3390/rs12223734.

Takeuchi, Kazuhiko. 2010. "Rebuilding the Relationship between People and Nature: The Satoyama Initiative". *Ecological Research* 25, no. 5: 891–97. https://doi.org/10.1007/s11284-010-0745-8.

Tang, Y.P., B.L.L. Linda, and L.W. Franz. 2013. "Proximate Analysis of *Artocarpus Odoratissimus* (Tarap) in Brunei Darussalam". *International Food Research Journal* 20, no. 1: 409–15.

Ulluwishewa, Rohana, Nick Roskruge, Garth Harmsworth, and Bantong Antaran. 2008. "Indigenous Knowledge for Natural Resource Management: A Comparative Study of Māori in New Zealand and Dusun in Brunei Darussalam". *GeoJournal* 73, no. 4: 271–84. https://doi.org/10.1007/s10708-008-9198-9.

Voeks, Robert A., and Samhan Nyawa. 2006. "Dusun Ethnobotany: Forest Knowledge and Nomenclature in Northern Borneo". *Journal of Cultural Geography* 23, no. 2: 1–31. https://doi.org/10.1080/08873630609478221.

Walker, Anthony R. 2010. "A Kingdom of Unexpected Treasures: Contributions to a National Ethnography of Brunei by UBD Sociology-Anthropology Students". *South East Asia: A Multidisciplinary Journal* 10: 11–38.

Wardah Haji Tuah, Kushan Udayanga Tennakoon, Salwana Md. Jaafar, and Rahayu Sukmaria Sukri. 2020. "Post-Fire Impacts on Tree Diversity in Coastal Heath Forests of Brunei Darussalam". *Scientia Bruneiana* 19, no. 1. https://doi.org/10.46537/scibru.v19i1.109.

Wasil, Wardi. 2018. "Agri Dept to Pilot Irrigation System, Seeks to Boost Rice Production". *The Scoop*, 28 September 2018. https://thescoop.co/2018/09/28/agri-dept-to-pilot-irrigation-system-seeks-to-boost-rice-production/ (accessed 14 April 2021).

Williams, C.N. 1978. "Fertilizer Responses of Cucumbers on Peat in Brunei". *Experimental Agriculture* 14, no. 4: 299–302. https://doi.org/10.1017/S0014479700008929.

Wong, Aaron. 2019. "How This Retired Lieutenant Colonel Led the Revival of Wasan, Brunei's Biggest Rice Farm". *BizBrunei*, 17 February 2019. https://www.bizbrunei.com/2019/02/how-this-retired-lieutenant-led-the-revival-of-wasan-brunei-biggest-rice-farm-hj-sahlan-koseka/ (accessed 15 April 2021).

Wong, K.M., Joffre Ali Ahmad, Y.W. Low, and Muhammad Ariffin A. Kalat. 2015. *Rainforest Plants and Flowers of Brunei Darussalam*. Brunei Darussalam: Forestry Department, Ministry of Industry and Primary Resources.

Wong, Marina. 2006. "Conserving Nature and Culture at Tasek Merimbun, Brunei Darussalam". *Tropics* 15, no. 3: 297–300.

Yakub, Khairunissa. 2012. "An Ethnographic Study of Wasan Rice Farm in Brunei Darussalam". Master's thesis, Ritsumeikan Asia Pacific University.

Yamada, Toshihiro, and Eizi Suzuki. 2004. "Ecological Role of Vegetative Sprouting in the Regeneration of *Dryobalanops Rappa*, an Emergent Species in a Bornean Tropical Wetland Forest". *Journal of Tropical Ecology* 20, no. 4: 377–84. https://doi.org/10.1017/S0266467404001300.

Yusoff, Aiman, Kushan U. Tennakoon, Salwana Md. Jaafar, Nur Amal Nazira Pg Zaman, and Rahayu Sukmaria Sukri. 2019. "Effects of *Acacia* Invasion on Leaf Litter Nutrient and Soil Properties of Coastal Kerangas Forests in Brunei Darussalam". *Scentia Bruneiana*, 18, no. 1: 1–9.

Yussof, Mahmud. 2005. "Global Forest Resources Assessment 2005: Brunei Darussalam, Country Report". Rome. http://www.fao.org/forestry/8921-02907faa744929ea15783f5a5baf8d641.pdf (accessed 15 April 2021).

Zunaidi, Adzrin Asikin, Lee Hoon Lim, and Faizah Metali. 2020. "Assessments of Heavy Metals in Commercially Available Fertilizers in Brunei Darussalam". *Agricultural Research* (November). https://doi.org/10.1007/s40003-020-00500-4.

4

ASEAN AND BRUNEI ENERGY TRANSITION

Jérémy Jammes and Marie-Sybille de Vienne

INTRODUCTION

The global energy landscape is undergoing a period of profound change. The first two decades of the twenty-first century may be remembered as the time in history when the world awoke to the fact that the costs—political, economic and environmental—of its 150-year addiction to coal and hydrocarbons might be unsustainable. A large-scale switch to a readily available supply of alternatives, including renewable energy, is perceived as the only viable solution moving forward, as well as changes into daily consumption and way of life. If this moderate pace is not followed by all countries, wars and neo-colonial campaigns to increase and better control the supply of strategic resources could be considered as an alternative by some big players.

Thanks to its hydrocarbons, Brunei, the smallest of all ASEAN[1] countries in population and gross domestic product (GDP), has known its "thermo-industrial revolution", a moment in mankind which decisively intertwines the relationship between modern energy and economic development (Fouquet 2008; Hamilton and Grinevald 2015; Mottet and Jammes 2020). Given the likely depletion of their reserves by 2040, Brunei's authorities have officially made diversifying production and, broadly speaking what they qualify as "energy transition", a so-called strategic objective since the mid-2000s (Energy Department 2014, pp. 12, 23, 27–28). Conversely, in 2019, the hydrocarbon sector generated 56.6 per cent of Brunei's GDP (current prices); oil and gas government revenue plus taxes (most of which induced directly or indirectly by the hydrocarbon sector) represented 21.7 per cent of GDP (*Brunei Darussalam Statistical Yearbook 2019*, tables 3.1 and 8.2). As such, Brunei's real "dependency rate" over hydrocarbons is presently around 80 per cent of GDP.

What does "energy transition" mean—if any—to Brunei, notwithstanding that the notion of "energy transition" is controversial and not unanimous (Jammes et al. 2020)? In the United States, energy transition is widely interpreted as the reduction in dependence on hydrocarbons from the Middle East (de Perthuis and Jouvet 2015), to the benefit of shale oil and gas of which extraction is highly polluting and costly. In Europe, energy transition is discussed more over the long term and is primarily related to climate change issues (Stern and Kander 2012).

Indeed, energy transition is hardly a new phenomenon if one considers the transition from wood and charcoal (already in use during the Bronze Age) to fossil fuels which took place over 200 years ago, and much earlier (ca. sixteenth century) in Europe (Low Countries, British islands) including another fossil fuel: peat.[2] The transition from one type of energy to another takes 80 to 400 years, depending on the kind of energy, the technology involved, the political commitment and the economic opportunities. In the short term, a transition can be influenced by the availability of energy, its cost, environmental and health constraints driven by its use, and technological innovations. Nowadays, with global warming becoming a real threat in addition to the need to reform economic and environmental global governance, the international community finds itself at a crossroads.

Talking about the energy transition in Brunei is tantamount to placing it at the threshold of both a historical and transitional relationship with energy resources, production and consumption in the ASEAN context. The energy policy taken by Brunei in terms of both consumption and renewable energy has first to be examined in the broader context of ASEAN energy development and strategic goals. We shall then draw an assessment of the main evolutions of the sector in Brunei since the 2010s, which will provide a better understanding of the sultanate's energy strategy as a whole, including the sultanate's recent response to greenhouse gas (GHG) emissions.

ENERGY TRANSITIONS FOR ASEAN

Resources, Production and Growth

With an average of 4.8 per cent GDP growth since 2014,[3] Southeast Asia can be considered as one of the most dynamic regions in the world. In regards to the energy sector, the area was expected before 2020 and the COVID-19 crisis to strongly increase its energy demand, up to 60 per cent by 2040. In addition, regional GDP was supposed to at least double for the same period, while its population should increase by some 20 per cent, reaching 767 million people (IEA 2019, p. 10).

As illustrated by the bulk of foreign direct investment or FDI (812 billion US dollars, i.e. an average of 135 billion FDI per year) during the years 2014–19 in ASEAN, the region offered a favourable investment environment (ASEAN Secretariat and UNCTAD 2017) for foreign companies seeking to establish a presence thanks to the political stability of eight out of ten of its member states,[4] a competitive workforce, an increasingly more open market, a strategic geographical position between the China sea and the Indian ocean, as well as abundant—but of course not infinite—natural resources. However, only a few studies address the energy developments in ASEAN countries (Peytral and Simon 2013; ISEAS 2019; Mottet and Jammes 2020) and the recent and contested upsurge—in comparison with the West—of the premises of an ecological "green thought".

The economic and energy landscape varies considerably among the Southeast Asian countries (see Table 4.1). Across the region, about 37 million people lived in 2019 without access to national electricity production and distribution networks, although electrification rates differ widely from one country to another and significant improvements have been made in the region during the last fifteen years. Several countries are endowed with energy resources to a greater or lesser extent. Brunei, Indonesia, Malaysia, Thailand and Vietnam share

TABLE 4.1
Key Economic and Energy Indicators in Southeast Asia

1-1 Key Economic Indicators	Population 2019 (in thousand)	GDP 2019 (in US$ billion)	GDP Growth 2014–19 (yearly average)	Primary Energy Supply (PES) 2018 (in Ktoe)
Brunei	423.200	13.87	0.26	3,696
Cambodia	16,487	26.79	7.1	8,068
Indonesia	270,626	1,134.82	5.0	231,008
Laos	7,169	18.85	6.5	8,057
Malaysia	31,950	366.82	4.9	93,562
Myanmar	54,045	79.33	6.5	24,035
Philippines	108,117	365.14	6.4	60,052
Singapore	5,804	361.71	2.8	37,752
Thailand	69,626	541.94	3.5	133,599
Vietnam	95,546	264.18	6.7	83,369
Southeast Asia	**564,247**	**3,171.45**	**4.8**	**683,198**

1-2 Energy Indicators	Electricity Consumption 2018 (TWh)	Electricity Consumption per capita 2018 (MWh)	Population Without Access to Electricity (2019, %)
Brunei	3.8	8.9	0
Cambodia	8.7	0.5	25.2
Indonesia	275.2*	1	0.5
Laos	5	0.7	5.2
Malaysia	157.2	5	0
Myanmar	18.8	0.4	49.4
Philippines	90.2	0.9	3.6
Singapore	52.6	9.3	0
Thailand	195.1	2.8	0
Vietnam	227.2	2.4	0.8
Southeast Asia	**1,033.8**	**2.3**	**6.6**

Source: Table compiled by the authors from UNCTAD (Key Economic Indicators 2019) and IEA databases (Energy Indicators). TPES: Total Primary Energy Supply. *Latest data available: 2019 for Indonesia, 2018 for other countries.

1.6 trillion tons of oil, representing 0.8 per cent of the world's proven reserves, which is quite modest. Indonesia, Malaysia, Myanmar and Brunei are also exporters of liquefied natural gas (LNG). Indonesia—now a net importer of hydrocarbons—has significant proven reserves of coal (2.2 per cent of world reserves), making it the world's second-largest exporter after Australia and the third-largest producer after China and India. Excepting Brunei, Malaysia, Vietnam and Indonesia, the remaining ASEAN is relatively poor in fossil fuels and rely massively on energy imports.

Since 2000 onwards, electricity demand in Southeast Asia has dramatically increased—at a speed faster than economic growth (Mottet and Jammes 2020, pp. 16–20). During the years 2000–19, Southeast Asia's GDP grew about 5 per cent per year, while the yearly rise in the demand for electricity reached about 6 per cent (IEA 2019, p. 31), leading to a production of 1,118 Terawatt/hour in 2018.[5] The progression of demand is expected to level off at nearly 4 per cent per year by 2040 (IEA 2019, p. 64). The top five consumers—Indonesia (26 per cent of ASEAN's consumption in 2018), Thailand, Malaysia, Vietnam and the Philippines—account for 90 per cent of Southeast Asia's energy demand. The main causes of this strong progression in electricity demand can be found less in the demographic growth than the steady pace of urbanization, high increases in industrial production, and the recent access to electricity (and internet) for most of the rural populations (Cornot-Gandolphe 2017, p. 17).

Gas is expected to play a growing role during the energy transition in Southeast Asia. Very versatile in its uses and less polluting, gas-fired power plants should gradually replace coal-fired power plants. Consequently, the demand for regional gas has grown rapidly from the 1990s onwards in connection with economic development and growing needs for electricity. Regional gas consumption increased from 74,000 Ktoe in 2000 to 141,000 Ktoe in 2018 (IEA database), mainly due to the electrical and industrial sectors. Though Southeast Asia had about 6,400 billion cubic metres of proven natural gas reserves as of 1 January 2016 (BP 2017, p. 26), or 3.5 per cent of global reserves, the cap on gas production has led to recurring shortages in all Southeast Asian producing countries,[6] even among main exporters such as Indonesia and Malaysia, which have reduced their exports. Essentially offshore, the reserves have a high cost of development, which, correlated with the low price of gas and the decline in the price of oil, has led to a reduction in investment spending on exploration and prospecting as well as a stagnation of production. The Trans-ASEAN Gas Pipeline Project (TAGP)[7] was originally intended to strengthen the security of gas supply in the region by interconnecting the pipelines of the various ASEAN countries (Shi and Malik 2013). From 2011 onwards, the region turned to the import of LNG (liquefied natural gas) to complete and secure its gas supply.

According to medium-term forecasts, the fossil fuel production of ASEAN countries will be unable to meet the strong progress in demand, especially for electricity.[8] Thus, in the context of sustained growth in energy demand prevailing up to the COVID-19 crisis, the increase of operating capacities could not be the only solution, particularly because they are limited in the Southeast Asian context. As a result, ASEAN member states planned the deployment of national energy policies that focused on two targets: 1) the promotion of renewable energies (firstly hydropower), thus reducing CO_2 emissions; and 2) the interconnectivity and integration of energy markets, especially with the so-called ASEAN Power Grid (APG) and Trans-ASEAN Gas Pipeline Project (TAGP).[9]

At the regional level, between 2000 and 2017, US$69 billion (IEA 2017, p. 45), an average of 3.8 billion per year have been invested in renewable energy, which thus represents 22.5 per cent of ASEAN's electricity production in 2018.[10] Hydropower is the main source (16.2 per cent), followed by biofuels (2.7 per cent) and geothermal energy (2.1 per cent), while waste, solar photovoltaic and wind turbines share the remaining 1.3 per cent. Four (Laos, Myanmar, Cambodia and Vietnam) out of the five countries of Peninsular Southeast Asia having large rivers originating in the Himalayas—Red River, Mekong, Menam, Salween and Irrawaddy—rely on hydroelectricity for 40 per cent (in 2018) of their electricity production.

Since 1999, ASEAN has overseen an independent intergovernmental organization, the ASEAN Centre for Energy (ACE). In this context, at the November 2014 ASEAN Summit in Naypyidaw, member countries adopted the ASEAN Plan of Action for Energy Cooperation 2016–2025 (APAEC), as a collective response to ASEAN's energy challenges through, among others, the development of renewable energy and integration of the electricity and gas markets (ACE 2015).[11] It aims at securing supply and making it more sustainable by the exploitation of various energy resources available in the region and their proper response to different energy demand profiles. Renewable energy and interconnection projects of production and distribution networks are part of the long-term goal of an energy transition[12] that tends towards a more sustainable energy system (Revault d'Allonnes 2008; Smil 2010).

To meet ASEAN's energy demand by 2040, investments required in the energy sector were estimated at US$2.08 trillion between 2017 and 2040 of which US$1.2 trillion should be dedicated to electricity production alone (including US$326 billion for renewable energy) and US$677 billion for its distribution (IEA 2017, p. 116).[13] Spread over twenty-three years, this huge amount represents an investment of about US$87 billion per year, or 2.7 per cent of Southeast Asia's GDP in 2019—notwithstanding that investment in energy as a whole in Southeast Asia decreased from US$72 billion in 2015 to 65 billion in 2018 (IEA 2019, p. 48). The USA seems to be here a quasi-unique exception within this world trend of decreasing investment, mainly due to the US development of shale hydrocarbons (Cornot-Gandolphe 2015).

Renewable Energies: Between Ambitions and Commitments

During the United Nations Climate Change Conference (COP21) meeting held in Paris in November–December 2015,[14] all the signatory countries pledged to respect the same legal framework in implementing their commitments to control greenhouse gas (GHG). Yet despite common efforts, each country will ultimately fulfil its own responsibilities, scaled on the basis of the levels of its GHG emissions as well as energy, industrial and economic specificities. These differences are particularly visible in Southeast Asia (see Table 4.2).

According to the Asian Development Bank (ADB), if the countries in the region do not reduce their GHG emissions by 30 per cent before 2050 (compared to the 2010 level), Southeast Asia could lose 11 per cent of its productive capacity by 2100 (ADB 2015). Faced with these alarming prospects—which span on a much too long period to be taken for granted—the adaptation to disasters as well as to the international regulations regarding GHG emissions remains on Southeast Asian states' agenda. This applies in particular to the

TABLE 4.2
Intended Nationally Determined Contributions (INDC) proposed by Southeast Asian countries at COP21

		Concerned GHG
Brunei	Suggests a series of sectorial measures (energy and transport sectors) by 2035.	No details available
Cambodia	Reduction of 27 per cent of GHG emissions by 2030, following a business-as-usual scenario,[15] conditional on financial and technological support.	CO_2, CH_4, N_2O
Indonesia	Reduction of 26–29 per cent of GHG emissions by 2030, following a business-as-usual scenario. Target raised to 41 per cent, conditional on international support.	CO_2, CH_4, N_2O
Laos	Proposes a series of sectorial measures (mainly energy, forestry and transport) by 2030, conditional on financial and technological support.	No details available
Malaysia	Proposes to reduce the carbon intensity of its economy by 35 per cent between 2005 and 2030. Target raised to 45 per cent, conditional on financial and technological support.	CO_2, CH_4, N_2O
Myanmar	Suggests a series of sectorial measures (mainly forestry and energy) by 2030, conditional on financial and technical support.	No details available
Philippines	Reduction of about 70 per cent of GHG emissions by 2030, following a business-as-usual scenario, conditional on financial and technological support.	No details available

TABLE 4.2 (continued)

Singapore	Reduction of 36 per cent in carbon intensity of its economy between 2005 (176 grams of CO_2 equivalent per Singaporean dollar of GDP (g CO_2/S$) and 2030 (113 g CO_2/S$).	CO_2, CH_4, N_2O, PFCS, HFCS, SF_6
Thailand	Reduction of 20–25 per cent of GHG emissions in 2030, following a business-as-usual scenario. Could raise the target to 25 per cent, conditional on financial and technological support.	CO_2, CH_4, N_2O, PFCS, HFCS, SF_6
Vietnam	Reduction of 8 per cent in GHG emissions by 2030, following a business-as-usual scenario. Could raise the target to 25–30 per cent, conditional on financial and technological support.	CO_2, CH_4, N_2O, PFCS, HFCS, SF_6

Source: UNFCCC (2015).

reduction of CO_2 emissions from forest fires and deforestation, which comprise the main contributors to regional emissions. To achieve this objective, the role played by the electricity production sector is essential, especially the development of renewable energies. With the exception of hydroelectricity (16.2 per cent of electricity production in 2018) and, to a much smaller extent, geothermal energy (2.1 per cent, mainly developed by Indonesia and Philippines), there is still a long way to go to develop renewable energies in the region. Also, nuclear power is expected to enter the electric power grid by 2036, with Thailand commissioning its first reactors (Cornot-Gandolphe 2017, p. 26; Mottet and Jammes 2020, pp. 27–30).

In 2017, the International Energy Agency (IEA) elaborated three scenarios depicting the future of energy policies in Southeast Asia (IEA 2017, pp. 136–37). Two years later, the third scenario was revised (IEA 2019, pp. 106–18). The three expected scenarios are the following:

the maintenance of current policies (CPS); the "new policies" scenario
(NPS), which adds to existing policies the state of achievement of the
national commitments pledged during the Paris Climate Agreement;
the sustainable development scenario (SDS), which goes further in
following the key energy goals of the United Nations agenda (see
Table 4.3).

According to the IEA's "new policies scenario", total electric power
production in Southeast Asia (1,139 TWh in 2018) is expected to double,
reaching up to 2,219 TWh by 2040. In order to meet the growing
demand for electricity, all sources of production will be explored and
intensified, with the exception of oil, to be virtually eliminated from
the electricity mix by 2040.

While efforts are being made to improve energy efficiency (40 per
cent by 2040) and foster development of renewable energies, experts
predict that fossil fuels will continue to dominate the regional energy
mix (between 52 per cent and 76 per cent in 2040, according to IEA's
three scenarios). Following the SDS, as the reserves are relatively well
distributed across the region, the share of coal will remain stable,
around 40 per cent up to 2040, meaning that the demand for coal
will increase by 80 per cent in 2040 because of its growing use for
electricity production, electricity representing then 26 per cent of the
energy mix against 18 per cent in 2018. The share of gas is expected
to remain stable, around 21 per cent in 2040, the demand for gas

TABLE 4.3
IEA's Scenarios for Electricity Generation: Prospective for 2030

	CPS	NPS	SDS
Renewables	22.5%	27.2%	46%
Hydro	13.5%	16.2%	20.7%
Bioenergy	3.2%	3.5%	4.6%
Wind	2.8%	1.3%	8.2%
Geothermal	1.8%	3.3%	7%
Solar	1.8%	2.6%	5.5%
CO_2 emissions (Mt)	2,039	1885	1,399

Source: IEA (2017), pp. 134–36; IEA (2019), pp. 110, 117.

growing by 80 per cent over the period, from 160 Bcm[16] in 2018 to 300 Bcm in 2040 (IEA 2019, pp. 98–99). As illustrated by Table 4.3, under the NPS, CO_2 emissions in Southeast Asia will reach 1,885 Mt, 7.5 per cent less than under the current policies (CPS), while under the SDS, they will decrease by 31.3 per cent to 1,399 Mt.

In recent years, policies and regulations have been adopted to promote the deployment of renewable energies and attract private investments in the sector, including purchase prices, tax breaks and subsidies. The target of increasing the share of renewable energies in the energy mix to 23 per cent by 2025 set by ASEAN countries in 2015 (ACE 2016, p. 8) is expected to be completed much earlier. Indeed, the share of renewable energies (including large—above 50 MWh installed capacity—hydropower plants) has already reached 22.5 per cent in 2018, indicating both awareness and the implementation of resources in this sector. According to NPS, in 2035, renewable energy could contribute up to 29 per cent to the electricity generation, largely dominated by hydroelectricity (347 TWh), followed by far by bioenergy (97 TWh), solar photovoltaic (85 TWh), geothermal (75 TWh) and wind turbines (55 TWh).

Hydropower is by far the most promising renewable energy source, with an estimated potential of 105 GW in 2040, compared to 41 GW of installed capacity in 2016 (IEA 2017, p. 136). In the ASEAN countries, the hydroelectric potential is very unevenly distributed and exploited. Many dam projects are either untapped—such as in Myanmar—or either under construction or study—such as in Thailand, Cambodia, Vietnam, Malaysia or Indonesia (International Hydropower Association 2015).

According to the IEA's new policies scenario (NPS), hydropower production capacity is expected to reach 61 GW in 2025, 82 GW in 2030, 96 GW in 2035 and 105 GW in 2040. IEA's sustainable development scenario (SDS) goes much further, mentioning a production of 151 GW in 2040.

With quite a number of volcanoes, Southeast Asia is home to a quarter of the world's geothermal electricity output, with the Philippines (10.7 TWh in 2018) and Indonesia (14.1 TWh) ranking third and second (IEA database). Southeast Asia's significant geothermal potential could represent up to 29 GW installed capacity in Indonesia (from 1.5 GW in 2016) and to 4 GW (from 1.9 GW) in the Philippines. To realize its potential, Indonesia has adopted a development plan promoting investment in the geothermal sector to reach a 6 GW capacity in 2020 and 13.5 GW in 2040. Following NPS, Southeast Asia could increase geothermal capacity to 11 GW in 2040. On the other hand, the IEA's sustainable development scenario (SDS) refers to a capacity of 27 GW in 2040 (IEA 2017, p. 91).

Located in the inter-tropical zone, Southeast Asia has a potential for photovoltaic energy too, which varies between 1,400 kWh/m^2/year and 1,900 kWh/m^2/year (IEA 2017, p. 89).[17] Climate conditions seem favourable for this type of energy, especially given the region's abundant sunlight for a large part of the year, joined with technological progress allowing up 2019 to produce solar electricity at a lower cost than coal. According to IEA's NPS, photovoltaics is expected to grow by around 11 per cent per year up to 2040, reaching an installed capacity of 53 GW, from 4 GW in 2016. The IEA's more optimistic SDS foresees a regional production capacity of 60 GW in 2030, followed by more than a doubling of that capacity by 2040 (161 GW).

Several ASEAN countries have ambitious targets for photovoltaics. Thailand projects an installed capacity of 10 GW in 2036; Vietnam, 12 GW in 2030; Indonesia, 5 GW in 2020; and Malaysia, 1 GW in 2020. In March 2016, the Philippines inaugurated the largest solar farm in Southeast Asia (Western Visayas), which has 425,000 solar panels installed over an area of 170 hectares (132 MW).

Moreover, ASEAN countries have diverse stocks of biomass from agriculture to forest products (7 GW in 2016). Playing an important role in isolated, mountainous and island regions, this biomass is expected to retain a significant part by 2040, whether one considers IEA's NPS scenario (19 GW) or the SDS (24 GW). In addition, there is an increasing use of biofuels in the transport sector, particularly those derived from palm oil cultivation (Malaysia, Thailand).

Recognizing that the regional coal, natural gas and oil resources will be unable to satisfy their national demand, several Asian member countries of the Asia-Pacific Economic Cooperation (APEC)—or at least those having mastered nuclear technology—are considering pursuing a domestic energy policy focusing on civilian nuclear power. The same are strongly encouraging Southeast Asian countries to examine the potential of this energy in the fight against climate change (Mottet 2016, pp. 122–25). ASEAN members, for their part, have been discussing this energy option since 2008 within the Nuclear Energy Cooperation Sub-Sector Network (NEC-SSN), a forum that provides information on safety issues through visits to nuclear power plants in South Korea, Japan, United States, Russia, China and Canada. Currently, there is no installed nuclear capacity in the countries of the region, and ASEAN members have little or no concrete nuclear power plant manufacturing projects. Nevertheless, the 2016–25 APAEC scenario makes it clear that nuclear power should be part of ASEAN's energy mix with a production of 1 GW in 2035 and between 2 GW (NPS scenario) and 5 GW (SDS scenario) in 2040, which corresponds to the installed capacity of two to five reactors.

Hydropower and, far behind, photovoltaics should thus dominate future renewable and non-fossil energy developments for the next half-century, but the ambition appears larger than the present commitment.

The Hydropower Environmental Dilemma

If hydropower is surely a renewable energy, its present and forthcoming developments remain a highly sensitive issue in Southeast Asia. Setting up photovoltaic farm is not prejudicial to the environment of the surrounding zone; it is not the case of dams, which are highly destructive for the local populations (Chandran 2018) as for biodiversity. The Mekong River is in the vicinity of 65 million people, 40 per cent of whom resides within a range of 15 km mainstream, and lives from the river, for irrigation, agricultural nutriments and fishing (Soukhaphon, Baird and Hogan 2021, p. 1). In Laos alone, 61 hydropower dams had already an installed capacity of 7.2 GW[18] in 2018, and 36 more dams should be completed beginning 2021, the government planning to develop an additional 20 GW by 2030. In Vietnam, the Yali river's Dam has considerably weakened food security and even health (due to toxic algae) of Cambodian people living downstream, similar to what the Lower Sesan 2 Dam has caused in Cambodia itself. In Myanmar, all dams are built in ethnic non-Bamar hill areas, of which populations have been in conflict with the central government since the years 1960s and even earlier for some of them, as illustrated by the highly controversial Myitsone Dam project on the Irrawaddy in the Kachin State,[19] developed by and for the Chinese to the detriment of local populations and suspended by President Thein Sein in 2011. The construction of the Myitsone Dam will probably resume "thanks" to the 2021 military coup, though the Kachin Independence Army is presently increasing its attacks against the Burmese army. Conversely, though China had postponed the building of 14 dams along the Salween (aka Thanlwin), Aung San Suu Kyi government decided to carry on six dams downstream, located in the Shan and Kayin (Karen) states, in partnership with the Chinese Sino-Hydro and Three Gorges Corporation, and Thai EGAT (Fawthorp 2016). Worse, due to the high level of stakes for both Southeast Asian states and the Yunnan province, proper regional cooperation does not work for hydropower (Soukhaphon, Baird and Hogan 2021, p. 11).

An Energy Transition between Regional Integration and Market Integration

It is all the more worrying that most countries are experiencing a high rate of energy wastage due to outdated technologies of exploitation, transmission and use. The overall losses of the entire power grid, arguably underestimated, are problematic in a region that suffers many power outages and other periods of energy shortage. The construction of the electricity market (ASEAN Power Grid or APG) and gas market (Trans-ASEAN Gas Pipeline or TAGP) has been slower than expected. Efforts toward bilateral and multilateral physical integration between member states are limited due to numerous financial, institutional, regulatory and technical obstacles that ultimately prevent the harmonization of the regional energy network. To address this problem, ASEAN is promoting the integration of energy markets and the construction of new interconnections, which require huge political and financial investments.

With this in mind, ASEAN is now orienting its energy strategy on market connectivity and works on creating the necessary conditions within the framework of its ASEAN Economic Community (AEC), which will ultimately allow multilateral trade in electricity and gas between its member states. The potential creation of an ASEAN electricity exchange system could accelerate the energy integration of the subregion, as illustrated by the system implemented in South Asia.

The ambition of the ASEAN Power Grid (APG) was initially to develop bilateral electrical interconnections, under the supervision of the leaders of the sector (HAPUA or Heads of ASEAN Power Utilities/Authorities). The adoption of the APAEC in 2014 accelerated the implementation of the APG for an integrated single market of

TABLE 4.4
Objectives and Installed Capacity of Renewable Energies in ASEAN Countries, 2017

Countries	Targeted year	Renewable energy objectives	Main Technology in 2018 & production	Installed capacity of renewable energies in 2017–18[20]	Renewable energy production (2018)	Achieved % of objective in 2017–18
Brunei	2035	954 GWh	Photovoltaics	1 MW	2 GWh	0.04%
Cambodia	2020	2,241 MW	Hydropower	1,055 MW	4,817 GWh	47%
Indonesia	2025[21]	46,307 MW installed capacity	Hydropower (21,161 GWh) Biofuels (10,713 GWh)[22]	9,378 MW	46,976 GWh	20.2%
Laos	2025	Small hydropower[23] (400 MW installed capacity) Others excluding large scale hydro (309 MW)	Big hydropower (22,328 GWh)	6,644 MW (small-hydro: 86.5 MW[24])	22,390 GWh	21.6% for small hydropower
Malaysia	2025	2,865 MW installed capacity excluding large-scale hydro	Hydropower (23.635 GWh) Biomass (1,352 GWh)	7,713 MW (small-hydro: 230 MW[25]; biofuels & others: 379 MW)	28,250 GWh	21.2% excluding large-scale hydro
Myanmar	2030[26]	12% for renewable in generation excluding large-scale hydro	Hydropower	3,255 MW (small-hydro: 33 MW[27])	12,129 GWh	8.3%

TABLE 4.4 (continued)

Philippines	2030	15,300 MW installed capacity	Geothermal (10,691 GWh) Hydropower (8,025 GWh) Solar (1.246 GWh) Wind turbines (1,042 GWh)	7,079 MW	21,495 GWh	46.2%
Singapore	2020	350 MW	Photovoltaics	369 MW	1673	105%
Thailand	2036	19,684 MW installed capacity	Small hydropower (6,000–10,000 MW) Biomass (5,570 MW) Hydropower (2,906 MW)	10,599 MW	33,958 GWh	53.8%
Vietnam	2030	45,800 MW	Small hydropower (27,800 MW) Photovoltaics (12,000 MW) Wind turbine (6,000 MW)	18,557 MW	84,748 GWh	40.5%

Source: ACE (2016); IEA database.

renewable (especially hydropower) energies, electricity border trade and greater access to energy services (ACE 2016, Phase I: 2016–20). APAEC identified three strategic areas of focus and action: 1) to allow free access to a system (import terminal/network) in at least one country (Singapore, in this case); 2) to make the destination clauses in the LNG contracts more flexible to encourage shipments to be redirected to markets offering a better price; and 3) to minimize the environmental impact of CO_2 related to gas production and transportation.

Looking beyond governmental rhetoric and public commitments, the implementation of energy transition is not self-evident for Southeast

Asian states, as for a significant number of countries. The United States withdrew from the Paris Agreement on Climate in November 2019, then deposited its instrument of acceptance on 20 January 2021. Turkey, Iran, Iraq, Libya and Yemen have not yet ratified it up to January 2021, which might be due to political instability for the latter three, but not for Turkey, or even for Iran which faced a diplomatic deadlock during the Trump presidency.

Though all ASEAN states ratified the Paris agreement, they implemented highly contrastive strategies as far as energy transition was concerned (see Table 4.4). Targeted years varied from 2020 (Cambodia, Singapore) to 2036 (Thailand). In 2017, Indonesia had already completed 20.2 per cent of its 2025 target of renewable energy and Malaysia, 53 per cent. Philippines realized 46 per cent of its 2030's objectives, and Thailand, nearly 54 per cent.

BRUNEI AS A CASE-STUDY

Brunei is lagging very far behind all other ASEAN states, having performed in 2018 only 0.04 per cent of its objective of 954 MW photovoltaics installed capacity; even if 2035 is far away, it could be interpreted as a lack of interest in energy issues other than increasing the productivity of oil and gas fields.

Brunei's Energy White Paper and NDC

To better understand Brunei's position towards energy transition, it is first necessary to present Brunei's strategy towards the energy sector as described in its 2014 Energy White Paper and thoroughly revised in the sultanate's first "National Determined Contribution" (NDC) in October 2019 (ACE 2020), then to describe its last developments in 2020–21.

Following the Energy White Paper (Energy Department 2014, pp. 9–13), the whole sector was supposed to grow at around 6 per cent on a yearly basis (in real terms) with a target of generating B$42 billion (US$31 billion) in 2035. New discoveries of exploitable hydrocarbons were expected to double the replacement ratio (based on proven reserves) from 0.5 to 1, with hydrocarbons production expanding from 408,000 barrels of oil equivalent (BOE) per day in 2010 to 650,000 in

2035—a 59 per cent increase in 25 years (de Vienne 2015, pp. 171–73). Gross income from downstream enterprises has progressed from B$300 million (US$ 220 million) in 2010 to B$3 billion (US$2.17 billion) in 2017 (multiplying tenfold) and should reach B$5 billion (US$3.6 billion) in 2035. In 2035, the number of locals working for the energy sector should thus double from 2017 and quadruple from 2010, locals[28] representing then four-fifths of the sector total employment (against only a half in 2010). According to *The 6th ASEAN Energy Outlook 2017–2040*, renewable energy would generate 124 GWh in 2017 and 954 GWh in 2035 (10 per cent renewable in installed capacity in 2035; ACE 2020, p. 56). Moreover, the ratio of primary energy demand to GDP, i.e., energy intensity,[29] would have decreased by 18 per cent between 2010 and 2017, and by one-third in 2035.

To realize these goals, the Department of Energy[30] gave priority to the exploration of unlicensed acreages and the implementation of new technologies relating to surveys and extraction. The major downstream project mentioned by the Energy White Paper was a refinery, which should generate in 2035 an output of B$16 billion, other downstream projects producing only B$5 billion.

A Net-Exporter of Hydrocarbons Suffering from Pandemic

Presently, the major issue is that the global economic slowdown induced by the pandemic has led to a world surplus in oil supply and, as a result, a 27 per cent fall in prices at the beginning of March 2020. After several weeks of negotiations, the Organization of Petroleum Exporting Countries or OPEC (of which Brunei is a member) and its partners decided to reduce production voluntarily by 23 per cent in April 2020 and again by 10 per cent from May. As the world supply of gas was already in excess before the pandemic, the fall in LNG prices was even worse than that of oil: –40 per cent (see Figure 4.1). In Brunei itself, demand for hydrocarbons dropped by 30 per cent in the first half of 2020; the situation deteriorated further in the second half of the year (de Vienne 2021). Current estimates suggest that the production of hydrocarbons in Brunei would not return to its 2019 level before 2023 or 2024. The fall of hydrocarbons prices (the trend beginning to slightly reverse in 2021) might have a direct impact on the replacement ratio, as it could be compensated by an increase of Brunei's export (and production) in volume.

FIGURE 4.1
Oil and Gas Prices, 2004–20

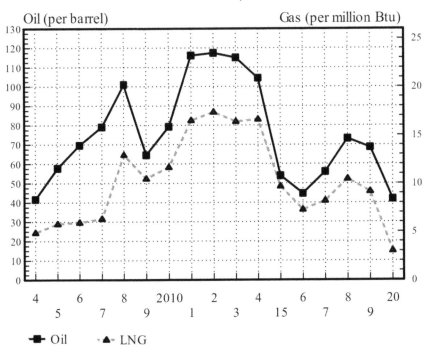

Oil (per barrel)   Gas (per million Btu)

◼ Oil   ▲ LNG

Source: *Brunei Darussalam Statistical Yearbooks 2004–19*; Statistical Database for 2020. All graphs are originals made by Marie-Sybille de Vienne for this specific chapter.

The "COVID-19 shock" remains all the more problematic for Brunei, as its finances have been in deficit since 2014–15 (fiscal year)—excepting a modest surplus of B$27.9 million (US$20.28 million) in 2018–19. Taxes on the hydrocarbon sector (including downstream industries) provide an average of 75 per cent of government revenues, compared to about 7 per cent for other taxes, 7 per cent for fees, charges and rents from government domestic assets, and around 10 per cent for return from investments and savings (*Brunei Darussalam Statistical Yearbook 2017–19*). Brunei thus forecasts a record deficit of minimum US$1.3 billion in 2020–21, which should persist in 2021–22—knowing that all hydrocarbons exporters will suffer worldwide.

A Growing Energy Consumption

After years of postponing, diversification has finally begun as
downstream hydrocarbons industries: a pioneer methanol plant was
first inaugurated in May 2010; a decade later, Hengyi Refinery[31] started
production (end-2019), with a processing capacity of eight million tons
of crude oil per year, geared to the production of fuels (petrol, diesel,
aviation fuel) in addition to by-products (500,000 tons of benzene and

FIGURE 4.2
Domestic Consumption of Hydrocarbons
('000 of cubic metres, excepting gas), 2006–19

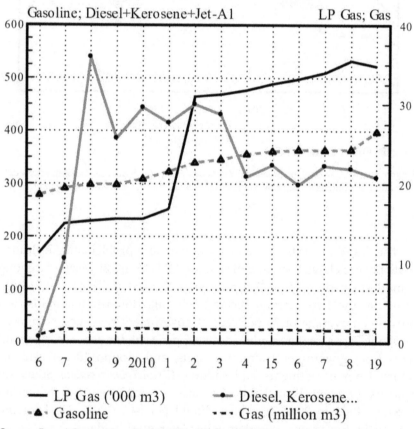

Source: Brunei Darussalam Statistical Yearbooks 2006–19.
All graphs are originals made by Marie-Sybille de Vienne for this specific chapter.

FIGURE 4.3
Electricity Production and Consumption, 2006–19

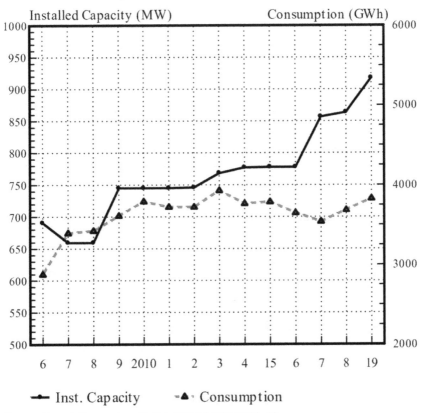

Source: Brunei Darussalam Statistical Yearbooks 2006–19.
All graphs are originals made by Marie-Sybille de Vienne for this specific chapter.

1.5 million tons of paraxylene). Brunei Fertilizer Industries (BFI), ASEAN's biggest fertilizer plant, is to be inaugurated mid-2021. Negotiations on the extension of Hengyi Refinery are progressing, which should represent an investment significantly bigger than those (US$3.45 billion) of the previous phase.

As a whole, Brunei's domestic consumption of hydrocarbons kept growing (see Figure 4.2), following the pace of industrial diversification (essentially downstream hydrocarbon production) (Brunei Economic Development Board 2017; Druce and Hai Julay 2018). Since 2006, gasoline consumption increased from 278,800 cubic metres (cm) in 2006 to 398,000 cm in 2019, a 43 per cent increase in 13 years; consumption of liquefied petroleum gas (LPG) more than doubled, from 14,000 cubic metres to 35,000. Conversely, the consumption of other fuels such as diesel and kerosene which had jumped to 539,000 cm in 2008, decreased to 311,000 cm in 2019. Even if LNG consumption remained stable (around 1.6 million cm per year), Brunei's importations of fuels regularly increased, from B\$43.79 million (US\$27.5 million) in 2006 to B\$176.1 (US\$129.2 million) in 2010, and to B\$2,341 million (US\$1.7 billion) in 2019, multiplying by 62 in 13 years.

Electricity (see Figure 4.3) followed: in the years 2006–19, electricity consumption grew from 2,900 GWh to 3,750 GWh; installed capacity, from 700 MG to nearly 900 MW.

2035: A Problematic Future?

Though Brunei's energy sector is presently not under threat, its future remains problematic, as the sultanate has been facing great challenges in achieving most of the goals identified by the Energy White Paper. As for hydrocarbons, Brunei remains today a net exporter, but its production is descending (see Figure 4.4) and will follow the same pace in absence of new discoveries. Oil production, which had reached 88 billion barrels in 1979, dropped to 48 billion in 1989, rose again to 80 billion in 2006, and finally declined to some 40 billion at the end of the 2010s. After rising up to 7.9 billion cubic metres in 1977, then to 12.5 billion in 2007, Brunei's liquefied natural gas (LNG) production dropped to 9.6 billion cm in 2019 too. Following the trends of the years 2009–19, the oil production is expected to decline to 37 billion barrels in 2025, then to 31 in 2035 while the LNG production would remain stable (see Figure 4.5).

Based on its 2019 production level (IEA 2020, pp. 14, 32), Brunei would have 24 years of oil reserves (up to 2043) and 18 years of gas (up to 2038). Though Brunei's energy supplies do not constitute even a middle-term issue, the government ordered in May 2020 the constitution of a strategic reserve equivalent to a minimum of 50 per cent of all producers' existing storage capacity to manage volatility in the crude oil market.

Employment in the energy sector (including electricity and downstream industries) increased, from around 10,200 in 2014 to 15,800 in 2019, meaning that at its present pace of development, reaching the Energy White Paper target of some 40,000 employed population in 2035 could be plausible.

Unfortunately, all targets relating to energy transition will not be fulfilled in the near future. Though the Energy White Paper presumed that energy intensity[32] would decrease from 18 per cent between 2010 and 2017, then from one-third from 2017 to 2035, it increased by 1.8 per cent in 2010–17 (ESCAP 2020, p. 92). Brunei's per capita energy consumption (1,700 kg oil equivalent in 2017) is the second largest after Singapore in ASEAN (ESCAP 2020, p. 2) though its population is less than one-tenth of Singapore's and its GDP 27 times smaller. Electricity consumption grew by 10 per cent from 2011 to 2019, though Brunei's

FIGURE 4.4
Brunei Hydrocarbons Production, 1965–2019

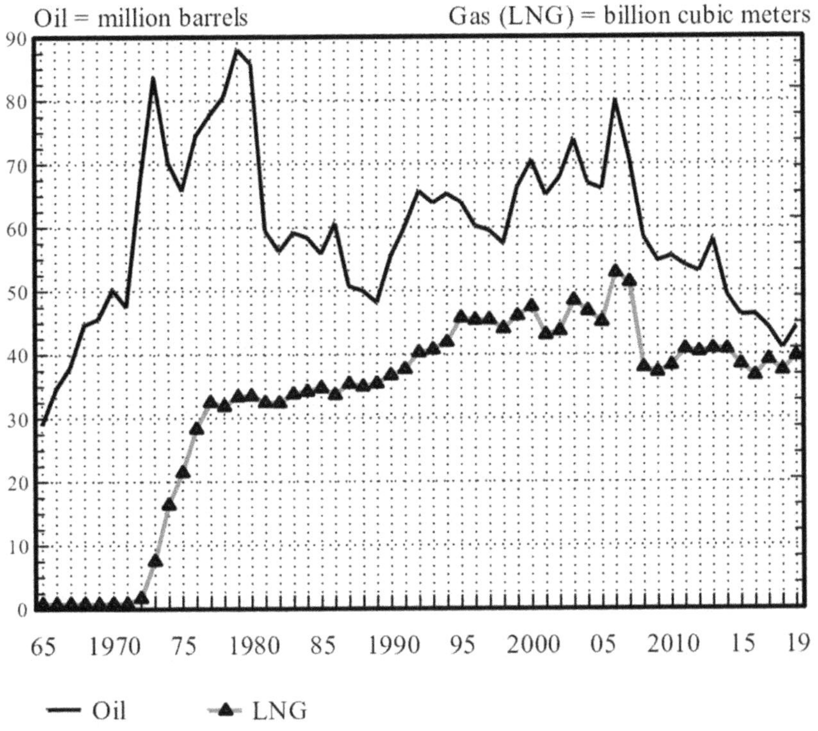

Source: *Brunei Darussalam Statistical Yearbooks 1965–2019.*
All graphs are originals made by Marie-Sybille de Vienne for this specific chapter.

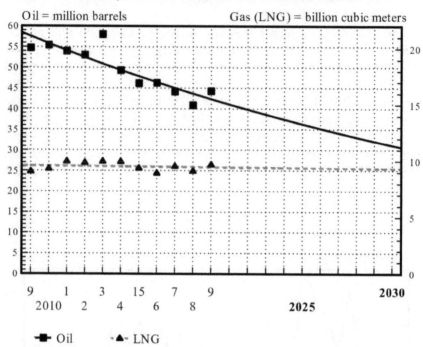

FIGURE 4.5
Brunei Hydrocarbons Production: Trends to 2025–30

Oil = million barrels   Gas (LNG) = billion cubic meters

▪■- Oil   ·▲· LNG

Source: Brunei Darussalam Statistical Yearbooks 2009–2019.
All graphs are originals made by Marie-Sybille de Vienne for this specific chapter.

most recent goal (as of ACE 2020, p. 55) is a 30 per cent decrease in all sectors by 2035, meaning a reduction of electricity consumption of minimum 10 per cent during the last decade. The development of downstream industries appears contradictory with the downsizing of electricity consumption in manufacturing.

Furthermore, Brunei has ASEAN's highest subsidization rate (36 per cent) for fossil fuels and electricity, which does not promote energy savings; regressive pricing and discounted tariffs for electricity pushes commercial consumers to increase energy intensity. Transport and residential represent 45 per cent of final energy consumption (ESCAP 2020, p. 102). In 2015, Brunei's average yearly electricity consumption per household was 15,780 kWh (ERIA, BNERI and Chiyoda Corporation 2020, p. 15), four times bigger than the average in the European Union

(4,000 kWh), and has not decreased since then. Air conditioning and fans totalize 60 per cent of Brunei household's energy consumption, but it increases to 70 per cent if one includes the use of refrigerators.

NEW BRUNEIAN ENVIRONMENTAL HOPES?

Though Brunei seemed to be suffering from an inertia syndrome as far as energy transition was concerned, things started to change at the end of the last decade. The authorities realized the effects of global warming in Brunei. Temperature is increasing at a rate of 0.25°C per decade and total rainfall of 100 mm, while forests and peat swamps (mostly in Belait district) suffer from devastating fires (*Brunei NDC 2020*, pp. 12–13). Not only does climate change threaten biodiversity, it also contributes to multiply mosquitoes that carry various plagues such as dengue fever.

Brunei's National Climate Change Policy

Awareness of the climatic stake started to change in 2018, the sultanate being endowed with a Secretariat on Climate Change[33] in July; two years later, two major documents were issued. In collaboration with the Brunei National Energy Research Institute (BNERI),[34] ERIA (Economic Research Institute for ASEAN and East Asia) published Brunei Energy Consumption Survey in June 2020. One month later, the Brunei Secretariat on Climate Change presented the National Climate Change Policy (NCCP).[35] In January 2021, Brunei exposed for the first time to the United Nations Framework Convention on Climate Change (UNFCCC)[36] its contribution (NDC) to a reduction in greenhouse gas emissions, with a target of –20 per cent by 2030, based on 2015 (11.6 Mt CO_2 equivalent, 0.025 per cent of world GHG emissions) and "business-as-usual" levels.

With 56 per cent of GHG being presently produced by power generation, 18 per cent by fugitive emissions and 13.6 per cent by land transport (Brunei Climate Change Secretariat 2020, p. 8), Brunei's climate policy aimed to boost renewable energy to 30 per cent of the power generation mix by 2035, mostly through photovoltaic (Brunei having presently only one small solar power plant in Seria), while improving supply management and distribution to reduce electricity consumption by 10 per cent. New power plants using combined cycle gas turbine (Tabrani 2015, p. 74) should have a minimum efficiency of 48 per cent, while the older single-cycle (diesel) power plants could be dismantled, such as the one in Temburong.

The price for economic diversification being that Brunei's GHG emissions should more than double by the next fifteen years, industries will have to comply with the new climate change policy (Rasidah 2020). Carbon reporting is to become mandatory by 2021; all plants emitting beyond a CO_2 emissions threshold should be taxed by 2025. The sultanate is now supporting the development of electric vehicles, with a target of 10 per cent electric vehicles[37] (i.e., 60 per cent of total annual vehicle sales) by 2035, but without studying the implementation of collective transportation such as tramways in Bandar Sri Begawan, where only a few (and irregular) city-buses are available, used by the poorest of the migrant workers. On 25 March 2021, a two-year pilot project for electric vehicles was launched in Bandar Seri Begawan, with the support of a new division from Shell offering electric charging service (Ministry of Energy 2021). Electricity tariffs for the commercial sector should be reviewed in the following years.

Given all these measures will not be sufficient to reduce GHG emissions, Brunei decided to increase its forest cover with a target of 500,000 new trees, hoping thus that some 85 per cent of its GHG production could be absorbed by this natural sink in 2035, provided that the forest cover would be maintained at a minimum 72 per cent. It implies enhancing full electrification (Brunei Climate Change Secretariat 2020, pp. 40–41) of the remote Temburong district (to prevent villagers from burning wood), using the new bridge linking the two parts of the territory across the mouth of the Brunei River to install a 66kV transmission device.

From Brunei's "Business-as-Usual" to APAEC Scenario?

Most of the target rates defined by Brunei's "climate change policy" in 2020 are in line with those presented by the ASEAN Plan of Action for Energy Cooperation (APAEC) as of 2035, notwithstanding that APAEC's early goal of 23 per cent of renewable energy by 2025 seems unreachable by Brunei. Brunei's climate change policy does not give a precise goal for increasing energy efficiency either (APAEC's target being a 30 per cent reduction by 2025), though it announced the introduction of energy standards and labelling for common electrical appliances.

The authorities are presently initiating an environmental campaign through the channel of education and compulsory meetings in administrations, to implement the practices described in the new *Protokol Hijau* or "Green Protocol" (Brunei Darussalam National Council on Climate Change 2021): segregating, reducing and reusing waste, promoting LED bulbs, switching off the lights and moderating air conditioners (23°C as a minimum threshold), all administrations having now received targets for planting trees in their surroundings.

If the authorities implement *Protokol Hijau* consistently, Bruneian locals could become in less than two decades the most committed to green environment in all ASEAN. Unfortunately, the authorities also consider carbon trading as an option (Brunei Climate Change Secretariat 2020, p. 44), while for the earth's sake there should be no other choice but to drastically curb GHG emissions at a world level, which implies banning all carbon trading. In Brunei, national concern about climate and energy transition must be triggered by political will.

CONCLUSION

In 2006, the economist, Nicholas Stern, of the Grantham Research Institute on Climate Change and the Environment, estimated in his famous *Stern Review: Economics of Climate Change*, that the measures adopted today will only have a limited effect on the climate over the next thirty years. On the other hand, "the investment that takes place in the next 10–20 years will have a profound effect on the climate in the second half of this century and in the next" (Stern 2006, p. vi). In other words, the energy issue, and, more broadly, the climatic and environmental issues, are related to the question of risks and uncertainties management, inevitably implying long-term "intertemporal equity" (Stern 2006, p. 41), and, more specifically, intra- and inter-generational commitment and moral considerations.

As illustrated by the case of Brunei, the ecological praxis observable in Southeast Asia remains multifaceted. In traditional societies such as Thailand, Myanmar and Cambodia, this praxis is well-implemented and even popularized by the millennial symbolic mode of representation and religious practices of hydro-agricultural civilizations, more or less in conflict with the Western-driven ideology of modernity. Unfortunately, in many Southeast Asian countries, it is also driven by the greed of local or national politicians as by pressures from dominating neighbour-states, while ecological concern in the civil society remains at the bottom of the agenda, compared with social or political issues considered as emergencies. There is a long way to go "to meet the needs of the present without compromising the capacity of future generations to meet their needs", as the 1987 Brundtland report so aptly demanded at the start of the United Nations awareness of the problem. Such a response and search for "intertemporal" or "intra- and inter-generational equity", at the level of each state and of international bodies, should ideally provide the ethical principle to be followed by every environmental policy in the world. In order to function effectively and in the long term, this principle requires to be based on political stability; it must also be relayed by moral and cultural codes, on the one hand, and consciousness of an interdependent relationship between humans and the environment on the other. Brunei's National Climate Change Policy (Brunei Climate Change Secretariat 2020, p. 3) reminds that Brunei's new policy for the climate is driven by the five *maqasid* (objectives) of the Quranic Law, *shari'ah*[38] (i.e., preservation of faith, life, intellect, progeny and wealth). The explicit citation of the said spiritual objectives in the formulation of the national energy transition policy did not appear at all in the 2014 Energy White Paper. On the one hand, this development can be explained as a continuation of more rigorous religious measures implemented in all sectors of the lives of Bruneian citizens in the last decade (de Vienne 2015). On the other hand, a new rationale seems to be emerging in Brunei's discourse on the environment, that of an ecological thought defined as a religious duty, while presenting ecological preservation as a way of following the divine Will. The following step will be a true implementation of the National Climate Change Policy.

NOTES

1. The Association of Southeast Asian Nations or ASEAN (Indonesia, Malaysia, Philippines, Singapore and Thailand) was established in 1967 to "accelerate economic growth [...] and strengthen the foundation for a prosperous and peaceful community" in Southeast Asia. Brunei joined in 1984, after independence, Vietnam in 1995, Laos and Myanmar in 1997 and Cambodia in 1999.
2. Used industrially for brickmaking and other kiln-operation (Park 2005, p. 36), while coal was more and more used to produce pig-iron.

3. Growth rate calculated by the authors using UNCTAD 2019 database (unctad.org/statistics) on GPB, constant US dollar.
4. Excepting Thailand and Myanmar.
5. With 1 Terawatt/h = 1,000 Gigawatt/h; and 1 Gigawatt/h = 1,000 Megawatt/h.
6. Indonesia, Malaysia, Brunei, Myanmar, Thailand and Vietnam.
7. The TAGP project entered into force in 2004 for a period of ten years. In 2013, it was extended by ten years, until 2024.
8. Electricity consumption is projected to grow by a factor of 2.5 from 82 Mtoe (million tons of oil equivalent) in 2015 to 207 Mtoe in 2040 (ACE 2015).
9. For further analysis on this electricity connectivity (APG) and gas cooperation (TAGP) projects, see Mottet and Jammes (2020, pp. 20–36).
10. All these data updated March 2021, have been calculated using statistics from the IEA website.
11. The key initiatives of this APAEC (ASEAN Plan of Action for Energy Cooperation) are based on seven axes of multilateral cooperation; see Mottet and Jammes (2020, p. 26).
12. An energy transition is measured in decades, given the great inertia of the energy system.
13. The IEA estimates that US$365 billion has been invested in Southeast Asia's energy sector since 2000, including US$195 billion for the expansion of distribution networks.
14. The Kyoto Protocol was binding only on developed countries, thirty-six in total, with the exception of the United States and Australia, which did not ratify it.
15. A business-as-usual scenario is designed based on both past trends that will be considered for continuation, and the policies, programmes or actions implemented that are likely to influence these past trends.
16. Billion cubic metres.
17. As for European cities, the average horizontal radiation is 940 kWh/m^2/year for Paris and 1,100 kWh/m^2/year for Lausanne (Switzerland).
18. 7,200 MW in 2019.
19. Located at the sources of the Irrawaddy, the dam (6,000 megawatts installed capacity), if completed, would have been the 16th largest in the world in 2017.
20. Calculated from ASEAN Energy Database System (AEDS), last year available: 2017, excepting Laos.
21. The target for 2050 is 171,000 MW.
22. Hydropower, solar photovoltaic, geothermal, biomass, wind turbines, tidal.
23. ≤ 15 MWh

24. World Bank (2017, annex 3–4). Calculation has added existing and under construction small hydropower in 2015.
25. See Poindexter (2018).
26. Based on ACE (2020, p. 56).
27. See Saw and Li (2019, p. 4).
28. Locals meaning Brunei citizens plus permanent residents.
29. Calculated in the Energy White Paper as tons of oil equivalent per million US$ of GDP, while according to ESCAP (2020) the ASEAN energy intensity (EI) value is based on total primary energy supply (TPES), in alignment with the global Sustainable Development Goals (SDG) indicator. However, the ASEAN indicator is based on data drawn from country submissions that have been standardized by the ASEAN Centre for Energy, whereas the SDG data is collected by and standardized by the United Nations Statistics Division and the International Energy Agency. The GDP base year used to calculate energy intensity also differs. ASEAN utilizes GDP 2005 PPP$, while the global indicator uses GDP 2011 PPP$.
30. Energy and Industry Department, Prime Minister's Office (PMO), upgraded in April 2018 to Ministry of Energy.
31. See de Vienne and Jammes (2020, pp. 908–9).
32. Primary Energy Demand/GDP (in million US$ or PPP$).
33. The National Council on Climate Change is co-chaired by the Minister of Development and the Minister of Energy.
34. Located in Universiti Brunei Darussalam (UBD).
35. http://www.climatechange.gov.bn/SitePages/BNCCP/index.html#page=1. The access to this volume is a good illustration of the methodological challenge researchers are facing when they work on Brunei. Indeed, this volume has been impossible to download, print or save as a pdf file, and it has required hours to print screen, page by page, before its contents could be analysed.
36. Created in 1994, UNFCCC is the UN entity working for the global response to climate change. It successively supported the 1997 Kyoto Protocol, its Doha Amendment (2012) and the 2015 Paris Agreement.
37. Brunei counting 253,000 active vehicles in 2020.
38. *maqāṣid al-sharīʿa.*

REFERENCES

ASEAN Centre for Energy (ACE). 2015. *ASEAN Plan of Action for Energy Cooperation (APAEC) 2016–2025, Phase I: 2016–2020.* Jakarta: ACE.
———. 2016. *ASEAN Renewable Energy Policies.* Jakarta: ACE.
———. 2020. *The 6th ASEAN Energy Outlook 2017–2040.* Jakarta: ACE.

ASEAN Secretariat and United Nations Conference on Trade and Development (UNCTAD). 2017. *ASEAN Investment Report 2017: Foreign Direct Investment and Economic Zones in ASEAN.* ASEAN@50 Special Edition. Jakarta: ASEAN Secretariat and UNCTAD.

Asian Development Bank (ADB). 2015. *Southeast Asia and the Economics of Global Climate Stabilization.* Manila: ADB.

BP. 2017. *BP Statistical Review of World Energy 2017.*

Brundtland, Gro Harlem. 1987. *Report of the World Commission on Environment and Development: Our Common Future.* Transmitted to the General Assembly as an Annex to document A/42/427 - Development and International Co-operation: Environment. New York. http://www.un-documents.net/wced-ocf.htm.

Brunei Climate Change Secretariat. 2020. *Brunei Darussalam National Climate Change Policy.*

Brunei Darussalam National Council on Climate Change. 2021. *Protokol Hijau* [Green Protocol], Vol. 1. Bandar Seri Begawan: Ministry of Development, Department of Environment.

Brunei Economic Development Board. 2017. "Downstream Oil and Gas". 18 November 2017.

Chandran, Nyshka. 2018. "Southeast Asia is Betting on Hydropower, but There Are Risks of Economic Damage". *CNBC*, 8 August 2018.

Cornot-Gandolphe, Sylvie. 2015. *The US Shale Oil Revolution: The Test of the Business Model is Underway.* Paris: IFRI.

_____. 2017. *L'énergie en Asie du Sud-Est. De l'intégration des réseaux à l'intégration des marchés* [Energy in South East Asia. From Integration of Networks to Integration of Markets]. Paris: IFRI.

Department of Statistics, Department of Economic Planning and Development (JPKE). 1966–2020. *Brunei Darussalam Statistical Yearbooks, 1965–2019.* Bandar Seri Begawan: Brunei: Department of Statistics, Department of Economic Planning and Development (JPKE).

_____. 2009–20. *Brunei Darussalam Key Indicators, 2010–2019.* Bandar Seri Begawan, Brunei: Department of Statistics, Department of Economic Planning and Development (JPKE).

Druce, Stephen C., and Abdul Hai Julay. 2018. "The Road to Brunei's Economic Diversification: Contemporary Brunei-China Relations". In *China and Southeast Asia in the Xi Jinping Era*, edited by Alvin Cheng-Hin Lim, and Frank Cibulka, pp. 139–52. Lanham, MD: Lexington Books.

Economic Research Institute for ASEAN and East Asia (ERIA), and Brunei National Energy Research Institute (BNERI). 2020. *Brunei Darussalam Energy Consumption Survey: Residential and Commercial and Public Sectors.* ERIA Research Project FY2019 No. 3. Jakarta: ERIA.

Economic Research Institute for ASEAN and East Asia (ERIA), Brunei National Energy Research Institute (BNERI), and Chiyoda Corporation. 2020. "Energy Outlook of Brunei Darussalam". In *Brunei Darussalam: Shifting to Hydrogen Society*. ERIA Research Project Report FY2020 No. 4, pp. 6–8. Jakarta: ERIA.

Energy Department. 2014. *Energy White Paper*. Bandar Seri Begawan: Prime Minister's Office (PMO).

Fawthorp, Tom. 2016. "Southeast Asia's Last Major Undammed River in Crisis". *The Third Pole*, 26 October 2016.

Fouquet, Roger. 2008. *Heat, Power and Light: Revolutions in Energy Services*. Cheltenham: Edward Elgar.

Hamilton, Clive, and Jacques Grinevald. 2015. "Was the Anthropocene Anticipated?" *The Anthropocene Review* 2, no. 1: 59–72.

International Energy Agency (IEA). 2017. *Southeast Asia Energy Outlook 2017*. Paris: IEA.

———. 2019. *Southeast Asia Energy Outlook 2019*. Paris: IEA.

———. 2020. *World Energy Investment 2020*. Paris: IEA.

International Hydropower Association. 2015. "Rapport 2015 sur le statut de l'hydroélectricité" [2015 Hydropower Status Report]. International Hydropower Association.

ISEAS – Yusof Ishak Institute. 2019. "Fuelling ASEAN's Energy Security". *ASEAN Focus*, no. 30. Singapore: ISEAS — Yusof Ishak Institute.

Jammes, Jérémy, Frédéric Lasserre, Éric Mottet, and Gauthier Mouton. 2020. "East and Southeast Asian Energy Transition and Politics: An Introduction". *CQEG Working Paper*, no. 2: 5–12. Conseil québécois d'Études géopolitiques with Asia Focus (IRIS) and Université Laval.

Ministry of Energy. 2021. "A Two-Year Pilot Project on Electric Vehicle Launched". 25 March 2021. Bandar Seri Begawan: Ministry of Energy and Industry.

Mottet, Éric. 2016. "Asie du Sud-Est: des programmes nucléaires civils bientôt opérationnels?" [Southeast Asia: Are Civilian Nuclear Programs Soon to Be Operational?]. *Monde Chinois, Nouvelle Asie* 44: 122–25.

Mottet, Éric, and Jérémy Jammes. 2020. "Towards and Beyond ASEAN Energy Transitions". *CQEG Working Paper* no. 2: 13–44. Conseil québécois d'Études géopolitiques with Asia Focus (IRIS) and Université Laval.

Park, Joonkyung. 2005. *Long-Run Economic Growth and Technological Progress*. Seoul: Korea Development Institute.

de Perthuis, Christian, and Pierre-André Jouvet. 2015. *Green Capital: A New Perspective on Growth*. New York: Columbia University Press.

Peytral, Pierre-Olivier, and Jean-Christophe Simon. 2013. "Défis énergétiques et climatiques en Asie du Sud-Est" [Energy and Climate Challenges in Southeast Asia]. In *L'Asie du Sud-Est 2013* [Southeast Asia 2013], edited by Jérémy Jammes, pp. 47–68. Paris: Les Indes savantes.

Poindexter, Gregory. 2018. "Companies Plan Mini-Hydropower Development in Peninsular Malaysia". *Hydro Review*, 8 August 2018. https://www.hydro review.com.

Rasidah Hj Abu Bakar. 2020. "Brunei to Introduce Mandatory Carbon Reporting in 2021". *The Scoop*, 25 July 2020. https://thescoop.co/2020/07/25/brunei-to-introduce-mandatory-carbon-reporting-in-2021/.

Revault d'Allonnes, M. 2008. "The Philosophical Implications of Sustainable Development". In *Europe and Sustainable Development*, Centre d'Analyse et de Prévision, pp. 136–46. Aubervilliers: La Documentation Française.

Saw, May Myat Moe, and Li Ji-Qing. 2019. "Review on Hydropower in Myanmar". *Applied Water Science* 9, no. 4.

Shi Xunpeng, and Cecilya Malik. 2013. *Assessment of ASEAN Energy Cooperation within the ASEAN Economic Community*. Jakarta: Economic Research Institute for ASEAN and East Asia (ERIA).

Smil, Vaclav. 2010. *Energy Transitions: History, Requirements, Prospects*. Santa Barbara: ABC-CLIO.

Soukhaphon, Akarath, Ian G. Baird, and Zeb S. Hogan. 2021. "The Impacts of Hydropower Dams in the Mekong River Basin: A Review". *Water* 13, no. 265: 1–18.

Stern, Nicholas, ed. 2006. *The Stern Review Report: The Economics of Climate Change*. London: HM Treasury.

Tabrani, A. 2015. "Brunei Darussalam Country Report". In *Energy Outlook and Energy Saving Potential in East Asia*, ERIA Research Project Report 2014–33, edited by Shigeru Kimura, and Han Phoumin, pp. 69–76. Jakarta: ERIA.

United Nations Economic and Social Commission for Asia and the Pacific (ESCAP). 2020. *Regional Energy Trends Report 2020 — Tracking SDG 7 in the ASEAN Region*. United Nations: ESCAP.

United Nations Framework Convention on Climate Change (UNFCCC). 2015. "INDCs as Communicated by Parties". Database. https://www4.unfccc.int/ sites /submissions/INDC/ Submission%20Pages/submissions.aspx.

──────. 2020. *Brunei Darussalam National Determined Contribution (NDC) 2020*. Bonn: UNFCCC.

de Vienne, Marie-Sybille. 2015. *Brunei: From the Age of Commerce to Rentier State*. Singapore: NUS Press.

──────. 2021. "Brunei, entre Tabligh et Covid" [Brunei between Tabligh and Covid]. In *Asie du Sud-est 2021*, pp. 169–90. Bangkok: IRASEC.

de Vienne, Marie-Sybille, and Jérémy Jammes. 2020. "China's Maritime Nexus in Southeast Asia: Economic and Geostrategic Challenges of the Belt and Road Initiative in Brunei". *Asian Survey* 60, no. 5: 905–27.

World Bank. 2017. *Small Hydro Resource Mapping in Lao PDR: Inception Report*. Washington, D.C.: World Bank Group.

5

BRUNEI'S TRANSITION POLICIES TO LOW CARBON ECONOMY: IMPLEMENTATION CHALLENGES AND GOVERNANCE IMPLICATIONS

Romeo Pacudan

INTRODUCTION

Being situated in the northwest coast of the island of Borneo with flat coastal plains and having an equatorial climate, Brunei is vulnerable to extreme weather events and rising sea levels. Since the 1970s, Brunei's annual mean temperature has been observed to increase by 0.25°C per decade; annual rainfall intensity has increased by 100 mm per decade, and; around 40 per cent of wildlife biodiversity were lost due to forest degradation (BCCS 2020). Coral bleaching was also observed in some shoals near Brunei-Muara district, and climate changes were expected to lengthen the transmission seasons of vector-borne diseases such as dengue, malaria and Zika (BCCS 2020).

In response to climate change threats, Brunei commits to international treaties and cooperation arrangements that address global climate change issues. The country acceded to the United Nations Framework Convention on Climate Change (UNFCCC) in 2007 and to the Kyoto Protocol in 2009. The country ratified the Doha Amendment to the Kyoto Protocol in 2014 and the Paris Agreement in 2016.

Brunei's climate change policy, launched in July 2020, would be the basis for developing a response framework for the requirement imposed on Parties of the Paris Agreement. This international agreement aims to strengthen global response to climate change threat and limit the global temperature rise to below 2°C above pre-industrial levels. Signatories to the Paris Agreement are required to submit a "nationally determined contribution" which specifies each country's efforts to reduce greenhouse gas emissions and adapt to impacts of climate change (UNFCCC 2015). A global stocktake will be undertaken every five years to monitor the progress in achieving the collective target.

Addressing climate change in Brunei requires a prudent approach to balance the interaction between key economic and environmental parameters. The country faces various economic and technical challenges in achieving a balanced mix of measures that satisfies various developmental concerns. While the new climate change policy appears to be skilfully designed to address the above concerns, its implementation, however, faces various challenges. In addition, the policy document states that the government pursues a whole-of-nation approach to policy governance, but the document does not present how the whole-of-nation approach was carried out to achieve these policy outcomes. The key questions thus raised in this chapter are the following: 1) how the cooperation among stakeholders was established during climate change policy formulation, and ii) as the country moves into policy implementation, what are the emerging challenges and their implications for climate change governance.

This chapter is organized as follows: the section immediately after this presents the challenges in the transition to a low carbon economy, the subsequent section highlights the intervention measures and emissions reduction potential, followed by a section on the collaborations in climate change governance. A separate section outlines the implementation challenges and implications on governance, with a subsequent section on perspectives on opportunities for policy refinement, and the final section concludes the chapter.

CHALLENGES IN THE TRANSITION TO LOW CARBON ECONOMY

The country's climate policy and strategies are formulated against the backdrop of long-standing national circumstances and economic policies that tend to encourage higher energy consumption and consequently higher carbon emissions. The main challenge for the government is to design policy measures that sustain these developmental trends but decouple economic development with environmental degradation and emissions.

Oil and Gas-based Economy

With high conventional energy resources relative to its population size, the oil and gas sector plays a dominant role in Brunei's economy. Contributing to around 57 per cent of the country's gross domestic product in 2019 (Department of Statistics 2020), the oil and gas industries are also envisaged to remain key pillars of Brunei's economy. Oil and gas production is projected to increase to 650,000 barrels of oil equivalent per day in 2035 from the baseline of 408,000 barrels of oil equivalent per day in 2010, and that the energy sector is expected to increase its contribution to the gross domestic product from B$10 billion in 2010 to B$42 billion in 2035 (EDPMO 2014).

Oil and gas production are dominant sources of fugitive greenhouse gas emissions. Fugitive emissions in oil and gas systems are defined to include flaring, venting and other greenhouse gas emissions except contributions from fuel combustion (IPCC 2006). Although the country's fugitive emissions had declined by 65 per cent during the period 2010 to 2018 due to rejuvenation projects in both onshore and offshore facilities, its contribution in 2018 remained high at around 18.1 per cent of the total emissions (BCCS 2020). Greenhouse gas emissions due to fuel combustion during the production, processing and transport of oil and natural gas are also important sources of greenhouse gas emissions in the country. With a projected increase in production, both fugitive emissions and fuel combustion emissions associated with the production, processing and transport of oil and natural gas will also increase.

Dependency on Fossil Fuels

Brunei is one of the countries in the world with a very high income per capita. This affluence combined with low prices for energy services (which is typical to most energy-exporting countries) creates a society with a very high domestic demand for energy services. Among the twenty-one countries under the Asia-Pacific Economic Cooperation, Brunei ranked seventh with 2.2 tons of oil equivalent per capita (APERC 2017). The top six countries are Canada (4.8 tons of oil equivalent per capita), the United States of America (4.2 tons of oil equivalent per capita), Australia (3.1 tons of oil equivalent per capita), Russia (2.9 tons of oil equivalent per capita), New Zealand (2.7 tons of oil equivalent per capita) and Korea (2.5 tons of oil equivalent per capita).

Due to the abundance of conventional energy resources in the country, power generation is almost 100 per cent fossil fuel based. Brunei's installed power generation capacity amounted to 902.3 megawatts in 2019. Of these, natural gas-fired power plants accounted for 98.5 per cent, followed by diesel power plants with 1.32 per cent and solar PV with 0.14 per cent (Ministry of Energy 2020a). Similarly, the domestic passenger transport is dominated by road transport. There were 446,393 registered vehicles in 2019 which translates to almost one vehicle per inhabitant (Ministry of Energy 2020b). The demand for fossil fuel-based energy supply would continue to increase with the increasing economic and population growth prospects.

Energy Intensive Industries

The plummeting international prices of oil and gas, and declining energy reserves indicate that there is an urgent need to diversify the economic base of the country. Aware of the risks related to high dependency on energy exports and with a growing population with high unemployment rate, the government continues to promote economic diversification in its economic development plan. The *Wawasan* Brunei 2035 (National Vision 2035) aims to shape Brunei into a dynamic and sustainable economy, and to transform the country into a well-educated economy with one of the world's top-ten highest standards of living, as well as having the highest income per capita worldwide ("Wawasan Brunei 2035", n.d.). Among the key pillars to achieve the goals to diversify the economy is the promotion of foreign direct investment and private sector investment in the downstream oil and non-oil industries, through joint venture arrangements with large international companies across various sectors.

With the abundance of hydrocarbon resources and low population densities, the emerging trend under economic diversification strategy is increased investments in energy intensive downstream industries. Important investments in energy intensive manufacturing industries include methanol production, fertilizer manufacturing, and refinery and aromatics cracker production facilities (Oxford Business Group 2016). These industries are associated with high carbon and air pollutant emissions per unit of gross domestic product.

Subsidized Energy Prices

Brunei pursues an energy pricing policy that sets energy prices, in the case of petroleum products, below the international market reference prices or in the case of electricity services, below the long-run marginal cost (Pacudan and Hamdan 2019). Low energy prices in the country have resulted in a rapid increase of energy consumption beyond what can be explained by factors such as rising income levels and population growth. Energy consumption per capita in Brunei is one of the highest in the Asia-Pacific region.

In addition, heavily subsidized energy prices distort investment decisions towards energy-intensive projects and encourage wasteful consumption of electricity. Lower energy prices, however, render investments in energy efficiency and renewable energy technologies less competitive with existing energy supply technologies (Pacudan 2018a, 2018b).

High Forest Cover and Pristine Forest Reserves

Aside from energy resources, the country also possesses a diverse and complex forest ecosystem. Since 2010, the country has managed to cease forest land conversions and maintain around 72 per cent of the land area with forest cover. On the other hand, 41 per cent of the land area have been gazetted as forest reserves (Ministry of Primary Resources and Tourism 2020). These resources are important carbon sinks and their preservation is an important strategy to mitigate climate change. Balancing conservation and sustainable management while optimizing resource benefits would remain a key challenge in managing natural resources in Brunei.

LOW CARBON INTERVENTION MEASURES AND EMISSIONS REDUCTION POTENTIAL

Greenhouse Gas Emissions

Between 2016 and 2017, climate change related policies and international negotiations were coordinated and carried out by the then Energy and Industry Department at the Prime Minister's Office. During this period, Brunei submitted its first and second national communications to the United Nations Framework Convention on Climate Change in 2016 and 2017, respectively. The first national communication covered greenhouse gas inventory for the year 2010 while the second estimated greenhouse gas emissions for the period 2010 until 2014.

In the process of preparing the Brunei Climate Change Policy (Policy), the Brunei Climate Change Secretariat (Secretariat) updated the greenhouse gas inventory and estimated the country's greenhouse gas emissions for 2015 and 2018. Compared with other ASEAN countries, Brunei's total gross emissions is relatively small (Global Carbon Atlas 2019). The gross emissions declined from 11.6 million tons of CO_2eq in 2015 to 10.1 million tons of CO_2eq in 2018. This is primarily driven by the reduction of emissions from the upstream oil and gas industries due to measures implemented to reduce natural gas venting and flaring.

While the country's gross emissions reached 10.1 million tons of CO_2eq in 2018, net emissions amounted to -1.3 million tons of CO_2eq indicating that Brunei is a net sink for emissions (BCCS 2020). The gap between the gross and net emissions represents the contribution of the forestry sector as a carbon sink. The energy sector contributed the highest share accounting for 91.2 per cent of the total gross emissions. Other sectors' contributions were marginal: waste sector contributed 2.2 per cent, agriculture and other land use 1.4 per cent, and residential sector 0.9 per cent. On the other hand, with 72 per cent of the country's land area is covered with forest, the forestry sector is estimated to absorb around 11.4 million tons of CO_2eq from the atmosphere (BCCS 2020).

Key Strategies

The new climate change policy outlines the country's emissions reduction targets for 2035 and stipulates ten strategies to achieve these targets and to transition Brunei into a low carbon economy. The transition policies consist of measures that reduce carbon emissions, increase carbon sink, and strengthen carbon resilience. The planned interventions and their performance indicators are summarized below.

Strategy 1 industrial emissions. Despite the decreasing emissions from oil and gas industries during the period 2010 to 2018 due to rejuvenation projects, industrial emissions remain relatively high accounting for around 18 per cent of the gross greenhouse gas emissions in 2018. The government aims to reduce overall emissions in the industrial sector (upstream and downstream oil and gas industries) through zero routine flaring, as defined by World Bank Standards and to As Low as Reasonably Practical (ALARP) level. The initiative of zero routine flaring was introduced by the World Bank in 2015 which aims to reduce wasteful release of associated gas from the extraction of crude oil.

Strategy 2 increasing forest cover. At present, around 72 per cent of the total land area is covered by forest. The government aims to increase the forest reserve from 41 per cent to 55 per cent of the total land area. Under this strategy, the government aims to plant 500,000 new trees by 2035 through reforestation and afforestation.

Strategy 3 electric vehicles. The country is highly dependent on private transportation. As of 2018, there were over 426,000 registered vehicles in the country. The number of vehicles was estimated to increase by 2 per cent per year from 2018 until 2035. The government aims to increase the penetration of electric vehicles accounting for 60 per cent of total vehicle sales in 2035.

Strategy 4 renewable energies. Electricity generation from renewable energies accounts for around 0.14 per cent of total generation at present. Among renewable energy resources, solar energy is the most abundant in the country and could be exploited using mature and commercially viable technologies. This strategy seeks to increase the total share of renewable energy to at least 30 per cent of total installed capacity in the power generation mix.

Strategy 5 power management. Over 99 per cent of the power generation in the country is generated from fossil fuel-based power plants mainly natural gas. The country's total installed power plant capacity in 2018 amounted to 889 megawatts. This strategy aims to reduce greenhouse gas emissions by at least 10 per cent through improving supply-side energy efficiency.

Strategy 6 carbon pricing. Carbon pricing will be implemented in a later stage once a proper monitoring, verification and reporting system is established. Carbon pricing will internalize external costs associated with carbon emissions. This strategy aims to introduce carbon pricing to industrial facilities and power utilities.

Strategy 7 waste management. Methane gas emissions from municipal solid waste will be reduced through waste minimization and adoption of waste-to-resource technologies. The strategy aims to reduce household waste to be disposed of in landfill sites to one kilogram per person per day.

Strategy 8 climate resilience and adaptation. Brunei is vulnerable to flooding, forest fires, strong winds and landslides. This strategy seeks to strengthen the country's resilience against climate change risks and increase its capacity to adapt to climate impacts.

Strategy 9 carbon inventory. This strategy requires all facilities that emit and absorb greenhouse gases to report their greenhouse gas data. The mandatory reporting promotes transparency and robustness in the national carbon emissions and sink data which provide a better understanding of the country's greenhouse gas emissions.

Strategy 10 awareness and education. This strategy seeks to promote awareness and educate stakeholders on the impacts and measures to mitigate and adapt to climate change. Specific measures include incorporating climate change mitigation and adaptation concepts in school curriculum and co-curriculum programmes; communicating, promoting and socializing the national climate change policy to all stakeholders.

Emissions Reduction Potential

Potential impacts of the above strategies were assessed with respect to emissions under the business-as-usual scenario. Gross emissions of greenhouse gases under the business-as-usual scenario were projected to increase by 4.9 per cent annually from 2015 until 2035 reaching 30.2 million tons of CO_2eq by 2035 from 10.1 million tons of CO_2eq in 2010 (see Figure 5.1).

As also shown in Figure 5.1, mitigation strategies (strategies 1 to 7) could potentially reduce the greenhouse gas emissions by more than 50 per cent in 2035 from business-as-usual emissions level. Measures

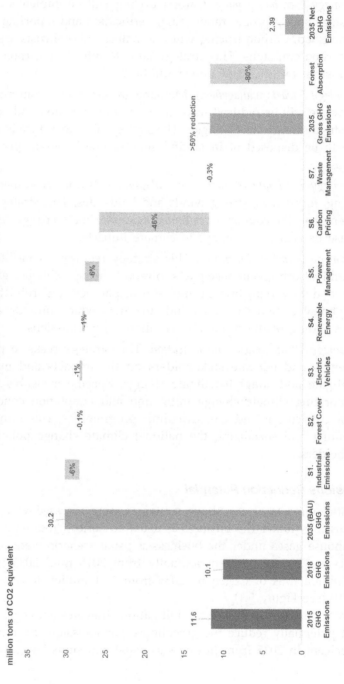

FIGURE 5.1
Greenhouse Gas Emissions Scenario

Source: Author's elaboration based on data from BCCS (2020).

under strategy 1 (industrial emissions) could reduce up to 6 per cent of the emissions; those under strategy 2 (increase forest cover) could reduce around 0.1 per cent; strategy 3 (increase deployment of electric vehicles) around 1 per cent; strategy 4 (renewable energies) also around 1 per cent; strategy 5 (improve energy efficiency in the power sector) around 6 per cent; strategy 6 (introduction of carbon pricing) around 46 per cent; and strategy 7 (waste management) at around 0.3 per cent. Among these measures, carbon pricing appears to contribute the biggest emissions reduction.

In addition to these measures, existing forests were also estimated to absorb CO_2 emissions from the atmosphere equivalent to around 50 per cent of the gross greenhouse gas emissions. With the combined effect of mitigation measures and existing forests, the net greenhouse gas emissions in 2035 would only amount to around 8 per cent of the gross business-as-usual greenhouse gas emissions.

COLLABORATIONS IN CLIMATE CHANGE GOVERNANCE

Whole-of-Nation Approach

The climate change policy document states that the government adopts a whole-of-nation approach in addressing adverse changing climate patterns as the country pursues to move towards a low carbon and climate-resilient economy through reducing carbon emissions, increasing carbon sink and strengthening carbon resilience (BCCS 2020). This all-encompassing climate change governance approach is in alignment with the current thrust of the government to involve all stakeholders, public and private, and the whole society to work together to achieve the economic development envisaged in the *Wawasan* Brunei 2035. The government recognizes that every stakeholder (public, private, non-government organizations) has a specific role to play and their active engagement would be crucial in achieving the long-term government vision.

The whole-of-nation approach appears to be a natural progression from the whole-of-government approach. The previous cabinet ministers used the concept of the whole-of-government to governance while the current ones are aligning themselves to the whole-of-nation concept. For example, the *Digital Government Strategy 2015–2020* stipulated the whole-of-government approach in innovation and service provision

(Prime Minister's Office 2015). The same progression can also be observed in Singapore as the public services go beyond the whole-of-government approach to the whole-of-nation approach (Low 2016; Yahya 2018). The whole-of-government approach (also known as intersectoral collaboration) refers to government agencies "working across boundaries to achieve shared goals and an integrated government response while the whole-of-nation approach widens this aperture to include all organizations to reach common goals" (Doyle 2019). The "whole-of-government focuses on internal stakeholder engagement while the whole-of-nation looks at external non-government stakeholder engagement" (WHO 2015).

Institutional Coordination

The complex nature of climate change mitigation and adaptation calls for a much broader response to climate change governance. Brunei established the first intersectoral collaboration platform spearheaded by the National Climate Change Council (Council) in 2010. It was co-chaired by the Minister of Energy and Minister of Development with members ranking from Deputy Ministers and Permanent Secretaries from the Prime Minister's Office and five other ministries (see Figure 5.2) with its Secretariat housed at the Ministry of Development.

With a new set of cabinet ministers installed in 2018, and through the initiative of the Minister of Energy, the Council was reorganized, with both the Ministers of Energy and Development remaining as co-chairs while the number of its members were reduced to the Minister of Primary Resources and Tourism, Minister of Transport and Infocommunications and Deputy Minister of Energy. One of the main lessons learned from the past structure is that convening a meeting with a bigger number of high-level government officials would be logistically difficult. Thus, the members of the new Council were limited to ministers of key sectors that would be the main target for climate change mitigation and adaptation. The Council's main mandate is to support global and national efforts to combat climate change and honour the country's commitments to climate change treaties including the Paris Agreement. The Council has the authority to formulate nationwide policies to address and adapt to climate change. The institutional arrangement of the Council, which convened its first meeting in October 2018, is also shown in Figure 5.2.

FIGURE 5.2
Brunei National Council on Climate Change

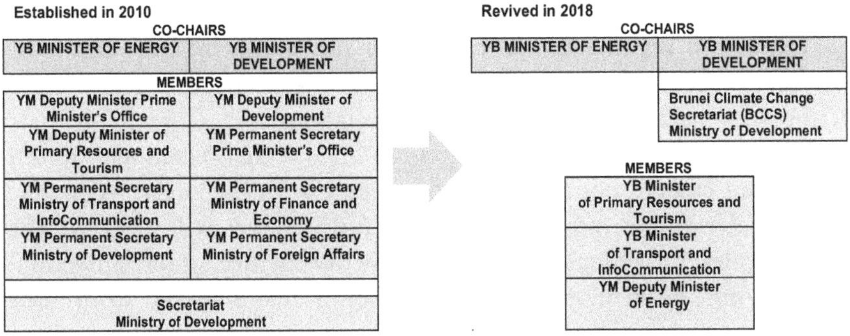

Established in 2010				Revived in 2018	
CO-CHAIRS				**CO-CHAIRS**	
YB MINISTER OF ENERGY	YB MINISTER OF DEVELOPMENT			YB MINISTER OF ENERGY	YB MINISTER OF DEVELOPMENT
MEMBERS				Brunei Climate Change Secretariat (BCCS) Ministry of Development	
YM Deputy Minister Prime Minister's Office	YM Deputy Minister of Development				
YM Deputy Minister of Primary Resources and Tourism	YM Permanent Secretary Prime Minister's Office			**MEMBERS**	
YM Permanent Secretary Ministry of Transport and InfoCommunication	YM Permanent Secretary Ministry of Finance and Economy			YB Minister of Primary Resources and Tourism	
YM Permanent Secretary Ministry of Development	YM Permanent Secretary Ministry of Foreign Affairs			YB Minister of Transport and InfoCommunication	
				YM Deputy Minister of Energy	
Secretariat Ministry of Development					

Source: Author's elaboration.

In the process, the Council established its secretariat, the Brunei Climate Change Secretariat, which at the same time serves as Brunei's national focal point to the United Nations Framework Convention on Climate Change. The Secretariat was initially created with selected officers from the Ministry of Energy. The Secretariat was recently moved to the Ministry of Development since the ministry represents the government in international environmental and climate change cooperation and international treaties. In addition, the Secretariat not only serves the Council but also the Executive Committee, and the three working groups (discussed in the next subsection). The Secretariat supervises the formulation of the country's long term emissions reduction target, with assistance from the Brunei National Energy Research Institute. It also takes the lead in the formulation of the Brunei National Climate Policy and the preparation of strategy road maps; development of a white paper that sets out detailed strategies and action plans in achieving the proposed long-term emissions reduction target; setting up a monitoring, reporting and verification system; and assessment of climate change impacts.

Inclusive Stakeholder Engagement Structure

Along with the revival of the Council, the Executive Committee on Climate Change (Committee) and three technical working groups were also established (see Figure 5.3 and Figure 5.4). Members of the Committee and the working groups were appointed to include representatives from key ministries, private sector as well as non-governmental organizations. It must be noted that at the outset the Committee considers that all stakeholders need to be engaged right at the very beginning from policy formulation.

The Committee's responsibility is to ensure that a national accord on climate change policy will be consistent with the social, economic and fiscal policies, strategies and activities, and will support the development of climate monitoring infrastructure, data collection, analyses and dissemination. Also, the Committee is tasked to provide

FIGURE 5.3
Executive Committee on Climate Change

CHAIR
PERMANENT SECRETARY Ministry of Energy

Brunei Climate Change Secretariat (BCCS) Ministry of Development

MEMBERS			
Chief Executive Officer Hengyi Industries	Managing Director Brunei Shell Petroleum	Permanent Secretary Prime Minister's Office	Permanent Secretary Ministry of Transport and InfoCommunications
Permanent Secretary Ministry of Primary Resources and Tourism	Permanent Secretary Ministry of Home Affairs	Permanent Secretary Ministry of Finance and Economy	Secretary General Attorney General's Chambers

AD HOC MEMBERS		
Managing Director Brunei LNG	Managing Director Petroleum Brunei	General Manager Mitsubishi Corporation
Co-Founder Green Brunei	President Institution of Engineers, Surveyors and Architects (PUJA)	President Brunei Automobile Trader's Association

Source: Author's elaboration.

FIGURE 5.4
Technical Working Groups

BRUNEI CLIMATE CHANGE SECRETARIAT Ministry of Development

MITIGATION WORKING GROUP	ADAPTATION & RESILIENCE WORKING GROUP	SUPPORT FRAMEWORK WORKING GROUP
	CHAIRS	
Deputy Permanent Secretary Ministry of Energy	Deputy Permanent Secretary Ministry of Home Affairs	Deputy Permanent Secretary

Source: Author's elaboration.

guidance to climate mitigation or adaptation proposals that will have an economic impact on Brunei.

Three technical working groups were also formed to discuss pertinent climate change issues. Each working group member, in addition to securing performance and achievement of all targets, must ensure that climate activities are aligned with the policies of their respective agencies (see Figure 5.4). These working groups will provide recommendations and implement climate policies and strategies in their respective sector. The Climate Change Mitigation Working Group examines alternative possibilities to reduce emissions in Brunei and determines the potential groundwork required for long-term climate change mitigation. The Adaptation and Resilience Working Group evaluates Brunei's vulnerability and its resilience to the effects of climate change and facilitates adaptation efforts to improve the country's resistance to climate change effects; and the Support Framework Working Group examines Brunei's technical and funding requirements for the effective operation of climate action, facilitates efforts to abate greenhouse gas emissions, and supports climate action in all sectors.

Drafting of Climate Change Policy and Operational Documents

The Committee established an ad-hoc committee, the climate policy drafting committee (CPDC), with representatives appointed from key stakeholders (public, private and non-governmental organizations) to prepare the climate change policy. A two-day workshop was held to draft the policy, and during this event, all stakeholders presented their views and alternative solutions and participated in constructive discussions. The main outcome of the workshop was a draft climate change policy. This draft policy document underwent further reviews and consultation iterations before it was finalized. The draft final version was also presented to youth representatives for further inputs. The final document was reviewed and endorsed by the Committee and the Council before it was submitted to the highest authority. The Policy document was approved and launched in July 2020.

A similar process was undertaken by the Committee in preparing for strategy road maps. Relevant stakeholders (public, private and non-governmental organizations) were identified and invited to participate in the preparation of strategy road maps. For each strategy, a two-day operational document task force workshop was organized to draft a strategy road map. Relevant units of each ministry assigned for policy implementation took the lead in outlining strategy road maps. These road maps are in fact strategic plans of government units that were assigned to implement climate change policy strategies.

IMPLEMENTATION CHALLENGES AND IMPLICATIONS ON GOVERNANCE

Each strategy presented above was assigned to relevant ministries including the Secretariat for implementation or for undertaking further studies. The Ministry of Energy was tasked to implement strategies 1 (industrial emissions), 4 (renewable energies), and 5 (power management); the Ministry of Primary Resources and Tourism for strategy 2 (increasing forest cover); Ministry of Development for strategy 7 (waste management); Ministry of Transport and Infocommunications for strategy 3 (electric vehicles); and the Secretariat was asked in coordinating and undertaking preparatory studies for strategy 6 (carbon pricing), 8 (climate resilience and adaptation), 9 (carbon inventory) and 10 (awareness and education).

For each strategy, the Policy document specifies tools and monitoring frameworks that identify performance indicators. In addition, the Secretariat together with all stakeholders prepared implementation road maps. Despite these, there remain challenges in the implementation of these policies. Some of the key challenges are discussed in this section.

Sectoral Coordination

The strategies outlined in the climate change policy encompass various sectors and governance structures. The Secretariat acts mainly as a focal agency and coordinator with respect to policy implementation. Intervention measures targeting the energy sector will be carried out by the Ministry of Energy, while those related to transportation, forestry and waste management will be under the Ministry of Transport and Infocommunications, Ministry of Primary Resources and Tourism, and Ministry of Development, respectively. In addition, various government ministries will be involved in climate change adaptation. Each ministry, however, has its own mandate and programmed activities, and that issues related to climate change may not be their main priority.

Effective coordination would be needed to ensure that climate change issues would be aligned with each ministry's central agenda and would be given equal priority in terms of budget allocation and implementation.

Financing

Brunei's public sector is a dominant economic sector in the country. In 2019, the government's consumption and capital formation accounted for more than 27 per cent of the country's gross domestic product (Department of Statistics 2020). Climate change intervention (and investment) measures in sectors whose services are mainly provided by the public sector (transportation and energy infrastructures and forestry) would potentially increase the financial requirement needed from the government. Required infrastructure investments include charging stations for electric vehicles, renewable power plants, energy-efficient power plants, adaptation measures, and reforestation/afforestation measures.

The government could tap the private sector in meeting some of these financial requirements. In the case of the forestry sector, some private companies through their corporate social responsibility departments have committed to supporting government reforestation programmes. The Brunei Shell Petroleum for example has taken the lead in rehabilitating a peat swamp forest (Badas Tree Planting Team 2020) in Belait district, while the Hengyi Industries has committed to reforesting around 200 hectares of land (Hengyi Industries 2020) in Brunei-Muara district.

Planting trees could easily attract private sector support but for other infrastructure projects, this may require the introduction of regulatory frameworks that would allow private sector participation in providing various services and ensuring them sufficient returns of their investments (Pacudan 2016). Public-private partnerships may take different forms in different sectors. For power generation this could be in the form of independent power producers, performance contracting in energy efficiency improvements, and perhaps private provision of vehicle charging stations. However, these would require some form of sectoral reforms and that each sector's reform process may not be easy and would take time to implement.

Regulatory Frameworks

Regulatory frameworks mentioned above are those that promote public-private partnerships while frameworks referred to in this section are those that promote energy efficiency or mandate industries and individuals to adopt practices that reduce carbon and other environmental emissions.

To reduce industrial emissions (strategy 1), the establishment of emission targets, as well as technology standards consistent with the World Bank's zero routine flaring in oil and gas extraction, is required. The deployment of electric vehicles (strategy 3) requires new or revision of existing vehicle regulations. Various frameworks need to be introduced such as net metering, green certificates and building integration of renewable energy to increase private sector deployment of renewable energy technologies (strategy 4). To improve electricity production efficiency on the supply-side, a regulation on power plant efficiency needs to be established (strategy 5). Carbon pricing regulations will be needed to provide the legal basis in internalizing carbon costs (strategy 6).

These regulations will be formulated and implemented by each concerned government ministry. Introducing a new regulation could take time in Brunei, along with aligning and prioritizing the required climate change related regulations with the other regulatory requirements and priorities of each ministry.

Carbon Pricing

As presented earlier, the potential contribution of carbon pricing in reducing carbon emissions is relatively high at around 46 per cent of the business-as-usual gross emissions in 2035. The policy indicated that the carbon pricing policy will be implemented not earlier than 2025 and that further studies will be carried out between now and that period.

Based on global experiences, the government could either introduce a carbon taxation or an emissions trading scheme (also known as cap-and-trade scheme). Under carbon tax policies, a price of carbon is introduced to power utilities and energy industries through a tax or fee on greenhouse gas emissions or the carbon content of fossil fuels (World Bank 2020). Under a cap-and-trade scheme, the total allowable volume of emissions in a particular time period from a specified set of sources is defined, and that economic actors are allowed to trade their emission rights (ICAP 2020; World Bank 2020). A carbon tax provides stable carbon prices while a cap-and-trade scheme provides certainty that the target emissions reduction would be achieved. Most of the countries that introduced carbon tax and/or emissions trading schemes are in Europe and North America as well as Australia and New Zealand. In Asia, Singapore and Japan have introduced carbon taxation while Korea and China have implemented various forms of emissions trading scheme.

Carbon taxes and cap-and-trade schemes have both advantages and disadvantages, but the selection of an appropriate carbon pricing mechanism for Brunei would depend on key economic, institutional and political factors. Whatever the choice of the government is, it remains to be seen whether the selected pricing mechanism could deliver around 46 per cent reduction of carbon emissions in 2035.

Governance Implications

As discussed earlier, Brunei's climate change governance in policy formulation involved a strong intersectoral collaboration at the highest level (Council) and stakeholder engagement at the working level particularly during the policy drafting stage where all stakeholders (public, private and non-government organizations) contributed to identifying and selecting appropriate strategies and measures that address climate change issues. The combination of institutional coordination and stakeholder engagement in policy formulation aims to secure public support and establish the legitimacy of the policy, empowering non-governmental organizations, and ensuring the sustainability of policy interventions.

Before these policy strategies could be implemented, mitigation strategies (reducing industrial emissions, increasing deployment of electric vehicles and renewable energies, improving energy efficiency under power sector management, introducing carbon pricing and managing wastes) require additional regulatory frameworks that will be formulated and implemented at the sectoral level. The institutional coordination at the Council level needs to be further strengthened by internal collaboration at the departmental level especially in the formulation of the sectoral policies and regulatory frameworks that support climate change mitigation. Similarly, the Secretariat who is responsible for carbon pricing, climate resilience and adaption, and support strategies (carbon inventory, and awareness and education) needs a stronger collaboration with other government agencies at the departmental level in preparing for additional regulatory frameworks for its assigned tasks as well as in anchoring some of its programmes and activities. In formulating additional policies and regulatory frameworks, each assigned government agency needs to embrace the whole-of-nation approach by engaging the private sector and non-governmental organizations, in addition to other government agencies.

Each stakeholder will then play different roles in the actual implementation of climate change policies and regulatory frameworks. Sectoral agencies will be responsible for the enforcement while the private sector would be involved in infrastructure and technology investments either as part of public-private partnerships or as compliance with the climate change mitigation regulations. Non-governmental organizations will be expected to support the implementation of government policies including education and awareness programmes. The Secretariat who will be responsible for reporting progress to various bodies of the United Nations Framework Convention for Climate Change will be working closely with key government agencies to monitor and verify compliance with the climate change related policies and regulations. Thus, the whole-of-nation collaboration arrangement in the implementation stage would be different from that during the policy formulation stage.

OPPORTUNITIES FOR REFINEMENT

Of the ten intervention measures discussed above, seven strategies are emission mitigation strategies (reducing industrial emissions, increasing forest cover, increasing deployment of electric vehicles and renewable energies, improving energy efficiency under power sector management, introducing carbon pricing and managing wastes), one adaptation strategy (climate resilience and adaptation), and two support strategies (carbon inventory and awareness and education). The seven mitigation strategies, except for managing wastes and increasing forest cover, have focused on the energy sector (transportation under the Intergovernmental Panel for Climate Change Guidelines is considered under energy sector). This focus is justified considering that, as presented earlier in this chapter, the energy sector contributed 91.2 per cent of the gross emissions in 2018.

The Secretariat specifies that the policy document is a live document and will be continuously revised at regular intervals (BCCS 2020). Being the first comprehensive national climate change policy, and the first to be implemented by a new team and a new coordination arrangement, the whole climate change governance system is on a steep learning curve. Policy strategies and targets would be modified and strengthened once learning experiences have been established.

While the policy document stipulates that the government pursues a strategy to reduce carbon emissions, increase carbon sink and strengthen climate resilience nationwide, it appears that the current focus is more on the mitigation rather than adaptation side. Mitigation measures are more prominent than those of adaptation, but this is also justified since the focus of the Paris Agreement is to stabilize the global concentration of carbon dioxide in the atmosphere by the end of this century. As the climate governance gains more experience eventually, and significant progress is achieved in climate change mitigation, perhaps more attention and resources could be allocated to adaptation measures especially when climate change impacts become more pronounced.

Since the policy document was prepared prior to the preparation of strategy road maps, some technologies or intervention measures were broadly defined and emissions targets by specific technological intervention were not determined. Under strategy 1 (industrial emissions) for example, technologies that comply with emissions reduction to as low as reasonably practical were not specified and hence it is not clear to what extent the emissions from oil and gas production industries would be reduced. Under strategy 6 (carbon pricing), the emissions reduction contribution from carbon pricing was estimated to be around 46 per cent from business-as-usual scenario. This appears to be very ambitious and that more studies need to be carried out to assess the potential contribution of carbon pricing. Similarly, under strategy 7 (waste management), the target of reducing one kilogram of waste per person per day needs to be further validated through an actual survey. The policy tools and the performance indicators would need to be fine-tuned and further elaborated once additional technical studies and strategic road maps are carried out and finalized.

In addition to strategic road maps, lead agencies also have their sectoral plans which contain policy measures that could contribute to reducing greenhouse gas emissions in a cost-effective manner. For example, the Ministry of Energy is also pursuing vehicle fuel economy standards, standards and labelling of household electrical appliances, building standards and others. Similarly, the Ministry of Transport and Infocommunications is also undertaking activities related to public transportation improvement, smart urban planning and others. Once regulatory frameworks and investment decisions have been finalized, these measures could be elevated and added to climate change policy strategies since these also represent national intervention measures that support the transition towards low carbon economy.

CONCLUSION

Brunei, being vulnerable to extreme weather events and sea level rise, responded to global climate change threats by committing to international treaties such as the Paris Agreement that aims to stabilize the global temperature rise to below 2°C above the pre-industrial levels by the end of this century. As part of this commitment, the country prepared a climate change policy that outlines its voluntary actions to reduce greenhouse gas emissions.

The planned climate change interventions between now and 2035 were carefully crafted to balance the country's developmental needs and global environmental protection. The ten strategies outlined in the climate change policy are consistent with the government's long-term vision ("Wawasan Brunei 2035", n.d.) but at the same time could decouple environmental emissions from economic development. These strategies address industrial emissions (strategy 1), increase forest cover (strategy 2), promote deployment of electric vehicles and renewable energy technologies (strategies 3 and 4), improve electricity supply-side and demand-side efficiency (strategy 5), internalize carbon dioxide damage costs through carbon pricing (strategy 6), reduce generation of municipal solid waste (strategy 7), ensure resilience and climate change adaptation (strategy 8), strengthen capacity to monitor carbon emissions (strategy 9), and increase awareness and education related to climate change mitigation and adaptation (strategy 10).

The balancing of economic and environmental objectives was made possible by adopting a whole-of-nation approach to policy formulation. The government established a climate change governing council which is represented by key ministries that would be instrumental in climate change mitigation and adaptation, established the Climate Change Secretariat, and created an executive committee on climate change and technical working groups that represented the government, private, and non-government sectors. The working groups supported in drafting the climate change policies and formulated operational documents for policy implementation.

While Brunei's whole-of-nation model appears to be effective in formulating a national climate change policy, it faces several challenges in the implementation of these policies and whether it can deliver an overall emissions reduction of around 50 per cent of the business-as-usual gross emissions. The main challenge for the whole-of-nation approach to climate change policy implementation is to demonstrate: i) effective coordination among ministries ensuring alignment and budget prioritization of climate change policies with those of core policies and programmes of key ministries; ii) timely introduction of regulatory frameworks promoting public-private partnerships and accessing private sector financing; iii) establishment of policy frameworks promoting investments of energy-efficient technologies and adopting practices that reduce carbon and other environmental emissions; and iv) introduction of carbon pricing framework that could effectively and significantly reduce greenhouse gas emissions.

Addressing these challenges requires a more complex approach to governance in policy implementation. The whole-of-nation approach to policy formulation needs to evolve with more defined internal collaboration arrangements at the working level of each ministry. As key strategies were assigned to various ministries, each ministry needs to further formulate supporting policies and regulations as well as to prioritize the climate change agenda in its specific sectoral agenda and in allocating financial resources. While the implementation and enforcement of these measures rest with the assigned ministries, the Secretariat needs to strengthen collaboration with these agencies in monitoring compliance with climate change policies and regulations. At the external level, cooperation and compliance would be required from the private sector while support in government programmes is expected from non-governmental organizations.

As a live document, opportunities exist for improving the Policy document in the future. In the long-term, as the climate change institutions gain more experience and important progress are achieved in implementing mitigation measures, climate change adaptation could be strengthened. In the short and medium terms, refinements related to technical details could be added in mitigation measures once studies have been carried out. Also, other sectoral policies being elaborated by key ministries which have positive impacts on the global environment could be integrated into the Policy.

REFERENCES

Asia Pacific Energy Research Centre (APERC). 2017. *APEC Energy Statistics 2017*. Japan: Energy Statistics and Training Office, Asia Pacific Energy Research Centre.

Badas Tree Planting Team. 2020. "Peat Swamp Rehabilitation Project". https://badastreeplanting.org/blog/ (accessed 20 December 2020).

Brunei Climate Change Secretariat (BCCS). 2020. *Brunei Darussalam Climate Change Policy*. Bandar Seri Begawan, Brunei: Ministry of Development.

Department of Statistics. 2020. *Gross Domestic Product Second Quarter 2020*. Bandar Seri Begawan, Brunei: Ministry of Finance and Economy.

Energy Department Prime Minister's Office (EDPMO). 2014. *Brunei Darussalam Energy White Paper*. Bandar Seri Begawan, Brunei: Energy Department, Prime Minister's Office.

Global Carbon Atlas. 2019. "Fossil Fuels Emissions". http://www.globalcarbonatlas.org/en/CO2-emissions (accessed 30 January 2020).

Hengyi Industries. 2020. "500 Trees Planted in Hengyi 3rd Reforestation Project". 10 September 2020. https://www.hengyi-industries.com/media/press-releases/500-trees-planted-in-hengyi-3rd-reforestation-project/ (accessed 20 December 2020).

International Carbon Action Partnership (ICAP). 2020. *Emissions Trading Worldwide: Status Report 2020*. Berlin: International Carbon Action Partnership.

Intergovernmental Panel on Climate Change (IPCC). 2006. "Fugitive Emissions". In *2006 IPCC Guidelines for National Greenhouse Gas Inventories*, Vol. 2. Intergovernmental Panel on Climate Change.

Low, James. 2016. "Singapore's Whole-of-Government Approach in Crisis Management". *Ethos* 16: 14–22.

Ministry of Energy. 2020a. "Strategy 4: Renewable Energy". Slide presented during the Operational Document Task Force Workshop, Brunei Darussalam, 2–3 September 2020.

_____. 2020b. "Strategy 3: Electric Vehicles". Slide presented during the Operational Document Task Force Workshop, Brunei Darussalam, 26 August 2020.

Ministry of Primary Resources and Tourism. 2020. "Strategy 2: Forest Cover". Slide presented during the Operational Document Task Force Workshop, Brunei Darussalam, 7–8 September 2020.

Oxford Business Group. 2016. *The Report: Brunei Darussalam 2016*. https://oxfordbusinessgroup.com/brunei-darussalam-2016 (accessed 20 December 2020).

Pacudan, Romeo. 2016. "Implications of Applying Solar Industry Best Practice Resource Estimation on Project Financing". *Energy Policy* 95: 489–97.

_____. 2018a. "Feed-in Tariff vs Incentivized Self-consumption: Options for Residential Solar PV Policy in Brunei Darussalam". *Renewable Energy* 122: 362–74.

_____. 2018b. "The Economics of Net Metering Policy in the Philippines". *International Energy Journal* 18: 283–96.

Pacudan, Romeo, and Mahani Hamdan. 2019. "Electricity Tariff Reforms, Welfare Impacts, and Energy Poverty Implications". *Energy Policy* 132: 332–43.

Prime Minister's Office. 2015. *Digital Government Strategy 2015–2020*. Bandar Seri Begawan, Brunei: Prime Minister's Office.

United Nations Framework Convention on Climate Change (UNFCCC). 2015. "The Paris Agreement". https://unfccc.int/process-and-meetings/the-paris-agreement/the-paris-agreement (accessed 20 December 2020).

"Wawasan Brunei 2035". n.d. https://www.gov.bn/SitePages/Wawasan%20Brunei%202035.aspx (accessed 20 December 2020).

World Bank. 2020. *State and Trends of Carbon Pricing 2020*. Washington, D.C.: World Bank Group.

World Health Organization (WHO). 2015. "Health in All Policies Training Manual". World Health Organization. https://www.who.int/social_determinants/publications/health-policies-manual/en/ (accessed 20 December 2020).

Yahya, Yasmine. 2018. "Public Service to Go from 'Whole-of-Government' To 'Whole-of-Nation'". *The Straits Times*, 9 May 2018. https://www.straitstimes.com/politics/public-service-to-go-from-whole-of-government-to-whole-of-nation (accessed 15 January 2021).

6

GEARING TOWARDS BUILDING A STRONGER DIGITAL SOCIETY

Muhammad Anshari, Mahani Hamdan and Hamizah Haidi

INTRODUCTION

All aspects of our lives have been significantly impacted by the ongoing digital revolution and advancement of modern technology. Such advancement has inevitably led towards the process of digitalization. Digitalization came to be crucial during the COVID-19 pandemic when many countries were forced to digitize to ensure the safety and well-being of their citizens. Brunei was one such country that had to undergo forced digitalization after an exponential rise of COVID-19 cases within a span of a few weeks after reporting its first case on 9 March 2020. Hence, it is critically important that the notion of "digital society" is intended to enable and provide a sustainable framework towards achieving the efficiency and effectiveness of the country's health system.

The Bruneian society is a high-degree digitalization adopter, as attested by the high internet and social media participation via smartphones by the people. Hence, this gives an indication that the people are ready to embark on a digital transformation. The AITI Business Report (2019) stated that 90 per cent of businesses in Brunei have access to the internet through social media utilization in tapping the digital market and engaging with their customers, and 58 per cent are aware of the advantages of Information and Communication Technology (ICT) integration into their businesses. However, businesses' digitalization through e-commerce is still low. Only 16 per cent of businesses have online sales activity, and much of these activities are attributable to their engagement with overseas traders or partners. Brunei's slow development in entrepreneurial activity is primarily due to its heavy dependency on the oil and gas industry which has been a long-standing problem since its first national development plan. Nevertheless, the fall of oil prices has made the country take precautionary or protective measures (Basir 2017).

In 2007, public recommendations of Brunei's expectations were published, which henceforth allowed the Bruneian society to envision a future that can fulfil long-term hopes and expectations (GOV.BN, n.d.). That vision was called *"Wawasan* Brunei 2035" or the National Vision 2035 as consented by His Majesty the Sultan of Brunei. This vision aims for the nation to be recognized through its educated and highly skilled people by international standards; and be placed among the top ten countries in the world with a high quality of life and a trustworthy economy (GOV.BN, n.d.). All entities across public and private sectors play a part in achieving the National Vision 2035 and safeguarding the strategies and policies that have been formulated to address issues and challenges. A Council for Long-Term Development Planning was formed and tasked to present a detailed account of technical, financial and strategic requirements needed for the vision to be realized (Hayat 2014).

This chapter discusses the readiness of Brunei and its initiatives to become a digital society. It focuses on several aspects of the nation's framework and presents the recent development and initiatives for a digital society. The chapter also addresses one important question: How efficient is Bruneian society in preparing and adapting to digitalization? Although there are numerous opportunities associated with digitalization, there are also challenges that the country must continue to overcome. This study is based on secondary data collected from various government-generated files, websites and extracted data from books, journals, government reports, and newspapers. Many sources also originated from official government publications in developing national strategy of a digital society.

DIGITAL SOCIETY

"Digital Society" is an important topic to be discussed because the optimization of digital technology can help in ensuring the efficiency and effectiveness of any organization's system. A digital society is a progressive society that is formed as a result of adaptation as well as integration of advanced technology into the society and culture (Paul and Aithal 2018). Digital systems can perform administrative procedures that may lead to cost-saving benefits. There are numerous potentials that can be explored, such as transforming public services into e-government services. These services are made available 24/7 to all citizens, which help support the governmental welfare system and transparency and hence develop a higher level of trust in the government framework.

Although there are advantages associated with the development of digital society, some social challenges also persist. Firstly, new policies need to be created to help develop a future of digital society. Therefore, it is necessary to establish a regulatory framework to manage areas such as liability, accountability, integrity and ethics that should not hinder further innovation. Secondly, a digital society can only be successful if the people are equipped to adapt to the changes in technology. Hence, the government needs to provide educational programmes that can help the society to acquire a sufficient level of digital skills to be able to fully utilize the e-services that will be offered. Thirdly, in building a digital society, every organization in the nation needs to be involved, hence trust and cooperation need to be built between private and public sectors. Such cooperation will then pave a solid foundation for sustainable and reliable digital society infrastructure. Finally, when information is available digitally, it is crucial to enhance cybersecurity to avoid any cybercrimes and accidents, especially in the banking and financial systems (Polak et al. 2019). The question of whether Bruneians are ready for a full transformation to a digital society is to be discussed in this chapter.

DIGITAL SOCIETY IN BRUNEI

Prior to the consolidation of the entire telecommunications infrastructure in Brunei through the establishment of Unified National Network (UNN), digital services were under the purview of three different companies (DST, TelBru (later named Imagine) and Progresif). Such consolidation was for the purpose of enabling equal access to network infrastructure (The Scoop 2019). Furthermore, UNN is also investing in the development of 5G as a form of network advancement. As ICT will be the main driver to realize Vision 2035, it is crucial for 5G technology to be implemented and developed. 5G implementation and development was first conceived in 2019 when the Authority for Info-communications Technology Industry of Brunei Darussalam (AITI) completed a study that assessed the country's readiness to embrace 5G (Hayat 2019). This was followed by the establishment of 5G regulatory sandbox by AITI in March 2020 and Brunei's first 5G Task Force Plenary Online Meeting in May 2020 (AITI 2020).

The 5G Taskforce is composed of three working groups that are composed of key stakeholders: ministries, government agencies, telecommunications service providers, equipment vendors, academia and industry. The first working group focuses on policy, regulatory and spectrum and is currently being co-chaired by a ministry and a government agency, that is, the Ministry of Transport and Infocommunications (MTIC) and AITI. The second working group looks into use cases, applications and infrastructure and is currently being chaired by the telecommunications service provider, Unified National Network (UNN). The third working group focuses on education and awareness, and is currently being co-chaired by a government agency and academia, that is, AITI and Universiti Teknologi Brunei (UTB). All the working groups are still in their planning stage to determine the country's increased readiness to adapt 5G technology with its AI and Robotic technology.

In general, the Bruneian society is very positive about the transformational shift towards digitalization and digital society ("smart nation") development pathways. This is seen in the "smart nation" initiative promoted by the government. The government aims to change its status into a smart nation that will drive its government agencies and private sectors towards achieving Vision 2035. Brunei is quite accepting in the governance, business and finance, and healthcare sectors, with the implementation of e-Darussalam, Digital Economy Masterplan 2020–2025, and Bru-HIMS respectively. Other targeted sectors in the framework have also been identified and need immediate execution of plan in order to complete the building blocks of a successful digital society, with greater cooperation and coordination between government agencies and private sectors.

Information and Communication Technology (ICT) is a key enabler to achieve the country's Vision 2035. It is thus imperative for the government to analyse for possibilities offered by these new technologies, and use them as tools to capture the interactions between the government and its stakeholders. More importantly, it is to achieve the country's sustainable development by increasing the efficiency, effectiveness, quality and accessibility of information and services (Digital Government Strategy, n.d.). In addition, ICT enables a seamless flow of information among government departments, citizens and businesses, which in return will manifest in greater transparency and better insights for informed decision making (Digital Government Strategy, n.d.). A *titah* by His Majesty the Sultan of Brunei in conjunction with His Majesty's 73rd Birthday Celebration on 15 July 2019 mentioned that Brunei needs to explore the potentials offered by a digital economy and he consented to the establishment of the Digital Economy Council for the purpose of preparing Brunei to become a Smart Nation.

With the establishment of the Digital Economy Council, Brunei aims to change its status into a Smart Nation. Smart Nation is driven by three key characteristics: a) a vibrant and diversified economy; b) improved competitiveness and economic growth by developing infrastructure, innovation, data capability, human capital and other resources; and c) an improved quality of life, public services, schools, safety, mobility of people and to achieve environmental sustainability. These characteristics can only be achieved via enhancing the nation's framework through leveraging digital technologies and equipping Bruneian society with the necessary skills and knowledge to embrace these changes (MTIC 2020). The Minister of Transport and Infocommunications further highlighted the significance of the Internet of Things (IoT) and data-driven decision-making and service delivery as key drivers of a connected and innovative society towards achieving the Brunei Vision (AITI 2018).

THE CRITICAL SUCCESS FACTORS FOR IMPLEMENTING DIGITAL SOCIETY

In general, there are major components that can contribute to the success of implementing a digital society. They are a) the government, b) the citizens or public, and c) the businesses. This means that good digitalization must be present and synchronized at governmental, business and citizenship levels. This section analyses Brunei's initiatives in becoming a digital society from the perspectives of governance, education, agriculture, healthcare, mobility services, business and economics, all of which form the building blocks for the planning and implementation of a digital society.

The Government

The journey of the government in transforming the nation into a digital society started in 1980 when Brunei first introduced personal computers in the public sector. This was followed by the building of multiple data centres and the introduction of multiple email systems in 2000. Since the early 2000s, Brunei has embarked on digitalization through e-government. The first e-Government Strategic Plan, together with Government Wide Network and structure were introduced in 2005 for the consolidation of services such as data centres, email systems and other ICT services. Indeed, numerous digitalization processes are currently in place within the government to increase its smart services to the public and businesses, including Secure Government Private Network and Citizen Services. The Internal Government system utilized data and analytics to help the government in making knowledge-based decisions in 2015 (Digital Government Strategy, n.d.), followed by the release of the Digital Government Strategy. The mission of the Digital Government Strategy is to "lead the digital transformation and make government services simpler, faster and more accessible".

Under the Digital Government Strategy, six focus areas have been identified. They are: a) service innovation, b) security, c) capability and mindset, d) enterprise information management, e) optimization, and f) collaboration and integration. In relation to service innovation, government offices must develop new and creative approaches to convey services to citizens and organizations with more prominent transparency and accountability. The government needs to maintain awareness of its digital assets and environment at all times, and continue to minimize the risks through a proper security system associated with digitalization and improve its capabilities to respond to cyber-incidents. Even with the advancement of technology, the capability and mindset of the Bruneian citizens are still key factors in ensuring the successful implementation of digital technology.

Therefore, it is important to develop a forward-thinking mindset, which will help increase the speed of implementing new systems, rate of utilizing the system and proficiency of government officials. It is also highly encouraged for the government to manage the data pool effectively using an enterprise information management system by structuring, describing and governing information assets so that they can be used to aid informed decision-making. With the implementation of various IT systems and platforms, it is time to optimize these digital assets to maximize effectiveness, minimize redundancy, and maximize value for money. Finally, it is also compulsory for government agencies to work alongside one another to face an increasingly complex environment, which requires a whole-of-government approach to increase collaboration and integration of government business processes (Digital Government Strategy, n.d.).

The roadmap towards becoming a digital society started with the implementation of "digital government". Through such implementation, it is apparent that Brunei has been making continuous efforts to achieve efficiency and effectiveness in its public services. Achieving operation excellence in public administration and management is one of the many benefits of digital government transformation. Once digitalization takes over human labour, it is safe to say that human errors would be reduced, especially in processes that involve recording and processing a large amount of data. Brunei is on the course of adjusting to the digitalization era that would be accommodating humans and machines. This adjustment could eventually lead in making new, more specialized and better jobs. Artificial intelligence will thus aid in facilitating employees instead of eliminating them (Maida 2019).

One of the most significant contributions towards building a digital government is the establishment of the official portal GOV.BN—also known as e-Darussalam—which is maintained by the E-Government National Centre at the Prime Minister's Office. This e-Darussalam portal is a one-stop shop for citizens, visitors as well as business organizations in Brunei. E-Darussalam provides centralized information on government online services, and in order to access these information and services, each citizen must create and activate their own e-Darussalam account. Some of the major benefits of e-Darussalam include public access to government information and online services anytime and anywhere; increased efficiency of government agencies in providing public services; and prevention of duplication of information and processes which leads to more effective service delivery. With the establishment of this online platform, Brunei was ranked 59th out of 193 countries in the E-Government Development Index (MTIC 2020).

On top of the e-Darussalam initiative, Brunei's current digital landscape portrays a high degree of internet penetrability in Brunei. Data on internet broadband usage showed 95 per cent of individuals in Brunei use such services, and there is a 50 per cent subscription of fixed broadband service per 100 businesses and households. In total, 61 per cent of households own laptops, and 88 per cent of households own smartphones. Though the percentage of laptop ownership was low compared to smartphone ownership, there is a 134 per cent subscription of mobile services per 100 inhabitants in Brunei, and 95 per cent of these subscriptions were covered by 4G network (MTIC 2020). The Digital Economy Masterplan 2025 report indicates that Bruneian society has the potential to quickly adapt to changes made in the system and be the driver of success in digital society transformation.

Healthcare

Several initiatives have been made by the government to improve the country's national health system. One such initiative is the introduction of the Brunei Darussalam Healthcare Information and Management System (Bru-HIMS). It is an e-Health initiative made by the Ministry of Health to improve the efficiency and effectiveness of healthcare information and management system (Almunawar et al. 2012; Anshari et al. 2013). Bru-HIMS comprises a centralized system that organizes patients' records and information that can automatically be retrieved using a unique BN number from any health facility. Thus, Bru-HIMS helps to replace the traditional manual system by integrating and managing patients' information and storing it electronically. This means that every individual will have their own electronic record that is accessible across hospitals and clinics in the country (Almunawar and Anshari 2014).

The establishment of Bru-HIMS since September 2012 has brought many benefits for healthcare service providers, such as improved efficiency in retrieving patients' files by doctors and nurses, significantly reduced probability of human errors caused by misplacing patients' records, improved ability to access previous treatment history from other hospitals or clinics, overall improvement of patient care and diagnosis, enhanced admission process and reduced paperwork. Bru-HIMS also facilitates monitoring and tracking of medication stock movement, and the availability of audit reports for any investigation. The Key Projects in the Digital Economy Masterplan 2025 noted that Bru-HIMS will be further enhanced in the year 2023 (MTIC 2020). Bru-HIMS is an example of how e-services can provide convenient access and savings to relevant stakeholders such as patients and healthcare providers. With the enhancement of Bru-HIMS, it is possible to also achieve digitalized prescription and digitized health data.

In response to the COVID-19 pandemic, a designated contact tracing app known as BruHealth was introduced by the government following the announcement on easing COVID-19 restrictions in the country. Canvassed as a refined monitoring mechanism in containing the COVID-19 spread, the Bluetooth-powered app presents authorities with data on individuals entering business premises as well as the number of people present at a specific location at a certain period (Han 2020). Specific Quick Response (QR) code has been issued to businesses, which needs to be printed and placed at the entrance of their premises. Customers and employees are required to download the app on their mobile phones and scan the QR code whenever they enter or exit. The app generates a five-colour classification system that indicates a user's mobility within the country (Han 2020). Users with green or yellow health codes are granted access to premises while those with red, blue and purple health codes (those having illness or diseases) will not be allowed to enter public areas.

Mobility Services

It is only logical for an advanced digital society to make travelling safer and provide an efficient transportation system. An initiative pertinent to the logistics and transportation system in Brunei was the introduction of an e-Hailing service application called Dart. The launching of Dart in May 2017, the first online booking ride in Brunei, takes advantage of the ride-sharing culture in Brunei by providing a cheap and reliable form of transportation (Dart Brunei 2020). Dart also eases the use of this public transportation service by introducing an online payment system. The local Bruneians are very supportive of this initiative. Other proposed initiatives to be launched in 2020 and 2021 are Public Transport Information System and Intelligent Transport System respectively. The two systems will disclose real-time information on public bus services with the use of GPS. Not much emphasis was laid on improving the digital public transportation system in Brunei because there is a high rate of private car ownership. In total, 80 per cent of 2,212 Brunei residents responded that they prefer using their own cars for transportation all the time (MTIC 2014). In summary, Brunei is quite slow in developing its mobility services and the country has a long way to go to develop digitalization in the logistics and transportation sector.

Agriculture

With a population of over 400,000, Bruneian society enjoys a relatively stable political climate since gaining its independence in 1984. It achieved a record-high gross domestic product (GDP) in 2012 (Department of Statistics 2012). However, the economy has since fluctuated and recently dwindled, affecting a majority of the people. With oil prices having dropped to US$77.3 per barrel in 2018 (Department of Statistics 2018), Brunei was forced to search for other alternatives to sustain its development and to fund the considerably excessive support given to the people. The government has launched several initiatives and schemes to encourage its people to delve into agriculture, and monitor efforts to further expand the existing farms to ensure self-sufficiency and reduce reliance on imports. Although a majority of farmers are struggling to achieve export standards and requirements, local supermarkets have taken the initiative to help the farmers sell their products at their business premises.

The government has begun to explore several e-services that can be provided by the Department of Agriculture and Agrifood (DoAA), under the Ministry of Primary Resources and Tourism of Brunei Darussalam (MPRT). DoAA is responsible for maintaining the productivity and sustainability of agricultural resources. Smart Agriculture in Brunei is in the emerging stage of e-government initiative and moving into the enhanced Web/Apps presence and with online services. However, some initiatives focusing on research and development between government agencies and private organizations such as AgromeIQ (local smart farming startup) have been started. The new advanced technologies such as IoT (Internet of Things), sensor technology, AI and Big Data will provide 24/7 facilities and increase crop health and machinery in use that could enhance sustainable agricultural development and food security. These technologies are expert systems that will increase the productivity of farming industries as they do not rely on human labours in processing routine farming activities. The digital development in this sector and its efficiency must not be taken for granted and underestimated, as statistics in the second quarter of 2017 showed the contribution of the agriculture, forestry and fishery sector at a current price worth B$47.2 million (Department of Statistics 2017). His Majesty the Sultan of Brunei further encouraged "smart farming" research to be conducted in order to improve the level of competitiveness (RTBNews 2020). Advanced technology is vital in agricultural activity as climate change issues, limited resources and environmental degradation call for the need to secure crop production and protection. Information gathered from IoT devices could be utilized to examine soil details, make forecasts and maximize theft protection (Anshari et al. 2019; Sangtrash and Hiremath 2017). According to Jayaraman et al. (2016), smart farming involves the use of ICT, IoT and other related big data analytics to address the challenges by means of the electronic monitoring of crops, environment, soil, fertilization and irrigation (Anshari and Sumardi 2020).

Education

Technology can be fully optimized if the society is equipped with sufficient digital knowledge, skills and resources. Hence, both public and private sectors need to develop education programmes that can cater to this increasing demand. The Ministry of Education (MOE) stated in their Strategic Plan 2018 that they recognized the importance of Big Data in aiding the collection, organization, analysation and interpretation of useful information to help the ministry with evidence-based decision-making, and by doing so, the ministry expects to deliver quality education with real-time data (MOE 2018). A policy has also been mandated by the Ministry of Education to strengthen the students, teachers and education officers' capacity in ICT including the integration of ICT in teaching and learning activities (Petra 2014). One of the collaborative government projects with the Ministry of Transport and Infocommunications is to enhance the education system in Brunei by introducing Innovation Lab in 2019. It is an intensive sixteen-week software development training programme organized by Universiti Brunei Darussalam (UBD) and FPT, Vietnam's largest IT company (UBD 2019). This programme was introduced to develop Brunei's manpower and talent and increase their proactive behaviour in digital transformation.

Smart Classroom Pilot was launched in 2020 to maintain a quality education despite the COVID-19 pandemic. Digital technologies such as group video call conferences in Zoom application and Microsoft Team were optimized to deliver class sessions online. While other countries have maximized the optimum performance of such systems today, Brunei's School Network Infrastructure and National Education Management System is only due to being completed and launched by 2023. The Ministry of Transport and Infocommunications is in collaboration with the Ministry of Education to launch this system which will innovate communication among parents, teachers and children and organize the necessary information to enhance the quality of education. Such delay would certainly affect the progress of Bruneian society in coping with and adapting to technological advancement particularly in the educational delivery system. Yet, the government must continually explore research fields that can further enhance the integration and management of ICT in all teaching and learning activities across various levels of education.

Business and Economics

Business and economics are backbones for achieving success in digital society transformation. Under the Digital Economy Masterplan 2025, the Digital Economy Council has laid out the vision for Brunei to become a "Smart Nation through Digital Transformation" and its mission is to drive and enhance the country's socio-economic growth through Digital Transformation (MTIC 2020). The highlights of the strategic thrusts of the Digital Economy Masterplan 2025 include industry digitalization to solve the unfamiliarity of Industrial Revolution 4.0 by undertaking industry awareness programmes across all stakeholders, especially Small and Medium Enterprises (SMEs), in order to help the people to adopt the technology through training and application, as well as government digitalization. These can be achieved by implementing a digital identity ecosystem and developing services for improved public experience. In addition, a thriving digital industry by implementing digital data policy can help provide governance and framework for data protection and sharing. Not only that, manpower and talent can be developed by enhancing the capabilities of the existing workforce by means of re-skilling and updating the education programmes to create a digital lifelong learning framework (Anshari 2020).

One of Brunei's strategies is to assimilate Micro, Small and Medium Enterprises (MSMEs) into regional and international markets. If these MSMEs can cater to Brunei's small population with stable purchasing power, they will be able to help diversify Brunei's economy and reduce reliance on imports. As asserted by Polsaram et al. (2011), Brunei should also be focusing more on the diversification of the private sector through various government initiatives. This includes attracting local and foreign investments through funding or grant supports, training and expansion of local business subsidiaries in business and financial services, hospitality and tourism, and other sectors.

A report produced by the Asia-Pacific Economic Cooperation (APEC) stated that government initiatives had taken place through promoting the use of e-commerce such as enforcing consumer protection laws by the Department of Economic Planning and Development (JPKE), conducting surveys on consumer behaviour by AITI, and classifying packages to facilitate delivery by the Royal Customs and Excise Department (RCED) (Pasadilla, Wirjo and Liu 2017). Initiatives for economic development through digital transformation include the introduction of One Common Billing System in 2020 which allows citizens to make online payments for their housing bills through their e-Darussalam account (Bakar 2020b). Digital payment in 2020 allows users to make payments using multiple options such as ATMs, CDMs and other online banking options such as electronic banking and mobile banking. Other initiatives that are in the pipeline include e-property tax, land payment, and the provision of National Welfare System as well as National Business Service Platform by 2022 (MTIC 2020).

Furthermore, the FinTech Unit established by Autoriti Monetari Brunei Darussalam (AMBD) in 2017 has resulted in several companies strongly venturing into the financial tech domains. This has contributed to an increase in Brunei-based digital payment solutions where firms and startups keenly move towards a cashless culture in Brunei. A number of these notable FinTech solutions mainly offer digital wallets that are operational in Brunei such as BIBD NEXGEN Wallet, Progresif Pay, and Pocket.

SMEs and E-Commerce

Brunei has developed a framework or roadmap to control the e-commerce activities in Small and Medium Enterprises (SMEs). Indeed, the adoption of e-commerce requires critical governmental support, which is important if these businesses were to enter foreign markets. OECD/ERIA (2018) reported that in 2017, Darussalam Enterprise (DARe), DHgate.com and UBD had launched an e-commerce bootcamp called the Asia Pacific Economic Co-operation Cross-Border E-Commerce Training, under the APEC Business Advisory Council. This was to encourage local businesses to sell their products in the foreign market through DHgate.com's digital marketplace. Such support can help local MSMEs to get a strong grasp of the digital marketplace. Furthermore, there were a total of 5,876 local SMEs in 2017, where 2,442 were micro-enterprises and 3,434 were small enterprises that consisted of the services industry (wholesale and retail trade, transportation), construction, and manufacturing (Othman 2020). This increasing number of SMEs can contribute to a large portion of GDP and provide employment. To ease costs of operation, SMEs can adopt e-commerce where there are online platforms for them to trade such as eKadaiBrunei.com. Bruneian SMEs are highly encouraged to take full advantage of e-commerce activities through social media considering that Brunei has over 90 per cent internet penetration rate and over 90 per cent of the population have at least one form of social media. Potential customers can be reached through e-commerce or even social commerce.

   Adoption of e-commerce by local SMEs is vital because more than 75 per cent of the national workforce is government-employed; this is unsustainable and perturbing for the future (Looi 2005). In addition, the government's financial capability to support this is limited due to the fall in oil and gas revenue and losses in the investment of Brunei's foreign reserves. A small percentage of the private sector establishments are large corporations like foreign banks, shipping, insurance companies and Brunei Shell Petroleum. They have used technology-based resources such as e-banking and e-business using business-to-business (B2B) and business-to-consumer (B2C) aspects of e-commerce. Othman (2020) reported that though the government supported the MSMEs by engaging them in government projects, some MSMEs are having difficulties to even enter the domestic market because of the lack of funding. The Ministry of Transport and Infocommunications (MTIC), Ministry of Home Affairs (MOHA), AITI, and DARe have recently launched eKadaiBrunei.com, an e-commerce directory for online marketplaces and delivery service providers such as Domo (mobile-based marketplace), Gomamam (mobile food delivery app), KadaiRuncit (online grocery store), and so forth (Wong 2020). eKadaiBrunei.com was launched prior to easing COVID-19 restrictions to allow businesses to connect with their customers without suffering a huge loss.

To expand e-commerce activities and develop the economy of MSMEs, it is perhaps essential for Brunei to consider Cross Border E-Commerce (CBE) as a business pathway. Fan (2019) defined CBE as an online import channel where consumers can purchase goods via the internet. In simpler terms, CBE is when consumers purchase goods from foreign countries through the electronic medium on the internet. Although CBE is frequently practised by foreign markets into Brunei rather than local companies going outside to foreign markets, better things may come along with strong government support and engagement with the private sector. Young (2019) articulated that global consumers spent about US$3.46 trillion online in 2019—an increase from $2.93 trillion in 2018—and is expected to grow 17.9 per cent yearly. Although online sales revenues increase annually, e-commerce penetration has been gradually rising unwaveringly from 10.5 per cent in 2016 to 12.3 per cent in 2017, and 14.4 per cent in 2018. Internet Retailer predicts 16 per cent in 2019, largely contributed by the world's leading online retailers (Young 2019). MSMEs in Brunei are managed within a small market where only a few penetrate the foreign markets and have yet to engage in the global value chains (Othman 2020). The value chains in agriculture are important as it involves food processing which, sustained by the Halal certification programme, ensure high export quality that can help to internationalize agribusiness (Othman 2020). Brunei's halal industry can thus be a channel for local SMEs to penetrate global markets.

Digital Wallet

The increasing trend of e-commerce activities in Brunei is mainly driven by millennials (Ahad and Anshari 2017; The Scoop 2018). AITI (2018) reported that the rise of online shopping activities was because most respondents found online shopping to be highly convenient. The statistics showed that the level of smartphone adoption, internet usage, and e-commerce activities are considerably increasing in the country, which would provide a solid platform for the adoption of eWallets. The adoption of eWallets is however not yet prominent in Brunei as people strongly prefer to utilize mobile banking channels (AMBD 2017). Many also prefer to make payments via swipe (credit card and direct debit) and online bank transfer rather than eWallets as the mode of payment (Anshari, Almunawar and Masri 2020b; Hamdan and Anshari 2020; Razzaq, Samiha and Anshari 2018).

Although there exists some resistance in embracing eWallets by individuals, this has not deterred FinTech companies in Brunei to establish their own local eWallets. Autoriti Monetari Brunei Darussalam (AMBD) hopes that this will aid in enhancing innovation, cost reduction, as well as improve the efficiency and effectiveness of mobile payments by streamlining both conventional face-to-face payments with online transactions between the consumer and businesses (AMBD 2017; Anshari, Almunawar and Masri 2020a). Some examples of local eWallets are Progresif Pay, an eWallet introduced by local telecommunications company, Progresif Cellular Sdn Bhd (PCSB) in collaboration with Bank Islam Brunei Darussalam (BIBD) in May 2018, as well as BIBD's QuickPay—an upgrade from their "e-*tunai*" mobile internet payment service platform that was introduced in 2013. The establishment of BIBD's QuickPay is aimed at revitalizing the growth of entrepreneurs within the country as a means to diversify and boost the economy, develop more opportunities for the growth of private sector, and create a greater competitive advantage (Al-Mudimigh et al. 2020; HAB 2018).

As for heading towards a cashless society, AITI has signed a memorandum of understanding to develop and implement a cashless society pilot programme, after a study they conducted in 2018 showed that 84 per cent of e-commerce users prefer to use a debit or credit card for their online purchases (The Bruneian 2020). Additionally, many businesses give the option of mobile bank transfer as yet another alternative cashless transaction for the convenience of their customers. Indeed, given that the World Health Organization (WHO) suggested that COVID-19 can be spread through dirty banknotes (Gardner 2020), it is likely that a cashless Bruneian society will be realized sooner rather than later.

CONCLUSION

The recent development and growing number of digital platforms in response to the COVID-19 pandemic somewhat indicate the positive acceptance of Bruneian society to embark on a digital transformation. The government's Digital Economy Masterplan entails the country's steps towards achieving a vibrant and sustainable economy, a digital and future-ready society and a digitally conducive ecosystem. Hence, a digital revolution will inevitably enhance economic diversification through job transformation (Mühleisen 2018) and the inclusive nature of the digital economy (Al-Roubaier, Hamdan and Sarea 2020). Such inclusivity might mean access to opportunities for many people (Al-Roubaier, Hamdan and Sarea 2020) and reduction of the digital divide (Wladawsky-Berger 2015). This may have the potential to reduce poverty and economic inequality. However, there is evidence of a wider digital divide between the rich and the poor countries that was exacerbated by the pandemic (Muggah, Rohozinski and Goldin 2020), and online learning due to school closure has also exposed the digital divide within the Bruneian society (Bakar 2020a). This incidence may be a reflection of the digital revolution as a whole, therefore it remains to be seen whether the digital revolution can reduce poverty in the country.

By optimizing digital technology, it could help ensure the efficiency and effectiveness of any organization's system. Brunei has also expressed its intention to change its status into a digital society ("smart nation") that will drive government agencies and private sectors to meet the goals of Brunei Vision 2035. Digital society is expected to improve all aspects and quality of life. However, this requires ICT literacy, public engagement and collaboration, integration systems, and knowledge sharing as competitive advantages. Brunei has initiated ICT integration in several key sectors such as governance, business and finance, and healthcare sectors. This includes, but is not limited to, the implementation of e-Darussalam, Digital Economy Masterplan 2020–2025, and Bru-HIMS. That said, immediate execution of the plan is needed to complete the building blocks of a successful digital society transformation.

REFERENCES

Ahad, Annie Dayani, and Muhammad Anshari. 2017. "Smartphone Habits among Youth: Uses and Gratification Theory". *International Journal of Cyber Behavior, Psychology and Learning (IJCBPL)* 7, no. 1: 65–75.

Al-Mudimigh, Abdullah, Muhammad Anshari, and Sumarsono. 2020. "Financial Technology and Innovative Financial Inclusion". In *Financial Technology and Innovative Financial Inclusion*, edited by Sumarsono, Abdullah Al-Mudimigh, and Muhammad Anshari, pp. 119–29. Hershey, PA: IGI Global.

Almunawar, Mohammad Nabil, and Muhammad Anshari. 2014. "Empowering Customers in Electronic Health (e-Health) Through Social Customer Relationship Management". *International Journal of Electronic Customer Relationship Management* 8, no. 1–3: 87–100.

Almunawar, Mohammad Nabil, Zaw Wint, Patrick Kim Cheng Low, and Muhammad Anshari. 2012. "Customer Expectation of e-Health Systems in Brunei Darussalam". *Journal of Health Care Finance* 38, no. 4: 36–49.

Al-Roubaier, Amer, Allam Hamdan, and Adel M. Sarea. 2020. "Economic Diversification in a Digital Economy". In *Proceedings of the International Conference on Artificial Intelligence and Computer Vision (AICV2020), Advances in Intelligent Systems and Computing (AISC) 1153*, edited by Aboul-Ella Hassanien, Ahmad Taher Azar, Tarek Gaber, Diego Oliva, and Fahmy M. Tolba, pp. 665–71. Cham, Switzerland: Springer. https://doi.org/10.1007/978-3-030-44289-7.

Anshari, Muhammad. 2020. "Workforce Mapping of Fourth Industrial Revolution: Optimisation to Identity". *Journal of Physics: Conference Series* 1477: 072023.

Anshari, Muhammad, Mohammad Nabil Almunawar, and Masairol Masri. 2020a. "Financial Technology and Disruptive Innovation in Business: Concept and Application". *International Journal of Asian Business and Information Management (IJABIM)* 11, no. 4: 29–43.

———. 2020b. "An Overview of Financial Technology in Indonesia". In *Financial Technology and Innovative Financial Inclusion*, edited by Sumarsono, Abdullah Al-Mudimigh, and Muhammad Anshari, pp. 216–24. Hershey, PA: IGI Global. doi:10.4018/978-1-5225-9183-2.ch012.

Anshari, Muhammad, Mohammad Nabil Almunawar, Masairol Masri, and Mahani Hamdan. 2019. "Digital Marketplace and FinTech to Support Agriculture Sustainability". *Energy Procedia* 156: 234–38.

Anshari, Muhammad, Mohammad Nabil Almunawar, Patrick Kim Cheng Low, and Abdullah Al-Mudimigh. 2013. "Empowering Clients Through e-Health in Healthcare Services: Case Brunei". *International Quarterly of Community Health Education* 33, no. 2: 189–219.

Anshari, Muhammad, and Wardah Hakimah Sumardi. 2020. "Employing Big Data in Business Organisation and Business Ethics". *International Journal of Business Governance and Ethics* 14, no. 2: 181–205.

Authority for Info-communications Technology Industry of Brunei Darussalam (AITI). 2018. *E-Commerce Survey for Consumers in Brunei Darussalam: 2018 Report.* https://www.aiti.gov.bn/Shared%20Documents/ECOMM%20 Survey%20Report%20v14.pdf (accessed 22 September 2018).

———. 2019. *ICT Household Report.* https://www.aiti.gov.bn/Shared%20 Documents/Final%20-%20ICT%20HOUSEHOLD%20REPORT.PDF (accessed 4 May 2021).

———. 2020. "Brunei Darussalam's 1st 5G Task Force Plenary Meeting". 6 May 2020. https://www.aiti.gov.bn/SitePages/News.aspx?AID=50 (accessed 8 January 2021).

Autoriti Monetari Brunei Darussalam (AMBD). 2017. "Request for Information: Retail Payments Infrastructure for Brunei Darussalam". http://ambd.gov. bn/SiteAssets/Request%20for%20Information%20-%20PSS%20Retail%20 Payment%20Infrastructure%20v1.1.pdf (accessed 15 August 2018).

Bakar, Rasidah. 2020a. "COVID-19 Lays Bare Digital Divide in Education". *The Scoop*, 29 September 2020. https://thescoop.co/2020/09/29/COVID-19-lays-bare-digital-divide-in-education/ (accessed 9 January 2021).

———. 2020b. "Gov't Rolls Out Online Payment Portal". *The Scoop*, 28 February 2020. https://thescoop.co/2020/02/28/govt-rolls-out-online-payment-portal/ (accessed 18 September 2020).

Basir, Khairul Hidayatullah. 2017. "Economic Issues in Brunei Prior to 2014 Oil Crisis". *Jurnal Sultan Alauddin Sulaiman Shah* 4, no. 1: 27–33.

The Bruneian. 2020. "AITI, Beep Digital Ink Partnership for Cashless Society Pilot Programme". *The Bruneian*, 30 November 2020. https://www.thebruneian. news/aiti-beep-digital-ink-partnership-for-cashless-society-pilot-programme/ (accessed 7 January 2021).

Dart Brunei. 2020. "Dart Driver Gathering". 21 September 2020. https://www. dartbrunei.com/news (accessed 18 September 2020).

Department of Statistics. 2012. *Brunei Darussalam Key Indicators 2012.* Bandar Seri Begawan, Brunei: Department of Economic Planning and Development,

Prime Minister's Office. http://www.deps.gov.bn/DEPD%20Documents%20 Library/DOS/BDKI/BDKI2012_R2.pdf (accessed 16 May 2021).

_____. 2017. *Gross Domestic Product Second Quarter 2017*. Bandar Seri Begawan, Brunei: Department of Economic Planning and Development, Prime Minister's Office. http://www.deps.gov.bn/DEPD%20Documents%20 Library/DOS/GDP/2017/1.%20GDP_Q22017.pdf (accessed 9 November 2017).

_____. 2018. *Gross Domestic Product Second Quarter 2018*. Bandar Seri Begawan, Brunei: Department of Economic Planning and Development, Prime Minister's Office. http://www.deps.gov.bn/DEPD%20Documents%20 Library/DOS/GDP/2018/GDP_Q22018.pdf (accessed 16 May 2021).

Digital Government Strategy. n.d. "Digital Government Strategy 2015–2020 Brunei Darussalam". http://www.digitalstrategy.gov.bn/Themed/index. aspx# (accessed 19 September 2020).

Gardner, Bill. 2020. "Dirty Banknotes May Be Spreading the Coronavirus, WHO Suggests". *The Telegraph*, 2 March 2020. https://www.telegraph.co.uk/ news/2020/03/02/exclusive-dirty-banknotes-may-spreading-coronavirus-world-health/ (accessed 7 January 2021).

GOV.bn. n.d. "*Wawasan* Brunei 2035". https://www.gov.bn/SitePages/ Wawasan%20Brunei%202035.aspx (accessed 4 May 2021).

Hab, Fizah. 2018. "BIBD Bolstering Efforts to Create Cashless Society". *Borneo Bulletin*, 18 August 2018. https://borneobulletin.com.bn/bibd-bolstering-efforts-to-create-cashless-society/ (accessed 24 September 2018).

Hamdan, Mahani, and Muhammad Anshari. 2020. "Paving the Way for the Development of FinTech Initiatives in ASEAN". In *Financial Technology and Innovative Financial Inclusion*, edited by Sumarsono, Abdullah Al-Mudimigh, and Muhammad Anshari, pp. 80–107. Hershey, PA: IGI Global. doi:10.4018/978-1-5225-9183-2.ch004.

Han, Shareen. 2020. "Gov't Rolls Out BruHealth Contact Tracing App as Restrictions Loosened". *The Scoop*, 14 May 2020. https://thescoop. co/2020/05/14/govt-launches-bruhealth-contact-tracing-app/ (accessed 4 May 2021).

Hayat, Hakim. 2014. "Work Together to Realise Brunei's Vision 2035 Goals". *Sultanate*, 9 October 2014. http://www.sultanate.com/news_server/2014/9_ oct_1.html (accessed 4 May 2021).

_____. 2019. "Brunei Getting Ready to Embrace 5G". *Borneo Bulletin*, 26 September 2019. https://borneobulletin.com.bn/brunei-getting-ready-embrace-5g/ (accessed 4 May 2021).

Jayaraman, Prem Prakash, Ali Yavari, Dimitrios Georgakopoulos, Ahsan Morshed, and Arkady Zaslavsky. 2016. "Internet of Things Platform for Smart Farming: Experiences and Lessons Learnt". *Sensors* 16, no. 11: 1884.

Looi, Hong Cheong. 2005. "E-Commerce Adoption in Brunei Darussalam: A Quantitative Analysis of Factors Influencing Its Adoption". *Communications of the Association for Information Systems* 15, no. 1: 3.

Maida, I. 2019. "Industry 5.0: Towards a New Revolution". *Criticalcase.* https://www.criticalcase.com/blog/industry-5-0-towards-a-new-revolution.html (accessed 4 May 2021).

Ministry of Education (MOE). 2018. *Ministry of Education Strategic Plan 2018–2022.* Brunei: Strategic Enterprise Performance and Delivery Unit, Ministry of Education. http://www.moe.gov.bn/DocumentDownloads/Strategic%20Plan%20Book%202018-2022/Strategic%20plan%202018-2022.pdf (accessed 19 September 2020).

Ministry of Transport and Infocommunications (MTIC). 2014. *Review to Formulate a Roadmap and Draft National Masterplan for a Sustainable Land Transportation System for Brunei Darussalam.* http://www.mtic.gov.bn/Resources/LAND%20TRANSPORT%20MASTER%20PLAN%20-%20Executive%20Summary.pdf (accessed 4 May 2020).

———. 2020. *Digital Economy Masterplan 2025.* Brunei: Digital Economy Council. http://www.mtic.gov.bn/DE2025/documents/Digital%20Economy%20Masterplan%202025.pdf (accessed 19 September 2020).

Muggah, Robert, Rafal Rohozinski, and Ian Goldin. 2020. "The Dark Side of Digitalization – and How to Fix It". World Economic Forum. https://www.weforum.org/agenda/2020/09/dark-side-digitalization/ (accessed 9 January 2021).

Mühleisen, Martin. 2018. "The Long and Short of the Digital Revolution". *Finance and Development* 55, no. 2: 4–8. https://www.imf.org/external/pubs/ft/fandd/2018/06/impact-of-digital-technology-on-economic-growth/muhleisen.htm (accessed 4 May 2021).

Organisation for Economic Cooperation and Development/Economic Research Institute for ASEAN and East Asia (OECD/ERIA). 2018. *SME Policy Index: ASEAN 2018: Boosting Competitiveness and Inclusive Growth.* Paris: OECD Publishing and Jakarta: Economic Research Institute for ASEAN and East Asia. https://doi.org/10.1787/9789264305328-en.

Othman, Azlan. 2020. "MSMEs Drive Brunei's Economy". *Borneo Bulletin*, 31 October 2020. https://borneobulletin.com.bn/msmes-drive-bruneis-economy/ (accessed 4 May 2021).

Pasadilla, Gloria O., Andre Wirjo, and Jiquan Liu. 2017. *Promoting E-Commerce to Globalize MSMEs.* Singapore: Asia-Pacific Economic Cooperation.

Paul, Prantosh, and P.S. Aithal. 2018. "Digital Society: Its Foundation and Towards an Interdisciplinary Field". In *Proceedings of National Conference on Advances in Information Technology, Management, Social Sciences and Education*, pp. 1–6. https://papers.ssrn.com/sol3/papers.cfm?abstract_

id=3397902#:~:text=A%20Digital%20Society%20is%20an,into%20the%20
society%20and%20culture (accessed 19 September 2020).

Petra, Fatimah. 2014. "An Introduction to Digital Literacy in Brunei Darussalam".
SHBIE article. https://www.researchgate.net/profile/Fatimah_Petra/
publication/263845406_An_Introduction_to_Digital_Literacy_in_Brunei_
Darussalam/links/02e7e53c0224de41d7000000/An-Introduction-to-Digital-
Literacy-in-Brunei-Darussalam.pdf (accessed 4 May 2021).

Polak, Petr, Christof Nelischer, Haochen Guo, and David C. Robertson. 2019.
"'Intelligent' Finance and Treasury Management: What We Can Expect". *AI
& SOCIETY* 35: 715–26.

Polsaram, Pussadee, Panid Kulsiri, Lissara Techasermsukkul, Thaw Dar Htwe,
and Kanittha Kwanchainond. 2011. "A Survey Research Project on 'Small and
Medium Enterprises Development Policies of 4 ASEAN Countries': Brunei
Darussalam, Cambodia, Lao PDR, Myanmar". Submitted to Japan Overseas
Development Corporation (JODC). https://www.asean.org/wp-content/
uploads/images/documents/SME%20Policies%20in%204%20ASEAN%20
Countries%20-%20Brunei%20Darussalam.pdf (accessed 4 May 2021).

Razzaq, Abdur, Yulia Tri Samiha, and Muhammad Anshari. 2018. "Smartphone
Habits and Behaviors in Supporting Students Self-Efficacy". *International
Journal of Emerging Technologies in Learning* (iJET) 13, no. 2: 94–109.

RTBNews. 2020. "Smart Farming is Good for Improving Competitiveness".
RTBNews, 2 November 2020. http://rtbnews.rtb.gov.bn/Lists/News%20
2018/NewDispForm.aspx?ID=22847 (accessed 5 Dec 2020).

Sangtrash, Heena M., and Anand S. Hiremath. 2017. "Review on IoT for Indian
Farmers". *International Journal of Scientific Research in Computer Science,
Engineering and Information Technology* (IJSRCSEIT) 2, no. 3: 236–39. http://
ijsrcseit.com/paper/CSEIT1722399.pdf (accessed 4 May 2021).

The Scoop. 2018. "Millennials Driving E-Commerce Says New Report from
AITI". *The Scoop*, 15 July 2018. https://thescoop.co/2018/07/15/millennials-
driving- ecommerce-report-aiti/ (accessed 15 July 2018).

———. 2019. "UNN Takes Over All Telco Infrastructure in Brunei". *The Scoop*,
4 September 2019. https://thescoop.co/2019/09/04/unn-takes-over-all-telco-
infrastructure-in-brunei/ (accessed 12 March 2020).

Universiti Brunei Darussalam (UBD). 2019. "Innovation Lab". https://innovation.
ubd.edu.bn/fptubd (accessed 19 September 2020).

Wladawsky-Berger, Irving. 2015. "Will the Digital Revolution Deliver for the
World's Poor?" https://www.brookings.edu/wp-content/uploads/2015/08/
wladawskybergerwillthedigitalrevoltiondeliver.pdf (accessed 7 January
2021).

Wong, Aaron. 2020. "eKadaiBrunei: Brunei's First Online E-Commerce Directory Launched". *Biz Brunei*, 1 April 2020. https://www.bizbrunei.com/2020/04/ekadaibrunei-bruneis-first-online-E-commerce-direc tory-launched/ (accessed 4 May 2021).

Young, Jessica. 2019. "Global Ecommerce Sales to Reach Nearly \$3.46 Trillion in 2019". *Digital Commerce 360*, 13 November 2019. https://www.digitalcommerce360.com/article/global-ecommerce-sales/ (accessed 4 May 2021).

PART III

Human Capital

7

CHANGING FACES OF BRUNEI POPULATION

Evi Nurvidya Arifin and Norainie Ahmad

UNDERSTANDING POPULATION DYNAMICS

Understanding population dynamics is very important for policymakers and business communities. They need to know the size, composition and geographical distribution of the population and how these have changed and will change over time. Population dynamics and its three main components (fertility, mortality and migration) affect various developmental sectors such as economy, politics, social and environment. Economic impacts of population dynamics operate through production, consumption and distribution. On the production side, the population provides capital and labour to the firms/institutions. In return, firms/ institutions provide salaries and produce goods and services to fulfil the needs of the population. On the other hand, the population consumes goods and services and pays the producers. Therefore, the population has two functions: as producers and consumers. Information on producers and consumers is needed for the distribution system of goods and services and labour allocation, making development policies and business strategies.

Socially, population dynamics may result in behavioural and norm changes. People may behave differently in densely populated areas compared to those in sparsely populated areas; living in areas with many older persons may be different from living in areas with mostly younger persons; living in areas with many visitors from other places may be different from living in areas where the members of the population are homogenous and have few visitors.

Coupled with rising income and wealth, population growth places increasing pressures on the planet's resources through consumption of water and air, clearing forests, and land use. This contributes to climate change and challenges environmental sustainability, with both global and local socio-economic-political implications.

There is a close relationship between population growth and economic growth. Expressed in percentage, economic growth is equal to population growth plus growth in per capita GDP (gross domestic product). However, to make effective targets of development, understanding the size of population is not sufficient—population composition matters more. Changing age composition from young to old, for instance, influences the labour market including pension and social protection systems, infrastructure, poverty, as well as demand for goods and services. This chapter describes and examines the population dynamics over time in Brunei. It shows how the Brunei population has been changing over these five decades. This change may continue in the next few decades.

The data is mostly compiled, calculated, and presented based on the published data of population census, produced by the Department of Statistics, Department of Economic Planning and Development, Ministry of Finance (2011, 2013, 2014 and 2018), Statistical Yearbook 2019, Vital Statistics 2019, and Mid-year Population Estimates 2020. The census in this country is conducted every ten years, with the latest one being the 2011 Population and Housing Census (BPP). The previous censuses were conducted in 1971, 1981, 1991 and 2001. In 2016, the government conducted an intercensal population survey.

The chapter starts with a discussion on the geographical distribution of the population, which can have important implications in policy-making for the whole nation. It is then followed by a section on population size, population growth, and migration. The next three sections focus on changing sex composition, changing age structure, and changing ethnic and religious composition. The chapter ends with a concluding remark.

GEOGRAPHICAL DISTRIBUTION

Brunei is entirely surrounded by the East Malaysian state of Sarawak with the South China Sea to the north (see Figure 7.1). Historically, as explained by Mohidin (2013), Brunei was administratively divided into six districts: Belait, Tutong, Brunei, Limau Manis, Muara and Temburong from 1909 to 1932. The country was then divided into five districts after the merging of Limau Manis and Brunei in 1932. Since 1938 up until now, Brunei has four districts: Belait, Tutong, Brunei-Muara and Temburong as ordered from the West to the East.

The Brunei population is scattered among its four districts with Brunei-Muara district as the centre where the capital, Bandar Seri Begawan, is located. This district is the most populous district

FIGURE 7.1
The Geographic Distribution of Brunei Population in 2020

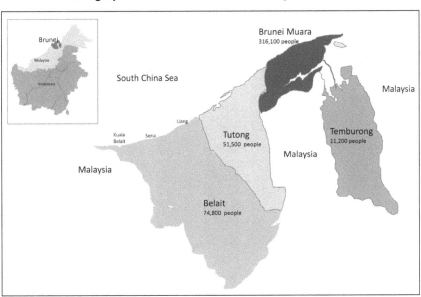

Source: Authors' autograph.

inhabited by more than 50 per cent of the total Brunei population as seen in Figure 7.2, and the percentage keeps increasing. People live in this district for close proximity to workplace and employment opportunities, schools, businesses and other facilities such as major ports (Tong 1989). The estimated population was about 320 thousand in 2019, which was 3.4 times higher than that of 1971 (see Table 7.1). In other words, the population in Brunei-Muara grew rapidly, even being the fastest among the four districts (see Table 7.1), especially in the period between 1971 and 2011. Since 2011, the population growth rate in this capital district has decreased. It was even the slowest in 2011–16 with an annual growth rate of 0.7 per cent (see Table 7.1). However, in recent years (2016–19), population has grown faster in this district (3.3 per cent) and also in other districts, with Temburong district being the fastest (3.5 per cent). However, Brunei-Muara and other districts experienced negative growth in 2019–20.

The size of population can change because of three components: births, deaths, and migrants (Poston and Bouvier 2010). There are two types of migrants: migrants into a region, which increases the size of population, and migrants out from a region, which reduces the size of population. Therefore, population can increase because of the number of births and migrants into a region. In contrast, population can decrease due to the number of deaths and migrants out from

FIGURE 7.2
Population Redistribution in Brunei Darussalam, 1971–2020

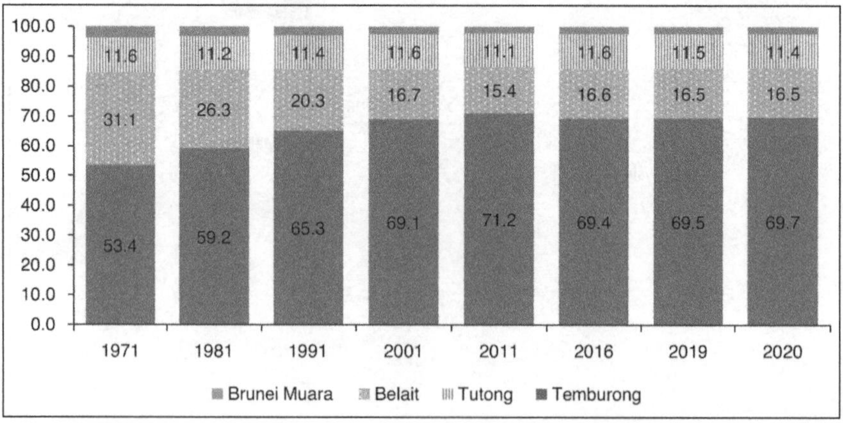

	1971	1981	1991	2001	2011	2016	2019	2020
Temburong	11.6	11.2	11.4	11.6	11.1	11.6	11.5	11.4
Tutong	31.1	26.3	20.3	16.7	15.4	16.6	16.5	16.5
Brunei Muara	53.4	59.2	65.3	69.1	71.2	69.4	69.5	69.7

■ Brunei Muara ▨ Belait ⫶⫶⫶ Tutong ■ Temburong

Source: Compiled and drawn from various publications by the Department of Statistics.

TABLE 7.1
Population and its Annual Growth Rate by District, 1971–2020

Year	Brunei-Muara	Belait	Tutong	Temburong	Total
1971	72,791	42,383	15,858	5,224	136,256
1981	114,231	50,768	21,615	6,218	192,832
1991	170,107	52,957	29,730	7,688	260,482
2001	230,030	55,602	38,649	8,563	332,844
2011	279,924	60,744	43,852	8,852	393,372
2016	289,630	69,062	48,313	10,251	417,256
2019	319,500	75,900	52,700	11,400	459,500
2020	316,100	74,800	51,500	11,200	453,600
Annual Growth Rate (%)					
1971–81	4.5	1.8	3.1	1.7	3.5
1981–91	4.0	0.4	3.2	2.1	3.0
1991–2001	3.0	0.5	2.6	1.1	2.5
2001–11	2.0	0.9	1.3	0.3	1.7
2011–16	0.7	2.6	1.9	2.9	1.2
2016–19	3.3	3.1	2.9	3.5	3.2
2019–20	−1.1	−1.5	−2.3	−1.8	−1.3
Population density (per Km^2)					
1971	127	16	14	4	24
1981	200	19	19	5	33
1991	298	19	25	6	45
2001	403	20	33	7	58
2011	490	22	38	7	68
2016	507	25	41	8	72
2019	560	29	45	9	80
2020	554	27	44	9	79
Area (Km)					
	571	2,724	1,166	1,304	5,765

Source: Compiled and drawn from various publications by the Department of Statistics.

a region. A natural increase is an increase in population when the number of births exceeds the number of deaths, without considering migration. However, historically, the natural changes in the number of births and deaths may take time, unless, unnatural deaths occur unexpectedly. On the other hand, migration can be more dynamic over time. This sudden change in the growth rate in the Brunei-Muara district within such a short period of time reflects the role played by migration rather than by the natural growth rate. The outbreak of the Coronavirus pandemic in 2019, known as COVID-19, has brought about a decline in the size of the Brunei population in all districts (see Table 7.1). There has been no sudden change in fertility and mortality rates in the past year. Yet, as reported by the Department of Statistics (2021), the travel restriction due to the COVID-19 pandemic has prevented the return of foreigners who had left Brunei when their contract finished and only limited sectors of employment can have a new batch of foreigners.

In terms of land size, Brunei-Muara district is the smallest, about one-fifth of Belait district, but it is the most densely populated area with more than 500 persons per square kilometre in 2020. The population density in this district has been increasing rapidly since 1971, when the density was only about 127 persons per square kilometre.

Belait district with the largest land area is an important district for oil production. Oil was first discovered there in 1929. Its commercial production began in 1932. It is the most important district for the establishment of oil and natural gas industries such as Brunei Shell Petroleum Company Sdn Bhd (BSP). BSP has been in existence for ninety years and has contributed to the growth and prosperity in Brunei. The gas industry at Lumut is one of the world's largest liquefied natural gas plants. The oil and gas development either inland or at offshore oil fields is one of the reasons that Belait is home to the second largest population after Brunei-Muara (Tong 1989).

Based on a series of decennial population censuses, Belait's population continuously increased from 42.4 thousand in 1971 to 50.8 thousand in ten years, and 53.0 thousand in 1991, 55.6 thousand at the turn of this millennium and 60.7 thousand in 2011. The latest estimated figure was about 75.9 thousand in 2019 and declined to 74.8 thousand in 2020.

In addition, Belait shares borders with Eastern Malaysia's city of Miri, the second largest city in Sarawak, Malaysia after the capital of Kuching. This close proximity in tandem with favouring currency exchange rate for Brunei currency has been known as a major appeal (Islam, Salleh and Sabli 2019) for Bruneians to reside in Belait. This enables cross-border mobility for Bruneians residing in Belait to Miri in just around a half an hour drive or about a two-hour drive from the capital of Brunei, Bandar Seri Begawan (Islam, Salleh and Sabli 2019; Koh 2019). The COVID-19 pandemic has forced the country to close its border since March 2020, turning the population mobility within the country only.

Although the size of Belait population is continuously increasing, the average annual growth had been decreasing from 1.8 per cent in 1971–81 to less than 0.5 per cent in two decades (1981–2001). The growth rate accelerated since 2001 and reached an annual rate of 2.6 per cent in 2011–16 and 3.1 per cent in 2016–19. The declining rate of population growth from 1971 to 1991 might be contributed by the decline in fertility rate and a continuing migration overseas from Belait (Tong 1994). As the decline of fertility rate is generally irreversible, the acceleration of population growth rate in recent years was more likely due to migration into Belait. Due to the border closure, Belait also feels the COVID-19 impact on its population as seen through a negative growth rate (–1.5 per cent) in 2019–20.

While Belait experienced a slower growth rate of population in the period of 1971–2011, other districts grew faster. As a consequence, the percentage of Belait population to the whole Brunei population was declining. The percentage declined from 31.1 per cent in 1971 to 15.4 per cent in 2001, and slightly increased to 16.5 per cent in 2019.

As the largest district in terms of land area, the population density of Belait increased steadily from 16 in 1971 to 29 persons per square kilometre in 2019 and declined to 27 in 2020. In 2016, temporary residents in Belait accounted for 17.8 per cent of Belait population, or 18.9 per cent of the total temporary residents in Brunei. Based on the 2011 census, they were mainly born in Indonesia, Malaysia, the Philippines and India. Permanent residents in Belait accounted for a higher percentage—18.9 per cent of the total population in Belait—and they were mainly born in Brunei (70.2 per cent) or in Malaysia (24.9 per cent). Located between Belait and Brunei-Muara, Tutong district has been experiencing a higher population growth than Belait. Yet, the size of population is smaller and the proportion is relatively stable at around 11.0 per cent. Its population density is higher than

Belait as Tutong's land area is smaller than Belait (see Table 7.1). Bruneians accounted for 87.0 per cent in 2016, and temporary residents accounted for 9.1 per cent, thus the remaining percentage comprised permanent residents. In 2011, temporary residents in Tutong were not as diverse as those in Belait, as more than half were born in Indonesia (58.0 per cent).

As the second widest district with the smallest size of population yet separated by the seas, Temburong district has become the least densely populated district (see Table 7.1). The unconnected location was the barrier for population mobility as well as distribution of goods and services. Bruneians accounted for 80.7 per cent, followed by permanent residents (12.0 per cent) and temporary residents (7.3 per cent) in 2016.

However, in 2020 this remote district was connected through the longest bridge in Southeast Asia, Temburong Bridge or named as the Sultan Haji Omar 'Ali Saifuddien (SOAS) Bridge, stretching along 30 km. The existence of this bridge is expected to increase population mobility from and to Temburong. This will have a lot of economic implications not only in Temburong but also in the other three districts. Not only that, UNISSA (Universiti Islam Sultan Sharif Ali) will develop a new campus in this district that will be a new source of growth for the population and economy of the district. The economy of the four districts will be better integrated, strengthening the domestic economy. The future geographical population distribution is likely to change due to the connectivity between Temburong and other districts.

SIZE, NATURAL GROWTH RATE AND MIGRATION

This section discusses the overall Brunei population. A small population can mean a small market under a closed economy when there are no economic activities linked to outside economies. However, when the small population has a high per capita income, the market (purchasing power) can be large. Although Brunei is the least populous country in Southeast Asia, Brunei economy is connected to the global market, catering to wider regions. By joining the Association of Southeast Asian Nations (ASEAN) on 7 January 1984[1] and the Brunei-Indonesia-Malaysia-Philippines East ASEAN Growth Area (BIMP-EAGA) in March 1994 (Mohidin 2013) as well as various trade agreements, Brunei market has become larger. Brunei has been part of the global supply chain and will continue to forge stronger international ties. In 2021, Brunei is the Chair of ASEAN; earlier sultanate chairmanships were in 2013 and 2001. The current chairmanship can be the opportunity to pave the way in achieving Aspiration 3 of the six aspirations of Brunei's economic blueprint (Ministry of Finance and Economy 2020), as an open and globally connected economy. "In this aspiration, we want our businesses to be able to penetrate external markets and attract foreign businesses..." (p. vii).

The following discussion presents an analysis of the Brunei market from the demographic point of view. It started with the first population census conducted in 1971. The data shows that Brunei was home to only 136.3 thousand persons based on *de-jure* population[2]. Ten years later, the population grew to reach 192.8 thousand. In other words, the population growth rate was 3.5 per cent annually for the period of 1971–81, which was when Brunei was a British protectorate. The population continued to grow to reach 260.5 thousand persons in 1991, six years after its independence in 1984.[3]

However, the growth rate of the population declined to 3.0 per cent annually in 1981–91. At the turn of the twenty-first century, Brunei's population was more than double the 1971 figure, precisely 332.8 thousand persons in 2001. In other words, the population grew annually at 2.5 per cent in 1991–2001, slower than the earlier period. The latest population census showed an increase to 393.4 thousand persons in 2011, and a slower growth rate of 1.7 per cent in 2001–11 (Department of Statistics 2012). In this century, Brunei's population grew much slower than before and continued to grow slower up to the present.

The year 2016 (from May to September) was the first time the government conducted an intercensal population survey (Department of Statistics 2018). Based on this survey, the population reached 417.3 thousand in 2016, or grew at 1.2 per cent in 2011–16. In 2019, it was estimated to be about 459.5 thousand (Department of Statistics 2020a), or on average, an annual growth of 2.4 per cent in 2016–19. This higher growth is seen especially in the past three years (2016–19). In a nutshell, the size of the domestic market has been increasing with a decreasing rate of growth until 2016 that has slightly increased after that. Only after the COVID-19 outbreak, the Brunei population declined for the first time.

This growth is determined by the number of births, deaths and net migrants (the difference between in-migrants and out-migrants). Therefore, the growth rate of population can be decomposed into natural population growth rate (crude birth rate minus crude death rate) and crude migration rate. As reported by the Department of Statistics (2020a), the increasing population growth rate on a year-on-year basis between 2016 and 2019 was as follows: 1.17 per cent, 2.89 per cent, 2.99 per cent and 3.78 per cent for each respective year. The natural population growth rates for the respective years were 1.15 per cent, 1.11 per cent, 1.04 per cent, and 0.96 per cent. The declining natural population growth rate is mainly due to the decline in the number of births as the crude death rates were relatively constant. Therefore, with the statistics on population growth rate and natural growth rate, the crude migration rate is calculated to be only 0.02 per cent in 2016, rising to 1.78 per cent in 2017, 1.95 per cent in 2018 and 2.83 per cent in 2019. The significant increase of crude migration rate may indicate rising labour shortage in Brunei, because of rising economic growth and/or unavailability of the locals to do the jobs. Brunei has a relatively open policy on international migration to benefit economic activities.

Migration involves time and place. There are two major types of migrants: life-time migrants and recent migrants (Poston and Bouvier 2010). These types of migrants have nothing to do with citizenship; they are only concerned with capturing information on population mobility, changing the place of residence at a certain time or period. Life-time migrants are defined as persons whose current place of residence is different from the place of birth. This has been adopted by the United Nations for many years (United Nations 2019a). By this definition, for instance, a person of a region (such as region A) in the present time is considered as a lifetime migrant in Region A if the person was born outside Region A. The weakness of this concept lies in its inability to track the person's migration trajectory from birth until the present time. On the other hand, recent migrants are defined as persons whose current place of residence is different from their places of residence five years earlier. This concept measures a more recent phenomenon, but still misses the migration trajectory within one to four years before the survey/census. A person who currently lives in Region A is a recent migrant if the person lived outside Region A five years earlier. However, a person who has lived in Region A for one year, or for six years and more is not considered as a recent migrant. Instead, this person is a non-migrant.

The latest available information on life-time migrants is from the 2011 Brunei population census. It indicates that foreign-born[4] population or life-time migrants constituted 25.6 per cent. This rate is lower than 27.8 per cent in 1981 (Tong 1989). However, there is no information to calculate recent migration.

The more often available time-series data is population composition by residential status which is defined as the status of the person residing in Brunei in relation to the immigration laws. The Department of Statistics (2020a) described that there are four statuses, namely Brunei citizen, that is a person holding a yellow identity card; a permanent resident, a holder of a purple identity card; a temporary resident, a holder of green identity card; and "Others", including relatives or friends who visited the households in Brunei during the census period. In other words, "Others" means persons holding a long-term social visit visa.

This categorization is different from the concept of migration mentioned earlier and generally applied in the global population census. The richness of the Brunei population lies in the availability of information on both residential status and country of birth. For instance, the 2011 data published the number of foreign-born in relation to residential status. The calculation shows that foreign-born consisted of 79.8 per cent temporary residents, 9.3 per cent Brunei citizens and 10.1 per cent permanent residents. Therefore, temporary residents are mostly foreign-born. There was also a limited percentage of Bruneians who were born in other countries. However, by the definition of life-time migrants, these citizens are migrants in Brunei. The calculation from this data shows that they accounted for 3.3 per cent of Brunei citizens. In contrast, temporary residents who were born in Brunei and still live in Brunei at the time of census date are not life-time migrants. As calculated, they accounted for 5.7 per cent of the total temporary residents.

Figure 7.3 depicts a significant percentage of temporary residents, larger than the percentage of permanent residents. The percentage fluctuated, from 17.4 per cent in 1971 to reach its peak at 27.1 per cent in 1991, and later declined to 15.6 per cent in 2016 and has been peaking up to 20.5 per cent in 2019. As expected, the share of temporary residents declined in 2020 which was 18.5 per cent.

FIGURE 7.3
Brunei Population by Residential Status, 1971–2020

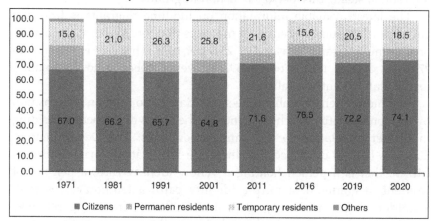

Source: Compiled and drawn from various publications by the Department of Statistics.

Based on the 2011 data, the foreign-born were at least from twenty-seven countries, more diverse than in 1981 as examined earlier by Tong (1989). Among the twenty-seven countries, Indonesia, Malaysia, Philippines, India, Bangladesh and Thailand were the six largest Asian origins. There were also foreign-born (life-time migrants) from non-Asian countries such as the United Kingdom, France, the Netherlands, the United States, Australia and New Zealand. In 1981, the foreign-born were mostly from the neighbouring country Malaysia, followed by China and Taiwan (Tong 1989). The presence of diverse migrant communities has shaped cultural exchanges and the market for final goods and services (Ullah and Asiyah az-Zahra 2019). Among Bruneians, the calculation shows that there were few of them (2.7 per cent) born in Malaysia based on the 2011 data. Figure 7.3 shows that overall Brunei citizens accounted for 67.0 per cent of the total population in 1971. The percentage slowly declined to reach 64.8 per cent in 2001. Since then, the percentage of citizens reached above 70.0 per cent, higher than the percentage in 1971.

CHANGING SEX COMPOSITION

Population composition by sex holds primary importance in understanding population dynamics and its consequences on society, economy and politics. Sex composition is important for partner availability in the marriage market (Schacht and Mulder 2015), and for security and safety through possible incidence of violence (Messner and Sampson 1991; Schacht, Rauch and Mulder 2014). Hobbs (2004) argued that different types of planning such as military planning, public services particularly health services, caregiving, sales and marketing require population data that are disaggregated into male and female groups. The sex ratio, sometimes called the masculinity ratio, is the principal measure of sex composition (Hobbs 2004). The sex ratio is usually defined as the number of males per 100 females. The ratio equals to one indicates the point of balance of the sexes. A sex ratio above one denotes an excess of males; a sex ratio below one, an excess of females.

Spoorenberg (2016) noticed that the sexual imbalance is a global phenomenon, where the world population has been masculinized since 1950. This is shown by the sex ratio of the overall population above one and higher than the sex ratio at birth. The sex ratio at birth is generally about 1.05, or five more baby boys per 100 baby girls. If they grow together across their lifespan, the sex ratio should remain around 1.05. However, there often exists different survival rates throughout the lifespan. Infant and child mortality among males is usually higher than females. When they are young adults, adults or older adults, the probability of death among men is also higher than women due to exogenous behavioural and environmental factors. This contributes in lowering the overall sex ratio of the population. However, there are other factors influencing the sex ratio of the population such as population policy, social norms, employment opportunity and migration.

According to this measure, Brunei shows a masculine population, i.e., men outnumber women or the sex ratio is far above the ratio at birth. Yet, as in many other countries in the world, women tend to have higher life expectancy than men. For instance, in 2015–20 Brunei life expectancy at birth was 76.9 for females and 74.5 for males (United Nations 2019b). The sex ratio in Brunei was higher than 1.0 throughout the period of 1971–2019. The sex ratio was far above the ratio at birth, 1.15 in 1971, meaning that there were 15 more men per 100 women in Brunei in 1971. The ratio remained the same in 1981, but declined to 1.12 in 1991, and reached slightly below the ratio at birth, 1.03, in 2001. Therefore, although Brunei had a masculine population, the trend started declining between 1971 and 2001 as the sex ratio was getting closer to the sex ratio at birth. However, it has turned to an upward trend since 2001. The sex ratio increased to 1.07 in 2011, declined to 1.05 in 2016, and went up to 1.14 in 2019, almost the same rate as in 1971.

This imbalance of sex ratio should be understood within the context of migration and job opportunities. Gender bias plays a role in migration, especially when determining reasons to migrate, how to and where to go, and the network they have. Risks in migrating and available opportunities at the destination determine who migrate, either men or women. The exceptionally high sex ratio of temporary residents seen in Figure 7.4 might be a reflection of the available opportunities from the hydrocarbon industries and other sectors, favouring men over women. Based on the 2011 population census, there were many types of occupations where males outnumbered females. The most predominantly male occupations among temporary residents were labourers in mining, construction, manufacturing and transportation;

FIGURE 7.4
Trend of Sex Ratio by Residential Status: Brunei Darussalam, 1971–2020

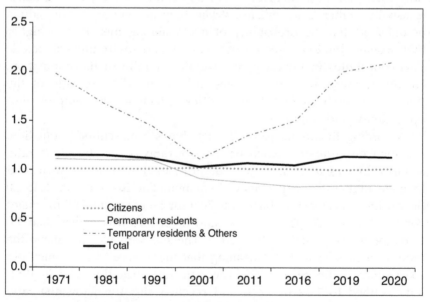

Source: Compiled and drawn from various publications by the Department of Statistics.

building and related trades workers; electrical and electronic trades workers; food processing, woodworking, garment and other craft and related trades workers; and agricultural, fishery and forestry related labourers.

Figure 7.4 indicates the masculinization of the Brunei population through migration. This contrasts with the sex composition of Brunei citizens which is relatively balanced with the sex ratio between 1.01 and 1.02 in 1971–2019. This is even lower than the biological ratio at birth. On the contrary, the gender composition of permanent residents has shifted from masculine (sex ratio above one) to feminine (sex ratio below one). For instance, in 2019, the ratio was 0.84, indicating 84 men per 100 women.

CHANGING AGE STRUCTURE: FROM YOUNG TO OLD POPULATION

The first demographic transition describes a shift from a regime of high levels of mortality and fertility to another regime of low levels of mortality and fertility. This results in the changing of population age-structure. The transition follows several stages. When the mortality rate starts to decline but the fertility rate remains high, the number of births rises and the age structure becomes younger due to an increase in the proportion of the young population. In the next step, the fertility rate follows the trend of mortality rate. Fertility decline reduces the number of births and the percentage of the young population to the total population. At the same time, the percentage of the working-age population increases as they continue to survive. The first demographic transition ends when fertility reaches replacement level, usually at Total Fertility Rate (TFR) at about 2.1.

The second demographic transition (Lesthaeghe 2010) describes changes when fertility continues to decline or fluctuate below the replacement rate. Marriage is not uniform, with high age at first marriage, high percentage of single persons, and disconnection between marriage and reproduction/procreation. Norms in family and society may change, with rising individual accentuation and aspiration. Percentage of children, young population, and possibly working-age population will decline. At the same time, the percentage of older persons will increase rapidly due to longer longevity among older adults in tandem with sustained below fertility rate. Population age structure thus shifts from young to old. This means changes in potential customers and producers. Shortage of young labour may also emerge. Many countries have undergone this age structural transition. GBD (Global Burden Diseases) 2019 Demographics Collaborators (2020) reported that the global TFR has been declining from 2.72 in 2000 to 2.31 in 2019, and 102 countries had reached below the replacement level of fertility shown by a TFR lower than 2.1.

The Brunei population is not an exception. High birth and death rates occurred a long time ago between 1931 and 1948 (Tong 1989). In the following years, birth rate continued increasing as a result of the post-war baby boom, and death rate gradually declined. This was an expansion period that occurred between 1949 and 1972 (Tong 1989). This is reflected in the age-sex population structure seen from the broader base which indicates a significant proportion of the young population (Azim 2002). Thus in 1971 and 1981, Brunei had a young population. Fertility rate then declined tremendously from 1973 to 1986 when the TFR was 5.46 in 1973, and down to 3.87 in 1981 and then 3.44 in 1986 (Neo 1989).

In 1971, the age structure showed a broader base (Azim 2002). This means the portion of population aged under five years old was large, accounting for about 16 per cent of the 1971 population, and this reflected a high fertility rate. As one of the consequences, the market and public services should cater to the needs of goods and services for this young generation. In 1981, the age structure indicated a change with a reduction in the proportion of this young population as fertility rate declined. The 1981 age structure remained an expansive base indicating high percentage of young population under five years old (see Figure 7.5). Fertility rate continued to decline; life expectancy increased (see Figure 7.6).

As seen in Figure 7.6, Brunei's TFR in 1970–75 was above Malaysia and Singapore, yet the decline in Brunei was faster than that of Malaysia. Thus, Brunei's TFR since then has been lower than Malaysia's TFR. The age structure has indicated the impact of the decline in fertility and mortality rates seen from narrower base of population pyramid to higher share of population at older ages.

Since 2005, Brunei has reached below replacement level when its TFR was below 2.1. Brunei currently has a very low fertility rate (1.6) accompanied by a declining number of births. The country is now undergoing its second demographic transition, with varying stages among districts and ethnic groups. It has been shifting from a very

FIGURE 7.5
Changing Age Structure: Brunei Darussalam, 1981, 2001, 2020 and 2035

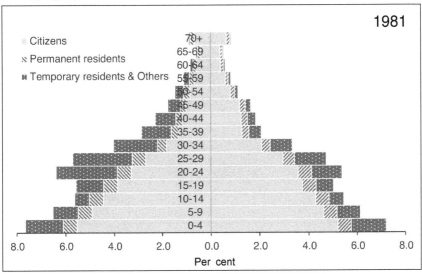

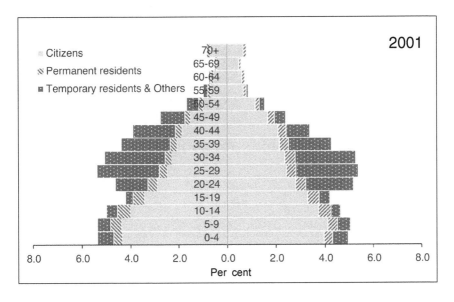

FIGURE 7.5 (continued)

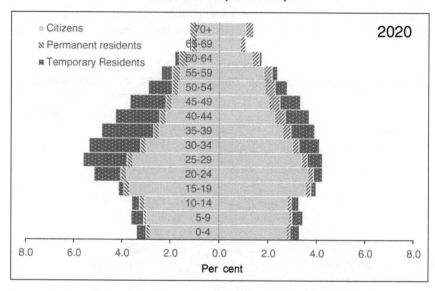

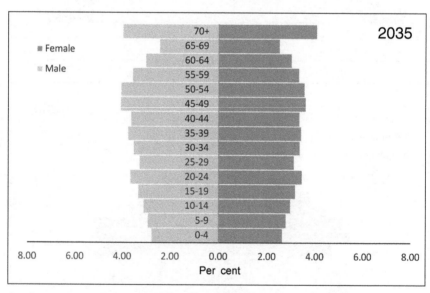

Sources: Compiled and calculated from the Department of Statistics (2020a) and United Nations (2019b).

FIGURE 7.6
Total Fertility Rate and Life Expectancy at Birth:
Brunei Darussalam, Malaysia and Singapore, 1970–2035

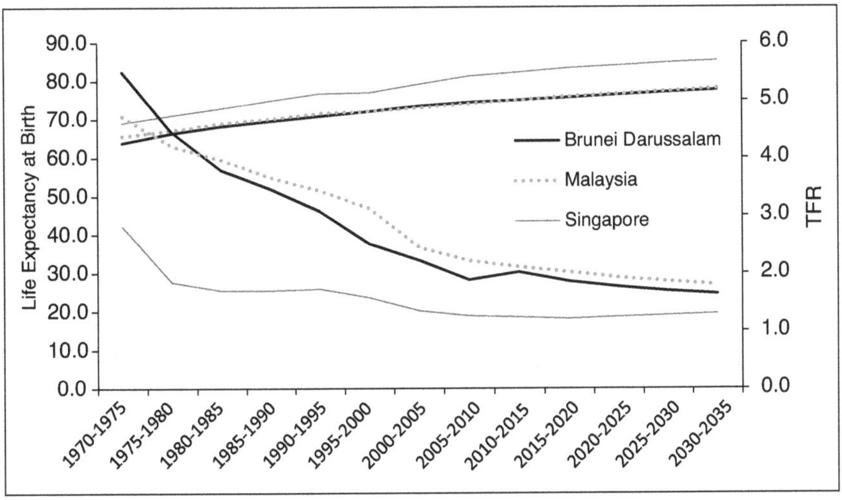

Source: Compiled from United Nations (2019b).

young age structure to the ageing structure. Table 7.2 shows that the number of registered live births was 6,680 babies in 2013 which steadily declined to 6,178 babies in 2019. The life births were mostly registered in Brunei-Muara district. In addition, the registered live births show that baby boys outnumbered baby girls, and the sex ratio at birth was also higher than 1.05. This high sex ratio at birth occurred particularly in Belait and Tutong districts. Different from some countries where the governments provide strong support to family planning programmes, Brunei's fertility decline is an example of "development as the best contraceptive" operating through improvement in women's education and their participation in the labour market (Ahmad 2018; Neo 1989). Due to high educational attainment especially among women, age at marriage among the locals (Bruneians and permanent residents) is high with the mean age at first marriage having always been above 22 years old during 1981–2011. More precisely, the mean age at first marriage among the local women was 24.3 years old in

TABLE 7.2
Number and Sex Ratio of Registered Live Births by District:
Brunei Darussalam, 2013–19

Districts	2013	2014	2015	2016	2017	2018	2019
	Number of Registered Births						
Brunei Darussalam	6,680	6,891	6,699	6,437	6,452	6,199	6,178
Brunei-Muara	5,506	5,654	5,446	5,349	5,440	5,218	5,251
Belait	976	1,020	1,031	894	963	902	862
Tutong	173	191	197	164	28	68	47
Temburong	25	26	25	30	21	11	18
	Sex Ratio of Registered Live Birth						
Brunei Darussalam	1.079	1.084	1.109	1.107	1.098	1.094	1.065
Brunei-Muara	1.082	1.089	1.103	1.098	1.084	1.080	1.047
Belait	1.081	1.073	1.148	1.165	1.159	1.163	1.177
Tutong	1.035	1.054	0.970	1.103	1.800	1.194	1.136
Temburong	0.786	0.733	2.571	1.143	1.100	2.667	1.000

Source: Compiled from the Department of Statistics (2020b).

1981 which steadily increased to 24.9 years in 1991 and 25.3 years in 2001. However, their mean age became younger (22.8 years old) in 2011. Yet, the mean age at first marriage among non-locals (temporary residents and others) was also younger than preceding years (22.5 years old in 2011 versus 25.4 years old in 2001). In contrast, men married at older ages, on average between two and three years older than women. Marriage at a younger age in 2011 was also seen among non-local men. With regards to ethnicity/race, mean age at first marriage increased in all groups for 1981–2001 and declined in the following decade. Chinese women have older mean age at first marriage than women of other groups (Malay and "Others"). The mean age at first marriage of Chinese women was 24.9 years in 2011 versus 22 years for Malay and others. The latest data shows that the overall age at first marriage in 2019 was 27.2 years old for males and 25.9 years old for females (Department of Statistics 2020b). This reflects a higher age for all ethnic groups.

In addition, Bruneians have expectedly lived for ten years longer. In 1970–75, life expectancy at birth was 63.9, increasing to 73.5 in 2000–5. This increasing trend is projected to reach 77.7 in 2030–35, indicating anticipated continuous improvement in the overall health of the population. This can be a result of better living conditions, better health facilities and care, sufficient knowledge of healthy lifestyle and nutrition. The provision of free medical and health services has very much helped in reducing the mortality rate and increasing life expectancy. Yet, the challenge remains in tackling non-communicable diseases such as cancer, heart disease and diabetes mellitus (Department of Statistics 2020b).

The smaller size of population aged below 15 years old indicates the impact of declined fertility rates on the size of population. In addition, the proportion of the older persons (population aged 60 years and above) is getting larger, accounting for 5.6 per cent in 2011 and increasing to 8.4 per cent in 2020. The United Nations projection shows that the percentage of older persons in Brunei will be 19.1 per cent in 2035 (United Nations 2019b). In other words, the ageing population in Brunei will accelerate in the next few decades. Population age structure in 2035 will be very different from the structures in 1971 and 1981. However, it should be noted that studies from other countries have shown that older persons, especially between 60 and 69 years old, are still capable to work (United Nations 2019b).

Another important factor of age structural transition is migration. Ananta and Arifin (2009) classified three patterns of ageing population considering the contribution of fertility and mortality on one hand and migration on the other hand. First is the "accelerated ageing population". Here the low fertility and mortality rates are accompanied by out-migration, resulting in an accelerated ageing process. This situation is seen in rural areas with unfavourable economic conditions, usually found in developing regions/areas with low fertility and mortality as well as high out-migration.

Second is the "slowed ageing population", usually found in rich regions. Fertility and mortality have been low for a long time resulting in a shortage of labour. Migration then changes the age structure. As the migrants are usually young, the influx of migrants slows down the ageing process. The age structure of this population would have been much older had there been an absence of in-migration.

The third is the "deferred ageing population", observed in regions with a long history of in-migrants. In this case, the emergence of ageing population is deferred by the long history of in-migration, usually consisting of mostly young, working-age population. Regions/countries with this pattern realize that without the in-migrants, they would have a rapid ageing population. Brunei is in this category. Its long history of migration has deferred the emerging ageing population in Brunei. The percentage of older persons was 4.3 per cent in 2001, rising to 8.4 per cent in 2019. However, excluding the temporary residents from the calculation, the percentage of local older persons was higher, 5.6 per cent and 10.1 per cent, respectively. In 2020, when the number of temporary residents declined, the percentage of older persons increased significantly to 10.0 per cent. Without them, the percentage would be even higher (11.8 per cent). The temporary residents do not grow old in this country (seen in Figure 7.5), while Bruneians remain and enjoy their old ages in the country. The rapid increase of ageing population has thus started, yet as Lesthaeghe (2010) argued, replacement migration cannot compensate ageing population. This may have important implications for the labour market and provision of services for the older persons, including retirement age, social security, culture and infrastructure. Facing the emergence of old population structure, Brunei should follow a life-course approach, which efforts to produce future independent, healthy and active older persons, and this should start from very young ages, even from embryos. In the meantime, the state has generously provided free healthcare, free education, no income tax, highly subsidized housing (if not free) and other programmes/policies. Then, as people live longer, higher retirement ages should be considered.

CHANGING RACE AND RELIGIOUS COMPOSITION

Racial Composition

Brunei is a small Malay Islamic sultanate and the Malay community accounts for the majority. Nonetheless, Brunei has a multi-ethnic population. Race in Brunei is often reported to consist of three groups: Malay, Chinese and Others. The Brunei Nationality Act 1961 defines the Malay group as consisting of seven ethnic groups, namely Brunei Malay, and six other groups (Belait, Bisaya, Dusun, Kedayan, Murut and Tutong). Brunei Malay is culturally and religiously similar to the Malay in West Malaysia who practise Malay culture and Islam (Loo 2009). Meanwhile, the other six groups are different in terms of religion, especially Tutong, Belait, Bisaya, Dusun and Murut who are not exclusively Muslim. They can be Christians or animists (Loo 2009). Kedayan is the closest to Brunei Malay, as both ethnic groups are Malay speaking groups and have a historically strong relationship (Maxwell 1996).

Although the Malays are found in Malaysia, Singapore and Indonesia, the definition of Malay is different in each of these countries. Race in Malaysia is broadly categorized into Bumiputera, Other Bumiputera and Other Malaysians (Nagaraj et al. 2015). Bumiputera includes Malay, Dusun, Murut and Iban ethnic groups. Other Bumiputera includes Chinese and Indian. Malay, as defined in Article 160 of the Constitution of Malaysia, refers to "a person who professes the religion of Islam, habitually speaks the Malay language, conforms to Malay custom..." (Nagaraj et al. 2015, p. 170).

As in Malaysia, Malay in Singapore is also defined by the state. Malays, as stated in Article 19B of the Constitution of the Republic of Singapore, are defined as "any person, whether of the Malay race or otherwise, who considers himself to be a member of the Malay community and who is generally accepted as a member of the Malay community by that community". Malay in the 2010 Singapore population census consisted of Malay, Javanese, Boyanese and Other Malays (Department of Statistics 2011).

Malay in Indonesia is also different; it is one of the many ethnic groups. In Indonesia, ethnicity is identified according to the perception of each individual and not defined by the state. The concept of ethnicity in Indonesia is very fluid. Javanese is the majority ethnic group in Indonesia, and Boyanese is another ethnic group in Indonesia. Dusun, Kedayan and Murut in Indonesia belong to the majority Kalimantan ethnic group known as Dayak, while Malay in Indonesia originated from some provinces in the Island of Sumatra. As shown in Ananta et al. (2015), Malay is the third largest ethnic group in Indonesia, accounting for 3.7 per cent in 2010, starkly in contrast to Javanese (40.1 per cent). Brunei Malay has some similarities with Indonesian Malay residing in Sumatra Island.

Racially, the Malays in Brunei, as the majority, accounted for 65.5 per cent in 1971. In its history, the Malays seem to be relatively stable at around 65 per cent of the Brunei population (see Figure 7.7), except in 1991 and 2001, with a slight increase. The Malay population grew by 3.4 per cent annually in 1971–81, and at relatively the same rate in the following decade. However, the rate began to grow slower since 1991, changing from 2.4 per cent annually in 1991–2001 to 1.5 per cent annually in 2001–11, and 1.7 per cent in 2011–19. The impact of COVID-19 is felt in all races as the latest figure showed a negative growth of Malays (–1.3 per cent) in 2019–20. This indicates that many Malay foreigners left the country and could not return as a consequence of the COVID-19.

Chinese in Brunei refers to all persons who belong to the Chinese ethnic group, while "Others" consists of the rest of the population not included in the Malay and Chinese groups, such as the South Asians, Filipinos, Europeans and other indigenous groups. The relative number

FIGURE 7.7
Racial Composition of Brunei Population, 1971–2020

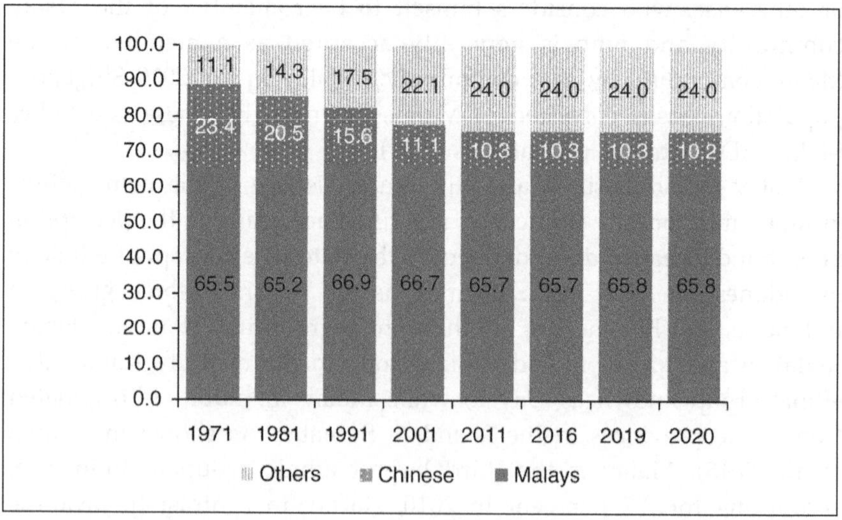

Source: Compiled and drawn various publications by the Department of Statistics.

of the Chinese has been significant, yet the share declined from 23.4 per cent in 1971 to 10.2 per cent in 2020. The number of Chinese grew at 2.1 per cent in 1971–81, and since then it grew very slowly (0.3 per cent in 1981–91) and even showed a negative growth rate (–0.9 per cent) in 1991–2001. The declining trend during this period is perhaps because of low fertility and out-migration among the Chinese. A reversed rate was shown in the following decades, with a positive rate of 0.9 per cent in 2001–11, 1.2 per cent in 2011–16 and 3.1 per cent in 2016–19. The impact of border closure also hit the Chinese whose size declined from 47.2 thousand in 2019 to 46.4 thousand persons in 2020. In other words, their number reduced by –1.7 per cent, faster than the Malays.

On the other hand, the number of "Others" increased the fastest in each period from 1971–2011, reflecting the influx of migrants into this country. In 1971–82, "Others" grew 6.1 per cent, almost double the Malays' growth rate. Over time, the growth rate has been declining, although it remains the highest rate in comparison to Malays and Chinese. "Others" grew 5.0 per cent in 1981–91 and 4.8 per cent in the following decade and grew much slower at 2.5 per cent in 2001–11. From 2011 to 2019, "Others" grew at the same rate as the Chinese. Similar to the Malay and Chinese, other ethnic groups did not grow but declined with –1.2 per cent in 2019–20.

Across districts, race composition shows a variation with the Malay being always the largest group (see Figure 7.8). In Brunei-Muara the race composition seems to remain constant, with the Malay constituting 66.0 and 68.0 per cent in 2011 and 2019 respectively; Chinese, about 10.0 per cent (2011–19); and "Others" between 23.0 and 24.0 per cent. On the other hand, Belait shows a dynamic race composition, where the percentage of Chinese declined significantly from 2011 to 2016, while Malay increased and "Others" declined. This is in contrast to two other districts (Tutong and Temburong), where the percentage of Chinese increased quite significantly during 2011–16, with a decline in Malay in Tutong and a decline in "Others" in Temburong. This may indicate internal migration within the country during 2011–16. This pattern deserves further study. The pattern of ethnic composition remained stable in all districts in 2016–20.

FIGURE 7.8
Racial Composition by Region, 2011–20

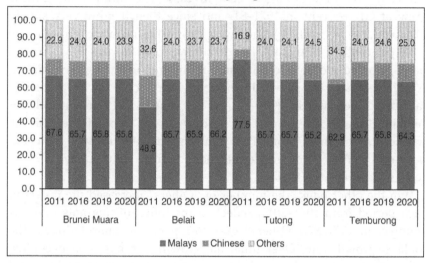

Source: Compiled and drawn from various publications by the Department of Statistics.

Religious Composition

Islam is the official religion and is embraced by the majority of the population. In 1971, Muslims accounted for 62.2 per cent, and steadily increased and reached 80.9 per cent in 2016. In contrast, Buddhists and Other religions (including free-thinkers, Hindus, Sikhs, Bahais, or undeclared) have been declining (see Figure 7.9) significantly, partly because of a faster decline in fertility rate among non-Muslims, as shown from the shape of age-sex population structure (see Figure 7.10). In particular, a decline in fertility among non-Muslims was seen from the declining percentage for each age group younger than 25 years old. This indicated the decline in fertility rate among non-Muslims since the late 1990s. The size and proportion of the young population among Christians, Others and Buddhists are much smaller than the Muslims. Fertility rate among Buddhists has indicated a decline even before the 1990s. Related to fertility and reproduction, interethnic-religious marriage is another possible explanation. Under MIB national philosophy, interethnic or interreligious marriage is seen as a process of assimilation to the notions of becoming Malay, *Masuk Melayu* or *Masuk Islam* (Hoon and Sahrifulhafiz 2021).

Another possible reason is religious conversion to Islam. As mentioned by Asiyah az-Zahra (2011), religious conversion to Islam in Brunei is not a new phenomenon and such conversion continues to increase. The Centre for Islamic Mission (Pusat Da'wah Islamiah) established in 1985 has emerged as a very active institution in disseminating Islamic knowledge through various channels such as television, radio, publication and public talks. This centre has been successful and conversion to Islam has been significant. Awg Asbol and Mansurnoor (2009) stated that the centre is "primarily to pursue internal Islamization and the spread of Islamic teaching to other segments of society".

It has been reported that the number of people having shifted to Islam as their new faith reached 15,697 between 1985 and May 2017.[5] According to the Islamic Dakwah Centre's statistics reported in Department of Statistics (2020a), the number of new converts was 2,586 persons between 2015 and 2020 with a declining trend seen up to 2019 from 513 people in 2015 to 472 people in 2016, and further declined in the following years: 409 people in 2017, 404 people in

FIGURE 7.9
Religious Composition of Brunei Population, 1971–2016

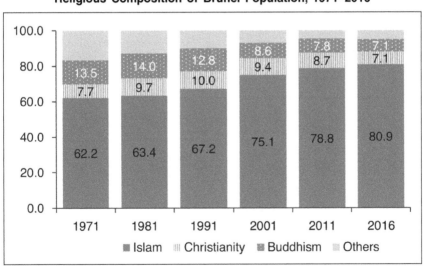

Notes: Data for 2019 and 2020 are not available.
Source: Compiled and drawn from various publications by the Department of Statistics.

FIGURE 7.10
Population Pyramid by Religion: Brunei Darussalam, 2016

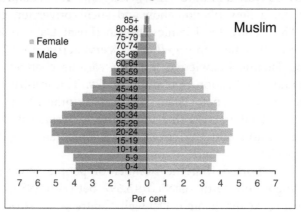

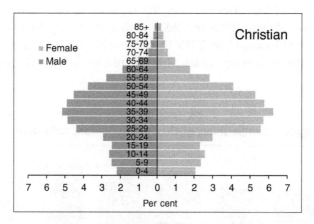

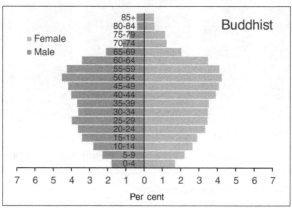

FIGURE 7.10 (continued)

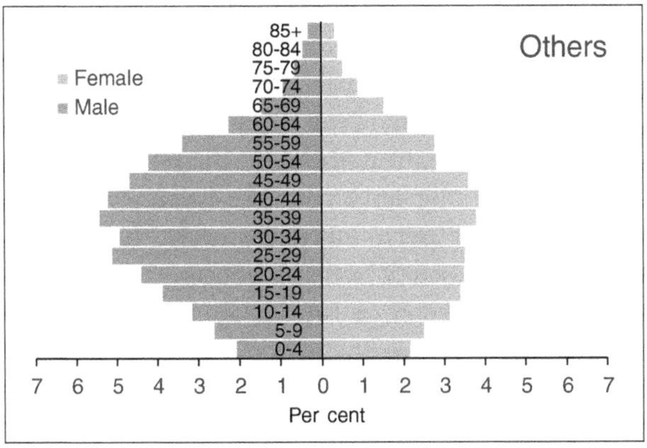

Source: Compiled and drawn from various publications by the Department of Statistics.

2018 and 349 people in 2019. The number increased to 436 people in 2020. Furthermore, it has also been reported that the new converts were mostly indigenous Malays with Dusun ethnics having the highest number of converts from 2015 to 2020. The second largest converts were Ibans, followed by the Filipinos and Chinese. As reported by RTB News,[6] these facts showed "positive effects toward the needs of the Bruneian constitution where Islam is the official religion of the nation".

CONCLUSION

The population of Brunei has been changing its faces due to the completion of its demographic transition and the start of the second demographic transition since 2005. In almost fifty years, 1971–2019, its size, age-sex-racial-religious composition and geographical distribution have been changing in tandem with its growing prosperity. Although the Sultanate has the smallest population in Southeast Asia, the population more than tripled from 136.3 thousand persons in 1971 to 459.5 thousand persons with relatively higher income in 2019. The growth rate of population is contributed more by migration than through natural growth rate. Moreover, Brunei has successfully lowered fertility rate through their people-centred national development. The closure of international borders around the world due to the highly infectious COVID-19 pandemic has brought about depopulation in Brunei for the first time in its history.

Among Southeast Asian countries, the Brunei population is unique as it has always been masculine. As a receiving migrant country, Brunei has experienced the masculinization of its population, contributed mainly by the influx of migrants who are mostly male. On the other hand, the population of permanent residents has been feminized. Brunei is a patriarchal society where women are liberated to attain higher education. The women of Brunei are seen to be working their way up to higher positions in the workforce.

Racially, Brunei remains predominantly Malay. Additionally, Brunei is becoming more Muslim predominant. Furthermore, its population has been increasingly concentrated in the more advanced district, Brunei-Muara, where the capital is located. As a commercial district, other public facilities such as ports, oil and gas facilities and marketing offices, and tourist attractions are located. Yet, the future will be different when the connection between the "used-to-be isolated" district of Temburong and other districts is heightened by the newly-built bridge. There will possibly be a shift in urban planning, economic planning and development moving away from the most densely populated area of Brunei-Muara. As the least populous districts, Temburong and Tutong may be selected for targeted industrial development. In addition, mobility within the country will increase and mobility across countries, especially Sarawak and Sabah, Malaysia will also accelerate in the next few decades when COVID-19 is over. In short, understanding population dynamics provides an understanding and recognition of the changing faces of the Brunei population in the past decades.

Moving forward, as in many other countries, the Brunei population is experiencing an age-structural transition from young to old amidst the presence of migration because most migrants are not retiring in this country. Although Brunei follows a deferred ageing process, ultimately by 2035, the Brunei population will have an old structure, especially with the success in reducing reliance on non-locals. This will influence socio-economic development and bring about the importance of social protection, pension system and caregiving. In contrast to many Southeast Asian countries, Brunei has been rich before its population becomes old. Increasing women participation in the labour market, delaying retirement age, moving toward automation, using robotic technology and artificial intelligence are other important steps to sustain the economy in the wake of an ageing population.

The population trends discussed here may be accompanying the journey toward *Wawasan* Brunei 2035 (Brunei Vision 2035) to achieve "a nation with a well-educated, highly skilled and accomplished people as measured by the highest international standard, enjoying a high quality of life among the top ten countries in the world, and having a dynamic and resilient economy which is ranked among the world's top ten countries in terms of per capita income" (Prime Minister's Office 2012, p. xxix).

NOTES

1. Brunei joined ASEAN in January 1984 as the sixth member. The five original members include Indonesia, Malaysia, Philippines, Singapore and Thailand. http://www.mfa.gov.bn/Pages/association-of-southeast-asian-nation-(asean).aspx.
2. The concept of *de-jure* population refers to the persons who have resided in Brunei for at least six months according to the usual place of residence. This concept has been used until now in the series of population survey or census (Department of Statistics 2018).
3. The 1991 population census is the first census since its independence.
4. It is mentioned that the number of foreign-born were 100,587 out of 393,372 people in 2011.
5. http://www.rtbnews.rtb.gov.bn/Lists/News/DispForm.aspx?ID=2213&ContentTypeId=0x0100AA1BCCD118BC9648BD0175EF8A615DAA.
6. http://www.rtbnews.rtb.gov.bn/Lists/News/DispForm.aspx?ID=2213&ContentTypeId=0x0100AA1BCCD118BC9648BD0175EF8A615DAA.

REFERENCES

Ahmad, Norainie. 2018. "Attitudes Towards Family Formation Among Young Adults in Brunei Darussalam". *Pakistan Journal of Women's Studies: Alam-e-Niswan* 25, no. 1: 15–34.

Ananta, Aris, and Evi Nurvidya Arifin. 2009. "Older Persons in Southeast Asia: From Liability to Asset". In *Older Persons in Southeast Asia: An Emerging Asset*, edited by Evi Nurvidya Arifin, and Aris Ananta. Singapore: Institute of Southeast Asian Studies.

Ananta, Aris, Evi Nurvidya Arifin, M. Sairi Hasbullah, Nur Budi Handayani, and Agus Pramono. 2015. *Demography of Indonesia's Ethnicity*. Singapore: Institute of Southeast Asian Studies.

Asiyah az-Zahra Ahmad Kumpoh. 2011. "Conversion to Islam: The Case of the Dusun Ethnic Group in Brunei Darussalam". PhD dissertation, Department of Sociology, University of Leicester, United Kingdom.

Awg Asbol bin Haji Mail, Haji, and Iik Arifin Mansurnoor. 2009. "Education, Religious Authority and Moderation: Muslim Scholars-Cum-Leaders in Brunei Darussalam". *TAWARIKH: International Journal for Historical Studies* 1, no. 1: 15–56.

Azim, Parvez. 2002. "The Ageing Population of Brunei Darussalam: Trends and Economic Consequences". *Asia-Pacific Population Journal* 17, no. 1: 39–54.

Department of Statistics. 2011. *Census of Population 2010 Statistical Release 1: Demographic Characteristics, Education, Language and Religion*. Singapore: Department of Statistics, Ministry of Trade and Industry.

——. 2012. *Population and Housing Census Report 2011: Demographic Characteristics*. Bandar Seri Begawan: Department of Statistics, Department of Economic Planning and Statistics (DEPS), Ministry of Finance and Economy.

——. 2013. *Population and Housing Census Update Report 2011: Demographic Characteristics*. Bandar Seri Begawan: Department of Statistics, Department of Economic Planning and Statistics (DEPS), Ministry of Finance and Economy.

——. 2014. *Population and Housing Census Report 2011: Economic Activity Characteristics*. Bandar Seri Begawan: Department of Statistics, Department of Economic Planning and Statistics (DEPS), Ministry of Finance and Economy.

——. 2018. *Population and Housing Census Update Final Report 2016*. Bandar Seri Begawan: Department of Statistics, Department of Economic Planning and Statistics (DEPS), Ministry of Finance and Economy.

——. 2020a. *Brunei Darussalam Statistical Yearbook 2019*. Bandar Seri Begawan: Department of Statistics, Department of Economic Planning and Statistics (DEPS), Ministry of Finance and Economy.

——. 2020b. *Brunei Darussalam Vital Statistics 2019*. Bandar Seri Begawan: Department of Statistics, Department of Economic Planning and Statistics (DEPS), Ministry of Finance and Economy.

——. 2021. *Report of the Mid-year Population Estimates 2020*. Bandar Seri Begawan: Department of Statistics, Department of Economic Planning and Statistics (DEPS), Ministry of Finance and Economy.

GBD 2019 Demographics Collaborators. 2020. "Global Age-Sex-Specific Fertility, Mortality, Healthy Life Expectancy (HALE), and Population Estimates in 204 Countries and Territories, 1950–2019: A Comprehensive Demographic

Analysis for the Global Burden of Disease Study 2019". *Lancet* 396, no. 10258: 1160–1203.

Hobbs, Frank. 2004. "Age and Sex Composition". In *The Methods and Materials of Demography*, edited by Jacob S. Siegel, and David A. Swanson, pp. 125–73. London: Elsevier Academic Press.

Islam, Saiful, Nurul Faizah Salleh, and Siti Nooraini Sabli. 2019. "Influence of Exchange Rate on Cross-Border Shopping of Bruneians in Malaysia". *Journal of Asian Business and Economic Studies* 26, special issue 01: 74–92.

Koh, Sin Yee. 2019. "Challenges and Opportunities of Comparative Urbanism: The Case of Brunei-Miri and Singapore-Iskandar Malaysia". In *Routledge Handbook of Urbanization in Southeast Asia*, edited by R. Padawangi, pp. 101–14. London: Routledge.

Lesthaeghe, Ron. 2010. "The Unfolding Story of the Second Demographic Transition". *Population and Development Review* 36, no. 2: 211–51.

Loo, Seng Piew. 2009. "Ethnicity and Educational Policies in Malaysia and Brunei Darussalam". *SA-eDUC JOURNAL* 6, no. 2: 146–57.

Maxwell, Allen R. 1996. "The Place of the Kadayan in Traditional Brunei Society". *South East Asia Research* 4, no. 2: 157–96.

Messner, Steven F., and Robert J. Sampson. 1991. "The Sex Ratio, Family Disruption, and Rates of Violent Crime: The Paradox of Demographic Structure". *Social Forces* 69, no. 3: 693–713.

Ministry of Finance and Economy. 2020. *Towards a Dynamics and Sustainable Economy: Economic Blueprint for Brunei Darussalam*. Brunei Darussalam: Ministry of Finance and Economy.

Poston, Dudley L., Jr., and Leon F. Bouvier. 2010. *An Introduction to Demography*. Cambridge: Cambridge University Press.

Prime Minister's Office. 2012. *Tenth National Development Plan (2012–2017) Brunei Darussalam*. Brunei Darussalam: Department of Economic Planning and Development, Prime Minister's Office. http://www.depd.gov.bn/DEPD%20Documents%20Library/NDP/RKN%20English%20as%20of%2011.12.12.pdf (accessed 3 February 2021).

Schacht, Ryan, Kristin Liv Rauch, and Monique Borgerhoff Mulder. 2014. "Too Many Men: The Violence Problem?" *Trends in Ecology & Evolution* 29, no. 4: 214–22.

Schacht, Ryan, and Monique Borgerhoff Mulder. 2015. "Sex Ratio Effects on Reproductive Strategies in Humans". *R. Soc. open sci.* 2: 140402.

Spoorenberg, Thomas. 2016. "On the Masculinization of Population: The Contribution of Demographic Development: A Look at Sex Ratios in Sweden over 250 Years". *Demographic Research* 34, article 37. https://www.demographic-research.org/volumes/vol34/37/34-37.pdf (accessed 5 February 2021).

Tong, Niew Shong. 1989. *Demographic Trends in Negara Brunei Darussalam*. Brunei Darussalam: Educational Technology Centre, Universiti Brunei Darussalam.

———. 1994. "Changing Economic Activities of the Chinese in Negara Brunei Darussalam". Paper presented at the International Conference on the Last Half Century of Chinese Overseas (1945–1994): Comparative Perspectives, The University of Hong Kong, 19–21 December 1994.

Ullah, AKM Ahsan, and Asiyah Az-Zahra Ahmad Kumpoh. 2019. "Diaspora Community in Brunei: Culture, Ethnicity and Integration". *Diaspora Studies* 12, no. 1: 14–33.

United Nations, Department of Economic and Social Affairs, Population Division. 2019a. *International Migration 2019: Report* (ST/ESA/SER.A/438).

———. 2019b. *World Population Prospects 2019*, Online Edition.

8

LEARNING AS BECOMING BRUNEI 2035: SHIFTING THE NATURE AND SCOPE OF TECHNICAL AND VOCATIONAL EDUCATION AND TRAINING

Adeline Yuen Sze Goh

PREAMBLE: HIGHER SKILLED AND MOTIVATED WORKFORCE FOR BRUNEI 2035

The acceleration of the inevitable disruptive changes to work due to rapid technological advancements will profoundly impact the employment landscape over the coming years for many countries, including Brunei. With such an evolving employment landscape, it would seem challenging to prepare workers for jobs that do not yet exist. These changes are not only non-linear and unpredictable, but are also imminent. The significant impact on jobs could range from job creation to job displacement and heightened labour productivity to widening skills gaps. One of the apparent signs of the changing employment landscape is many in-demand occupations that exist now did not exist several years ago. According to the World Economic Forum (2016), approximately 65 per cent of today's children will find themselves working in jobs that do not exist now. This salient statement has urgent implications on future jobs which will require a new set of technical and soft skills.

Advances in digitalization could lead to revolutionary changes such as a significant disruption to the labour market, where many sectors will face chronic unemployment due to the replacement of routine human jobs involving repetitive and regimented tasks. On the other hand, these revolutionary changes could also present unprecedented business opportunities, job creation and sustainable economic growth (Chui, Manyika and Miremadi 2016; Frey and Osborne 2017; OECD 2016). These changes raise new challenges for i) the preparation of future higher skilled and motivated workforce through education and training, and ii) maintaining the employability of the existing workforce through continuing education and workplace learning, in order to upskill or reskill to remain relevant to the needs of the labour market.

The purpose of this chapter is to illuminate the contribution of Brunei's Technical and Vocational Education and Training (TVET) in promoting vocational competence of the future and existing workforce in realizing *Wawasan* 2035. The initial part of the chapter will describe the concept of "vocational education and training" and its significant position within Brunei's education system. The subsequent section provides an overview of the developments focusing on key milestones of Brunei's TVET landscape. The chapter will present and examine various aspects of the current provisions offered by Brunei's TVET in response to the changes in the labour market. The final section discusses suggestions for future TVET developments and initiatives to prepare our Bruneian workforce for the years to come. Against this backdrop, one critical question which drives this chapter is: "With an unchartered digital future, how can we prepare our existing and future workforce in realizing *Wawasan* 2035 through TVET?"

TECHNICAL AND VOCATIONAL EDUCATION AND TRAINING

Technical and Vocational Education and Training (TVET) can play an important role in the socio-economic development in many countries. It should be oriented towards preparing young adults with relevant knowledge, skills and competencies for work and life through an overall lifelong learning framework (UNESCO 2015). Increasingly, many countries recognize that high-quality vocational education and training can contribute to economic development and international competitiveness (OECD 2015). This contribution becomes imminent when the world is experiencing unprecedented impacts due to global disruptions like the Fourth Industrial Revolution (IR 4.0). These disruptions are driving demand for skilled labour and spurring an upgrading of skills across the economies. Hence, despite being marginalized in the past, TVET has gradually gained its prominence and is recurrently cited in many countries' human resource development policy discussions. On a practical level, TVET provides an alternative pathway that attracts a diverse range of students who seek technical skills to enter the labour market and students who prefer to progress to higher education. TVET also provides opportunities for adults who wish to re-enter the labour market or develop their skills further to increase their employability.

The field of TVET has changed throughout history, which has always been dependent on the demands of the labour market and the structure of the economy it serves. Different terms to describe TVET are used in different countries such as Career and Technical Education in the United States; Further Education in the United Kingdom, and Technical and Vocational Education (TVET) in ASEAN countries. For the purpose of this chapter, TVET terminology is used. One recurrent theme emerging from these definitions point to the training and skills development as part of a country's lifelong learning agenda.

Technical and vocational education and training is defined as:

> ...comprising education, training and skills development relating to a wide range of occupational fields, production, services and livelihoods. TVET, as part of *lifelong learning*, can take place at secondary, post-secondary and tertiary levels and includes work-based learning and continuing training and professional development which may lead to

qualifications. TVET also includes a wide range of skills development opportunities attuned to national and local contexts. Learning to learn, the development of literacy and numeracy skills, transversal skills and citizenship skills are integral components of TVET. [italics added by author] (UNESCO-UNEVOC 2015)

The Organisation for Economic Cooperation and Development (OECD) defines vocational education and training programmes as:

...programmes [that] is mainly designed to help participants acquire the practical skills, know-how and understanding necessary for employment in a particular occupation or trade, or class of occupations or trades... includes apprenticeship programmes that involve concurrent school-based and work-based training, and programmes that involve alternating periods of attendance at educational institutions and participation in work-based training. (OECD 2010, p. 2)

TVET can be categorized into two: initial and continuing. Initial TVET includes programmes mainly designed for and used by young people at the beginning of their careers and commonly before entering the labour market. It includes many upper secondary and tertiary programmes. Continuing TVET includes enterprise training of employees and training explicitly provided for those who have lost their jobs (OECD 2010). Following this categorization, there is an acknowledgement that TVET can be represented at different qualification levels and across different occupational structures, and with different training programmes. These programmes can be formal, non-formal or informal. Formal programme is a structured training programme which leads to a recognized qualification and is accredited. Non-formal programme is a structured training programme which does not lead to a recognized qualification and is not accredited. Informal programme describes learning resulting from daily activities related to work, family or leisure (UNESCO-UNEVOC 2011). TVET recognizes learning before entry to the labour market and learning on the job are parts of an individual's lifelong learning journey (Goh 2015). These days, workers learn many workplace skills through informal or formal training, as skill requirements are volatile and keep on changing due to rapid technological change. An example is IR 4.0, as mentioned earlier.

In Brunei, TVET offers a wide range of programmes involving formal, informal or non-formal learning. One of the key purposes of these programmes is to serve Brunei's future human resource needs, in view of Brunei's long-term development plan—Brunei's 2035 Vision or *Wawasan* Brunei 2035, which aims to create a nation that is widely recognized for its world-class education and highly educated and skilled workforce, high quality of life, and dynamic and sustainable economy by 2035. Brunei's vision of a diversified, knowledge-based economy recognizes the importance of a quality education system to compete in an increasingly integrated global market. Amongst several other aims (MOE 2013), a new education system launched in 2009 aims to fulfil the needs and challenges of the social and economic development of the twenty-first century. The next section presents a brief introduction of Brunei's education system and how TVET has been integrated into mainstream education in the endeavour to embrace *Wawasan* 2035.

BRUNEI'S EDUCATION SYSTEM

The vision of the Ministry of Education (MOE) of Brunei is "Quality Education, Dynamic Nation" which guides its mission to provide holistic education to achieve the fullest potential by providing quality education to all. This vision aims to realize the nation's aspirations and provide equitable access to education. This vision also aims to equip the country's future generation with values inherent in the Malay Islamic Monarchy (MIB) or *Melayu Islam Beraja* philosophy together with twenty-first-century skills. The Ministry of Education has a policy of providing a minimum of twelve years of education: seven years in primary education that is inclusive of one year in pre-school, and five years in secondary education. As Brunei places high importance on education, it is made mandatory and accessible for every citizen to have the opportunity to receive a quality basic twelve-years education (MOE 2013). With support from the government in financial subsistence, free schooling is made available for all levels including TVET. Scholarships are given to Bruneian nationals enrolled at TVET and they are also provided with allowances (MOE 2020, p. 69).

In response to Brunei's 2035 Vision, the national education system was restructured in 2009, now known as the National Education System for the 21st Century or *Sistem Pendidikan Negara Abad ke-21* (SPN 21) (see Figure 8.1). It was imperative for Brunei to introduce this new national education system in order to develop individuals who are competitive and remain relevant in a globalized world. There are three key changes made to the national education system, which are education structure, curriculum and assessment, and the repositioning of technical and vocational education in the whole education system. All these three changes are interrelated but in view of this chapter's scope, changes to TVET system are focused on in this chapter.

FIGURE 8.1
Brunei's National Education System

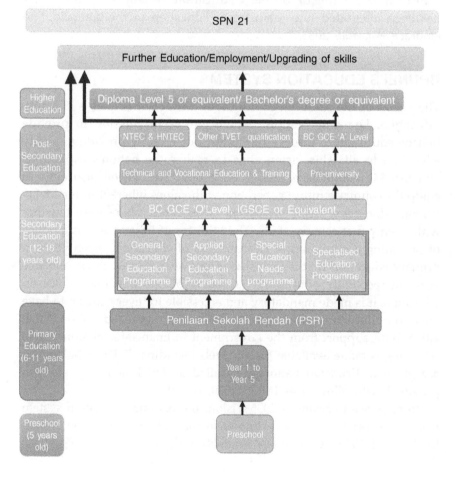

Technical and Vocational Education and Training (TVET) as Part of the National Education System

The move to reposition TVET within the national education system provides an increase in students' access and participation in post-secondary education, which aims to produce graduates equipped with the relevant and marketable skills needed to be employable in the labour market. The technical and vocational education and training provides crucial and alternative pathways to develop competencies required for employment in the labour market. Given its importance in contributing to Brunei's skilled workforce and its potential in reducing unemployment, the integration of TVET is key to SPN 21 and Brunei's Vision 2035. In line with SPN 21, TVET is offered at different educational levels: secondary level, post-secondary level and higher education level. The range of TVET programmes at these different levels will be discussed in detail in the following sections.

DEVELOPMENT OF TECHNICAL AND VOCATIONAL EDUCATION IN BRUNEI

In many countries, Technical and Vocational Education and Training (TVET) is instrumental in each country's workforce development. In Brunei, TVET makes a significant contribution to skilling the workforce in view of its vision of a diversified economy. However, the development of TVET in Brunei is relatively recent compared to other countries. Based on the 1959 Baki-Chang report, practical and technical subjects were recommended to be introduced in the school curriculum. This recommendation was triggered by the economic progression in the late 1950s when local skilled workforce was required to work in different occupation sectors in the country (Jumat 1989).

Since then, several key milestones have marked significant progress in TVET development. These milestones, as you might interpret, come in tandem with the economic development of the country. Formal vocational training began in 1970 at two trade schools: Sultan Saiful Rijal Building Trade School and Jefri Bolkiah Engineering Trade School. These establishments marked the beginning of a separate TVET system under the jurisdiction of the organizer of technical education, a section of the then education department. These schools offered UK-based craft level programmes catered to the needs of Form Three (now known as Year 9) secondary school leavers. Subsequently, in 1977, the UK-based technician level programmes were introduced to cater to the needs of Form Five (now known as Year 11) secondary school leavers. In the same year, Brunei Technical Training Centre was established. The TVET system continued to expand, and many more TVET institutions were introduced to meet the country's workforce demands. In 1982, the two trade schools were upgraded to college level; Sultan Saiful Rijal Technical College and Jefri Bolkiah Engineering College, which offered many UK-based Business and Technology Education Council (BTEC) technician level programmes to further cater to the needs of Form Five secondary school leavers. Later in 1986, the mechanical training centre, or commonly known to many as Pusat Latihan Mekanik (PLM), was set up to offer a programme in heavy vehicle machinery mechanics. In the same year, two institutions were established namely, Institut Teknologi Brunei (ITB) which offered higher technician level programmes and Pengiran Anak Puteri Rashidah Sa'adatul Bolkiah Nursing College offering programmes in the field of nursing. Two more vocational colleges, Nakhoda Ragam Vocational School and Sultan Bolkiah Vocational School were built in 1992 and 1995 respectively to offer trade-level programmes. The diversification of programmes provided opportunities for students to enrol in different level qualifications and played a crucial role in ensuring that TVET could meet labour market needs in Brunei.

The expansion of TVET system continues with many more institutions being built to meet the workforce requirements. In an attempt to move away from dependence on foreign accrediting bodies based in the UK, the establishment of a vocational programme development centre which is now known as the programme development section of Institute Brunei of Technical Education (IBTE) was established to develop locally accredited programmes. In support of these programmes, the Brunei Darussalam Technical and Vocational Education Council (BDTVEC) was formed in 1991 and formally oversees the accreditation and awarding of qualifications. This shift from foreign to local accreditation provided flexibility and autonomy to develop the locally trained workforce to meet the specific demand of the local economy. Given the changing demographic situation and rapid expansion and diversification of local economic and industrial developments, this move was imperative (Jamil 2000). Hence, there was a dire need of expanding the number and range of programmes offered.

Due to the growing emphasis on TVET in meeting the country's workforce requirements, a separate department of technical education was formed within the Ministry of Education in 1993. Recognizing the importance of learning on the job, the Department of Technical Education expanded its training options by offering a dual system apprenticeship scheme. This dual system apprenticeship scheme integrates training on-the-job at a designated company and off-the-job at a vocational institution. The Apprenticeship and Trade Testing Section was formed in 1995 which was then upgraded to Industrial Training Development Division in 2009. In 1996, two establishments, namely the Youth Development Centre (PPB) and Navy Technical Training School (NTTS) were formed and operated by the Ministry of Culture, Youth and Sports and the Royal Brunei Armed Forces respectively.

Beyond the public TVET institutions, private formal higher education institutions were also established to contribute to the country's human resource development such as Kolej International Graduate Studies (KIGS), Laksamana College of Business (LCB), Kemuda Institute (KI), Cosmopolitan College of Commerce and Technology (CCCT), Micronet International College, BICPA-FTMS Accountancy Academy in early years of the 2000s. These private TVET providers offer programmes mainly in business, information technology and film and visual arts.

In 2005, the Business School was formed to offer business-related programmes, and in 2006, Wasan Vocational School was formed to cater to students who intend to work in the agricultural sector. Students can access TVET programmes at higher education institutions such as Universiti Teknologi Brunei (UTB), previously known as ITB, and Politeknik Brunei (PB) that was established in 2012. Both of these higher education institutions are aimed to contribute and accelerate human resource development in view of Brunei's Vision 2035.

In 2014, Brunei Maritime Academy (BMA) was established to offer a range of competency-based qualifications in maritime. In the same year, we saw the transformation of the TVET system leading to the establishment of the Institute of Brunei Technical Education (IBTE). In addressing the country's socio-economic demands within a globalized competitive society, this transformation is of paramount importance and deemed necessary to produce a skilled and knowledgeable workforce for a competitive knowledge-based economy (IBTE 2013a). The system also acknowledges the importance of being responsive and relevant to the changes in the labour market. Hence, there is a need to strengthen cooperation between technical education providers and stakeholders. This move is to ensure that students are trained and developed with the relevant industrial skills bases. In 2017, the Centre of Capacity Building or *Pusat Pembangunan Kapasiti* (PPK), a multi-programme vocational skills training centre under the jurisdiction of the Ministry of Energy (ME) was formed to develop vocational skills training and professionalization of skilled labour for local youth. In line with previous roles of vocational and training education, PPK collaborated with the industry in offering industry-driven skills training. Mahakarya Institute of the Arts Asia, a private TVET provider that offers programmes in film and screen, was established in 2019.

CONTRIBUTION OF TVET TO SKILLING BRUNEI'S WORKFORCE

Over fifty years, TVET has been instrumental to Brunei's socio-economic development by addressing the labour market demands. For the past three years in Brunei, up to 15 per cent of the labour workforce is made up of technical and vocational graduates (Department of Statistics 2017, 2018, 2019). This section highlights the contribution of TVET to skilling Brunei's workforce through the current TVET provisions.

Current TVET Provisions

The 2007 restructuring of the national education system to SPN 21 had brought about significant changes to the TVET system. This was deemed essential to produce highly skilled people. In Figure 8.2, we can see the shift in TVET provisions to broadly prepare the Bruneian youth to meet the changing socio-economic demands in the twenty-first century. A three-tier qualification TVET system was introduced in place of the pre-SPN 21 framework. This system provides multiple pathways, which increase students' access to participation in higher education and create a more dynamic TVET system (MOE 2013).

FIGURE 8.2
Changes in TVET System: Pre-SPN 21 and Post-SPN 21

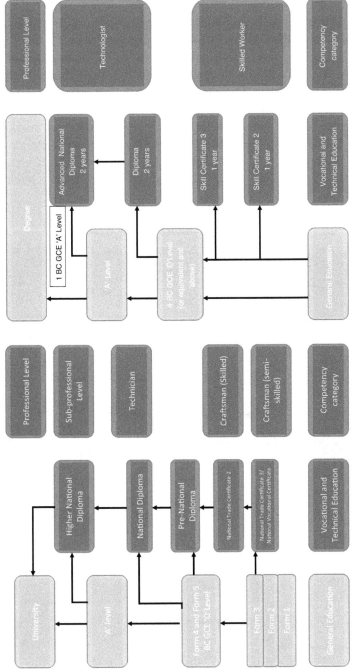

Another major review of the TVET system (see Figure 8.3) was done in 2012 to evaluate its relevancy and responsiveness to the demands of the industry. Considering the labour market priorities and students' access to participate in TVET, a transformation plan of the TVET system was implemented. Through this initiative, wider opportunities have been made available for post-secondary school students, who have an inclination for technical subjects to pursue TVET training, in the view of being employed in the labour market. In the past, TVET was perceived as inferior compared to general or academic education. The transformation serves as a key step in changing the societal mindset about TVET. The transformed TVET system ensures

FIGURE 8.3
Transformation of TVET System

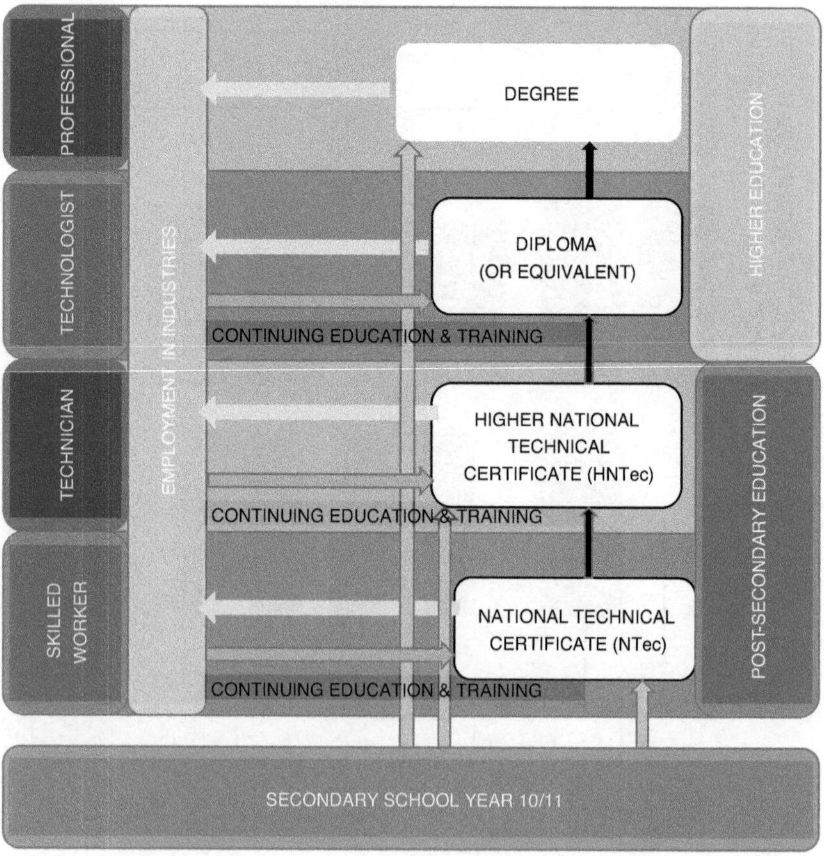

multiple pathways with clear progression opportunities for students to produce a highly skilled human resource to support the nation's economic development (IBTE 2013a).

Initial Training Programmes

One of the central roles of TVET in Brunei is to provide training for new entrants to the labour market, particularly young people. As shown in the previous section, TVET provides an alternative progression pathway for post-secondary school leavers who are not interested in pursuing higher education level education, to the labour market. There are several TVET providers in Brunei, which can either be public or private institutions under the purview of the Ministry of Education. These TVET institutions offer various training programmes relevant to the needs of the industries and occupations listed on the Brunei Darussalam Standard Industrial Classification (BDSIC) 2011. These programmes can be formal, which lead to a qualification upon completion and can be off-the-job training for the apprentices.

TVET programmes are offered at different educational levels; secondary education, post-secondary level and higher education level. Various TVET programmes are offered and can be categorized into different competency levels, which correspond to the different Brunei Darussalam Qualification Framework (BDQF) levels.

In the secondary education level, students are channelled to Business and Technology Education Council (BTEC) vocational programmes after undergoing the Student Progress Assessment (SPA) at the end of Year 8 of their secondary education. These vocational programmes, which primarily focus on practical skills, are catered for students who are vocational oriented. Secondary schools offer a few training levels such as BTEC levels 1, 2 and 3 and recently a new BTEC +5 was introduced.

Programmes offered at the post-secondary level of training leads to:

1. Industrial Skills Qualification (ISQ), a programme offered in collaboration with Registered Training organizations from the industries to prepare workers at artisan level,
2. National Technical Education Certificate or NTec to prepare workers at the skilled level, and
3. Higher National Technical Education Certificate or HNTec to prepare workers at the technician level.

One of the central focus of the shift from the previous SPN 21 TVET system to this new transformed TVET system is skills development through the use of a competency-based training framework. Recently, iSkill, a new qualification programme, was launched in August 2020. iSkill was developed by the Ministry of Education, with close collaboration between the relevant industry with the support of the Manpower Industry Steering Committee Working Group (Energy) and IBTE (Kon 2020). This iSkill is a rebranding and improvement of the programmes previously offered by the Centre of Capacity Building or known as *Pusat Pembangunan Kapasiti* (PPK). This programme was rigorously reviewed to match and align industry requirements and the country's local workforce's expectations, where individuals are provided with a pathway to develop their career in the relevant skill pools.

IBTE is the main provider for TVET programmes at the post-secondary level and manages nine schools; School of Agrotechnology and Applied Sciences, School of Aviation, School of Business, School of Building Technology Services, School of Hospitality and Tourism, School of Information and Communication Technology, School of Energy and Engineering Central, School of Energy and Engineering Satellite and Brunei Maritime Academy.

TVET Diploma programmes are also offered at the higher education level, which provides post-secondary students with progression opportunities. Politeknik Brunei (PB) is the main provider for TVET diploma programmes. There are four schools under PB: School of Business, School of Information and Communication Technology, School of Science and Engineering and School of Health Sciences. It is in the transformation plan that there should also be more progression opportunities for those who aspire for tertiary education.

There are TVET institutions under the jurisdiction of other ministries like the Prime Minister's Office and the Ministry of Youth, Culture and Sports. These institutions such as the Centre of Capacity Building or *Pusat Pembangunan Kapasiti* (PPK) and Youth Development Centre or *Pusat Pembangunan Belia* (PPB) offer value-added programmes which are catered mainly to youths who are unemployed. These programmes aim to develop their vocational skills which could help them find employment. In Brunei, the Brunei Darussalam National Accreditation Council (BDNAC) is responsible for the quality assurance and standards of programmes.

Apprenticeships

Prior to the introduction of Dual System Apprenticeship programmes, the Department of Technical Education drew on four apprenticeship training models with different arrangements of employment and sponsorship. These apprenticeship training models were then strengthened to a Dual System Apprenticeship programmes (DSA) with employment-based training model. These programmes require apprentices to be employed by a company and spend time in the workplace for six months and at a Registered Training Organization (RTO) for six months where they are required to undertake "off-the-job" training during a period of block release (IBTE 2013b). IBTE plans to increase the range of dual system apprenticeship programmes.

In the past, each year, there were sixty students undertaking the old apprenticeship programme. In the transformation plan, there are plans to increase the enrolment from sixty to two hundred with this dual system apprenticeship to meet the demands of industries, particularly in the oil and gas sector. In order to increase the enrolment, a range of sixteen new dual-system apprenticeship programmes have been proposed. For these programmes, consultation with the respective apprenticeship training advisory committee (ATAC) is conducted to understand the demands and needs of the employers.

Continuing Education and Training (CET)

IBTE CET offers lifelong learning opportunities in the form of short courses, programmes and workshops to the community, which allow adult learners to acquire further knowledge and skills in relevant fields. These courses or programmes help 1) to assist adult learners with academic upgrading in order to meet the admission requirements for post-secondary programmes, 2) as a form of community development to help learners to learn new skills, 3) workforce development—train workers to upskill for employment, and 4) provide bespoke professional certificates to improve employees skills gap as a requirement by the industry.

TVET CHALLENGES

Based on the latest global research, Brunei is in good company facing similar challenges due to the rapid changes to the labour market. For this chapter, we focus on two of these challenges.

Skills Mismatch

In order to investigate and monitor the employment of graduates, Public TVET institutions like the Institute of Brunei in Technical Education (IBTE) and Politeknik Brunei (PB) have been conducting graduates' employment studies since 2014 and 2016 respectively. These studies' key focus is to investigate the employability and employment of the graduates six months after their convocation in the labour market. Over the last few years, there has been a decline in the employment of TVET graduates in the government sector due to the limited job vacancies. As a consequence, a majority of the graduates found employment in the private sector or started their own business. There is an increase in the number of graduates who started their own business as they are supported by the government, as part of the entrepreneurship development agenda (MOE 2020). Overall, there is a decrease in the employment rate for TVET graduates in the year 2016, 2017 and 2018 due to skills mismatch. According to ILO (2020), "Skills mismatch is a discrepancy between the skills that are sought by employers and the skills that are possessed by individuals. Simply put, it is a mismatch between skills and jobs. This means that education and training are not providing the skills demanded in the labour market or that the economy does not create jobs that correspond to individuals' skills."

Figure 8.4 presents an overview of the supply and demand of TVET employment prospects grouped by BDSIC across industries in the year 2019. Supply refers to the number of TVET graduates and demand refers to the number of job vacancies available. The figure presents five important findings (arranged from i to v): i) when the supply of TVET graduates satisfies the demand of the industries, ii) an undersupply of TVET graduates, where the number of vacancies was more than the number of TVET graduates especially in the wholesale and retail including the repair of motor vehicles and motorcycles industry, iii) an oversupply of graduates, where the number of vacancies was less than the number of TVET graduates especially in the information and communication industry, iv) where there were no jobs available but there were TVET graduates, v) where there were job vacancies with no suitable graduates (MOE 2020). This is an overview of skills mismatch in 2019 where the statistics are only limited to those vacancies listed for companies registered under JobCentre Brunei. This overview provides us with an indication of skills mismatch in a few concerned industries which should be addressed in the future.

FIGURE 8.4
Supply and Demand

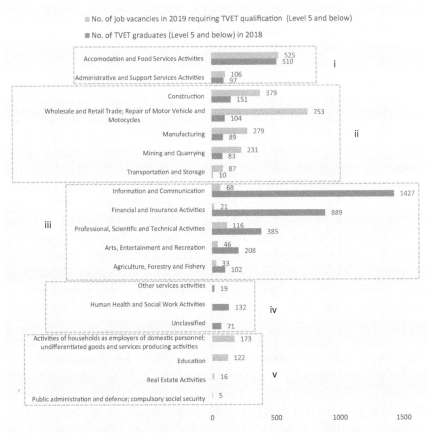

■ No. of job vacancies in 2019 requiring TVET qualification (Level 5 and below)

■ No. of TVET graduates (Level 5 and below) in 2018

Source: Re-adapted from JobCentre Brunei (2019).

Research revealed that growing labour market imbalances could potentially lead to higher structural unemployment rates if skills mismatch worsens (Cedefop 2015). Hence, to maintain a thriving economy to remain competitive in the global arena, it is of utmost importance to produce a skilled workforce and preserve a functional labour market to reduce skills mismatch. In order to do so, industry collaboration is needed in several areas, including curricula planning, development and implementation of apprenticeship schemes, provision of competency-based training and assessment. By shifting the focus of curricula towards the demand side as opposed to the supply side, it is hoped that TVET institutions will be able to better match students' skills with the competencies required in the industry. This shift could also promote a more diverse array of occupations.

Countries worldwide, including Brunei, recognize the need to integrate work-based learning, particularly apprenticeships in their policy agenda. Work-based learning refers to all forms of learning that take place in real work settings. Hence, there are wider apprenticeship options in the current TVET system. It recognizes the potential for reducing skills mismatch and meeting the skills demand of a fast-changing labour market. Apprenticeship also supports students by smoothing the transitions from education to the world of work.

As one of the steps to address skills mismatch, the Manpower and Industry Steering Committees (MISC) were established in 2019 under the Manpower Planning and Employment Council (MPEC) at the Prime Minister's Office. One of MISC's roles is to support the MPEC's vision to have a strategic workforce planning to ensure employability amongst the local graduates by identifying current and future sectoral jobs that are high in demand and to develop competency standards in these sectors. The MISC focuses on five industrial sectors which are Energy, Construction, Information and Communication Technology, Marine, and Hospitality and Tourism. IBTE has been working closely with MISC and other relevant parties such as JobCentre Brunei to identify new training programmes to reduce skills mismatch and to produce industry-ready workforce (Borneo Bulletin 2020; MOE 2020). To address this in the future, there should be a strategic and systematic process through which labour market information can be made available to avoid potential gaps between skills demand and supply. This information could then assist TVET, policymakers and employers in offering relevant training programmes and assisting youth and employees to make better educational choices for a higher chance of getting employed. Such a strategy could minimize the wastage of skills, and instead, capitalize the use of skills and improve human capital development.

TVET Teachers with Limited Industrial Exposure

TVET teaching profession within the broader sector is differentiated by the way TVET provision is manifested in each country, the TVET institutions within each country, and the purpose of what and how

TVET seeks to serve at a particular time in the country's socio and economic development. Hence, the kinds of roles that TVET professionals undertake are likely to be varied, given the different educational purposes, as well as the contexts and sectors they practise in. In Brunei, a large part of TVET teachers' role includes teaching and learning at TVET institutions and supervision of learners in workplaces. Due to the changing landscape of TVET as a result of technology and globalization, the roles of TVET professionals are also subject to change. In addition, due to economic imperatives that need to be reflected in TVET, the degree and focus of changes to the roles of TVET professionals are likely to be incessant and frequent. Given these changes, it is inevitable that TVET professionals should maintain their competencies in different areas such as occupational subject matter expertise and the ability to apply occupational knowledge in different contexts, and the pedagogical expertise to teaching and learning (Attwell 1999). Hence TVET professionals are inscribed with having a dual identity, being a professional in their occupational field and a teacher.

One of the challenges that TVET teachers face in Brunei is limited industrial exposure, which would seem to be a barrier when creating situational learning experiences in the classroom. They need to maintain their industry skills and competencies as they play a critical role as "connective specialists" (Young and Guile 1997) to contextualize theoretical knowledge into practical knowledge. This is why it is fundamental for TVET teachers to maintain the currency of industry changes and developments through industrial exposure.

Due to rapid technological advances as mentioned at the beginning of the chapter, the world of work is changing as it manifests in workplaces. Digitalization at work is one of the technological advances that have changed the nature of work and occupations in many sectors. Hence, future workers would need to have digital literacy—the skills required to achieve digital competence, the confidence and critical use of ICT for work, leisure, learning and communication (European Commission 2017). This suggests that teachers should be rethinking their pedagogies with the use of digital technologies to prepare learners for the digital future of jobs. Thus, teachers should be equipped with competencies through professional learning to develop their digital technology skills to enhance their delivery.

Workplace contexts and changes can only be understood through industrial exposure. It is vital for TVET teachers to gain industrial exposure as returning to the industry helps develop their knowledge and skills and, more importantly, learn how to apply occupational knowledge in different and changing contexts. In Engeström's (1995) terms, they could develop poly-contextual skills to move between different work contexts.

Given the importance of occupational knowledge and competencies, arrangements for industrial attachments must form part of an overall professional development plan for TVET teachers and should also be a part of the pre-service training (UNESCO-UNEVOC 2020), especially in this ever-changing industrial environment. Broadly, TVET teachers should continue to assess their skills and competencies and to have self-empowerment for learning.

FUTURE-FOCUSED TECHNICAL AND VOCATIONAL EDUCATION SYSTEM IN BRUNEI

Brunei's economy depends largely on the oil and gas industry. In an attempt to move away from the heavy reliance on these resources, the country has been striving and working towards achieving economic diversification. TVET has a critical and significant role in preparing a resilient, adaptable and agile workforce that is skilled and employable in a prospective oil and non-oil economy. We work on the premise that globalization and rapid changes in technology are accelerating social, economic and environmental challenges at an unprecedented pace, which will shift the skills required by future graduates. So this returns us to the central question: given an unchartered digital future, how can we prepare our existing and future workforce through TVET considering the evolving employment landscape?

On the Path to 2035

To begin early, we need to foster a high-quality, future-focused TVET system which can support teaching and learning for the future of work. We need to (re)assess the position of TVET as a part of the whole human resource development plan taking into account the technological, socio-economic and demographic advancements. Simultaneously, the future directions of TVET also depend on local, regional and international socio-economic forces that can influence and shape the future TVET provisions in the country. This chapter suggests broad strategies to chart out a future-focused TVET system.

Redesigning Our Curriculum

In an increasingly uncertain world, a traditional education model that categorizes knowledge into specialized fields is no longer adequate for today's fast-changing workplaces. The continuous change to the workplaces today calls for a more holistic and cross-disciplinary mode of thinking. Hence, it is important to develop our students' ability to comprehend, navigate and be agile to a world of uncertainty through practising "strategic foresight". Practising continuous strategic foresight will also be important for curriculum designers in designing ideal programmes including resources and learning spaces to prepare students for future changes.

The paradigms of globalization and digitalization will create many new cross-functional roles, where workers will need more than technical skills. The demand for social, analytical, transversal and applied skills is most likely to grow in these coming years. Given this premise, there is a need to redesign our curriculum towards an education that is "future-oriented, globally informed and locally contextualised" (OECD 2020). This points toward the use of labour market and skills intelligence (LMSI) which can help to transform information on skills into powerful evidence for decision-making, e.g., to inform our curriculum to address the changing labour needs. Labour market and skills intelligence is the "outcome of an expert-driven process of identifying, analysing, synthesising and presenting quantitative and/or qualitative skills and labour market information" (Cedefop 2019). In tandem, we need to acknowledge that initial training for an occupation will no longer suffice to enter and stay in employment.

Intermediate-skill occupations that generally require specialized vocational education and on-the-job training will be at most risk of displacement as technologies can replace them. Therefore, this would mean that any occupations most likely to be affected by labour market changes due to Artificial Intelligence are integrally linked with TVET. This signifies the impending changes of skill sets which we should be aware of, that is to be taken into account in TVET. Given these changes, digital and transversal skills must be integrated into the curriculum to ensure students' employability. Equally important, students will need to foster a lifelong learning mindset throughout their career and life (Goh 2015) in their journey to "becoming" a professional.

Cultivate Lifelong Learning Culture

The digital revolution has rapidly transformed the world of work and the skill profiles of many occupations. Many jobs and occupations will undergo a fundamental transformation resulting either in job displacement or job creation. The synergistic forces which result from technological, socio-economic, geopolitical and demographic developments will transform the work organization and work practices which require new skill sets. Inevitably, this impending transformation necessitates continuous skilling and reskilling, which could be reinforced in the TVET lifelong learning policies for the future. In the recent World Economic Forum on ASEAN 2018, a key point strongly advocated by the distinguished panel was the importance of promoting lifelong learning of individuals to embrace IR 4.0. Hence, lifelong learning, including workplace learning, should be aggressively endorsed to address the displacement of jobs by a shift in the division of labour between humans and machines.

Lifelong learning will need to be embedded in TVET if sustainable development is to be achieved, especially in this climate of technological change. Initial TVET will no longer suffice to prepare workers for a lifelong career as changes to required skill sets at work keep on shifting due to digitalization. Firstly, one of the suggested ways is to continue to put forward the significance of work-based learning. In the form of apprenticeship, work-based learning has the potential to prepare learners for incessant changes in the workplace.

Secondly, as an essential component of lifelong learning which is intrinsically linked with professional development, Continuing Technical and Vocational Education and Training (CTVET) is key to addressing any technological, social and economic challenges, ensuring that workers are guided and equipped with necessary skills. All workers, regardless of whether they are employed or unemployed, old or young, irrespective of their background and qualifications, will require to have access to opportunities to upskill, retrain, and reskill to keep up with rapidly changing work demands and practices. Simultaneously, workplaces need to recognize the significance of lifelong learning and promote it by incentivizing and investing in their workforce training. Hence, a robust CTVET will demand complex institutional arrangements and coordinated policies and practices. Collaborative partnership with multi-stakeholder/industries ranging from major to small organizations in the public and private sectors and learning providers should also be strengthened. This means ensuring that employers are recognized for their contribution and that they understand themselves to be a crucial part of the education and skills development ecosystem. Whilst CTVET is an integral part of lifelong learning systems, it must recognize that it cannot be an extension of TVET, rather it requires a robust organization, structure and governance arrangements.

Thirdly, in order to broaden the access to CTVET, stronger emphasis should be placed on work-based learning and informal learning in any work organization. Excepting these emphases, workplace affordances and individual engagement must be encouraged as research findings have shown that valuable workplace learning is the outcome of the interrelationship between individuals and the workplace environment (Billett 2001; Goh 2014, 2020; Hodkinson et al. 2008).

These two strategies for a future-focused TVET aim to foster a system fit for the challenge of transitions ahead. For these strategies to be successfully implemented, the current TVET system will need to reassess its position in terms of infrastructure, resources and provisions using the national TVET baseline study that was recently conducted (MOE 2020). Simultaneously, practising strategic foresight is necessary as it will help engage key stakeholders such as policymakers, relevant ministries and industries to form a shared vision of the future.

CONCLUSION

This chapter has highlighted the past and present contributions of TVET in building a resilient workforce in realizing *Wawasan* 2035. Given how the rapid technological advancement will continue to infiltrate our work organizations, the nation needs to be lifelong learners as we are always "learning to becoming" (Goh 2015; Hodkinson et al. 2008) in order to adapt and be agile to the demands of the work practices. In achieving Brunei's Vision 2035, there are enormous opportunities provided by the digitalization of work that can bring about economic and social progress. This, however, depends crucially on the extent of collaborative effort by all relevant stakeholders, including TVET, to reassess and initiate reforms such as the curriculum in education and training systems, labour market policies, workforce development policies and employment policies.

REFERENCES

Attwell, Graham. 1999. "New Roles for Vocational Education and Training Teachers and Trainers in Europe: A New Framework for Their Education". *Industrial and Commercial Training* 31, no. 5: 190–200.
Billett, Stephen. 2001. "Learning Throughout Working Life: Interdependencies at Work". *Studies in Continuing Education* 23: 19–35.
Borneo Bulletin. 2020. "Keeping Tabs on Manpower Development". *Borneo Bulletin*, 11 August 2020. https://borneobulletin.com.bn/keeping-tabs-on-manpower-development-2/ (accessed 12 January 2020).
Cedefop. 2015. *Tackling Unemployment While Addressing Skill Mismatch: Lessons from Policy and Practice in European Union Countries*. Cedefop Research Paper, no. 46. Luxembourg: Publications Office.
———. 2019. "Crafting Skills Intelligence: How Cedefop Transforms Information on Skill into Powerful Evidence for Decision-Making". 25 September 2019. https://skillspanorama.cedefop.europa.eu/en/blog/crafting-skills-intelligence (accessed 18 January 2021).
Chui, Michael, James Manyika, and Mehdi Miremadi. 2016. *Where Machines Could Replace Humans—and Where They Can't (Yet)*. San Francisco, CA: McKinsey & Company.
Department of Statistics. 2017. *Report of Summary Findings: Labour Force Survey 2017*. Brunei Darussalam: Department of Statistics, Department of Economic Planning and Development, Ministry of Finance and Economy. http://www.deps.gov.bn/DEPD%20Documents%20Library/DOS/Labour%20force%20survey_KTK/2017/Sum_FindingsLFS2017.pdf (accessed 11 December 2020).
———. 2018. *Report of Summary Findings: Labour Force Survey 2018*. Brunei Darussalam: Department of Statistics, Department of Economic Planning and Development, Ministry of Finance and Economy. http://www.deps.gov.bn/DEPD%20Documents%20Library/DOS/Labour%20force%20survey_KTK/2018/Summary%20Report%20of%20the%20Labour%20Force%20Survey%20(LFS)%202018.pdf (accessed 11 December 2020).
———. 2019. *Report of the Labour Force Survey 2019*. Brunei Darussalam: Department of Statistics, Department of Economic Planning and Development, Ministry of Finance and Economy. http://www.deps.gov.

bn/DEPD%20Documents%20Library/DOS/Labour%20force%20survey_
KTK/2019/KTK_2019.pdf (accessed 11 December 2020).

Engeström, Yrjö. 1995. *Training for Change: New Approach to Instruction and
Learning in Working Life*. Geneva, Switzerland: International Labour
Organization.

European Commission. 2017. "Digital Competence Framework for Educators".
https://ec.europa.eu/jrc/en/digcompedu (accessed 10 January 2021).

Frey, Carl Benedikt, and Michael A. Osborne. 2017. "The Future of Employment:
How Susceptible are Jobs to Computerisation?" *Technological Forecasting
and Social Change* 114: 254–80.

Goh, Adeline Yuen Sze. 2014. "Insights from a Bourdieusian Lens: The
Relationship between College-Based and Workplace Learning in Becoming
a Vocational-Technical Education Teacher in Brunei". *Journal of Workplace
Learning* 26: 22–38.

———. 2015. "An Individual Learning Journey: Learning as Becoming a
Vocational Teacher". *International Journal of Lifelong Education* 34, no. 6:
680–95. doi:10.1080/02601370.2015.1096311.

———. 2020. "Learning Cultures: Understanding Learning in a School-University
Partnership". *Oxford Review in Education*. doi:10.1080/03054985.2020.1825368.

Hodkinson, Phil, Gert Biesta, and David James. 2008. "Understanding Learning
Culturally: Overcoming the Dualism between Social and Individual Views
of Learning". *Vocations and Learning* 1: 27–47.

Institute of Brunei Technical Education (IBTE). 2013a. *Transforming Technical
and Vocational Education: A White Paper*. Brunei Darussalam: Department
of Technical Education, Ministry of Education. https://ibte.edu.bn/ibte-
white-paper/ (accessed 11 December 2020).

———. 2013b. "Upgrading Plan". Brunei Darussalam: Department of
Technical Education, Ministry of Education. https://ibte.edu.bn/cet/
academicupgrading/ (accessed 11 December 2020).

International Labour Organization (ILO). 2020. "What is Skills Mismatch and
Why Should We Care? A Key Question to Ensure a Decent Future of
Work". 1 April 2020. https://www.ilo.org/skills/Whatsnew/WCMS_740388/
lang--en/index.htm (accessed 12 December 2020).

Jamil, A. 2000. "Vocational and Technical Education in Brunei Darussalam:
Policy Directions for the 21st Century". Proceedings of the Fifth Annual
Conference of the Department of Science and Mathematics Education,
Universiti Brunei Darussalam, 15–18 May 2000.

JobCentre Brunei. 2019. "Unpublished Report for MOE: JCB Jobseekers Data
(Q4 2019 for MOE)".

Jumat, Ahmad Haji. 1989. "A Chronological Study of the Development of
Education in Brunei Darussalam from 1906–1984 with Special Reference

to Education Policies and Their Implementation". PhD dissertation, School of Education, California Coast University.

Kon, James. 2020. "New Offerings from IBTE". *Borneo Bulletin*, 13 June 2020. https://borneobulletin.com.bn/new-offerings-from-ibte/ (accessed 12 December 2020).

Ministry of Education (MOE). 2013. "National Education System for the 21st Century (SPN 21)". Bandar Seri Begawan: Ministry of Education Brunei Darussalam. https://www.moe.gov.bn/Pages/spn21.aspx (accessed 21 December 2020).

———. 2020. *Brunei Darussalam TVET Report*. Bandar Seri Begawan: Ministry of Education Brunei Darussalam.

Organisation for Economic Co-operation and Development (OECD). 2010. *Learning for Jobs: Synthesis Report of the OECD Reviews of Vocational Education and Training*. Paris: OECD Publishing.

———. 2015. "Focus on Vocational Education and Training Programmes". *Education Indicators in Focus*, no. 33. Paris: OECD Publishing.

———. 2016. *Tax Policy Reforms in the OECD 2016*. Paris: OECD Publishing.

———. 2020. *What Students Learn Matters: Towards a 21st Century Curriculum*. Paris: OECD Publishing.

United Nations Educational, Scientific and Cultural Organization (UNESCO). 2015. *EFA Global Monitoring Report 2015 (Education for All 2000–2015: Achievements and Challenges)*. Paris: UNESCO.

UNESCO-UNEVOC. 2011. "TVETipedia Glossary". https://unevoc.unesco.org/home/TVETipedia+Glossary/filt=all/id=306 (accessed 12 December 2020).

———. 2015. "TVETipedia Glossary". https://unevoc.unesco.org/home/TVETipedia+Glossary/filt=all/id=474 (accessed 12 December 2020).

———. 2020. *UNESCO-UNEVOC Study on the Trends Shaping the Future of TVET Teaching*. UNESCO-UNEVOC International Centre for Technical and Vocational Education and Training. https://unevoc.unesco.org/pub/trendsmapping_futureoftvetteaching.pdf (accessed 20 October 2020).

World Economic Forum. 2016. *The Future of Jobs: Employment, Skills and Workforce Strategy for the Fourth Industrial Revolution*. Geneva, Switzerland: World Economic Forum.

Young, Michael, and David Guile. 1997. "New Possibilities for the Professionalisation of VET Professionals in the UK". *Journal of European Industrial Training* 27, no. 6/7: 203–12.

9

POPULATION HEALTH LANDSCAPE: CHALLENGES AND OPPORTUNITIES

Nik Ani Afiqah Tuah

INTRODUCTION

Parallel to demographic transition, Omran (1971) showed an epidemiologic transition, describing an expected change in mortality and the cause of deaths. It starts with the "age of pestilence" when the mortality rate is very high and fluctuates. Death mainly occurs because of infectious/communicable diseases. The second stage is the "age of receding pandemics", when countries have well-managed the pandemics, and then mortality starts to decline. The third and last stage is when the primary cause of death shifts to degenerative/non-communicable diseases (NCDs). Olshanky and Oult (1986) added the fourth stage, the so-called "age of delayed degenerative diseases", when people live much longer, and the degenerative diseases are compressed in shorter periods of the remaining years of life.

However, people in developing countries may not be able to successfully manage communicable diseases. At the same time, they experience the emergence of degenerative diseases as the cause of death, thus facing a "double burden of disease" (Tyagi 2014). The prevalence of degenerative diseases has aggravated the impact of the COVID-19 pandemic, often known as the co-existence of co-morbidities (Collins et al. 2020).

This epidemiological trend often goes together with the transition in nutrition. Popkin (1993) argued that there are five stages of nutrition transition. The first is the "food gathering" stage. Individuals consume high carbohydrate foods in this stage, followed by the second stage, known as the "famine" stage. People are hungry and then die. The third is "receding famine" when people have sufficient amount of food. They start consuming fruits, vegetables and animals. The fourth is the "degenerative disease" stage, sometimes called the "western" diet, in which individuals consume high meat diet accompanied by a sedentary life. The fifth is the stage of behavioural changes toward healthy lifestyles, including consuming healthy food.

Therefore, with this framework as the background, this chapter examines trends of population health outcomes and the determinants in Brunei, a high-income country with the second-highest per capita income in Southeast Asia, and its related health policies. It focuses on the landscape, challenges and opportunities related to population health in Brunei. It discusses mortality rates, non-communicable diseases, communicable diseases (especially the COVID-19), people with disabilities, and the ageing population. It also examines health policies and systems in delivering high-quality care. Population health is a vital element of people's capability, productivity and welfare to achieve *Wawasan* Brunei 2035 or Brunei Vision 2035.

Brunei has shown improvements towards achieving the United Nations (UN) Sustainable Development Goals (SDGs) in 2030, primarily for SDG3 on good health and well-being. The goal consists of high quality maternal and child health services, universal health coverage and high immunization coverage. However, the nation still faces formidable and continuous health challenges. The selected health achievements for Brunei are antenatal coverage of more than 95 per cent and essential services coverage of more than 80 per cent (Ministry of Finance and Economy 2020). Unfortunately, an ageing population, unhealthy lifestyles, and behavioural encumbrance have resulted in the emergence of mortality and morbidity from NCDs and the emergence and re-emergence of infectious pathogens. In addition, climate change and environmental pollution have further worsened human health conditions. Brunei has so far well-managed the coronavirus disease (COVID-19) pandemic, yet it has aggravated public health challenges, adverse social and economic impacts on the kingdom, people and livelihood. Brunei still needs a sufficient and robust healthcare workforce to respond to current and future health problems adequately. The recent global pandemic of COVID-19 has made the issue more critical than ever. The health facilities comprise government medical care, health services, dental services and private health services. Doctors, nurses and midwives are the fundamentals of human resources in health, especially today with the global spread of COVID-19.

HEALTH STATUS

Brunei's total population has remarkably increased from 412,400 people in 2015 to 459,500 people in 2019 (Department of Statistics 2020). The total live birth was 15.3 per 1,000 population, while the life expectancy was 76.3 years for males and females was 78.3 years in 2017. The Infant Mortality Rate (IMR) significantly declined from 50.8 per 1,000 live births in 1962 to 17.5 in 1980 and further declined to 9.5 per 1,000 live births in 2017. Since 1990, the IMR has remained stable in Brunei and on par with figures in developed nations. From 2004 to 2017, the country reported that over two-thirds of deaths occurred during early and late neonatal periods, mainly due to perinatal conditions and congenital abnormalities. Also, the Under-5 Mortality Rate (U5MR) has gradually decreased from 30 deaths (1976) to 11.5 deaths (2017) per 1,000 live births (Ministry of Health 2018a).

Abortion in the nation is only legal when it will save a woman's life. The prohibition does not permit a pregnancy termination even when there is a high risk to the baby's life; for example, in certain conditions originating in the perinatal period or congenital malformations, the leading causes of infant mortality in the country.

Immunization coverage has steadily been above 95.0 per cent for all vaccinations for all ages in the National Immunisation Programme that has met the World Health Organization's target (Ministry of Health 2018a). The immunization coverage consists of Diphtheria, Tetanus,

Pertussis, Influenza, Polio, Hepatitis (DTP-Hib-IPV-HepB 3), Mumps, Measles, Rubella and Hepatitis B (birth dose) (Ministry of Finance and Economy 2020).

The Maternal Mortality Ratio (MMR) had shown a marked decline from 487.2 (1960) to 0 (1990) per 100,000 live births in Brunei. However, there was slight variation and constantly very low MMR from 26.7 (2000) to 62.0 (2017) per 100,000 live births. Thus, the low rate of MMR over the last 57 years has been comparable to other developed countries. The factors attributing to low MMR in the nation include high access to reproductive healthcare and immunization programmes. Also, a high percentage of skilled health personnel (doctors, nurses and midwives) attend the majority of deliveries and provide high-quality care for newborn children. Thus, the improvements profoundly impact the high quality of maternal and child health services in the country (Ministry of Health 2018a).

NON-COMMUNICABLE DISEASES: BURDEN AND RISK FACTORS

Cancer, heart disease, diabetes mellitus, stroke and hypertension are the common causes of death in the nation (Ministry of Health 2018a). A total of 1,696 deaths in 2017 comprised of cancer (19 per cent), heart diseases (15 per cent), diabetes mellitus (10 per cent), stroke (8 per cent), hypertension (5 per cent) and others (42 per cent). These non-communicable diseases (NCDs) accounted for 52.5 per cent of the country's total deaths in 2017 and about 47 per cent of total deaths aged 30–69 years. The top four types of cancer deaths among males were trachea, bronchus and lung, rectum/anus and stomach, whereas among females were breasts, trachea, bronchus and lung, and rectum/anus (Ministry of Health 2018a).

Obesity and smoking are the common risk factors for NCDs in Brunei. The prevalence of obesity in Bruneian adults was one of the highest in Southeast Asia. Also, the prevalence of tobacco smoking in the nation is among the highest in high-income countries; nearly one-third (32 per cent) of adult males smoke (World Health Organization 2018). The overall smoking prevalence in Bruneian adults was 20 per cent in 1997, and adult male smokers contributed to 31.1 per cent. The overall smoking prevalence decreased to 17 per cent in 2011, however, adult male smokers increased to 32.8 per cent (Ministry of Health 2013).

The prevalence of obesity in adults was 12 per cent in 1997 and increased to 27.2 per cent in 2011. However, the prevalence of overweight adults increased marginally from 32.4 per cent in 1997 to 33.4 per cent in 2011. In 2011, the prevalence of overweight (as defined by BMI for age $\geq$ 1 SD) and obese (as defined by BMI for age $\geq$ 2 SD) among children was 33.5 per cent and 18.3 per cent (Ministry of Health 2013). Overall, the prevalence of obesity and overweight among adults had increased from 1997 to 2011 with no indication of downward trends. One out of two children is either overweight or obese.

The prevalence of hypertension increased from 28.6 per cent in 1997 to 33.8 per cent in 2011. The prevalence of hypertension in adult males increased from 35.4 per cent in 1997 to 36.4 per cent in 2011; in adult females, it increased from 23 per cent in 1997 to 31.7 per cent in 2011 (Ministry of Health 2013). Thus, the prevalence of hypertension steadily increased among adults (males and females) from 1997 to 2011.

The prevalence of diabetes was 12.5 per cent in 2011, comprising 12.2 per cent for adult males and 12.7 per cent for adult females. On the other hand, the prevalence of hypercholesterolemia in 2011 was 11.6 per cent—12.4 per cent among adult males and 10.8 per cent adult females (Ministry of Health 2013). In other words, diabetes and hypercholesterolemia remain public health problems in the country.

Brunei reported 26.7 per cent exclusive breastfeeding rates at zero to six months in 2011. Additionally, 8.7 per cent of children aged one year and below were already consuming sweetened drinks. Some children also consumed high amounts of saturated fats and sugary drinks while their intakes of fibre and fruits and vegetables were too low. The country highlighted poor nutrition among children two to five years old. Some children had inadequate fruit and vegetable intake leading to a deficient dietary fibre intake of 6.2 g (SD±2.1) for males and 6.1 g for females (SD±2.1) (Ministry of Health 2013). Generally, Bruneian children (two to five years) have poor nutrition and inadequate fibre, fruits and vegetables.

Therefore, about 1.0 per cent of the two to five-year-old population met 70 per cent of most internationally recommended dietary intakes for fibre. The National Dietary Guidelines recommend two to three servings of fruits and two to three servings of vegetables per day to prevent chronic diseases (Ministry of Health 2013). The 2nd National Health and Nutritional Survey (NHANSS) reported that the prevalence of malnutrition among children was gradually rising in 2012. About 20 per cent of children with stunting, 10 per cent were underweight, 3 per cent of young children were wasting, overweight was 9 per cent, and 11 per cent had low birth weight (Ministry of Health 2014; World Health Organization 2014). Breastfeeding is one of the most practical means to guarantee child health and survival. The World Health Organization (WHO) and United Nations International Children's Emergency Fund (UNICEF) suggested that children initiate breastfeeding within the first hour of birth and up to two years. The WHO recommended exclusively breastfed children for the first six months of life (World Health Organization 2021a).

In 2011, the Prime Minister's Office of Brunei introduced "Maternity Leave Regulations" that provide 15 weeks of maternal leave for all government servants and citizens and permanent residents in both public and private sectors. This policy aims to enable the environment for nutrition and food security to address the relevant nutrition issues in the country and strengthen the Ministry of Health's existing policies (World Health Organization 2014). As a result, the prevalence of exclusive breastfeeding (EBF) among mothers increased after extending paid maternity leave, with the most significant increases seen among employed mothers in Brunei. In addition, evidence showed that EBF of infants in their first six months postpartum is beneficial (Alhaji et al. 2018).

In 2011, only females aged between 30 and 60 years and males aged 40–60 years met the daily recommendations for vegetable intake. In addition, there is a failure to meet the daily recommendations for vegetable intake for males aged 39 and below and females aged 29 and below. The most deficient intakes were among children and adolescents. On average, in terms of fruit intake, only two servings of fruits per week were consumed by males and three servings by females for all age categories—significantly lower than the recommended 14–21 servings per week. Overall, the dietary fibre intake is insufficient among Bruneians of all ages. Only 7.8 per cent of Bruneian males and 3.4 per cent of females met most international dietary recommended amounts for fibre intake of 18–30 grams per day. The breakfast meals were taken daily in all age categories for both males and females. However, this is an exception for males aged 15–29 years and females aged 15–19 years who tend to miss their breakfast two times per week. The situation showed that adolescents do not meet essential nutrients for peak growth and development and this may negatively impact scholastic achievements.

The prevalence of physical activity in adults (≥ 20 years) from NHANSS is 45.3 per cent, with 42 per cent of males and 48.1 per cent of females performing more than 150 minutes of moderate physical activity in a week. In the same population study, the prevalence of physical activity for children (aged 5–19 years) is much lower than the adults at 28.3 per cent, with 28.2 per cent being males and 28.4 per cent females. Another 21.8 per cent of adults, with 38.9 per cent males and 7.4 per cent females, performed between 75 and 150 minutes of moderate physical activity per week. These figures are lower for all children at 15.8 per cent, with 27 per cent males and 4.6 per cent females performing between 75 and 150 minutes of moderate physical activity per week (Ministry of Health 2013). In general, the prevalence of physical activity is lower in children aged 5 to 19 years compared to adults (≥ 20 years) in Brunei.

Depression, personality disorder and anxiety are the most commonly diagnosed mental illnesses in Brunei. The neuropsychiatric disorders in the nation are estimated to contribute to 18.9 per cent of the disease's global burden in 2008. In 2012, the government reported that about 11,000 people were registered with the country's mental health services (Commonwealth Network 2020). The Ministry of Health (MOH) highlighted recent reports of suicides or attempted suicides in the community and offered advice and reassurance to the public (Ministry of Health 2018b). It aims to support people with mental health problems living in the community. As a result, mental health facilities, including six mental health outpatient facilities, three day treatment facilities, and forty psychiatric beds in general hospitals, have been provided (World Health Organization 2011). On 1 November 2014, the government introduced Mental Health Order 2014 to consolidate laws relating to mental disorders and provide the admission, detention, lodging, care, treatment, rehabilitation and protection of mentally disordered persons and other related matters (Ministry of Health 2017).

COMMUNICABLE DISEASES AND THE COVID-19 OUTBREAK

The nation has achieved remarkable success in eliminating infectious diseases. The World Health Organization declared Brunei free from malaria in 1987, poliomyelitis in 2000 and measles in 2015. Also, there are low incidences of HIV/AIDS, tuberculosis and other infectious diseases in the country (Ministry of Health 2018a).

However, the emergence and re-emergence of infectious pathogens become continuous threats to the country's population health. In today's time, the coronavirus (COVID-19) pandemic has resulted in 3,899,172 deaths globally (World Health Organization 2021b). SARS-CoV-2 has caused COVID-19, and this, in turn, has resulted in a range of clinical manifestations from mild flu-like symptoms to fatal acute respiratory distress syndrome (Guan et al. 2020). Thus, the COVID-19 pandemic has negatively affected public health and the economy and society at large.

Brunei detected the first COVID-19 case on 9 March 2020 (Ministry of Health 2020a) and had 259 infected cases with three fatal cases. To date, about 20,575 individuals have completed their Mandatory Self Isolation from March 2020, and the Ministry of Health has conducted a total of 139,503 laboratory tests (Ministry of Health 2021b).

The BruHealth mobile application was created on 28 May 2020 by the Ministry of Health to engage its residents during the COVID-19 pandemic, trace community contact and control a possible outbreak. A total of 395,164 individuals have registered in the BruHealth system. The application also integrates with the health data of patients (Ministry of Health 2020c). It serves as an information platform on COVID-19 development and related policy measures. Moreover, it enables the monitoring of health conditions through the self-assessment function and tracks risk exposure of residents using Bluetooth and GPS tracking tools (Ministry of Health 2021a).

Brunei has implemented various mitigation measures, including social and physical distancing, travel/border restrictions, quarantine of affected households, isolation of infected or suspected individuals, mass gathering ban, contact tracing, closure of workplaces and schools and promotion of preventive behaviour (such as personal hygiene). Arguably, the widely used public health strategies of "flattening the epidemic curve" for COVID-19 help reduce disease transmission, lessen the burden of the healthcare system/workers, and decrease infection likelihood in high-risk populations (Anderson et al. 2020).

Simultaneously, Brunei has ramped up its COVID-19 testing capacity and rate by setting up a new viral testing laboratory facility and expanding the National Isolation Centre (Ministry of Health 2020b). In addition, the MOH implemented risk communication strategies in the country. The strategies include a constant stream of health information and updates on the national and global pandemic situation through daily media conferences by the Minister of Health with online press releases (Ministry of Health 2020c), and supported by a 24-hour health advice line service 148 (Ministry of Health 2020b) to address public concerns related to COVID-19. Furthermore, laws and regulations, including The Infectious Diseases Act [Cap 204] and The Infectious Diseases [Quarantine] Regulations, are brought into force to prevent the introduction, spread and transmission of infectious diseases in Brunei. The latter also includes procedures on quarantine measures which infected vessels arriving at any port in Brunei may be subjected to (Ministry of Health 2017).

PEOPLE WITH DISABILITIES (PWDs)

About 10 per cent of the world's population, or approximately 650 million people, experience some form of disability (World Health Organization Western Pacific Region 2008). The World Health Survey reported that around 785 million people (15.6 per cent) aged 15 years and above are living with a disability, although the Global Burden of Disease estimated around 975 million people (19.4 per cent). The global increase in chronic health conditions such as diabetes, cardiovascular diseases, chronic respiratory diseases, cancer and mental disorders contribute to disability among individuals. The trends of health conditions and environmental factors include road traffic crashes, natural disasters, conflict, diet, and substance abuse (World Health Organization and The World Bank 2011). The specific disabilities are associated with chronic conditions, including cardiovascular diseases, chronic respiratory diseases, cancer, diabetes, injuries (road traffic crashes, falls, landmines and violence), mental illness, malnutrition, HIV/AIDS and other infectious diseases (World Health Organization Western Pacific Region 2008).

In Brunei, the Department of Community Development estimated 7038 registered individuals with disabilities (PWDs) in 2019, consisting of 4,381males and 2,628 females (Roslan and Mohamad Diah 2020). Brunei's Old Age and Disability Pensions Act [Cap 18], introduced on 1 January 1955, states that individuals can receive monetary payments through old age pensions and other pensions for persons with blindness. The dependents of persons who have Hansen's disease and mental illness are entitled to obtain such allowances based on this act. Disability pensions, other pensions and allowances as prescribed, and all matter incidental are also included (Attorney General's Chamber 2017).

Brunei reviewed this act to further include disability allowances for those below 15 years, as of 1 January 2018 (Ministry of Finance and Economy 2020). On 18 December 2007, the country signed the Convention on the Rights of Persons with Disabilities (CRPD) and ratified it on 11 April 2016 (Office of the High Commissioner for Human Rights 2021). As a result, 3,630 and 38,290 recipients received disability pensions and allowances and old age pensions respectively in May 2020. The government spent over BND$10 million on disabilities pensions and allowance expenditures, and BND$111 million on old age pension payments from April 2019 to March 2020 (Ministry of Finance and Economy 2020).

The government is currently working towards integrating the CRPD into *Wawasan* Brunei 2035 to ensure PWDs' equal rights, opportunities and participation are fully exercised in the society. The National Council on Social Issues (MKIS) implements the Plan of Action under the Special Committee on the Elderly and PWDs for developing strategies on the development, well-being, welfare and support system for PWDs (Ministry of Finance and Economy 2020). The country practises a whole-of-nation approach in ensuring the involvement and progress of the PWDs, alongside robust social welfare support. Evidently, there is a profound paradigm change on disability from medical to social models in society. The medical model of disability ("personal tragedy" model) emphasizes curative treatment of disability exploiting in-depth clinical perspective; hence, a caring and decent society devotes resources to healthcare and related services to offer PWDs a "normal" life. The social model of disability recognizes that the main attributable factors in disabling individuals are systemic barriers, negative attitudes and social exclusion (Retief and Letšosa 2018).

The Welfare of PWDs Council (MKOKU) advocates and empowers the differently-abled in Brunei. It consists of nine non-governmental organizations (NGOs) representing differently-abled people. In addition, there is the Centre for Children with Special Needs; Paraplegic and Physically Disabled Association, Pusat Ehsan Al-Ameerah Al-Hajjah Maryam; Brunei Down Syndrome Association; Special Olympics Brunei Darussalam; Society for the Management of Autism; Learning Ladders; Brunei Darussalam National Association of the Blind (BDNAB); and National Association of the Hearing Impaired (Ministry of Finance and Economy 2020). BDNAB, furthermore, has introduced braille and sign language courses to promote greater awareness and public empathy on the challenges faced by PWDs, including those with visual and hearing impairment. In 2019, BDNAB had conducted nine workshops on "Braille, Orientation and Mobility" in collaboration with other agencies. About 450 participants comprising PWDs, parents, government agencies, non-governmental bodies, the private sector, and individuals attended the workshops (Ministry of Finance and Economy 2020).

In terms of employment, the Ministry of Culture, Youth and Sports (MCYS) reported that 75 and 25 PWDs were employed in the government and private sectors, respectively. Pusat Bahagia, under the Department of Community Development, MCYS, is a skill training (job coaching) centre for PWDs, focusing on living, social, work and basic vocational skills. In addition, Pusat Bahagia was established in each of the four districts to assist PWDs. In 2019, there was a total of 433 PWDs registered in these centres. Pusat Bahagia and the strategic partnership work together to raise awareness to prevent harassment of PWDs in the workplace and ensure their open access to the general labour market (Ministry of Finance and Economy 2020).

The Youth Development Centre (YDC) had also organized a programme, "Program Pendedahan Kemahiran OKU" in 2019 for differently-abled youth to participate in short-term skills training courses. The programme aims at providing equal opportunities as well as developing marketable and employable skills to PWDs such as in tailoring, baking, pastry-making, and beauty courses with assistance and guidance from professional instructors in these respective areas (Ministry of Finance and Economy 2020).

The Special Education Unit (SEU) at the Ministry of Education (MOE) and government secondary schools collaborate with employers from various industries to provide differently-abled students with various work attachments during the Pre-Vocational Programme in their final years. The Pre-Vocational Programme equips them with appropriate work-related skills at various placements according to their abilities and skills. The government also assists in promoting and marketing goods or products made by PWDs, and provides entrepreneurial spaces for such products in public premises, including government buildings (Ministry of Finance and Economy 2020).

The National Education System for the 21st Century (SPN21), which commenced in 2009, provides students, including PWDs, with multiple pathways according to their capabilities, interests, inclinations, growth and development, thereby catering to their needs. On top of that, MOE offers education services to PWDs which are delivered by Special Education Needs Assistance (SENA) teachers and aides accessible in many schools.

The government introduced the Model Inclusive Schools (MIS) project in 2008. It embarked on a significant centralization initiative in 2019 to set up two Centres of Excellence for students with special needs in the Temburong district. MIS project is a significant initiative introduced and implemented in selected primary and secondary schools to meet students' needs with different abilities, including those with autism. These selected schools provide students with different abilities relevant learning and adaptive skills to participate alongside their same-age peers in the regular classroom actively.

The Religious Special Education Unit, Religious Schools Division, Ministry of Religious Affairs (MORA) also offers Intervention Programme by Pull-Out System. This programme provides individual learning through a structured learning approach using the Picture Exchange Communication System (PECS) system and guidance in establishing a healthy study-play balance. Others are religious internships and cued speech programmes. NGOs partner with the government to advocate for the inclusion and empowerment of PWDs (Ministry of Finance and Economy 2020).

Pusat Ehsan Al-Amerah Al-Hajjah Maryam (Pusat Ehsan) is a non-governmental and non-profit charitable organization committed to providing quality education, rehabilitation and vocational training programmes for PWDs. It serves individuals with Cerebral Palsy, Down Syndrome, Autism Spectrum Disorder, Hearing Impairment, Visual Impairment, and individuals with Global Developmental Delays and

Intellectual Disabilities. Pusat Ehsan was established in 2000 and has two centres. It is currently serving more than 300 PWDs.

The Society for the Management of Autism Related issues in Training, Education and Resources (SMARTER) Brunei is a family support organization run by parents and family members for persons with autism. Its mission is to provide close collaboration and closely work with parents, families, therapists and other professionals to help children develop their fullest potential. It provides lifelong services, with its own pre-vocational, vocational and employment programme that caters towards each person's individualistic needs through their centres, supporting the Ministry of Education's Special Education Unit. It launched its Brunei Autism Centre for Adults in 2008.

The Brunei Darussalam National Association of the Blind (BDNAB) was established in 2001 and aimed to empower the blind and partially sighted by promoting equality and full participation (Ministry of Finance and Economics 2020).

Furthermore, the Ministry of Development issued the Different Abilities Design Guidelines under the Building Control Order in 2018. The guidelines aimed to ensure all new buildings provide facilities and access for PWDs (Ministry of Finance and Economy 2020).

In sports, Brunei's para-athletes participated and had outstanding achievements in various regional and international competitions, including the 2019 World Para Bowling Tour Championship in the Philippines and the 2019 Arafura Sports Games in Australia (Ministry of Finance and Economy 2020).

TRENDS, OPPORTUNITIES AND CHALLENGES OF AGEING POPULATION

While today's proportion of older people increases and life expectancy improves, Brunei's fertility rate is decreasing. The trends depict an upward or increasing trend towards the ageing population. The changing composition of the population has significant implications for the government. Individuals at old age tend to have low incomes and require income support from the government. The greying population may slow economic growth, heighten social tension and weaken cohesion in the community. In addition, pension and social services budgets may impose strains upon government finance. Therefore, the government should encourage more voluntary welfare organizations and private operators to provide community-based healthcare services (Azim 2002). NCDs are common health problems affecting the ageing population in Brunei.

The Ministry of Culture, Youth and Sports (MCYS) of Brunei implemented a strategic plan which is driven by the national philosophy of Malay Islamic Monarchy (MIB) and guided by the five objectives (*maqasid*) of the *"Syariah"*. The critical mission of MCYS is to improve the lives and well-being of the people through the provision of service excellence, while the vision is to aspire to a future state of excellence (*Bangsa Brunei Cemerlang*). The MYCS established two new Senior Citizens Activity Centres (PKWE) in Belait and Temburong districts, collaborating with the Ministry of Home Affairs, Yayasan Sultan Haji Hassanal Bolkiah Brunei Shell Petroleum (Ministry of Culture, Youth and Sports 2020a). The protection and social empowerment efforts implemented are in line with the Senior Citizens Action Plan. The plan fosters a proactive attitude, high commitment and strong cooperation from all parties, especially PKWE, organizations, and senior citizens' associations. It also intended and implemented beneficial activities at the level of ministries, associations, volunteers and individuals towards the progress and inclusion of the elderly in a whole-of-nation effort (Ministry of Culture, Youth and Sports 2020b).

In 2020, the MCYS introduced National Welfare System (SKN) to facilitate access and relevant assistance applications for senior citizens. The system provides a more comprehensive picture of the assistance ecosystem in Brunei. The government has also introduced "in-kind" assistance, namely disposable diapers and milk, to individual senior citizens in order to help family members care for the elderly. The Department of Community Development continues to work with the Ministry of Health (MOH), associations, and volunteers to increase support for the Caring for the Elderly Project. It is an initiative to care for, identify and implement health screening for the elderly on an ongoing basis (Ministry of Culture, Youth and Sports 2020b).

The MCYS has implemented the "Dementia Disease Awareness Programme" in collaboration with the MOH and Dementia Brunei. Physical exercise and aerobics training, gardening and handicrafts are activities conducted with PKWE to improve healthy lifestyle practices. These health-promoting activities implemented using the whole-of-nation approach support an active ageing lifestyle that focuses on mental and physical health (Ministry of Culture, Youth and Sports 2020b).

Brunei recognizes the importance of empowering the elderly and supporting the needs of lifelong learning (inclusive learning) through capacity-building, skills and entrepreneurship programmes. The MCYS and its strategic partners are also committed to providing space and opportunities to enable senior citizens to start and implement enterprises optimally. In collaboration with the Authority for Info-Communications Technology Industry (AITI) and telecommunication companies, the ministry introduced the Information Technology Programme in 2020, ensuring that senior citizens will uphold the country's aspirations towards Industrial Revolution 4.0 (Ministry of Culture, Youth and Sports 2020b).

During the COVID-19 outbreak, 2,100 youths from various backgrounds and ages participated in the COVID-19 Volunteer Operations Centre. They played a critical role, including distributing food rations and protective equipment to those in need, like the elderly, to continue to be cared for and remembered while facing the risk of a pandemic.

The social protection efforts such as the payment of Old Age Pensions through online banking were introduced as an optional method by the government to deliver social services by avoiding any risk of infection to the elderly. In addition, the introduction of the BruHealth application has enabled the authorities to monitor the elderlies' safety, health and well-being by utilizing digital technology. MCYS also collaborated with Universiti Brunei Darussalam for health research projects and raised awareness on the effects of COVID-19 among the elderly population (Ministry of Culture, Youth and Sports 2020b).

A SUMMARY OF HEALTH POLICIES AND SYSTEMS

His Majesty Sultan Haji Hassanal Bolkiah Mu'izzaddin Waddaulah ibni Al-Marhum Sultan Haji Omar 'Ali Saifuddien Sa'adul Khairi Waddien, the Sultan and Yang Di-Pertuan of Brunei Darussalam has called upon for better discipline and sustainable actions to promote healthy lifestyles and progressively tackle NCDs. Therefore, there is high urgency to address NCDs prevention and control (Ministry of Health 2013).

The UN General Assembly High-Level Meeting has highlighted the importance of the whole-of-government and whole-of-society efforts to respond to NCDs' challenges. Effective prevention and controls of NCDs require multisectoral approaches across all government sectors, including health, education, energy, agriculture, sports, transport, communication, town planning, environment, labour, employment, industry and trade, finance, social and economic (United Nations 2012).

The increasing NCDs' burden over time has led MOH to revisit and formulate their strategies, policies, and programmes to address NCDs' prevention and control accordingly. The policies and programmes include National Dietary Guidelines (2000), National Breastfeeding Policy (2002) and Health Promotion Blueprint 2011–2015. The national and multisectoral committee on prevention and control of NCDs include the Healthy Lifestyle Promotion Committee (2012) and Maternal, Infant and Young Child Nutrition (MIYCN) Task Force (2013). The Health Promotion Blueprint 2011–2015 was developed in line with the MOH's strategic plan to work towards a healthy nation. It offers a framework to tackle the growth of NCDs. In 2012, MOH established the National NCD Prevention and Control Strategic Planning Committee to strengthen the NCD initiatives and develop Brunei National Multisectoral Action Plan for the Prevention and Control of Noncommunicable Diseases (BruMAP-NCD) 2013–2018 (Ministry of Health 2013).

The ministries and sectors have a role to play for NCDs prevention and control, requiring a holistic, integrated and multilevel approach. The goal of BruMAP-NCD 2013–2018 was to achieve an 18 per cent reduction in premature mortality from NCDs by 2018, requiring robust and continuous commitment and actions from all sectors. The World Health Organization's Global Action Plan for NCD Prevention and Control has guided this policy. Also, it is consistent with the UN High-Level Meeting's political declaration on NCD Prevention and Control in New York, 2011. BruMAP-NCD 2013–2018 sets up recommended actions for the MOH and other ministries. It accounted for existing policies and strengthening others and provided detailed guidance to achieve various goals and targets. The five strategic actions of the National Multisectoral Action Plan comprise reducing tobacco use, promoting a balanced and healthy diet, increasing physical activity, sufficiently identifying and managing people at high risk of NCDs, and improving the quality of care and outcome of NCDs management (Ministry of Health 2013).

The policies help to address critical public health issues such as undernutrition, low birth weight, maternal undernutrition, childhood obesity and adulthood obesity. Besides, it provides a connection and continuity of actions identified in the Health Promotion Blueprint 2011–2015, particularly in addressing the first three objectives: reducing tobacco use, promoting a balanced and healthy diet, and promoting physical activity. The "National Strategy for MIYCN in Brunei Darussalam 2014–2020" is implemented to focus on optimum child nutrition status, such as promoting exclusive breastfeeding for the first six months of life. The MOH is steadfast to monitor and achieve the key targets in reducing stunting among children under five, reduction in low birth weight, controlling childhood obesity, promoting EBF in the first six months and reducing childhood wasting.

Furthermore, in 2017, Brunei introduced excise taxes on food products with high sugar and monosodium glutamate (MSG) contents (Ministry of Finance and Economy 2020). These policies have positive impacts on population health as highlighted in the national NCD target from 2019 to 2023, including a reduction in tobacco use among adults from 19.9 per cent to 14.0 per cent, reduction in sweetened beverage consumption among students from 46.2 per cent to 23.1 per cent, reduction in the prevalence of physical inactivity for adolescents from 87.0 per cent to 74.0 per cent, and reduction in the prevalence of physical inactivity for adults from 25.3 per cent to 20.0 per cent (Ministry of Health 2019). In addition, Brunei's Public Health [Food] Act [Cap 182] offers social protection related to the population's food or nutrition aspects (World Health Organization 2014). The legislation commenced on 1 January 2001 to call for this act to also make specific provisions to regulate public health regarding food and relevant matters (Ministry of Health 2017).

There is a strong impetus in strengthening primary healthcare (PHC) within the health sector based on universal healthcare coverage. The Government of Brunei Darussalam generously subsidizes medical and healthcare to its citizens via government hospitals, health centres and health clinics. The PHC provides services via a network of health centres and clinics in the country. In addition, the Flying Medical Services provide PHC in remote areas that are difficult to access by land or water. In 2000, MOH implemented decentralization of PHC services to aid healthcare access to all in the nation (Ministry of Health 2013).

The health facilities consist of 4 government hospitals, 14 health centres, 3 health clinics, 4 maternal health and child health clinics, 3 travelling health clinics and 2 flying medical services as of 2017. The MOH offers dental services in 4 hospitals, 1 health centre, 16 health clinics, 44 static school clinics and 9 mobile squads. Moreover, 2 hospitals, 1 health centre, 33 health clinics and 8 dental clinics have also offered private health services in the country. The human resource in health comprises 683 doctors, 106 dentists, 73 pharmacists, 2,713 nurses and 289 midwives (Ministry of Health 2018a).

The Department of Medical Services is accountable for delivering hospital services in all districts in the country. The hospital services have developed and progressed tremendously in providing both secondary and tertiary care. The MOH also provides highly specialized care in almost all areas of specialities in line with the current disease trends and enables patients to access medical care. Raja Isteri Pengiran Anak Saleha (RIPAS) Hospital is the primary referral government hospital located in the capital city. RIPAS Hospital offers an extensive and comprehensive range of medical and surgical services, covering almost 30 different specialities and subspecialties (Ministry of Health 2018a).

Brunei has also dealt with the harmful impacts of climate change and environmental pollution on public health. It is a hot and wet country with an equatorial climate throughout the year, with the most decadent rainfall period from October to January and May to July. Therefore, it is hugely affected by climate change, and there are several risks such as increased flooding, heat-related mortality, occupational health hazards, water scarcity, and reduced agricultural production (World Health Organization 2016).

The *Wawasan* Brunei 2035 (Brunei Vision 2035) has stated the nation's social, economic and environmental goals. The strategies emphasize enhancing climate resilience, adaptation and mitigation measures that are essential for the health and well-being of the population and the country's natural resources. The government has identified six priority sectors for further climate change adaptation actions: 1) biodiversity, 2) forestry, 3) coastal and flood protection, 4) health, 5) agriculture, and 6) fisheries. The country's mean annual temperature increased about 3.9°C from 1990 to 2000 due to high global carbon emissions. Besides, the risk of vector-borne diseases is likely to increase towards 2070 in the case of high emissions. Furthermore, the heat-related deaths in the elderly (65+ years) will increase to about 51 deaths every 100,000 people in 2080 compared to the estimated baseline of zero death every 100,000 people annually between 1961 and 1990. Therefore, a rapid reduction in global emissions could limit heat-related deaths in the elderly to about seven deaths per 100,000 in 2080 (World Health Organization 2016).

In 2002, the Pollution Control Guidelines for Industrial Development in Brunei were adopted to control emissions, effluents, and discharge from various development and construction activities. Brunei Darussalam ratified the United Nations Framework Convention on Climate Change (UNFCCC) in 2007 and the Kyoto Protocol in 2009. In addition, the nation introduced several environmental acts and guidelines, for example, "Environmental Protection and Management Order 2016" and "Hazardous Waste (Control of Export and Transit) Order 2013". The Brunei Darussalam National Council on Climate Change (BNCC) launched the nation's first climate change policy, the Brunei Darussalam National Climate Change Policy (BNCCP), on 25 July 2020 (Department of Environment, Parks and Recreation 2020).

CONCLUSION

Brunei has markedly shown improved overall health status and life expectancy of the population over the last five decades. However, NCDs and the risk factors remain significant public health issues in the country. The common causes of death among adults are cancer, heart disease, diabetes mellitus, stroke, and hypertension. Children have low physical activity and inadequate intake of fibre, fruits and vegetables. Mental health issues and ageing are raising concerns in the nation. Brunei has to address social determinants of health and may benefit from using the whole-of-nation approach. There is a profound paradigm shift on disability from medical to social models to ensure PWDs' equal rights, opportunities and participation are fully exerted in Bruneian society. The health and social policies implemented in the country have positive impacts on population health and citizens' quality of life. The emergence and re-emergence of infectious pathogens, including the COVID-19 pandemic, become continuous threats to the country's population health and worldwide. The nation has implemented effective strategies, including exploiting digital platforms and artificial intelligence (BruHealth) in "flattening the epidemic curve" for COVID-19. Brunei faces a "double burden of disease" with a growing ageing population and environmental threats that pose various challenges and opportunities.

REFERENCES

Alhaji, Mohammed, Roslin Sharbawi, Adrian Kay, and Nik Tuah. 2018. "Paid Maternity Leave Extension and Exclusive Breastfeeding Practice: Evidence from Brunei". *Asian Biomedicine* 11 (December): 435–42. https://doi.org/10.1515/abm-2018-0020.

Anderson, Roy M., Hans Heesterbeek, Don Klinkenberg, and T. Déirdre Hollingsworth. 2020. "How Will Country-Based Mitigation Measures Influence the Course of the COVID-19 Epidemic?" *Lancet* 395, no. 10228: 931–34. https://doi.org/10.1016/S0140-6736(20)30567-5.

Attorney General's Chamber. 2017. "Old Age and Disability Pensions Act [Cap 1] Revised Edition". Brunei Darussalam: Prime Minister's Office. http://www.agc.gov.bn/AGC%20Images/LAWS/ACT_PDF/Cap18b.pdf.

Azim, Parvez. 2002. "The Ageing Population of Brunei Darussalam: Trends and Economic Consequences". *Asia-Pacific Population Journal* 17, no. 1: 39–54. https://doi.org/10.18356/f356c493-en.

Commonwealth Network. 2020. "Mental Health in Brunei Darussalam". Commonwealth Network: Commonwealth Education Online Commonwealth Governance Online Commonwealth Health Online. https://www.commonwealthofnations.org/cho/asia/brunei_darussalam/mental_health_in_brunei_darussalam/.

Department of Environment, Parks and Recreation. 2020. "Environmental Acts and Guidelines". Brunei Darussalam: Ministry of Development. http://env.gov.bn/SitePages/Environmental%20Acts%20and%20Guidelines.aspx.

Department of Statistics. 2020. *Report of the Mid-Year Population Estimates 2020*. Brunei Darussalam: Department of Economic Planning and Statistics, Ministry of Finance and Economy. http://www.deps.gov.bn/DEPD%20Documents%20Library/DOS/POP/2020/RPT_MidYr_2020.pdf.

Guan, Wei Jie, Zheng Yi Ni, Yu Hu, Wen Hua Liang, Chun Quan Ou, Jian Xing He, Lei Liu, et al. 2020. "Clinical Characteristics of Coronavirus Disease 2019 in China". *The New England Journal of Medicine* 382: 1708–20. https://doi.org/10.1056/NEJMoa2002032.

Ministry of Culture, Youth and Sports. 2020a. *Strategic Plan 2020–2024*. Bandar Seri Begawan, Brunei Darussalam: Ministry of Culture, Youth and Sports. http://www.kkbs.gov.bn/Documents/MCYS_Strategic_Plan_2020_2024_Eng. pdf.

———. 2020b. "Warga Emas NBD Terus Catat Pencapaian Signifikan". 1 October 2020. http://www.kkbs.gov.bn/Lists/News/NDispForm.aspx?ID=883& ContentTypeId=0x0100ECC89185A7F5E74A8CA7B999A4454ABE.

Ministry of Finance and Economy. 2020. *2020 United Nations High-Level Political Forum on Sustainable Development: Voluntary National Review Report of Brunei Darussalam*. Bandar Seri Begawan: Ministry of Finance and Economy. https:// sustainabledevelopment.un.org/content/documents/26410VNR_2020_ Brunei_Report.pdf.

Ministry of Health. 2013. *National Multisectoral Action Plan for the Prevention and Control of Non-Communicable Disease (BruMAP-NCD)*. Bandar Seri Begawan, Brunei Darussalam: Ministry of Health.

———. 2014. *The 2nd National Health and Nutritional Status Survey (NHANSS)*. Bandar Seri Begawan, Brunei Darussalam: Ministry of Health.

———. 2017. "Acts and Regulations". Brunei Darussalam: Ministry of Health. http://www.moh.gov.bn/SitePages/Acts%20and%20Regulations.aspx.

———. 2018a. *Health Information Booklet 2017 (Revised as of 11 December 2018)*. Bandar Seri Begawan, Brunei Darussalam: Department of Policy and Planning, Ministry of Health Brunei Darussalam. http://moh.gov.bn/ Downloadables/Health%20Information%20Bookler%202017%20(revised%20 as%20of%20January%202019).pdf.

———. 2018b. "Mental Health Services in Brunei Darussalam". 4 August 2018. http://www.moh.gov.bn/Lists/Latest%20news/NewDispForm.aspx?ID=187.

———. 2019. *Ministry of Health Strategic Plan 2019–2023. Investing for Our Future*. Bandar Seri Begawan, Brunei Darussalam: Department of Policy and Planning, Ministry of Health Brunei Darussalam. http://www.moh. gov.bn/Shared%20Documents/Strategic%20Plan%20MOH%202019-2023/ FINAL%20MOH%20Strategic%20Book%202019-compressed%20(5MB).pdf.

———. 2020a. "Detection of the First Case of COVID-19 Infection in Brunei Darussalam". Press Release, 9 March 2020. http://www.moh.gov.bn/ Shared%20Documents/2019%20ncov/press%20releases/FINAL%20Press%20 Release%20(eng)%20-%20First%20Case%20COVID-19%20in%20Brunei%20 Darussalam%20(2).pdf.

———. 2020b. "Media Statement on the Current COVID-19 Infection in Brunei Darussalam". Press Release, 30 March 2020. http://www.moh.gov.bn/Shared Documents/2019 ncov/press releases/Media statement on the current situation of COVID-19 in Brunei Darussalam (30.03.2020).pdf.

_____. 2020c. "Press Releases & Press Info on Coronavirus Disease 2019 (COVID-19)". http://www.moh.gov.bn/SitePages/pressreleaseCOVID-19.aspx.

_____. 2021a. "BruHealth". http://www.moh.gov.bn/SitePages/bruhealth.aspx.

_____. 2021b. "Press Release on the Current Situation of the COVID-19 Infection in Brunei Darussalam". 26 June 2021. http://www.moh.gov.bn/Lists/Latest%20news/NewDispForm.aspx?ID=926.

Office of the High Commissioner for Human Rights. 2021. "Conventions on the Rights of Persons with Disabilities: Brunei Darussalam". *UN Treaty Body Database*. https://tbinternet.ohchr.org/_layouts/15/TreatyBodyExternal/Treaty.aspx.

Retief, Marno, and Rantoa Letšosa. 2018. "Models of Disability: A Brief Overview". *HTS Teologiese Studies/Theological Studies* 74 (March). https://doi.org/10.4102/hts.v74i1.4738.

Roslan, Nurul Nabilah, and Nurazzura Mohamad Diah. 2020. "To Work or Not to Work: The Struggle for Employment Among Youth with Disabilities in Brunei". In *Proceedings of the 1st Progress in Social Science, Humanities and Education Research Symposium (PSSHERS 2019)*, pp. 1050–56. Atlantis Press. https://doi.org/10.2991/assehr.k.200824.232.

United Nations. 2012. "Resolution Adopted by the General Assembly on 19 September 2011. 66/2. Political Declaration of the High-Level Meeting of the General Assembly on the Prevention and Control of Non-Communicable Diseases". *General Assembly*, 24 January 2012. https://documents-dds-ny.un.org/doc/UNDOC/GEN/N11/458/94/PDF/N1145894.pdf?OpenElement.

World Health Organization. 2011. "Mental Health Atlas 2011 Country Profiles: Brunei Darussalam". Geneva, Switzerland: Department of Mental Health and Substance Abuse, World Health Organization. https://www.who.int/mental_health/evidence/atlas/profiles/brn_mh_profile.pdf?ua=1.

_____. 2014. "Brunei Darussalam - Food and Nutrition Security Profiles". Geneva, Switzerland: World Health Organization. http://www.fao.org/3/at705e/at705e.pdf.

_____. 2016. "Climate and Health Country Profile 2015: Brunei Darussalam". Geneva, Switzerland: World Health Organization. https://www.who.int/publications/i/item/health-and-climate-change-country-profile-2015-brunei-darussalam.

_____. 2018. "Non-Communicable Diseases (NCD) Country Profiles 2018: Brunei Darussalam". Geneva, Switzerland: World Health Organization. http://awareness.who.int/nmh/countries/brn_en.pdf.

_____. 2021a. "Breastfeeding". https://www.who.int/health-topics/breastfeeding#tab=tab_2.

_____. 2021b. "Coronavirus Disease (COVID-19) Pandemic". 25 June 2021. https://www.who.int/emergencies/diseases/novel-coronavirus-2019.

World Health Organization, and The World Bank. 2011. *World Report on Disability*. Geneva, Switzerland: World Health Organization. https://www.who.int/teams/noncommunicable-diseases/sensory-functions-disability-and-rehabilitation/world-report-on-disability.

World Health Organization Western Pacific Region. 2008. *Asia-Pacific Consultation on the World Report on Disability and Rehabilitation*. Manila, Philippines: World Health Organization Regional Office for the Western Pacific. https://apps.who.int/iris/bitstream/handle/10665/208456/RS_2008_GE_13_PHL_eng.pdf?sequence=1&isAllowed=y.

PART IV

Business, Economy and Welfare

10

CHANGING BUSINESS LANDSCAPE IN BRUNEI: ENTREPRENEURSHIP AND INNOVATION

Mahani Hamdan

INTRODUCTION

Innovation is now the buzzword in the world of business, and entrepreneurship is an area critical for global economic development particularly in developing countries. Innovation and entrepreneurship are not confined to start-ups and new ventures, but rather, they allude to dynamic and holistic processes in all aspects of social and economic development. Thornton, Ribeiro-Soriano and Urbano (2011) highlighted that entrepreneurship is on the rise due to a number of cultural and economic factors. For most entrepreneurs, innovation is not just about creating new ideas but making those ideas happen. While invention is an important source of technology (Weber, Dixon and Llorente 1993), Schumpeter (1934) asserted that innovation is more than invention, and technological innovation can help to create opportunities and give entrepreneurs access to a wider swath of the population.

The complementary relationship between entrepreneurship and innovation can be explained via two perspectives. Schumpeter's (1934) notion of business in innovation described how entrepreneurs' new ideas can lead to the overhaul of a market and link them to economic growth and development ("creative destruction"). On the other hand, Kirzner (1973) looked at how entrepreneurs find gaps, recognize opportunities and make the most of the opportunity by trial and error and market feedback. No doubt that the world today is dominated by innovative ideas and technology, but innovation alone cannot facilitate entrepreneurship success because success does not take place in a vacuum. Entrepreneurs require a healthy entrepreneurial ecosystem comprising the mix of attitudes, resources and infrastructure to grow and sustain. It has been years since the Global Entrepreneurship Index ranked the United States of America top in the list because of its attractive ecosystem, showing that the success of entrepreneurship hinges on the context in which it operates.

In the context of oil and gas high income developing economies, entrepreneurship and innovation have continuously been an important agenda in their national economic development plans. Even more today, the role of entrepreneurship and innovation intensifies as the reduction in oil prices and their volatility pose strong challenges to these economies. While it may be a blessing to have an abundant supply of natural resources, in the long run, diversified economies perform better than mono-sector economies (Cherif, Hasanov and Zhu 2016). Carter and Jones-Evans (2006) argued that economies with many small firms are more innovative than those with large firms because small firms are less bound by convention and more flexible. However, not all new and small firms are equal in innovation. Although the landscape of today's economy accommodates the growing number of start-ups, entrepreneurs and venture companies, the highly innovative and high growth potential firms that can make a huge impact on jobs and productivity make up only a small minority of all small and medium-sized enterprises (SMEs) (OECD 2010). Moreover, not all entrepreneurs venture into the same business lines. This is a beneficial advantage because strong economies are primarily based on different kinds of business. Hales (2016) pointed out that a diversified economy can support multiple businesses and they can continually feed off one another for financial gain and grow larger as the economy grows.

In the case of Brunei, its business landscape is ever-evolving and continually changing. Globalization, digitalization and the recent global pandemic COVID-19 have affected not only the way businesses are conducted in this country and how the locals perceive the purpose of doing business, but also job availability and opportunities for workers displaced by COVID-19. These circumstances probe the positive engagement of the private sector with the state (government) in sustaining the drive towards entrepreneurship and innovation, and set to create new jobs and displaced jobs because of digitalization. To reduce Brunei's heavy reliance on oil and gas and adequately prepare for the future, the country has made economic diversification the prime economic agenda since its independence in 1984, yet the progress in achieving this goal has been much slower than expected (Siddiqui, Athmay and Mohammed 2012). For example, one of the objectives tied to the diversification and development projects is the promotion of investment, foreign and domestic, both in downstream industries and economic clusters beyond the oil and gas industry. Although Brunei is on the right track with the establishment of Monetary Authority of Brunei Darussalam in 2011 and the issuance of *Sukuk* (bond), its capital market development has been slow due to the lack of secondary market and conservatism of Bruneian investors (Global Capital 2011). About ten years ago, Lawrey (2010) claimed that Brunei's efforts to diversify had failed because the country was still faced with the problem of how to rely less on the production of non-hydrocarbons. Regardless, what remains important today is how the country addresses the main challenges of diversification (Mishrif 2018), not whether their diversification efforts have succeeded or failed.

Economic diversification remains a challenge for Brunei. The government has been talking about shifting from a non-hydrocarbon to hydrogen society but hydrogen's supply cost is much higher than that of oil and gas (Kimura et al. 2020). A further shift from a resource-based to a knowledge-based economy also appears less feasible without the government investing in emerging new technologies and technology transfers (Mohammad Sofian 2016). To increase the country's diversification efforts, many initiatives, programmes and projects had been introduced. Policies were formulated and regularly revised. Financing facilities were provided, and standard operating procedures had also been simplified. That said, it is yet to be known how impactful all these efforts to boost entrepreneurial and innovation activities are.

This chapter carries three main objectives. Firstly, it identifies some of the government's key initiatives and support measures that cut across all levels to accelerate the development of entrepreneurship and innovation. Secondly, it highlights the achievements and the need for cooperation for progress to continue, and thirdly, it addresses several issues and challenges that Brunei faces, particularly amid the dwindling global oil prices and COVID-19 pandemic, with some recommendations for improvement. Both secondary data and observation are employed to support the findings of the study. Overall, the chapter highlights the importance of building and strengthening innovation and entrepreneurship which go hand in hand with wider benefits to all society in shaping the country's future and helping to create sustainable economic growth.

ENTREPRENEURSHIP AND INNOVATION HOLDS THE KEY TO ECONOMIC DIVERSIFICATION

Economic diversification in the Brunei context infers three issues. Firstly, to create "revenue streams" from non-oil and gas sectors that will help the country to generate extra income. Secondly, to develop "industrialization" in order to decrease its dependency on oil and gas as well as reliance on public sector employment, and thirdly, to strengthen the development of "local human capital" as Brunei needs to move away from dependency on outside experts for assistance. Many studies have looked into the progress of Brunei's economic diversification in general terms across time and space, and the focus ranged from strategic and operational to future strategies (Bhaskaran 2010; Lawrey 2010; Yunos 2014). Only a few provided specific emphasis to the development of entrepreneurship as a tool for economic diversification (Low, Hussin and Ang 2013; Siddiqui, Athmay and Mohammed 2012), and that innovation as a tool of entrepreneurship (Drucker 1985).

Yunos (2014) indicated that entrepreneurship has been on the national agenda for economic diversification even before Brunei gained its full independence from the British colonial system in 1984. The agenda became transparent only when the government started to operationalize it through its first and subsequent five-year national development plans (NDP) as early as in the 1950s. At that point in time, the main objective of the NDP was to develop the non-oil and gas sectors. Most of the plans and reforms had, however, failed to be implemented effectively because of the lack of coordination, ownership and accountability (Yunos and Milojevic 2016). Innovation, on the other hand, became ostensible only in 2014 when the Prime Minister's Office announced a plan to foster a knowledge-based society through the establishment of new institutions, provision of support services, and identification of projects for research and development along with investment in technology and training as a means to support innovation (Oxford Business Group 2014).

Before delving into the development of innovation and entrepreneurship, there is one perception that begs clarification. That is, Bruneian society has long been criticized by western observers for their apparent complacency over the diversification issue. It was argued that Bruneians have little or no motivation to improve themselves and the economy because much of what they need is provided for them (Bhaskaran 2010). The word "complacency" is synonymous with what local journalists, bloggers and academic writers regard the Bruneian society for a decade or so. Is this still relevant to describe Bruneians today? Based on the researcher's informal conversations with nearly 100 respondents working and studying across sectors in different fields, two viewpoints are formulated:

Firstly, the argument that the Bruneian society is complacent due to not having a need for conscious self-improvement thanks to a subsidized life can no longer be considered appropriate, but rather to acknowledge that people today sincerely appreciate the government's continual efforts to strengthen the economy through various economic diversifications. Bruneians have also become more aware of the stream of challenges and issues that the country is experiencing, and strive to unlock energies and entanglements of initiatives in ways that are helpful. Public acknowledgement and local contributions in national programmes, projects and events where appropriate is attributable to the government's positive governance efforts in promoting transparency, accountability and participation, although much work still needs to be done to bring the benefits of open governance to the society. Secondly, the Bruneian society holds strong values for stability, protection and security which makes them less competent, dynamic and risk-averse, to some extent. These are not bad things at the margin, but if the society does not take enough risk, over the longer run, there will come a time where people start moving backwards in life. In essence, taking risks is closely associated with entrepreneurship, while innovation and opportunity are tied to risks (Genever 2020).

THE MODERN ERA OF ENTREPRENEURSHIP AND INNOVATION: PUTTING IT INTO PERSPECTIVE

The word "entrepreneurship" has evolved over time, changing people's understanding and perception of that term. No single definition of entrepreneurship is definitive (Lichtenstein 2011), and Blackburn (2011) regarded entrepreneurship as multi-dimensional because "it involves analysing people and their actions together with the ways in which they interact with their environments, be these social, economic or political, and the institutional, policy, and legal frameworks that help define and legitimise human activities" (p. xiii).

A three-perspective approach to understanding entrepreneurship in the Brunei context can be identified. Firstly, *entrepreneurship subsists in different types of entrepreneurial ventures*. Entrepreneurs who become business owners in any form of business entities come up with new business ideas, and they turn those ideas into different types of entrepreneurial ventures based on five business occupations: (a) business, (b) trading, (c) industrial, (d) corporate and (e) agricultural (Drucker 2014). Prior to Brunei's independence, a number of local entrepreneurs had ventured into fisheries, timbers, food and traditional delicacies and weaving that were primarily undertaken by those who resided in Water Village. Animal farming, poultry and rice plantation were largely operated by those who lived on dry land. These primary business activities generally aimed at fulfilling people's basic needs. Local entrepreneurs in the past perceived doing business as "doing a family business to make a living". Business was seen as a necessity rather than an option, and they were committed to growth and sustainability. Few of the family businesses still exist today with new brands or images. The businesses expanded across the country and have been passed down from one generation to the next, such as Hua Ho and Soon Lee Department Stores.

Secondly, *entrepreneurship as a way to generate extra income*. After Brunei gained its independence, the situation changed. The government created many job opportunities for people to work in the public sector and provided them with good salaries and fringe benefits, which could account for the gradual decline in entrepreneurial activity. Job search was easy in the late 1980s and early 1990s because demand for labour in the public sector employment was higher than the supply, and many Bruneians worked for the government in search of job security and stability (Cleary and Francis 1994). Only a small number of working population in the public sector, especially women, continued to do small home-based businesses ranging from food catering services, bakery, tailoring, furniture making to handicraft, in their free time as a hobby. During that time, the government had not yet imposed any restriction for public servants to conduct a business, and these part-time entrepreneurs perceived entrepreneurship as a part-time job and a way to generate extra income. As a matter of fact, this could be the starting point of people's complacency as they began to enjoy the benefits of working for the government and became more comfortable and satisfied in the workplace.

Thirdly, *entrepreneurial spirit drives innovation*. From the mid-1990s until today, the meaning of entrepreneurship is less likely seen as a source of employment or income but rather as a means to inculcate the spirit of independence, self-reliance, resourcefulness and innovation ("value inculcation"). It is more of individuals' self-development and personal growth including willingness to take risks which can be inculcated through education and coaching (Mahani and Masairol 2015), careful planning and having the ability to take calculated risks. It is also the change of mindset that risk-taking is a rewarding strategy and to accept risk as a cost of opportunity and innovation. Certainly, not all risks will pay off but individual entrepreneurs must believe that they can still recover and keep their reputation intact. Sowbhagya (2017) emphasized the importance of education in building up values and attitudes of mind in the people to enable their active participation in life. Entrepreneurship education was first introduced by Universiti Brunei Darussalam (UBD) in 2009 through its Discovery Year activities, followed by the establishment of Entrepreneurship Village and National Entrepreneurship Agenda (NEA) in 2014, the introduction of an upgraded programme (Brunei Entrepreneurship Education Scheme Second Chapter 2016) and the integration of entrepreneurship education into Core Education (grades K–12). Under NEA, entrepreneurship education is to be taught in schools, colleges and higher education institutions across all age groups with various means such as curriculum, classroom instruction, plays, movies and stories. By providing early training in entrepreneurship, Brunei's national education system is preparing students for the future of work. The Ministry of Finance and Economy (2020) reported that about 16 per cent of graduates have successfully become entrepreneurs, with 300 start-ups founded by UBD graduates. In relation to innovation, it can be understood from three perspectives as well. Firstly, *entrepreneurs as innovators*. Schumpeter (1934), who was among the first to highlight innovation in entrepreneurship development, defined innovators as those who implement entrepreneurial change within markets, including introducing new or improved products, new methods of production, opening of a new market, exploitation of a new source of supply and re-engineering or organization of business management process. Although Brunei's innovation ecosystem is still very much in its infancy, the growing number of social enterprises and their strong social media presence have helped to create jobs and provide innovative services and products. Secondly, *innovation-led sustainable entrepreneurship in local SMEs*. It implies that innovation plays an important role in the process of transformation towards the sustainable development of enterprises (Soltysik, Urbaniec and Wojnarowska 2019), thus building a competitive advantage for entrepreneurs (Porter 1990). In fact, innovation itself is the new competitive advantage (Jacobsen 2020), as it can be a threat to existing jobs and subsequently, technological change creates uncertain economic growth. Thirdly, *innovation and entrepreneurship are complementary fit* because "innovation is the source of entrepreneurship and entrepreneurship allows innovation to flourish and helps to realise its economic value" (Brem 2011, p. 13). Both concepts have been identified as conditions for economic growth, diversification and sustainable development in Brunei's political discussion, which lead to various conclusions concerning the role of the private sector and opportunities affecting the development in these areas.

EMPOWERING THE PRIVATE SECTOR

The government alone cannot diversify and sustain the economy without the help of the private sector. Hence, the need to mobilize the private sector is at the heart of discussions around how to engage with civil society partners and harness its resources while combining them with the talent and initiatives of Bruneian society. A local business development strategy intended as a catalyst for growth in an effort to achieve the goals[1] of Brunei Vision 2035 has outlined several policy directions and initiatives with a focus primarily on SMEs development as they represent over 90 per cent of businesses in Brunei (Iqbal and Rahman 2015). The government's initiatives include introducing grants and funded programmes to finance local entrepreneurs to gain business skills and become more competitive; developing incubation centres to assist and promote local entrepreneurs in high-skilled sectors such as ICT; maximizing the indirect benefits of foreign direct investments; encouraging the use of local products, suppliers and contractors by major businesses and industries; privatizing, commercializing and outsourcing of government services as a way of expanding opportunities; reducing the cost of doing business for local entrepreneurs by simplifying government procedures; and ensuring prompt government decisions and payment to local contractors and suppliers.

Though much of Brunei's diversification effort over the years is government-led, Lebdioui (2019) emphasized the need for greater collaboration between the private and public sectors to seek out new activities and share costs where necessary. The post-financial crisis (2008) period shall be used in the study to examine the contribution of private-public engagement to Brunei's economic diversification. Selective attention revolving around the need to nurture the country's entrepreneurial and innovation activities can be manifested into two eras.

In the first era (1980s, 1990s and 2000s) the focus was largely on "financing" and "the growth of local SMEs" in the country. The government introduced financial assistance schemes through grants and loans to develop SMEs. While in the second era (2010s onwards), the impetus shifted towards increasing "investment" and "fostering engagement" to facilitate SMEs access to international markets. The government explored actively outside Brunei for global business community outreach, which in many things were largely carried out by the Brunei Economic Development Board (BEDB), to look for potential investors or partners and promote innovative local SMEs in a global economy. To reflect on the progress and changes in entrepreneurship development and innovation, the next section provides analyses on several key initiatives and support measures (including but not limited to) that have been specifically undertaken in the second era (2010s onwards). This era is chosen because the year 2011 is the first year Brunei's data was made available for Global Innovation Index (GII). The country was ranked 13th among 17 economies in Southeast

Asia, East Asia and Oceania; and 71st globally in the GII 2020 report (Azlan 2020a).

DIVERSIFICATION INITIATIVES: A TEN-YEAR REVIEW WITH KEY STAKEHOLDERS

Brunei's diversification efforts over a ten-year period (from 2010 until 2020) had only marginally improved the overall economic performance. Although the country's gross domestic product (GDP) and GDP per capita had declined from US$18.3 billion in 2011 to US$13.47 billion in 2019; and from US$47,056 in 2011 to US$31,087 in 2019, respectively, the country recorded a positive economic growth rate of 1.3 per cent in 2017, which later increased to 3.9 per cent in 2019.[2] The recent statistics showed that the economy has continued to grow by 2.8 per cent in the second quarter of 2020, and the growth was contributed by the increase in the non-oil and gas sector by 8.1 per cent—a sign of economic diversification (Borneo Bulletin 2020a). For ease of analyses, these ten-year diversification efforts are split into two five-year periods: investment (2011–15) and engagement (2016–20) periods.

Investment Period: 2011–15

The value of Brunei's foreign direct investment (FDI) net inflows has gradually declined after the global financial crisis in 2008, with the JPKE[3] reporting that FDI has fallen below 2010 levels. Investment reached a peak in 2012, before falling to approximately US$171.32 million in 2015 and declining further in 2016 to negative US$150.44 million.[4] Though the FDI net inflows rose to US$460.15 million and US$503.89 million in 2017 and 2018 respectively, the value fell back again to US$374.62 million in 2019. During this period, there has been an increase in the government's efforts to attract new FDI in strategically important industries by strengthening the growth and localization of entrepreneurship, and giving grants and assistance schemes for local SMEs to go overseas but then some entrepreneurs just do not want to. Few investment funds administered by BEDB were aimed at providing funding support for early-stage companies in hi-tech growth areas such as ICT and engineering.

Also, there has been a plethora of public policy reforms such as the reduction of corporate tax rate from 22 per cent in 2011 to

18.5 per cent in 2015, the Investment Incentive Order (2001) and the Brunei Competition Order (2015). Financial institutions including both Islamic and conventional banks have offered various microcredit financing schemes for micro and SMEs (MSMEs) to commercialize their products, export and expand overseas. The cooperation between government and such public-interest entities is based on agreement or government's directive, top-down approach. The directive sets guidelines for facilitating the government's cooperation with the private sector and consultation, and the progress of cooperation depends on the level of trust between the involved parties through transparency and integrity (Thindwa 2015).

Innovation spurs technology applications to support economic diversification in agriculture, fisheries, forestry and related processing and creative industries. For example, Brunei Agro-Technology Park (later known as Bio-Innovation Corridor in 2015) was established to increase investment in fields such as Brunei Halal Brand. Anggerek Desa Technology Hub in 2014 was to cater to local and international companies in the creative and information technology industry. Creative Arts Facilities in 2012 was to provide capacity development programmes such as seminars and training workshops for students from Institutes of Higher Learning as well as local industry players, followed by Universiti Brunei Darussalam's art and creative technology degree programme to buttress the creative industries (Geiger-Ho and Ho 2016). In summary, many of these initiatives generally took a "whole-of-government" approach to skills development and identifying conditions to foster innovation success.

Engagement Period: 2016–20

This is the period of active engagement across government departments and agencies, as well as inter-ministerial coordination with responsibility for resource allocation. Programmes and financial grants that were administered by different agencies were coordinated by BEDB, and the FDI Action and Support Centre (FAST) was established by the Prime Minister's Office specifically to facilitate FDI. Darussalam Enterprise (DARe) in 2016 was formed to work along with iCentre to develop local entrepreneurs, and Bank Usahawan in 2017 to meet the financial ambitions of entrepreneurs across various industries that will help the government's aim to diversify the economy (The Bruneian 2018).

I-Usahawan initiative led by the Ministry of Energy was introduced in 2018 in collaboration with Brunei Shell Petroleum to give opportunities to Youth SMEs to compete for a three-year contract with Brunei Shell Joint Venture Credit Facility Programme.

Although the government is still taking the lead in this endeavour, the approach has changed to involve the private sector, local communities and stakeholders, youth participation, and integrative leadership and cross-sector structural reforms in the public sector, to speed up the process of economic diversification. This change in approach further calls for an urgent paradigm shift from a predominantly "whole-of-government" approach to a "whole-of-nation" approach. The latter involves community engagement, which requires the government to be willing and able to implement appropriate policies or internal processes that effectively incorporate feedback derived from stakeholders (McCabe, Keast and Brown 2006). Evidently, Brunei's Ease of Doing Business has improved over the years. The country was ranked 66th out of 190 economies in 2019 and still maintained the number one ranking in "Getting Credit" (Borneo Bulletin 2019). Brunei was ranked 44th for the Global Innovation Index 2020 as one of the most innovative countries among 49 high-income economies. The country had performed better in innovation inputs (39th) than innovation outputs (113th) (Azlan 2020a). Whereas, in the Global Talent Competitiveness Index 2020, Brunei ranked 3rd place in Southeast Asia, 7th in the Asia-Pacific region and 38th place globally (The Star 2020).

The government has also pushed for the creation of a country-wide infrastructure (government leads by example), development of impactful programmes such as Elevate and Energy Business Academy, and coaching in practice on financial investments through apprenticeship schemes, to create an appetite to take risks and stimulate innovation. Brunei's government formed a joint venture with the leading foreign direct investor, Hengyi Industries Sendirian Berhad (Hengyi), to build Pulau Muara Besar Refinery and Petrochemical Plant (PMBRPP). Hengyi signed a commercial agreement with Brunei Shell Marketing in 2019 to supply refined fuel products for domestic market distribution (Hengyi 2020). The refinery is expected to contribute B$1.3 billion to GDP in 2020 (Bandial and Rasidah 2019) and create more downstream industries in the next phase of development. These industries are further expected to provide at least 50 per cent of over 2,000 new jobs to local Bruneians in the second phase of the refinery (Wong 2019), which in turn can help to reduce the high unemployment rate recorded at 9.12 per cent in 2020. As the intensity of collaboration increases, costs and control over the process decrease. Therefore, cross-cultural understanding and communication are keys to foster the country's collaboration with international partners.

The agricultural sector that received greater attention in 2018 with the introduction of the Contract Farming Programme[5] to stimulate youth in agriculture, especially in hi-tech farming, is expected to boost the country's GDP from 1 per cent in 2015 to 5 per cent by 2020 (Rasidah 2020). Yet, this still begs the question of how Brunei's business landscape will look like by 2035. In the next decade or so, a much greater focus should be continually directed towards building innovative and entrepreneurial ecosystems (Rasidah 2018). Strategic public-private partnerships by sector can possibly be employed to facilitate more informed and tailored decisions with the diversification process. In view of public contention that Brunei's diversification efforts have not been considered rapid, drastic or massive enough to accelerate the growth of entrepreneurship and innovation, His Majesty the Sultan and Yang Di-Pertuan of Brunei has addressed two major concerns that deserve attention for all ministries to act upon.

Firstly, the government has poor data collection which made it difficult to determine the economic growth of targeted key industries, and secondly, poorly managed privatization efforts as part of collaborative governance have hurt rather than helped nations (Rasidah 2020). It is understood that the ecosystems for innovation and entrepreneurship have different needs and specifications, but they are not mutually exclusive (Xu and Maas 2019). Brunei's government will not be able to create this single-handedly, and to rely on outside experts for innovative talent is also not sustainable. Hence, both "whole-of-government" and "whole-of-nation" approaches are necessary to enhance the collaboration between public and private sectors in fulfilling their respective roles to build a more innovative, resilient and self-reliant society. However, this does not come easy as there are challenges, and Bruneian society must do more and act faster than ever before in creating the cultural shifts to enable transformational entrepreneurship and digital transformation for sustainable economic growth.

THE CHALLENGES AND HOW TO MANAGE THEM

Challenges that hinder the development of entrepreneurship and innovation in Brunei are identified as follows. Firstly, the "classic" perception that Bruneian society has been previously labelled as—lazy, too choosy about jobs and too dependent on the government (Deseret News 1997)—can break the youth's reputation or credibility. To begin with, it is not fair to generalize that people are still behaving as such because there has been active participation of Bruneian youth in entrepreneurial and innovation activities (Kon 2020). Moreover, the number of local SMEs has increased, along with the establishment of social enterprises which are more apparent today than before (Azlan 2019). These enterprises venture into food and beverage, construction, real estate properties, technology and consultancy businesses for the greater social good and not just the pursuit of profits. More importantly, they have played a big part in Brunei's COVID-19 response.

Secondly, despite the active youth participation in entrepreneurship and innovation activities, there lies a huge yet resolvable problem. That is the mindset of local entrepreneurs, which can be described in three things: (a) short-term thinking, (b) not willing to take risks, and (c) lack of self-confidence. Short-termism has become pervasive among the local entrepreneurs because of their value system. They prefer to play safe in doing business and are not willing to take risks or conflicts because they value stability and security, and the social structure of Brunei society also somewhat influenced their personality (Asiyah az-Zahra, Siti Norkhalbi and Noor Azam 2017). Local entrepreneurs are concerned with short-term profits and costs which may generate long-term problems as the country's economic growth depends on long-term investments that will pay out over time. OECD (2018) reported that most of the local SMEs are concentrated in the wholesaling and trading businesses, usually considered less costly, risky and innovative than other businesses. Clearly, they are also not investing in their employees, research or technologies. For a start, the government is setting an example by applying risk-taking behaviour to its own activities by diversifying the economy through FDIs in big national projects such as PMBRPP and Brunei Fertilizer Industries at the Sungai Liang Industrial Park.

Thirdly, many initiatives revolve around policies that have necessitated local entrepreneurs to attract potential investors. For instance, non-pioneer and pioneer enterprises can apply for tax relief on export profits from eight to eleven years respectively. Yet, only very few MSMEs have the desire to build value for long-term investments. This indicates that "investment culture" is still deficient in Brunei. Young entrepreneurs may have considered financial investments as important, but they have a preference for low-risk investments (Tang and Lee 2020). The government thus needs to build financial infrastructure that is sustainable, and partners with the local business community to increase connectivity and provide research and advisory services on infrastructure development and project finance. The local business community can help to provide a highly trained programme and an apprenticeship scheme for new start-ups to stimulate their long-term thinking into business.

Fourthly, there are too many "what if" questions which infer that the MSMEs are not only afraid to lose but also fail. It is observed that a performance-orientation goal with a failure (risk)-avoidance appears to be the motivational orientation adopted by today's generation (Hussain, Farooq and Akhtar 2012). Nonetheless, taking risks does not mean going into business blindly and expecting great results. Local entrepreneurs must work hard and prepare careful planning. Generally, their businesses are unable to grow successfully because they lack experimentation with new ideas. One way to induce risk-taking behaviour and encourage innovation is through education and incentivizing entrepreneurs to invest in assets for longer, and this calls for increased government spending on research and development activities. Lack of (or low) self-confidence also proves to be a major hurdle for local entrepreneurs, which can be enhanced through proper mentorship and coaching.

Next is culture. Bruneian society is known for its caring and supportive culture. Although they show support for local products and services, many have spent money on imported goods or products particularly from Malaysia due to currency rate differences and bulk discounts (Islam, Salleh and Sabli 2019). It remains a fact that it is cheaper to shop overseas in neighbouring countries, which provide more options and wider selection of goods and services. Thus, it is the economic rather than cultural constraint that has a greater influence on local consumer behaviour and prospective purchase decisions in a dynamic pricing competition. Despite the government's successful effort to reducing reliance on imports in which the total value of

Brunei's imports had reduced from US$3.61 billion (2013) to US$2.68 billion (2016), the value of exports had also significantly fallen from US$13 billion (2012) to US$4.88 billion (2016) due to a drop in global oil prices.[6] The values of exports and imports have moved in the same direction after 2016, but the former fell by 3.5 per cent in 2020 due to the declining global oil demand as COVID-19 weighs heavily on markets (Borneo Bulletin 2020b). There are also instances where people provide adverse criticisms to the creation of local products, disparaging the youth entrepreneurs to innovate and be productive. Thus, the society must understand that emotional distress cannot be recovered quickly and having a strong support system from families, communities, government and society as a whole is critical for entrepreneurship development and innovation to thrive.

Another challenge is that most of the initiatives or measures to promote entrepreneurship and innovation are government-led and overlapped within, between and across ministries. The ministries might come up with different programme titles but the goals and objectives are relatively similar, leading to wasted efforts and resources. Some elements of decentralization may be favourable because it allows ease of communication. Accountability transfer is vital for governmental performance when collaborating with the private sector and wider community to eliminate unnecessary confusion to the public, cost ineffectiveness and inefficiencies (Mulgan 2000), and the government should set targets and allocate budgets to examine the impacts of the programmes or projects on the entrepreneurial society. As innovative as the government should be, new programmes and initiatives must continually develop to meet subsequent objectives towards achieving the ultimate strategic goal of Brunei Vision 2035.

Finally, the country does not have many local innovators. It takes time to develop talents. It is therefore timely for the government to set the minimum salary or wage rate in a business field appropriate to individuals' qualifications and sectors. This can help to reduce the unemployment rate as well as boost the development of the private sector. National awards that were introduced at various levels are not sufficient to create a culture of innovation, and the achievement of local entrepreneurs is often seen as a one-off thing. Thus, a holistic sustainable development plan beyond national strategy is necessary at all levels, and real collaborative effort from the private sector and local communities are directly needed to maintain the spirit of nationhood towards economic diversification amid growing challenges to private sector growth, competitiveness and innovation.

FUTURE PROSPECTS

There are five key trends set to redraw and shape the future of the business landscape in Brunei by 2035, identified as follows:

a. *The accelerating growth of e-commerce*: Local MSMEs have maximized social media platforms like Facebook and Instagram as a way to promote their products or goods. While this promotes fair competition among entrepreneurs, customers now have a wider choice to choose from. They become more aware of the market brands and far-sighted in their purchasing decision. Azlan (2020b) reported that Brunei is the fourth country with the highest penetration rate in social media of 94 per cent internet users. In addition, the COVID-19 pandemic has accelerated the growth of online and mobile banking and the shift towards a cashless society.

b. *Digital innovation*: Using digital technologies to enable and empower innovation. The perception that information and communication technology (ICT) is for the young generation is proven to be off beam. In fact, local entrepreneurs need to prepare themselves to adapt successfully to a rapidly changing business environment, and ICTs are not a panacea in themselves (OECD 2004). Entrepreneurs can cultivate innovation and use ICT to grow their businesses (Mahani and Anshari 2020).

c. *Proliferation of lifelong learning*: This is no longer restricted to formal education and academic interest because the formal educational system cannot respond to the challenges of modern society. Non-formal educational practices on entrepreneurship as a de facto partner in the lifelong process must be accessible for all.

d. *Making industrialization work*: Local MSMEs should venture into primary and creative industries other than wholesaling and trading businesses, and inject "modernity and enthusiasm" to attract local employment in the private sector. Corporate leaders and local corporations are to champion and lead the targeted key industries including fishing, agriculture, banking, downstream industries in oil and gas sector and IT. The industrialization is designed for the domestic market, but with some degree of internationalization to diversify the country's export portfolio.

e. *Public-private partnerships (PPP)*: This form of collaborative governance model between the public and private sectors could help to create a healthy ecosystem for innovation and developing sustainable entrepreneurship (Sudiyono et al. 2017). For PPP to succeed, it needs to be done right and well.

CONCLUSION

Despite the many advances Brunei has made toward economic diversification in the past few decades, progress has been slow. The government cannot be left alone to tackle the issues and challenges of economic growth and development, but rather the future of the economy lies in the hands of today's youth. Whereas, the future of Bruneian society lies in its leadership's hands in both public and private sectors. As entrepreneurship works hand in hand with innovation, the whole-of-nation must continue to coordinate all their economic activities effectively, lead and work together towards sustainable economic growth. The entrepreneurial society in the youth economy needs to be agile, and must be able to take full opportunity of their surroundings and create business opportunities. The body responsible for resource allocation must be present and good governance to be practised in national development discussions. Hence, plans can be directed towards creating a balance between what stakeholders are keen to do and what they are actually capable of doing, and building a healthy ecosystem for entrepreneurship and innovation activities. More importantly, as Brunei progresses, the government clearly accentuates that Islam and modernity must go along in tandem. Local entrepreneurs are highly expected to conduct their businesses with the values of justice, equity and compassion, and innovators to solve real problems and nurture the next generation for the greater benefit of society.

NOTES

1. The goals include achieving a dynamic and sustainable economy; a high quality of life; and producing highly educated, skilled and accomplished people by 2035. Brunei as an Islamic nation that has long based on its national philosophy of Malay Islamic Monarchy, strongly upholds Islamic values, principles and practices as a way of life, and thus, its vision is moulded towards achieving Maqasid Shariah (as an Islamic system of governance) for the worship of Allah (Negara Zikir).
2. https://www.statista.com/statistics/526777/gross-domestic-product-gdp-per-capita-in-brunei-darussalam/
3. Jabatan Perancangan Ekonomi dan Statistik (JPKE).
4. https://www.statista.com/statistics/607432/brunei-foreign-direct-investment-net-inflows/
5. The government gives agricultural entrepreneurs a piece of land to do farming, and assure that their products will be bought by local companies and major retailers in the country.
6. https://trendeconomy.com/data/h2/Brunei/TOTAL

REFERENCES

Asiyah az-Zahra Ahmad Kumpoh, Siti Norkhalbi Hj Wahsalfelah, and Noor Azam Hj-Othman. 2017. "Socio-Cultural Dynamics in Bruneian Society". In *Comparative Studies in ASEAN Cultures and Societies*, pp. 1–44. Bangkok: Semadhma Publishing House.

Azlan Othman. 2019. "Social Enterprise, Yayasan's New Initiative to Assist Needy". *Borneo Bulletin*, 29 April 2019. https://borneobulletin.com.bn/2019/04/social-enterprise-yayasans-new-initiative-to-assist-needy/ (accessed 16 December 2020).

———. 2020a. "Brunei 44th Most Innovative among High Income Economies". *Borneo Bulletin*, 7 September 2020. https://borneobulletin.com.bn/2020/09/brunei-44th-most-innovative-among-high-income-economies-2/ (accessed 14 December 2020).

———. 2020b. "Bruneians Rank High in Social Media Usage". *Borneo Bulletin*, 10 February 2020. https://borneobulletin.com.bn/2020/02/bruneians-rank-high-social-media-usage/ (accessed 15 December 2020).

Bandial, Ain, and Rasidah Hj Abu Bakar. 2019. "Hengyi Refinery to be Operational by End of 2019". *The Scoop*, 1 March 2019. https://thescoop.co/2019/03/01/hengyi-refinery-to-be-operational-by-end-of-2019/ (accessed 16 December 2020).

Bhaskaran, Manu. 2010. "Economic Diversification in Brunei Darussalam". *CSPS Strategy and Policy Journal* 1: 1–12.

Blackburn, Robert. 2011. "Foreword". In *World Encyclopedia of Entrepreneurship*, edited by Leo P. Dana. Cheltenham, UK: Edward Elgar Publishing Limited.

Borneo Bulletin. 2019. "Brunei Goes Up in 'Ease of Doing Business' Rating". *Borneo Bulletin*, 25 October 2019. https://borneobulletin.com.bn/brunei-goes-ease-business-rating/ (accessed 14 December 2020).

———. 2020a. "Brunei Economy Continues to Grow By 2.8pc in Q2 2020". *Borneo Bulletin*, 21 September 2020. https://borneobulletin.com.bn/brunei-economy-continues-to-grow-by-2-8pc-in-q2-2020/ (accessed 15 December 2020).

———. 2020b. "Brunei Notches 12.5pc Total Trade Increase in September 2020". *Borneo Bulletin*, 16 December 2020. https://borneobulletin.com.bn/brunei-notches-12-5pc-total-trade-increase-in-september-2020/ (accessed 15 December 2020).

Brem, Alexander. 2011. "Linking Innovation and Entrepreneurship—Literature Review and Introduction of a Process-Oriented Framework". *International Journal Entrepreneurship and Innovation Management* 14, no. 1: 6–35.

Carter, Sara, and Dylan Jones-Evans. 2006. *Enterprise and Small Business: Principles, Practice and Policy*, 2nd ed. Harlow, UK: Pearson Education.

Cherif, Reda, Fuad Hasanov, and Min Zhu. 2016. "Breaking the Oil Spell: The Path to Diversification". *Voxeu*, 3 September 2016. https://voxeu.org/article/breaking-oil-spell-path-diversification (accessed 15 December 2020).

Cleary, Mark, and Simon Francis. 1994. "Brunei: The Search for a Sustainable Economy". *Southeast Asian Affairs* 1994: 59–75. Singapore: ISEAS – Yusof Ishak Institute.

Deseret News. 1997. "Lazy Kids, Jobless Rate Worry Clerics in Brunei". *Deseret News*, 25 March 1997. https://www.deseret.com/1997/3/25/19302483/lazy-kids-jobless-rate-worry-clerics-in-brunei (accessed 14 December 2020)

Drucker, Peter. 1985. *Innovation and Entrepreneurship: Practice and Principles*. New York, NY: Harper & Row.

———. 2014. *Innovation and Entrepreneurship*. New York: Routledge.

Geiger-Ho, Martie, and Kong Ho. 2016. "Nurturing the Creative Industries in Brunei Darussalam as a Form of Cultural Studies". *Southeast Asia: A Multidisciplinary Journal* 16: 103–19.

Genever, Harriet, 2020. "Why Entrepreneurs Should Take Risks". *LivePlan* (blog), 5 May 2020. https://www.liveplan.com/blog/why-risk-takers-are-winners-and-why-all-entrepreneurs-should-take-risks/ (accessed 5 December 2020).

Global Capital. 2011. "Brunei's Drives Economic Diversification Forward". *Global Capital*, 18 July 2011. https://www.globalcapital.com/article/k3cqdktqyf0k/bruneis-drives-economic-diversification-forward (accessed 14 December 2020).

Hales, Reagan. 2016. "The Importance of a Diversified Economy". *Amarillo Economic Development* (blog), 12 May 2016. https://www.amarilloedc.com/blog/the-importance-of-a-diversified-economy (accessed 15 December 2020).

Hengyi. 2020. "First Domestic Supply of Refined Fuel Products from Hengyi". *Hengyi Press Releases*, 18 May 2020. https://www.hengyi-industries.com/ media/press-releases/first-domestic-supply-of-refined-fuel-products-from-hengyi/ (accessed 17 December 2020).

Hussain, Iftikhar, Zeeshan Farooq, and Waheed Akhtar. 2012. "SMEs Development and Failure Avoidance in Developing Countries through Public Private Partnership". *African Journal of Business Management* 6, no. 4: 1581–89.

Iqbal, Badar A., and Mohd Nayyer Rahman. 2015. "Contribution of ASEAN-6 SMEs to Economic Growth of ASEAN". *Economics World* 3, no. 11–12: 258–69.

Islam, Saiful, Nurul Faizah Salleh, and Siti Nooraini Sabli. 2019. "Influence of Exchange Rate on Cross-Border Shopping of Bruneians in Malaysia". *Journal of Asian Business and Economic Studies* 26, no. 1: 74–92.

Jacobsen, Marianne D. 2020. "Innovation is the New Competitive Advantage". *Knowit.* https://www.knowit.eu/services/experience/digital-strategy-and-analysis/strategy-and-digitalization/knowits-take-on-tomorrow/innovation-is-the-new-competitive-advantage/ (accessed 15 December 2020).

Kimura, Shigeru, Osamu Ikeda, Hirazaku Ipponsugi, Takeshi Miyasugi, Sakwi Kim, Romeo Pacudan, and Muhammad Nabih Fakhri Matussin. 2020. "Brunei Darussalam: Shifting to a Hydrogen Society". *ERIA Research Project Report 2020, No. 04.* Senayan, Indonesia: Economic Research Institute for ASEAN and East Asia (ERIA). https://www.eria.org/uploads/media/ Research-Project-Report/RPR-2020-04-Brunei-Shifting-Hydrogen-Society/ Brunei-Darussalam-Shifting-to-Hydrogen-Society-new.pdf (accessed 16 December 2020).

Kirzner, Israel M. 1973. *Competition and Entrepreneurship*. Chicago, USA: University of Chicago Press.

Kon, James. 2020. "International Cooperation Remains Key to Youth Empowerment". *Borneo Bulletin*, 5 November 2020. https://borneobulletin. com.bn/2020/11/intl-cooperation-remains-key-to-youth-empowerment/ (accessed 3 December 2020).

Lawrey, Roger Neil. 2010. "An Economist's Perspective on Economic Diversification in Brunei Darussalam". *CSPS Strategy and Policy Journal* 1 (July): 13–28.

Lebdioui, Abdelkader A. 2019. "Economic Diversification and Development in Resource-Dependent Economies: Lessons from Chile and Malaysia". PhD dissertation, University of Cambridge.

Lichtenstein, Benyamin B. 2011. "Complexity Science Contributions to the Field of Entrepreneurship". In *The Sage Handbook of Complexity and Management*, edited by Peter Allen, Steve Maguire, and Bill McKelvey, pp. 471–93. Thousand Oaks, CA: SAGE Publications.

Low, Kim Cheng P., Habrizah Hussin, and Sik-Liong Ang. 2013. "Being Entrepreneurial, the Brunei Perspective". *International Journal of Economy, Management and Social Sciences* 2, no. 3: 44–55.

Mahani Hamdan, and Masairol Masri. 2015. "The Development of Entrepreneurship Education in Brunei Darussalam". Paper presented at the Proceedings of the 3rd Convention of the World Association of Business Schools in Islamic Countries (WAiBS), Malaysia, November 2015.

Mahani Hamdan, and Muhammad Anshari. 2020. "Paving the Way for the Development of FinTech Initiatives in ASEAN". In *Financial Technology and Disruptive Innovation in ASEAN*, edited by Muhammad Anshari, Muhammad N. Almunawar, and Masairol Masri, pp. 80–107. Hershey, PA: IGI Gothamlobal.

McCabe, Angela, Robin Keast, and Kerry Brown. 2006. "Community Engagement: Towards Community as Governance". *Governments and Communities in Partnership*. University of Melbourne, Melbourne VIC.

Ministry of Finance and Economy. 2020. "Sustainable Development Goals: Voluntary National Review Report of Brunei Darussalam". *2020 United Nations High-Level Political Forum on Sustainable Development*. Brunei: Ministry of Finance and Economy, Government of Brunei Darussalam.

Mishrif, Ashraf. 2018. "Challenges of Economic Diversification in the GCC Countries". In *Economic Diversification in Gulf Region, Volume II, The Political Economy of the Middle East*, edited by Ashraf Mishrif, and Y. Al Balushi, pp. 1–19. UK: Gulf Research Centre Cambridge.

Mohammad Sofian bin Haji Awang Radzuan. 2016. "Evolving Brunei Darussalam's Economy Towards Technology-Based Industries". PhD dissertation, University of Sussex.

Mulgan, Richard. 2000. "Comparing Accountability in the Public and Private Sectors". *Australian Journal of Public Administration* 59, no. 2: 87–97.

Organisation for Economic Co-operation and Development (OECD). 2004. "ICT, E-Business and SMEs (Report)". The Second OECD Conference of Ministers Responsible for SMEs, 3–5 June 2004. https://www.oecd.org/sti/34228733.pdf (accessed 16 December 2020).

_____. 2010. "Small Businesses, Job Creation and Growth: Facts, Obstacles and Best Practices". https://www.oecd.org/cfe/smes/2090740.pdf (accessed 10 December 2020).

_____. 2018. "Structural Policy Country Notes: Brunei Darussalam". *Economic Outlook for Southeast Asia, China and India 2019: Towards Smart Urban Transportation*. https://www.oecd.org/dev/asia-pacific/saeo-2019-Brunei_Darussalam.pdf (accessed 16 December 2020).

Oxford Business Group. 2014. "Investing in Innovation in Brunei Darussalam". *Oxford Business Group*, 13 August 2014. https://oxfordbusinessgroup.com/news/investing-innovation-brunei-darussalam (accessed 4 December 2020).

Porter, Michael E. 1990. *The Competitive Advantage of Nations*. New York: Free Press.

Rasidah Hj Abu Bakar. 2018. "Brunei Retooling Entrepreneurship Ecosystem". *The Scoop*, 1 August 2018. https://thescoop.co/2018/08/01/brunei-retooling-entrepreneurship-ecosystem/ (accessed 15 December 2020).

————. 2020. "Brunei Still Failing to Meet Agriculture, Fisheries Targets: HM". *The Scoop*, 27 February 2020. https://thescoop.co/2020/02/27/hm-outlines-shortcomings-in-agriculture-fisheries-sectors/ (accessed 15 December 2020).

Schumpeter, Joseph A. 1934. *The Theory of Economic Development*. London: Oxford University Press.

Siddiqui, Shamim A., Alaa Aldin Abdul Rahim Al Athmay, and Hamdan Mohammed. 2012. "Development and Growth through Economic Diversification: Are there Solutions for Continued Challenges Faced by Brunei Darussalam?" *Journal of Economics and Behavioral Studies* 4, no. 7: 397–413.

Soltysik, Mariusz, Maria Urbaniec, and Magdalena Wojnarowska. 2019. "Innovation for Sustainable Entrepreneurship: Empirical Evidence from the Bioeconomy Sector in Poland". *Administrative Sciences* 9, no. 3: 1–21.

Sowbhagya, G. 2017. "Inculcation of Value in Education". Paper presented at the Proceedings of 72nd ISERD International Conference, Bangkok, Thailand, 5–6 May 2017.

Sudiyono, Krist A., Tirta Mursitama, Boto Simatupang, and Mohammad Hamsal. 2017. "The Governance of Public-Private Ties Model: How to Govern the PPPs Infrastructure Project Effectively (An Indonesia Case)". Paper presented at the International Conference on Business and Management Research, Atlantis Press, 2017.

Tang, Jack L., and Francis L.F. Lee. 2020. "Understanding Investment Culture: Ideologies of Financialization and Hong Kong Young People's Lay Theories of Investment". *Consumption Markets & Culture* 23, no. 6: 537–52.

The Bruneian. 2018. "Bank Usahawan Joins BSP Credit Facility Program". *The Bruneian*, 3 November 2018. https://www.thebruneian.news/bank-usahawan-joins-bsp-credit-facility-program/ (accessed 13 December 2020).

The Star. 2020. "Brunei Ranks Third in Southeast Asia for Talent Competitiveness". *The Star*, 24 April 2020. https://www.thestar.com.my/news/regional/2020/04/24/brunei-ranks-third-in-southeast-asia--for-talent-competitiveness (accessed 16 December 2020).

Thindwa, Jeff. 2015. "Multi Stakeholder Initiatives: Platforms of Collective Governance for Development". *World Bank* (blog), 7 July 2015. https://blogs.worldbank.org/governance/multi-stakeholder-initiatives-platforms-collective-governance-development (accessed 14 December 2020).

Thornton, Patricia H., Domingo Ribeiro-Soriano, and David Urbano. 2011. "Socio-Cultural Factors and Entrepreneurial Activity: An Overview". *International Small Business Journal* 29, no. 2: 105–18.

Weber, Robert J., Stacey Dixon, and Antolin M. Llorente. 1993. "Studying Invention: The Hand Tool as a Model System". *Science, Technology & Human Values* 18, no. 4: 480–505.

Wong, Jeffrey. 2019. "China-Brunei Joint Venture Provides Training, Employment for Local Bruneians". *Xinhuanet*, 10 July 2019. http://www.xinhuanet.com/english/2019-07/11/c_138215762.htm (accessed 15 December 2020).

Xu, Zimu, and Gideon Maas. 2019. "Innovation and Entrepreneurial Ecosystems as Important Building Blocks". In *Transformational Entrepreneurship Practices*, edited by Gideon Maas, and Paul Jones, pp. 15–32. USA: Palgrave Pivot, Cham.

Yunos, Haji Mohd Rozan. 2014. *The Golden Warisan Brunei Darussalam*, Vol. 2. Brunei: Dewan Bahasa dan Pustaka, Bandar Seri Begawan.

Yunos, Haji Mohd Rozan, and Ivana Milojevic. 2016. "Strategic Planning in Brunei Darussalam: History, Experience and Lessons Learned". *CSPS Strategy and Policy Journal*: 1–23. http://www.bfi.org.bn/JournalArticles/StrategicPlanningBrunei.pdf (accessed 15 December 2020).

11

OIL AND GAS DEPENDENCE OF BRUNEI ECONOMY: CURRENT PROGRESS AND CHALLENGES

Ly Slesman and Roslee Baha

INTRODUCTION

The Sultanate of Brunei Darussalam is a small but rich country that is most notably known for hydrocarbon resource abundance. Its economy heavily relies on oil and gas, accounting for over 91 per cent of total commodity export and 76 per cent of government revenue. It has a relatively large share of public sector that supports a population of 459,500 (2019) with a generous welfare system that subsidizes staple food, petrol, water and electricity, while providing free education, affordable healthcare services, low-cost government housing scheme and subsidized land purchase, and old-age pensions for those above 60 years old. Its accumulated wealth from oil and gas has propelled the Sultanate into a high-income country, with the 2019 real gross domestic product (GDP) per capita of US$62,100 international purchasing power parity (internationally comparable purchasing power of the income per person). Life expectancy has increased from 62.6 years in 1970 to 70.2 years and 75.7 years in 1990 and 2018, respectively, while educational attainment and literacy rate of its population aged 15 years old and older has also increased over time from 85.1 per cent in 1981 to 97.2 per cent in 2018 (UNDP 2020; UIS 2021). These improvements led Brunei to rank 47 (out of 189 countries and territories) and score 0.838 on the United Nations' Human Development Index (HDI) in 2019.

Despite being wealthy, Brunei economy has been growing at slower rates, with an average GDP growth of 1.7 per cent over 1975–2019 (1.2 per cent during 1986–2019, and 3.9 per cent in 2019). Its non-oil-and-gas private sectors are still relatively small (less than 30 per cent share in GDP) and are dominated by Micro, Small and Medium Enterprises (MSMEs) that are mainly concentrated in the service sector. The manufacturing sector is dominated by downstream oil and gas production while the agriculture sector accounts for just 1 per cent of the total output. The Brunei government has been actively seeking, through its National Development Plans (NDPs), to diversify the economy towards non-resource sector with various policy initiatives and institutional reforms, as well as large investment projects and modernizing its business and economic infrastructures. This is guided by the Brunei National Vision or *Wawasan* 2035 to transform its economy into a dynamic and sustainable economy.

This chapter has three objectives. First, it seeks to provide an assessment of the oil-gas and non-oil-gas structures of the Brunei economy using various economic indicators to gauge their evolvement over time. Second, the chapter provides a concise discussion on the National Development Plan (NDPs) and further assesses the country's economic diversification with the help of relevant economic indicators. The conventional policy wisdom suggests that structural economic transformation from oil-and-gas towards non-oil-and-gas based economy would promote long-run sustainable economic progress. This chapter takes stock of such structural transformation in the Brunei economy. Finally, the chapter provides empirical analysis with reference to Brunei's data over the period 1975–2018 to evaluate whether Brunei experiences a natural resource curse or natural resource blessing. Natural resource curse view refers to countries that are endowed with abundant natural resources but tend to grow more slowly than those without the abundance of natural resources. Whereas the "resource blessing" view argues that sub-soil (e.g., oil and gas) resources can be transformed into surface-assets that benefit the development of the natural-resource rich countries.

THE ECONOMIC STRUCTURE

Oil and Gas Sector

Oil and gas have been the dominant sector in Brunei's economy. Since the oil discovery in 1929 and the establishment of the Brunei Liquefied Natural Gas (LNG) plant, the Brunei economy has been highly dependent on the export earnings of oil and gas. Figure 11.1 shows, after earlier fluctuations, oil production has picked up speed slowly and settled higher at 221,2448 barrels per day (b/d) in 2006, after which it declined to 111,6231 b/d in 2018 as oil reserve has depleted from 1.35 billion barrels in 2006 to 1.1 billion barrels since 2007. The oil export has closely been moving together with the production of oil, reflecting

FIGURE 11.1
Total Crude Oil Production and Export, and Oil Price

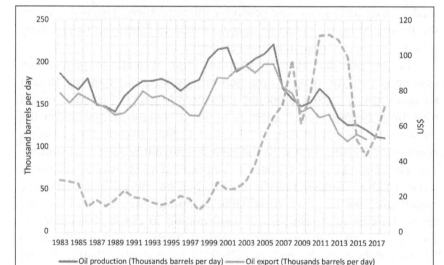

Source: US Energy Information Administration (n.d.) and British Petroleum (2020).

the high content of export (in total oil production) relative to small but highly subsidized domestic oil consumption. At least until 2006, there is a clear positive relationship between oil prices and oil production and export. Then, such relationship pattern becomes less visible.[1]

This pattern of correlations may expose Brunei economy to volatility caused by the changing oil prices that may affect its fiscal policy (government expenditure) as most government revenue comes from oil and gas earnings. Koh (2017b) showed that any unanticipated decline in oil price would negatively affect Brunei government expenditure and non-oil GDP. With low oil production and price, the revenue (more than 70 per cent raised from the oil and gas sector) was reduced by nearly one half from around B$9 billion in 2013/14 financial year to around B$3.7 billion since 2015/16 (DEPD 2019). Starting from the 2014/15 financial year, Brunei has experienced an annual fiscal deficit of around B$2.6 billion between 2015/16 and 2016/17. To reduce the deficit, the government has cut the expenditure by $1 billion annually, from B$7.6 billion in 2013/14 to less than B$6.5 billion from 2015/16 onwards (DEPD 2019).

The important component of the cut is development expenditure, reducing to below B$1 billion annually since 2014/15 financial year. In the 2018/19 financial year, it has further been reduced to around B$500 million—lowering the expenditure on public buildings, security, research and development, technology, and innovation (DEPD 2019). Moreover, the consequent reduction in government spending to tackle the deficit has also negatively affected the private sector activities in the country. Most of the large-scale joint-ventures projects with foreign investors are led by the government. Similarly, most large-scale private sector projects are also government-initiated projects such as housing schemes and building new infrastructures. The end results of the low-oil price induced reduction in government expenditure are the reduction in government-led private economic activities and growing unemployment. The Brunei Labour Force Surveys shows the unemployment rate at 6.8 per cent in 2019 (a reduction from 8.7 per cent [2018] and 9.3 per cent [2017]), the highest among ASEAN member countries.

Furthermore, the sectoral share in GDP of oil and gas sector has been very high at about 66 per cent during 2010–14, but the share declined to 54.5 per cent during 2015–19. The decline in the share of oil and gas sector in recent years is mainly caused by the decline in oil production since 2013 and the decline in oil price since the third quarter of 2014. The dominance of the oil and gas sector can be seen from Figure 11.2, showing GDP shares of sub-industry sector of oil and gas mining with an average of 47 per cent during 2010–19.[2] The second largest GDP share of sub-industry is in the downstream sector (manufacture of liquefied natural gas and other petroleum and chemical products) with an average of 13.5 per cent during the same period.[3]

The Brunei Economic Development Board (BEDB) has actively promoted the development of downstream oil and gas sector through several initiatives. For example, the development of the Sungai Liang Industrial Park (SPARK) that currently houses Brunei Methanol Company with an annual production of 850,000-tonnes of methanol; and the development of Pulau Muara Besar which is currently home to an oil refinery and aromatics cracker plant, Chinese Zhejiang Hengyi Group, with the production capacity of refined 175,000 b/d of crude oil for export. Since its operation in November 2019, the Hengyi industries has exported US$4.08 billion worth of petrochemical products, surging in 2020 at 323.9 per cent (Han 2021). This may explain the reversing trend in the share of oil and gas related manufactured goods

FIGURE 11.2
Sub-sectoral Shares of Industry in GDP (%)

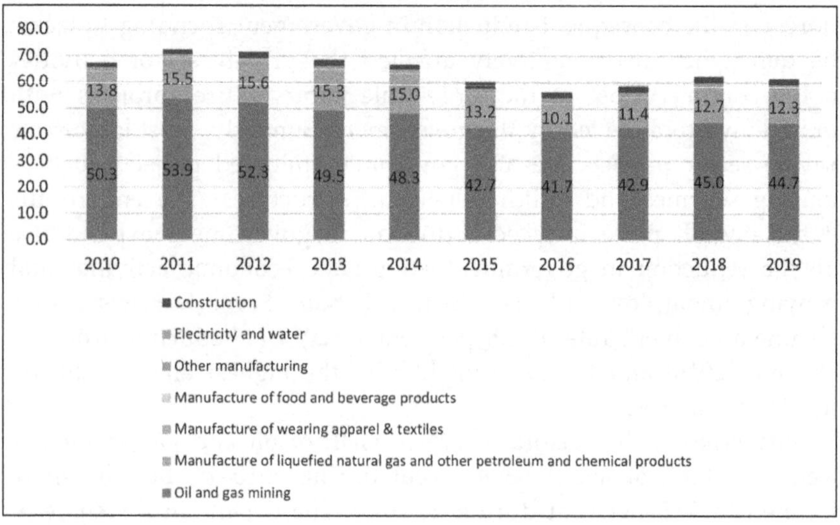

Source: DEPS, MoFE.

from a trough of 10 per cent in 2016 to 12.3 per cent in 2019. The centrality of hydrocarbon sector is also evident in the utilities sector as Brunei's electricity is sourced entirely from its natural gas. Brunei also subsidizes most of its domestic energy consumption. The retail motor gasoline (premium 97 fuel) and diesel are priced at B$0.53 and B$0.31 per litre respectively, making fuel prices in Brunei the lowest in Southeast Asia. This again shows a high dependency of Brunei economy on oil and gas sectors, though at a lesser degree on oil and gas mining but with increasing downstream activities.

The dependency of Brunei economy on the non-renewable oil and gas sector can be approximated using the ratio of total natural resource rents or total rents—the sum of oil, natural gas, coal (hard and soft), mineral, and forest rents. It is the percentage GDP share of the net market monetary values of total natural resource production including oil and gas. With the availability of data for earlier periods, Figure 11.3 plots total, oil, and gas rents along with real GDP per capita (measured using 2010 US$) for 1975–2017 to gauge their historical trends and possible correlations.

Firstly, the figure shows that the total rents, and oil and gas rents move almost in an identical manner confirming the fact that most rents

FIGURE 11.3
Natural Resource Rents and GDP per capita in Brunei Darussalam

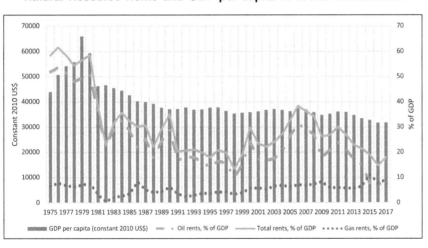

Source: Constructed by authors using data from World Bank's World Development Indicator (WDI).

are from oil, with gas rents accounting for less than 10 per cent of the total rents share of GDP. Secondly, as expected, we observe that the movement of these natural resource rents variables over time are similar to the oil production and export, reported in Figure 11.1. They correlate (or co-move) with oil prices especially towards 2006, after which such correlation is less apparent. Thirdly, it is visible that real GDP per capita and total and oil rents have been relatively high in the pre-1980s, a period marked by a sharp spike in oil prices, but drop to lower trend since the 1980s. There were moderate correlations (or co-movements) between them especially during 1981–2017.[4] It follows that, after a bottom in 1983 from the peak in 1976, resource rents share in GDP has fluctuated between the two peaks of 1984 (36 per cent of GDP) and 2006 (38 per cent) hitting a trough (13.3 per cent) briefly in 1997, coinciding with the 1997–98 Asian financial crisis. Since then, the rents have decreased to about 18 per cent in 2017. These trends may suggest possible dynamic correlations between the natural resource rents including oil and gas rents and real income per head for the past forty-one years.

Non-oil and Gas Sector

With the slow declining shares of the resource sector, the non-oil-and-gas private sector has seen a modest increase from 34 per cent share of GDP in 2010–14 period to 45.5 per cent shares in GDP during 2015–19, most of which occurred in the service sectors with a 9.2 per cent increase between the two periods. The increase includes the business, financial, real estate, and communication services. The government services also increased by 2.4 per cent during this same period. Overall, the non-oil and gas sector comprises 62 per cent of the private sector and 38 per cent of the public sector over 2010–19, with a modest five-year average or medium-term decrease in the public sector and the corresponding increase in the private sector from 2010–14 to 2015–19 periods. During this period, Brunei has made significant improvement in its ranking in the ease of doing business (EDB) index published by the World Bank over the years.

Brunei's EDB ranking has considerably increased from 97th in 2016 to 72nd (2017), 56th (2018), and 55th (2019). However, its 2020 ranking dropped to 66th, which is mainly due to the decline by 0.8 from the previous year in the EDB's component of "registering property" score. Despite an overall drop in the ranking, the notable 2020 reforms made contracts enforcement and resolving insolvency in Brunei now easier. Moreover, the EDB's component of ease of starting a business (ESB) indicator has a structural break from the past trend of lower average of 50 scores (2007–15) to the higher average of 90 scores (2016–20). Similarly, the cost of starting a business (number of days and procedures used to get necessary licenses and permits) also show a similar trend—dramatically reducing from more than 100 days to less than 20 days—during the same periods. These favourable institutional and policy reforms would be expected to spur growth in the private sector—including the inflows of foreign direct investment (FDI)—going forward.

Data from the World Bank's entrepreneurship survey shows, over the last eight years, Brunei's business density or new formal business creations has grown considerably from 1.3 shares of new limited liability companies (per 1,000 adult population age 15–62)—a measure of new formal business creations—in 2011 to 2.4 in 2018. This corresponds to the uptake in the EDB and ESB. Figure 11.4 shows that the private sector is dominated by MSMEs, accounting for 97 per cent of total enterprises. Again, most of these enterprises are in the service sector.

FIGURE 11.4
Private Enterprise Share by Business Size and Industry, 2015–17 (%)

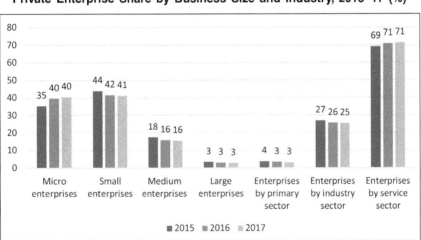

Source: Annual Census of Enterprises (ACE), DEPS, MoFE.

Furthermore, conventionally, the inflows of foreign firms especially the greenfield FDI—defined as the newly established subsidiary firms in the host country by the (parent) foreign multinational corporation (MNCs)—can have spillover effects on domestic economy and entrepreneurship through the exposures of local firms/entrepreneurs to new knowledge and advanced technological transfer and know-how, efficient and better managerial practices, new supply chains and international markets for export, access to international networks, learning-by-doing and observing, and other backward and forward spillover effects brought over by foreign MNCs. With these potential growth-enhancing benefits, the Brunei government has initiated policies to attract FDI into five key priority sectors: business clusters in halal goods, technology and creative industry, business services, tourism, and downstream oil and gas sectors. Figure 11.5 shows the distribution of the actual stock of FDI in Brunei for the period 2010–19. FDI is concentrated in mining and quarrying (as traditionally embodied in the presence of Brunei Shell Petroleum and its sister companies), manufacturing, financial and insurance activities, wholesale and retail trade, construction, and others. The average share of mining and quarrying (oil and gas) over 2010–19 shows that the sector absorbs half of the total stock. The only percentage share that shows an increasing

FIGURE 11.5
Foreign Direct Investment Stock by Economic Activity

Source: DEPS, MoFE.

trend is manufacturing from just 9.6 per cent in 2010 (or an average of 10.5 during 2010–14) to 34.3 per cent in 2019 (or an average of 21 per cent during 2015–19) reflecting the overall increasing trend in the stock of FDI, especially in the downstream sector.

The figure also shows a dramatic shrinking of financial and insurance activities from 51.5 per cent in 2010 (or 32 per cent during 2010–14) to 10 per cent in 2019 (or 13 per cent during 2015–19). This may reflect the withdrawal of HSBC with nine branches in 2017 after selling all its retail and commercial banking portfolio to Baiduri Bank (Bandial 2017). All in all, the inflows of FDI are mainly concentrated in the oil and gas sector and its related downstream activities. In 2020, the Brunei government put forward six economic aspirations in its economic blueprint that specifically aims to make the Brunei economy dynamic and sustainable. It aspires to have (1) productive and vibrant business; (2) skilled, adaptive and innovative people; (3) open and globally connected economy; (4) sustainable environment; (5) high quality and competitive economic infrastructure; and (6) good governance and public service excellence. At least four of these aspirations clearly aim to promote private sector growth. Many of the policy directions to support these aspirations emphasize the transformation of non-oil-and-gas private sectors by attracting FDI inflows. For example, policies to realize the first economic aspiration involve policies to promote FDI and encourage MSMEs and innovation (policies 3–5) which clearly link to (or support) other policies, e.g., strengthening priority sectors (policy 1), encouraging entrepreneurship (policy 2), creating high-value jobs (policy 7), and promoting export-oriented firms (policy 6). Moving forward, when these policies and reforms take effect, the constraints removed, and progress made (as reflected in EDB and ESB), further growth in high value-added local enterprises and FDI inflows that create jobs would be expected to take place.

NATIONAL DEVELOPMENT AND ECONOMIC DIVERSIFICATION

National Development Plans

Socio-economic development has always been emphasized in national development planning, especially the post-independence twenty-year long-term development plan (LTDP) that comprises four five-year medium-term National Development Plans (NDP). It is the continuation of the previous pre-independence NDPs. This twenty-year LTDP started with the 5th NDP (1986–90) and the 6th NDP (1991–95) that prioritized human resource development and economic diversification through industrial development and encouraging private sector participation in the economy. The 7th NDP (1996–2000) aimed to further improve the quality of life of the people and further strengthen the economy. It incorporated the importance of balanced socio-economic development with the implementation of social development projects, protecting the environment, and utilizing technologies. The twenty-year LTDP ended with the introduction of the 8th NDP (2001–5) which aimed at strengthening and expanding both oil and gas sector and the economic diversification plans.

In 2007, Brunei devised a Brunei vision or *Wawasan* 2035 with the support of the 9th NDP (2007–12) as the first five-year plan of the next thirty-year LTDP. *Wawasan* Brunei 2035 is an aspiration for Brunei to become a dynamic and sustainable economy, provide a high quality of life for its people, and produce a well-educated and highly skilled workforce. By the year 2035, Brunei aims to be ranked among the top ten countries globally in terms of the quality of life of its people and per capita income. To ensure all goals of *Wawasan* Brunei 2035 are achieved, all strategies are outlined and planned through the five-year national development plans (NDPs) starting from the 9th NDP where strong emphasis was placed on, among others, economic diversification, knowledge-based economy, and human resources, as the vital trusts of the development plan. Apart from that, the government also focused on developing tourism and communication sectors.

Those emphases were further enhanced under the 10th NDP (2012–17), where various goals were put forward to enhance economic productivity and provide a more conducive business environment, improve quality of life through comprehensive healthcare and medical services, access to a clean and healthy environment and necessities. The current ongoing 11th NDP (2018–23) continues to emphasize the strengthening of non-oil-and-gas sector by focusing on improving the private sector's dynamism and developing the workforce and human capital in the country. It also emphasizes on improving the welfare of the people by improving healthcare, public infrastructure and strengthening national security. Under the 11th NDP, all the proposed projects need to be assessed by the *Wawasan* Champions Committee to ensure they are in line with the goals of *Wawasan* Brunei 2035 (DEPS 2020). In many respects, the recently released 2020 Economic Blueprint mentioned above reflects closely the thrusts of the 11th NDP that focus on non-oil-and-gas private sector and human capital development, attracting FDI, good governance and a conducive business environment.

Economic Diversification: Achievements and Challenges

Economic diversification is one of the four long-term goals prescribed in the Brunei Economic Blueprint to achieve *Wawasan* 2035's economic dimension of becoming a dynamic and sustainable economy (MoFE 2020). The other three long-term goals are high sustainable economic growth, macroeconomic stability and low unemployment. Indeed, economic diversification may be the most important goal to achieve a dynamic and sustainable economy in the context of heavy dependency of the Brunei economic structure on the oil and gas sector. While standard policy advice for resource-rich economies centres on the short run "fiscal stabilization" which can be achieved through diligent fiscal rules and with the help of sovereign wealth fund (SWF). Recent research argues that economic diversification "is the best way to achieve macroeconomic stability in the long run, to sustainably escape the devastating effects of commodity price volatility, and to smoothen consumption over time" (Chang and Lebdioui 2020, p. 1).

In this sense, Brunei has been actively and cautiously pursuing economic diversification from a hydrocarbon-based economic structure toward a more diversified economic base. Beutel (2021, p. 108) defined economic diversification as "the diversification of exports and domestic production away from extreme dependence on a single dominant industry or a few natural-resource-based products, as well as towards increased complexity and quality of output". There are two conventional reasons for economic diversification (Alsharif et al. 2017). First is the reduction in dependency on volatile oil and gas sectors that generally move in tandem with international oil and gas prices. Second is the growing share of non-resource private economy, especially the export-oriented ones, which would benefit a small country through a more sustainable development path and employment generation.

Data from Brunei's DEPS show that there is a reduction in the oil and gas sectoral shares in Brunei economy from 74.6 per cent of the industrial sector share, 96.5 per cent of the export share, and 51.2 per cent of GDP in 2010 to 68.5 per cent, 91.4 per cent, and 46.2 per cent in 2019, respectively. As Figure 11.6 shows, this corresponds with the increase in the total share of non-oil-and-gas sector from 35.9 per cent in 2010 to 44.3 per cent in 2019. Furthermore, the private content of non-oil-and-gas sector increased from 21.4 per cent to 28 per cent while that of the public (government) slightly increased from 14.5 per cent to 16.3 per cent during the same period. This suggests that the increase in the non-oil-and-gas share of GDP is driven by the private sector which is growing at an average rate of 2.6 per cent since 2010 (MoFE 2020). Thus, there is an incremental structural change towards the growing share of private non-oil-and-gas sector.

Table 11.1 further shows the industrial shares in real gross value added (GVA)[5] in the last ten years. The bulk of shares in output produced are from the industrial sector followed by service and agriculture sectors. On average, the share of the industrial sector in GVA has reduced by about 10 per cent from 2010–14 to 2015–19 periods. This reduction appears to be driven by oil and gas mining (−9.5 per cent) and oil and gas related manufacturing (−7.5 per cent)

FIGURE 11.6
Resource vs. Non-Resource Shares in Current GDP (%)

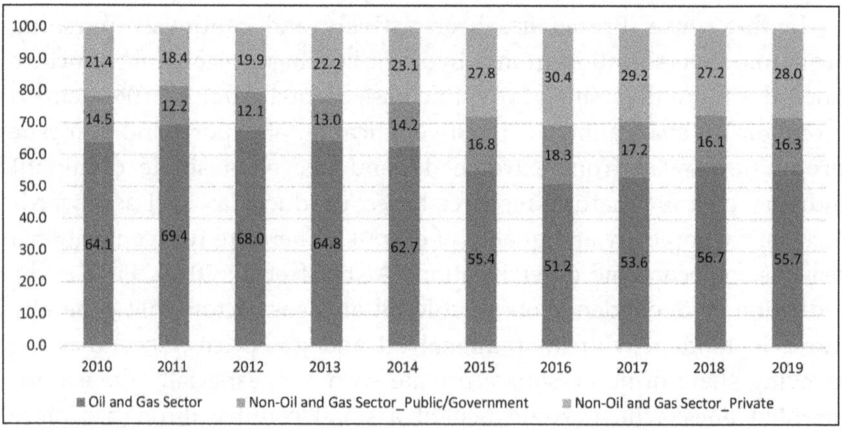

Source: DEPS, MoFE.

TABLE 11.1
Shares of Economic Activity in Real Gross Value-added (%)

Classification according to DEPS, Ministry of Finance and Economy	Classification according to ADB (ADB 2018)	2010 – 2014	2015 – 2019
Agriculture, Forestry and Fishery	**Primary sector**	**0.7**	**1.1**
Vegetables, fruits & other agriculture	Primary sector	0.1	0.2
Livestock and poultry	Primary sector	0.3	0.4
Forestry	Primary sector	0.1	0.2
Fishery	Primary sector	0.2	0.4
Industry	–	69.4	59.8
Oil and gas mining	Primary sector	50.9	43.4
Manufacture of liquefied natural gas and other petroleum and chemical products	High and medium tech	15.0	11.9
Manufacture of wearing apparel & textiles	Low tech	0.1	0.2
Manufacture of food and beverage products	Low tech	0.1	0.2
Other manufacturing	Low tech	0.5	0.8
Electricity and water	Utilities/Low tech	0.6	0.9
Construction	Low tech	2.1	2.5
Services	**–**	**29.9**	**39.1**
Wholesale and retail trade	Business services	3.9	5.1
Land transport	Business services	0.1	0.1
Water transport	Business services	0.7	0.9
Air transport	Business services	0.3	0.3
Other transport services	Business services	0.5	0.5
Communication	Business services	1.2	1.5
Finance	Business services	3.8	5.5
Real estate & ownership of dwellings	Business services	2.9	3.8
Hotels	Business services	0.1	0.1
Restaurants	Business services	0.6	1.0
Health services	Public and welfare services	1.1	1.5
Education services	Public and welfare services	2.5	3.5
Business services	Business services	2.0	2.2
Domestic services	Public and welfare services	0.3	0.4
Other private services	Business services	0.5	0.6
Government Services/Public Administration	Public and welfare services	9.6	12.0

Note: The number are five-year average value for 2010–14 and 2015–19.
Source: DEPS, MoFE and ADB's Input-Output Table (ADB 2018)

during the same periods. The corresponding increase in the shares of non-oil related manufacturing are, however, small. In the same period, the share of the service sector has also increased by 9 per cent mainly in the wholesale and retail trade (1.2 per cent), finance (1.7 per cent), and a modest increase in other Service sub-sectors. Government services increased by 2.4 per cent. Lastly, the agricultural sector showed a small increase to 1.1 per cent of its share in GVA, which indicates that the country's over-reliance on imported goods may pose serious national food security challenges in the long term. However, this agricultural share is expected to pick up as the government vested interests in agricultural projects such as the phase one of the 500-hectare commercial paddy plantation at Kandol Agricultural Development Area in Belait district (operated in 2019), and the current development of Brunei Agro-Technology Park (BATP)—the advanced technology business-oriented site and agro-research centre to promote agricultural products including the halal industry.

Data from the Asian Development Bank's (ADB) input-output table further shows that the GVA content of domestic final demand has steadily increased from 40 per cent in 2010 to 56 per cent in 2017 (ADB 2018). This may be due to the increasing size and growth of Brunei's market as the population increases. It corroborates with Figure 11.7 that shows the corresponding growth in domestic final demand

FIGURE 11.7
Sectoral Shares of Gross Value-added Content in
Domestic Final Demand, 2010–17

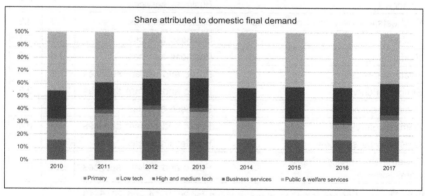

Source: Asian Development Bank Multiregional Input-Output Database (ADB 2018).

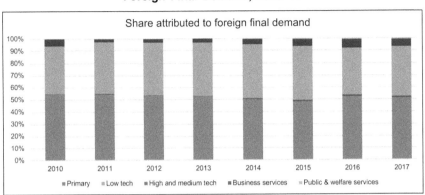

FIGURE 11.8
Sectoral Shares of Gross Value-added Content in
Foreign Final Demand, 2010–17

Source: Asian Development Bank Multiregional Input-Output Database (ADB 2018).

which centred on public and welfare services, business, and primary and low-tech sectors.

Interestingly, Figure 11.8 shows that foreign final demand share in GVA is mainly concentrated in oil and gas related products (primary, and high and medium tech sectors), and the export of these products constitutes Brunei's biggest foreign final demand. The challenge now is to also increase the content of non-oil-and-gas products for export. The third aspiration of the 2020 Economic Blueprint thus aims to penetrate external markets through the promotion of local products internationally, export-oriented domestic firms and establishing marketing networks with the help of foreign firms.

This chapter plots the product concentration index data from the United Nations Conference on Trade and Development (UNCTAD) that captures the degree of concentration of goods exported and imported for Brunei. The index ranges from zero to one; number closer to one indicates higher degree of product concentration. Confirming the observation in Figure 11.8, Figure 11.9 shows that Brunei export is considerably concentrated in a few products, e.g., oil and gas, albeit at a lesser degree since 2006, while its imports are sourced from a variety of goods, mostly food, manufacturing goods, machinery, and transport equipment.

FIGURE 11.9
Product Concentration in Export and Import for Brunei Darussalam

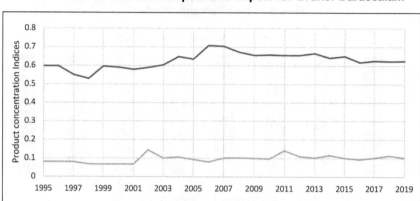

Source: Statistics from UNCTADstat (n.d.).

International trade theories dictate that high export concentration reflects specialization of Brunei economy with oil and gas products as its comparative advantage. Thus, high export concentration is as expected. However, the volatile nature of its prices in the world market and its spread to domestic macroeconomic variables are some of the actual reasons why export diversification from a few products to more diverse and quality products is important. At its current rate, Brunei's economic structure is still dominated by oil and gas sector and exports.[6] Though the non-oil-and-gas private sector is growing in its share of the national economy, it is still relatively small (less than 30 per cent of GDP).

Furthermore, data from the DEPS's Annual Census of Enterprises shows that oil and gas sector (mining and quarrying and its related downstream manufacturing) employed about 10–16 per cent of the labour force during 2015–17. In the private sector, as Figure 11.10 shows, 43.7 per cent of employment is concentrated in only a handful of large firms, while the remaining 31.5 per cent and 24.7 per cent shares are absorbed by medium (16.3 per cent) and micro-small (80.6 per cent) enterprises, respectively. It is expected that with the diversification process gaining steam, the private sector would absorb a larger share of employment, hence reducing unemployment. Thus,

FIGURE 11.10
Private Enterprise by Business Size and Employment Share, 2015–17

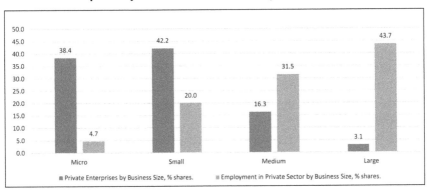

Source: Annual Census of Enterprises (ACE), DEPS, MoFE.

policy directions of the Brunei Economic Blueprint that aim to encourage entrepreneurship and promote FDI and export-oriented firms, and good governance, among others, to spur "Productive and Vibrant Businesses" are crucial. Recent empirical studies (e.g., Munemo 2017; Slesman et al. 2020) that look at Brunei (within a pool of other countries), show that the inflows of FDI crowd-in (induce) more new business creation (or entrepreneurial activities) as Brunei has relatively better developed financial services and markets (Munemo 2017) and possesses a relatively higher level of overall governance quality (Slesman et al. 2020).[7] This suggests that Brunei is in a better position—having a relatively conducive environment—to attract more greenfield FDI and MNCs (as advocated in the 2020 Brunei Economic Blueprint) and contribute to private sector growth (more new business creations).

All in all, to achieve the goal of a dynamic and sustainable economy enshrined in *Wawasan* 2035, the Brunei government places important emphases on economic diversification, among other important goals, to transform the economy from an oil-and-gas based economy into a vibrant non-oil-and-gas private-led economy. Progress has been made, though modest, in increasing the share of the private sector in the economy that are in line with long-term aspirations outlined in MoFE's (2020) economic blueprints.

Challenges remain, however. A research conducted by Monitor Group in 2003 identified slow government decision-making, a lack of government transparency, significant bureaucracy, a lack of an entrepreneurial culture and an underdeveloped private sector as the main bottlenecks to further growth in the private sector (Koh 2020). Moving forward, policy reforms to remove these constraints are imperative. Indeed, many policy directions proposed in the recent MoFE economic blueprints precisely aim to minimize these constraints which will further enlarge the share of private sectors, promoting entrepreneurship and the inflows of FDI into the private non-oil-and-gas sectors.

In addition to this assessment, this chapter proceeds to provide an empirical assessment on the long-run and short-run effects of oil and gas rents and abundance on real GDP per capita grounded within the empirical (and theoretical) literature.[8]

OIL AND GAS RENTS AND ECONOMIC DEVELOPMENT

The Views: Resource Blessing vs. Resource Curse

Generally, there is a cross-country divergence of experiences in using the natural resources endowments and abundances including hydrocarbons and minerals to promote long-term sustainable economic growth and development. Wright and Czelusta (2004) argued using historical accounts that the United States' natural-resource-based economic transformation and development had helped propel it into a world leader in non-resource-based manufacturing industries and technology. The United Arab Emirates has also been cited as an example where the oil resource endowment is turned into a blessing: small government debt, low inflation, modernized infrastructure, and a generous welfare system (Fasano 2002). The success stories seem to cluster around the experiences of developed countries while similar success has been lacking in some resource-rich developing countries across the Middle East, Latin America, and Africa. The seemingly straightforward transformation of the sub-soil assets (non-renewable natural resources, e.g., oil and gas) into surface assets (various development outcomes, e.g., high output growth and income, better health, highly educated workforce, modernized infrastructure, employment, among others), in practice, can be paradoxically difficult (Venables 2016). The tendency of the natural resource abundant economies to have worse development outcomes than the non-resource-based economies has become known as the "resource curse" as opposed to the "resource blessing". Sachs and Warner (1995) sparked the economic literature by showing empirical support for the "resource curse" hypothesis. They found a negative correlation between resource export intensity (GDP share of natural resource export) and economic growth during the 1970–90 period. Since then, there have been opposing evidences that either support "resource curse" or "recourse blessing" views. Ben-Salha et al. (2018) who examined the nexus between resource rents and economic growth using time-series information over 1970–2013 with a panel sampling of top eight resource-rich countries found that the positive effect of resource rents on economic growth was only statistically significant in the long-term, supporting a "resource blessing" view. Causal analysis further reveals a bi-directional (feedback) causality between resource rents and economic growth. Similar results were identified in Haseeb et al. (2021) for five Asian countries—Malaysia, Indonesia, Thailand, China and India. Overall, the literature suggests that the "resource curse" is far from being universal, and some scholars even argue that this may be a "statistical mirage" (Alexeev and Conrad 2009; James 2015).

In the literature, there is no quantitative country-case study conducted for Brunei on the relationship between oil and gas rents and real income per capita growth over the short and long run. Earlier attempts have only investigated the drivers of economic growth in Brunei. For example, Anaman (2004) examined the long-run effects of government expenditure, total investment, labour force, and export on Brunei output growth during 1971–2001. The study found that only the growth of export followed by a moderate size of government promotes growth in the long run. Koh (2011) provided a sectoral macro-econometric analysis and forecast on key macroeconomic variables. His findings highlight the potential transmission of exogenous oil price volatility induced fluctuation in export and government revenues, government expenditure and GDP growth. His findings also emphasized the important short-run role of government expenditure in promoting growth and employment. Based on quarterly data between 2003 and 2014, Koh (2016) observed that the Brunei fiscal policy tends to be procyclical, and the transmission effect of declining oil prices on the country's government expenditure and non-oil-and-gas sector was negative (Koh 2017b). Thus, smoothing out government expenditure is important and one strategy to do this, as suggested by Koh (2017a,

2017b) and Venables (2016), is by using oil fund or SWF to support budget deficit during the downturns and low-oil-price period to support economic growth and development.

Though these studies draw attention to external shocks influencing macroeconomic volatilities which warrant macroeconomic policy responses—including fiscal policy and economic diversification strategies, they do not provide a direct test on the resource "curse" vs. "blessing" hypothesis along economic development outcome for Brunei. The next sub-section aims to fill this gap.

Long-run Effects and Causality

Table 11.2 reports the empirical results on the long run (and short run) effects of total resource rents ($RENT_t$), oil-and-gas rents ($ORGENT_t$), oil export per capita ($OILXPC_t$), oil production per capita ($OILPPC_t$), and oil reserve per capita ($OILPRC_t$) on real GDP per capita during 1975–2018. All the empirical models, i.e., Autoregressive Distributed Lag (ARDL) models (Model 1–5), are well specified. The ARDL bound test confirms that there exists a long-run relationship between measures of natural resource dependence (and endowments) ($NRESOURCE_t$) and real GDP per capita. A detailed explanation of the ARDL model and estimation and measurement for each variable are provided in Appendix 11.1. Long-run coefficients are all statistically significant at the 1 per cent level. Coefficient assessments on the long-run effects suggest the following:

— *Models 1 and 2.* A one per cent increase in the GDP shares of $RENT_t$ and $ORGENT_t$ would be associated with 1.47 per cent and 1.48 per cent increases in real GDP per capita in the long run, respectively. Thus, total natural resource rents, particularly oil and gas rents, have been an important driver of long-term economic development process in Brunei. Using resource rents to finance government expenditure and developments of non-resource sectors (diversification), and socio-economic development including generous welfare benefits have been an integral part of long-term development goals in Brunei (Abdul Amin 2010).

— *Models 3, 4 and 5.* A one per cent increase in $OILXPC_t$, $OILPPC_t$ and $OILPRC_t$ would be associated with the respective 0.24 per cent, 0.23 per cent and 0.20 per cent increase in real GDP

Ly Slesman and Roslee Baha

TABLE 11.2
Natural Resource Abundances and Economic Growth in Brunei Darussalam, 1975–2018

	Model 1	Model 2	Model 3	Model 4	Model 5
	$NRESOURCE_t$ $= RENT_t$	$NRESOURCE_t$ $= ORGENT_t$	$NRESOURCE_t$ $=$ $lnOILXPC_t$	$NRESOURCE_t$ $=$ $lnOILPPC_t$	$NRESOURCE_t$ $=$ $lnOILRPC_t$
Long Run Effects *(Dependent variable:* $lnOILXPC_t$*)*					
$NRESOURCE_t$	0.0147*** (0.000)	0.0148*** (0.0000)	0.2388*** (0.0000)	0.2283*** (0.0000)	0.1997*** (0.0009)
Constant	10.1017*** (0.0000)	10.1022*** (0.0000)	9.0339*** (0.0000)	9.0736*** (0.0000)	8.8374*** (0.0000)
Short Run Effects *(Dependent variable:* $\Delta lnRGDPPC_t$*)*					
ECT_{t-1}	-0.3089*** (0.0001)	-0.3089*** (0.0001)	-0.2976*** (0.0000)	-0.2742*** (0.0000)	-0.2031*** (0.0009)
$\Delta lnRGDPPC_{t-1}$	–	–	0.2713** (0.0273)	0.2583** (0.0321)	0.4009*** (0.0042)
$\Delta NRESOURCE_t$	0.0051*** (0.0001)	0.0052*** (0.0001)	–	–	–
$\Delta NRESOURCE_{t-1}$	-0.0034*** (0.0036)	-0.0033*** (0.0037)	–	–	–
Crisis	0.0134 (0.3540)	0.0132 (0.3608)	-0.0086* (0.0905)	-0.0077 (0.1358)	-0.0019 (0.7613)
Cointegration Tests					
ARDL Bounds test (F–stat)	5.9391**	5.8971**	10.5490***	9.5411***	4.2132*
Optimal lag length (AIC)	ARDL (1, 2)[a]	ARDL (1, 2)[a]	ARDL (2, 0)[a]	ARDL (2, 0)[a]	ARDL (2, 0)
Diagnostic tests					
χ^2 NORMAL (p–value)	5.5477 (0.062)*	5.6571 (0.059)*	0.1278 (0.938)	0.4118 (0.813)	0.2326 (0.890)
χ^2 SERIAL (p–value)	1.6475 (0.438)	1.6401 (0.440)	9.3765 (0.01)**	5.8697 (0.053)*	3.8324 (0.147)
χ^2 ARCH (p–value)	0.2659 (0.606)	0.3004 (0.583)	0.5409 (0.462)	1.1787 (0.277)	2.2907 (0.130)

TABLE 11.2 (continued)

χ^2 WHITE (p-value)	18.4 (0.002)***	18.6 (0.002)***	0.9227 (0.9213)	0.8847 (0.9267)	0.2993 (0.9899)
F–stat. RAMSEY (p-value)	0.1560 (0.695)	0.1325 (0.717)	0.6708 (0.507)	0.5601 (0.579)	0.1258 (0.725)
CUSUM	Stable	Stable	Stable	Stable	Stable
CUSUMSQ	Stable	Stable	Stable	Stable	Stable
F–statistics (p-value)	91.7 (0.000)***	91.5 (0.000)***	173 (0.000)***	209 (0.000)***	151 (0.000)***
Adjusted R^2	0.9152	0.9150	0.9541	0.9597	0.9449
Durbin–Watson Statistics	1.7118	1.7203	1.8125	1.9796	1.8632
Period (T)	1975–2017	1975–2017	1983–2016	1983–2018	1983–2018
Granger Causality Test (Lag 2 of all right-hand side variables are used)	$RENT_t \rightleftarrows RGDPPC_t$ (Bidirectional causal effects)	$OILGASRENT_t \rightleftarrows RGDPPC_t$ (Bidirectional causal effects)	$OILXPC_t \rightarrow RGDPPC_t$ (Unidirectional causal effect)	$OILPPC_t \rightarrow RGDPPC_t$ (Unidirectional causal effect)	$OILRPC_t \rightarrow RGDPPC_t$ (Unidirectional causal effect)
F Test Statistics (p-value) for H_0: $NRESOURCE_t$ does not Granger cause $lnRGDPPC_t$	4.1648** (0.0234)	4.1248** (0.0241)	4.7880** (0.0160)	7.9562*** (0.0016)	2.2060 (0.1271)
F Test Statistics (p-value) for H_0: $lnRGDPC_t$ does not Granger cause $NRESOURCE_t$	6.1128*** (0.0051)	6.1594*** (0.0049)	0.4774 (0.6251)	0.1407 (0.8693)	2.4856* (0.0997)

Note: p-values are reported in the parenthesis. Finite-sample bounds F critical values are based on Narayan (2005) methods. ARDL models are estimated with restricted constant. Optimal lag length is determined by Akaike information criteria (AIC). ***, ** and * indicate significance level at 1 per cent, 5 per cent and 10 per cent respectively. ARDL (p, q) with [a] superscript indicates the model is estimated with Newey-West correction on the residual variance-covariance matrix after it was confirmed to have either serial correlation and/or heteroscedasticity problems.. → indicates unidirectional causal effect from one variable toward another. ⇌ indicates bi-directional (or feedback) causal effects between the two variables.

per capita in the long run. These findings confirm that oil abundances and endowments are important for Brunei's long-term real income per capita growth.

The findings of positive long-run impacts corroborate with the "resource blessing" view that Brunei's oil and gas dependence, abundance, and endowment have promoted its long-run economic growth. Granger causality tests further show that there exist bi-directional (feedback) causal effects running between the natural resource dependences ($RENT_t$ and $ORGENT_t$) and ln$RGDPPC_t$: increase in rents would lead to an increase in real GDP per capita growth which in turn lead to higher rents, possibly due to, as economic historians suggested, further development in resource sectors along more advanced technology and appropriate knowledge (Wright and Czelusta 2004). Interestingly, $OILPRC_t$ Granger cause ln$RGDPPC_t$ in unidirectional way which conforms with the expectation that more oil production per capita cause high real GDP per capita. In a similar finding, ln$RGDPPC_t$ is found to unidirectionally Granger cause $OILPRC_t$ implying that a growing Brunei economy may make it economically viable to finance further discovery of oil resources which may, in turn, lead to increase in oil reserve.

All in all, the data confirms that oil and gas dependency, abundance, and endowment have a positive long-run relationship with Brunei's real income per capita, in line with the recent growing literature on resource blessing (Ben-Salha et al. 2018; Haseeb et al. 2021). The long-run equilibrium effect suggests more oil and gas rents promote economic growth, but it may not be sustainable in the long term since oil and gas are non-renewable, and their prices are volatile. Thus, this finding implies that diversification of the economic base to further grow the non-resource private sector would promote long-term sustainable economic growth.

Short-run Effects

Evaluation of the short-run coefficients reported in Table 11.2 reveals the following dynamics. First, the negative signed coefficients on lagged error correction term (ECT_{t-1}) in all models are statistically significant at 1 per cent level implying annual adjustment from short-run deviations towards long-run relationship between oil and gas rents and economic growth. The annual speeds of adjustments are 30.89 per cent, 30.89 per cent, 29.76 per cent, 27.42 per cent and 20.31 per cent for Model

1 to 5 respectively implying that it will take approximately 3 years (for Model 1–3), 3½ years for Model 4, and 4¼ years for Model 5 for any short-run deviations (from long-run relationship) to disappear completely to restore long-run equilibrium relationship between the variables. Thus, any short-run shocks that put the relationship off the long-run equilibrium path will take about three years to revert.

Second, Model 1 shows the immediate mixture of positive and negative impacts of a change in total resource rents ($\Delta RENT_t$) and oil and gas rents ($\Delta ORGENT_t$) on a change in income per capita. A one per cent increase in the current resource rents contributes to about 0.51 per cent increase in income per capita. However, its previous year increase was associated with 0.34 per cent reduction effect in income per capita. The net accumulated (multiplier) effects of changing GDP share of resource rents is a 0.17 per cent increase in short-run real income per capita in Brunei. The net accumulated effect for oil and gas rents is higher at 0.19 per cent. These findings shed important insight on the dynamic short-run impacts of resource rents on income per capita. The well-specified ARDL models for $OILXPC_t$, $OILPPC_t$ and $OILPRC_t$ further suggest no short-run effects from these resource abundance and endowment variables, except in the long run. Overall, only oil-and-gas rents (or dependency) have a net positive impact on Brunei's economic growth in the short run.

CONCLUSION

Rich in natural resource endowment has led Brunei to specialize in oil and gas production and export since the oil discovery in 1929. This allows Brunei to transform its sub-soil hydrocarbon resources into surface wealth and become a high-income country. Due to the high volatility of oil and gas prices, like other resource exporting countries, its non-renewable natural resource skewed economy is not sustainable over the long run. To sustain economic growth over time, structural transformation would need to rebalance towards increasing the share of the non-resource private sector, which is presumed to be dynamic and job-generating and capable of adapting to changing economic circumstances. Thus, economic diversification is imperative and has been the focus since the twenty-year LTDP (1986–2006). However, structural change has been slow. Hence, one of the next thirty-year

LTDP (2007–38) goals is to further diversify the economy, which is enshrined as one of the four pillar-outcomes of *Wawasan* 2035 towards achieving a dynamic and sustainable economy. To do this, in 2020, the Brunei government has put forward six aspirations with the supports of thirty-eight policies directions and strategies that mostly centre on strengthening private sector growth and viability.

Based on various economic indicators, the assessment of oil-and-gas and non-oil-and-gas economies shows that progress has been made in the last ten years or so. The non-oil-and-gas private sector, though small, has grown at an annual average of 2.6 per cent during the last decade. The growth of entrepreneurship has increased resulting from the establishment of policy initiatives and institutional reforms. These are in line with the 11th NDP's focus on increasing the size of non-oil-and-gas private sector in the economy. The challenges, however, remain in further accelerating the non-oil-and-gas sector including non-resource manufacturing, modern services, and agriculture sectors. Specifically, efforts to attract more FDI into the non-oil-and-gas sectors, promote vibrant and value-added employment-generating SMEs and entrepreneurial culture, skills and activities are crucial to enlarge the share of economic growth from the non-oil-and-gas sector in the long run. These challenges are addressed in the 2020 Economic Blueprint with clear policy directions.

Finally, the empirical analyses on the effects of resource rents and abundance on economic growth during 1975–2018 reveal that Brunei's experience has been in line with the "resource blessing" hypothesis in both the short and long run. The causality analysis reveals a (two-way) feedback relationship between resource rents and real income per capita in the long run. In the short run, fluctuation in rents from oil and gas have a mixed effect but with net positive. All in all, the oil and gas rents have been an important driver of Brunei's economic development process for the past decades. However, since oil and gas are non-renewable, and their prices are volatile, heavy reliance on this narrow export base would not be sustainable. Thus, the finding of resource blessing suggests that natural resource blessing (rents) can be used to develop the non-resource private sector to diversify the productive structure of the economy to grow more sustainably in the long term.

APPENDIX 11.1

The Dynamic Effects of Oil and Gas Rents on Brunei Economic Growth: A Dynamic Modelling Approach

In this appendix, we briefly explain the dynamic relationship between resource rents (including oil and gas rents) and economic growth using the dynamic modelling approach, i.e., ARDL model proposed by Pesaran et al. (2001) and Pesaran and Shin (1998), to test the resource "curse" vs. "blessing" hypothesis for Brunei. We specify the long-run and the implied short-run dynamic relations between natural resource ($NRESOURCE_t$) and real gross domestic product (GDP) per capita ($\ln RGDPPC_t$) over the 1975–2018 sampling period. $\ln RGDPPC_t$ (real GDP per capita in constant 2010 US$) is dependent variable, expressed in natural logarithmic value. $NRESOURCE_t$ is independent variable proxied with five different measures.

— $RENT_t$ is total natural resource rents as percentage share of GDP. It is computed as the sum of oil, natural gas, coal (hard and soft), mineral, and forest rents. Before the sum, each component of rents is computed as the difference between the market value of its production at world prices (total revenue) and its total costs of production (total cost), and then divided by GDP. It captures total natural resource dependence of the Brunei economy. Data is taken from World Bank's World Development Indicator (WDI).

— $OGRENT_t$ is oil and gas rents as percentage share of GDP. Since $OGRENT_t$ constitutes the main component of $RENT_t$ in Brunei, we also examine it separately. $OGRENT_t$ proxies the oil and gas dependence. Data is taken from WDI.

— $\ln OILXPC_t$ is the oil export per capita (expressed in natural logarithm). It is the total export of crude oil including the lease condensate (millions of barrels) divided by total Brunei population. It captures oil dependence of the Brunei economy. Data is from the US Energy Information Administration (EIA).[9]

— $\ln OILPPC_t$ is the total oil production per capita (expressed in natural logarithm). It is the total petroleum and other liquids production divided by total population.[10] It captures Brunei's oil resource abundance. Data is taken from EIA.

— In$OILRPC_t$ is the crude oil reserve per capita (expressed in natural logarithmic value). It is crude oil reserve (billions of barrels) divided by total population. It captures Brunei's oil resource endowment. Data is taken from EIA.

Panel A of Table 11.A summarized each variable, sources of data and the purported proxy it seeks to represent. To avoid spurious or nonsensical finding on the nexus of $NRESOURCE_t$ and In$RGDPPC_t$ using

TABLE 11.A
Measurement and Unit Root Tests

	A. Measurements		
Variables	**Unit of Measurement**	**Sources of Data**	**Proxy for**
$RGDPPC_t$	Constant 2010 US$	WDI, World Bank	Level of real income per head
$RENT_t$	Percentage share of GDP	WDI, World Bank	Natural resource dependence
$OGRENT_t$	Percentage share of GDP	WDI, World Bank	Oil and gas dependence
$OILXPC_t$	Barrels/day per capita	US EIA and WDI, World Bank	Oil dependence
$OILPPC_t$	Barrels/day per capita	US EIA and WDI, World Bank	Natural Resource abundance
$OILRPC_t$	Million barrels per capita	US EIA and WDI, World Bank	Natural Resource endowment

	B. Unit Root Tests					
	Augmented Dickey-Fuller (ADF) Test			**Phillips and Perron (PP) Test**		
	Level	First Differenced	Result	Level	First Differenced	Result
In$RGDPPC_t$	−2.9321	−5.4118***	I(1)	−2.4383	−5.4542***	I(1)
$RENT_t$	−3.4068*	−4.8915***	I(0)	−3.2116*	−5.3754***	I(0)
$OGRENT_t$	−3.4181*	−4.8869***	I(0)	−3.2115*	−5.3854***	I(0)
In$OILXPC_t$	−0.9806	−5.2791***	I(1)	−1.0015	−5.2791***	I(1)
In$OILPPC_t$	−1.3053	−6.1914***	I(1)	−1.2540	−6.4414***	I(1)
In$OILRPC_t$	−2.9886**	−6.4393***	I(0)	−3.3570**	−6.6821***	I(0)

Note: In$RGDPPC_t$, In$OILXPC_t$, In$OILPROPC_t$, and In$OILRESPC_t$ are variables expressed in natural logarithmic values. Data is from World Development Indicators (WDI) of the World Bank and the US Energy Information Administration (EIA).

time-series data, we conduct unit root tests (ADF and PP tests) to check for nonstationary of each variable. Panel B of Table 11.A shows the variables are a mixture of stationary at the level [integrated of order zero, I(0)] and first differenced [I(1)]. This justifies the application of ARDL model to estimate the long-run and short-run effects of $NRESOURCE_t$ on $lnRGDPPC_t$. The ARDL (p, q) model can be expressed as Error Correction Model (ECM):

$$\Delta \ln RGDPPC_t = \beta_0 + \sum_{i=1}^{p} \gamma_i \Delta \ln RGDPPC_{t-i} + \sum_{j=0}^{q} \lambda_j \Delta NRESOURCE_{t-j}$$
$$+ \sigma CRISIS + \lambda ECT_{t-1} + \varepsilon_t$$

Where Δ is the first-difference operator. p and q are the optimum lag length for the ARDL which is determined by Akaike Information Criteria (AIC). CRISIS capture the impacts of financial and oil crisis on $lnRGDPPC_t$.[11] The λ coefficient on the one-year lagged error correction term (ECT_{t-1}) captures the speed of adjustment towards long-run equilibrium from the short-run shocks/deviations. ARDL (p, q) model is estimated using Ordinary Least Square (OLS) criteria.[12] The ARDL bound test is conducted to determine the existence of cointegrating/ long-run relationship between the level variables. If confirmed, we can then estimate short-run effects and dynamics determined by λ. To determine causal relationship between $NRESOURCE_t$ and $lnRGDPPC_t$, we further test the direction of the causality using the (F-statistics based) Granger causality test.

NOTES

1. Respectively, correlation coefficients between oil price and oil production and export are 0.61 and 0.73 during 1983–2006 but decline to 0.53 and 0.12 during 2007–18.
2. Few firms are involved in oil and gas production in Brunei, but the main player is Brunei Shell Petroleum (BSP), a joint venture with equal shares between the Brunei government and the Royal Dutch Shell Group. Other major companies that dominate Brunei natural gas and oil supply chains include Brunei Liquefied Natural Gas (BLNG), Brunei Shell Tankers (BST), Brunei Gas Carriers (BGC) and Brunei Shell Marketing (BSM). BLNG operates the country's sole liquefaction plant and LNG export terminal, BST transports LNG (sold to Japan and the Republic of Korea), BGC

manages the LNG carriers, while BSM is the sole supplier of petroleum products for the Brunei domestic market (Koh 2020).

3. The shares of oil and gas mining in the *industry* are more than 70 per cent and 20 per cent for that of the related manufacturing downstream sector.

4. Correlation coefficient between total rents and real GDP per capita is −0.4 for 1975–80 but turn 0.5 for 1981–2017.

5. GVA measures the contribution to GDP made by an individual producer, industry, or sector in Brunei. It is the value of output less the value of intermediate consumption, i.e., the value of the raw materials, components, and partly manufactured goods going into a given product, as well as other services used in the production of a good or a service (ADB 2018; Lequiller and Blades 2014).

6. Some studies argue that existing indicators of economic diversification may be biased in reflecting the extent of diversification as it is complicated by the fluctuation in oil prices. According to Luciani (2021), whenever oil prices are high, the value added in upstream oil and gas increases, more so than the value added from other sectors, hence making the economy appears to lose economic diversification. The opposite also is true when the oil prices are low, economy may appear diversified.

7. In the context of Brunei with governance quality (GQ)—measure with International Country Risk Guides—ranges from the scores of 73 (2006) to 84 (2016) over the maximum 100 scores. According to Slesman et al.'s (2020) panel data estimate, at GQ score of 73, a 1 per cent increase in FDI inflows would draw in Brunei domestic firm creations by 0.08 (share of newly registered private and formal firms per thousand of working-age population). The share further increases to 0.14 as Brunei GQ scores increase to 84, a GQ level it possessed in 2016.

8. Conventionally, long run denotes a period over which full adjustment to changes takes place: all markets are in equilibrium, and all prices and quantities have fully adjusted and are in equilibrium. At the microeconomic level, firms can enter or leave an industry and capital stocks can be replaced at the macroeconomic level, all prices, wage contracts, tax rates, and expectations can fully adjust. In contrast, short run denotes a period over which not all factors can adjust fully; the capital stock and other fixed inputs cannot be adjusted, and firm entry is not free in the short run (microeconomics); while prices, wage contracts, tax rates, and expectations may not fully adjust (macroeconomics). For details, see Samuelson and Nordhaus (2010). In this chapter, long-run and short-run effects (estimated using the time-series dynamic model of Autoregressive Distributed Lag

(ARDL), technically involve the nonstationary property of each variable) capture along these essences: the equilibrium long-run effect of resource rents on real GDP per capita (if such relationship exists)—the final effect after all adjustment take place; and short-run dynamic effects (due to variables not fully adjusted to changing economic conditions)—whereby, in one point of time, the effects might be below and, in another, above (or hover around) the long-run equilibrium value over the short time horizon. ARDL estimation also provides an estimate of speed (amount of time needed) of adjustment from this short-run (disequilibrium or deviation from equilibrium path) to the long-run equilibrium path, the so-called error correction term (ECT).

9. Due to data unavailability, the sample period is limited to 1983–2018.

10. This includes a wide range of sub-categories of petroleum: crude oil, NGPL, other liquids, refined petroleum products such as motor gasoline, jet fuel, kerosene, distillate fuel oil, residual fuel oil, liquefied petroleum gases, and other petroleum liquids.

11. We allow crisis episodes (*CRISIS*) to influence the ln*RGDPPC*$_t$ in the short run. *CRISIS* is a dummy variable that captures the periods of crisis: oil price crisis (1973, 1979, and 1990–91), Asian financial crisis of 1997–98 and the global financial crisis of 2007–8.

12. To ensure the estimated ARDL model is well-specified, we diagnosed it with various diagnostic tests—normality distribution in residuals (Jarque-Bera Normality test), residual serial correlation (Breusch-Godfrey LM test), autoregressive conditional heteroscedastic (ARCH) effect, heteroscedastic residuals (White test), model misspecification (Ramsey RESET test), and model stability (CUSUM and CUSUM of Squares, CUSUMSQ) tests.

REFERENCES

Abdul Amin Haji Hashim. 2010. "Challenges in Achieving *Wawasan* 2035 Goals: Economic Diversification in Perspective". *CSPS Strategy and Policy Journal* 1, no. 1: 29–54.

Alexeev, Michael, and Robert Conrad. 2009. "The Elusive Curse of Oil". *Review of Economics and Statistics* 91, no. 3: 586–98.

Alsharif, Nouf, Sambit Bhattacharyya, and Maurizio Intartaglia. 2017. "Economic Diversification in Resource Rich Countries: History, State of Knowledge and Research Agenda". *Resources Policy* 52: 154–64.

Anaman, Kwabena A. 2004. "Determinants of Economic Growth in Brunei Darussalam". *Journal of Asian Economics* 15, no. 4: 777–96.

Asian Development Bank (ADB). 2018. *Economic Indicators for Southeastern Asia and the Pacific: Input-Output Tables.* Manila. http://dx.doi.org/10.22617/TCS189780-2.

Bandial, Ain. 2017. "HSBC Shutters All Branches in Lead Up to Brunei Exit". *The Scoop*, 11 November 2017. https://thescoop.co/2017/11/11/hsbc-shutters-branches-lead-brunei-exit/ (accessed 2 May 2021).

Ben-Salha, Ousama, Hajer Dachraoui, and Maamar Sebri. 2018. "Natural Resource Rents and Economic Growth in the Top Resource-Abundant Countries: A PMG Estimation". *Resources Policy.* https://doi.org/10.1016/j.resourpol.2018.07.005.

Beutel, Joerg. 2021. "Economic Diversification and Sustainable Development of GCC Countries". In *When Can Oil Economies Be Deemed Sustainable?* edited by Giacomo Luciani, and Tom Moerenhout, pp. 99–151. Singapore: Palgrave Macmillan.

British Petroleum (BP). 2020. "Statistical Review of World Energy". https://www.bp.com/en/global/corporate/energy-economics/statistical-review-of-world-energy.html (accessed 15 March 2021).

Chang, Ha-Joon, and Amir Lebdioui. 2020. "From Fiscal Stabilisation to Economic Diversification: A Developmental Approach to Managing Resource Revenues". *WIDER Working Paper Series*, no. wp-2020-108. World Institute for Development Economic Research (UNU-WIDER).

Department of Economic Planning and Development (DEPD). 2019. *Brunei Darussalam Statistical Yearbook 2018.* Brunei Darussalam: Department of Statistics, Prime Minister's Office.

Department of Economic Planning and Statistics (DEPS). 2020. *Eleventh National Development Plan (2018–2023) Brunei Darussalam.* Bandar Seri Begawan: Ministry of Finance and Economy.

Fasano, Ugo. 2002. "With Open Economy and Sound Policies, U.A.E. Has Turned Oil 'Curse' into a Blessing". *IMF Survey* 31, no. 19: 330–32.

Han, Shareen. 2021. "Gov't Set to Cut Spending on Development Projects as Fiscal Deficit Hits $2.98 Billion". *The Scoop*, 17 March 2021. https://thescoop.co/2021/03/17/govt-set-to-cut-spending-on-development-projects-as-fiscal-deficit-hits-2-98-billion/?fbclid=IwAR2om8e253KVclKjPGZCyayXcs8W4UpK0hvDHLqKZGGiQYOI89mRJxTKeOM (accessed 2 May 2021).

Haseeb, Muhammad, Sebastian Kot, Hafezali Iqbal Hussain, and Fakarudin Kamarudin. 2021. "The Natural Resources Curse-Economic Growth Hypotheses: Quantile-On-Quantile Evidence from Top Asian Economies". *Journal of Cleaner Production* 279, no. 10: 123596.

James, Alexander. 2015. "The Resource Curse: A Statistical Mirage?" *Journal of Development Economics* 114: 55–63.

Koh, Wee Chian. 2011. "A Macroeconomic Model of Brunei Darussalam". *CSPS Strategy and Policy Journal* 2: 55–72.

———. 2016. "Fiscal Cyclicality in Brunei Darussalam". *Journal of Southeast Asian Economies* 33, no. 1: 83–94.

———. 2017a. "Fiscal Policy in Oil-exporting Countries: The Roles of Oil Funds and Institutional Quality". *Review of Development Economics* 21, no. 3: 567–90.

———. 2017b. "The Effects of Macroeconomic Shocks on the Brunei Economy: A Sign Restriction Approach". *Journal of the Asia Pacific Economy* 22, no. 3: 414–28.

———. 2020. "Brunei: Economy". In *The Far East and Australasia 2020*, 51st ed. Routledge.

Lequiller, François, and Derek Blades. 2014. *Understanding National Accounts*, 2nd ed. Paris: Organisation for Economic Co-operation and Development.

Luciani, Giacomo. 2021. "Framing the Economic Sustainability of Oil Economies". In *When Can Oil Economies Be Deemed Sustainable?* edited by Giacomo Luciani, and Tom Moerenhout, pp. 9–30. Singapore: Palgrave Macmillan.

Ministry of Finance and Economy (MoFE). 2020. *Towards a Dynamic and Sustainable Economy: Economic Blueprint for Brunei Darussalam*. Brunei Darussalam: Ministry of Finance and Economy. http://deps.gov.bn/ DEPD%20Documents%20Library/NDP/BDEB/Econ_Blueprint.pdf.

Munemo, Jonathan. 2017. "Foreign Direct Investment and Business Start-up in Developing Countries: The Role of Financial Market Development". *Quarterly Review of Economics and Finance* 65: 97–106.

Pesaran, M. Hashem, and Yongcheol Shin. 1998. "An Autoregressive Distributed-Lag Modelling Approach to Cointegration Analysis". In *Econometrics and Economic Theory in the 20th Century: The Ragnar Frisch Centennial Symposium (Econometric Society Monographs)*, edited by Steinar Strøm, pp. 371–413. Cambridge: Cambridge University Press.

Pesaran, M. Hashem, Yongcheol Shin, and Richard J. Smith. 2001. "Bounds Testing Approaches to the Analysis of Level Relationships". *Journal of Applied Econometrics* 16, no. 3: 289–326.

Sachs, Jeffrey D., and Andrew M. Warner. 1995. "Natural Resource Abundance and Economic Growth". *National Bureau of Economic Research Working Paper*, no. 5398.

Samuelson, Paul A., and William D. Nordhaus. 2010. *Economics*, 19th ed. New York: McGraw-Hill.

Slesman, Ly, Yazid Abdullahi Abubakar, and Jay Mitra. 2020. "Foreign Direct Investment and Entrepreneurship: Does the Role of Institutions Matter?" *International Business Review*: 101774. https://doi.org/10.1016/j. ibusrev.2020.101774.

UNCTADstat. n.d. https://unctadstat.unctad.org/EN/ (accessed 15 March 2021).

UNESCO Institute of Statistics (UIS). 2021. "Brunei Darussalam". http://uis.unesco.org/en/country/bn (accessed 15 March 2021).

United Nations Development Programme (UNDP). 2020. *Human Development Report 2020*. New York: United Nations Development Programme.

US Energy Information Administration. n.d. https://www.eia.gov/international/data/world (accessed 15 March 2021).

Venables, Anthony J. 2016. "Using Natural Resources for Development: Why Has It Proven So Difficult?" *Journal of Economic Perspectives* 30, no. 1: 161–84.

Wright, Gavin, and Jesse Czelusta. 2004. "Why Economies Slow: The Myth of the Resource Curse". *Challenge* 47, no. 2: 6–38.

12

EMPLOYMENT AND WELFARE

Siti Fatimahwati Pehin Dato Musa and Aris Ananta

INTRODUCTION

There are three main characteristics of a rentier state. First, oil revenues are paid to governments in the form of rent. Second, oil revenues are externally generated from exports. Third, oil revenues are directly accumulated by the state (Benli 2014). Furthermore, in order to qualify as a rentier state, oil should account for at least 40 per cent of the country's gross domestic product (GDP). Usually, only a small percentage deals directly with the extraction of the natural resources. The majority participates in the distribution and utilization of the natural resources (Belbawi 1987).

Brunei is therefore a rentier state; its vast income from oil and natural gas provides its basis as a rentier state. It is among the world's most dependent economies on oil and gas, which accounts for around half of its GDP and 90 per cent of export revenues (Department of Economic Planning and Statistics 2020a). Revenues from oil and gas have made the GDP per capita levels in Brunei the second highest in Southeast Asia (Organization for Economic Co-operation and Development 2018).

Mahdavy (1970) and Beblawi (1987) argued that overdependence on oil revenues can have negative political, economic and social impacts on a rentier state. On the economic side, it can cause enclaved development which is termed a "resource curse" or "Dutch Disease" whereby the booming oil sector distorts the growth of other sectors. The role of most rentier states is largely limited to the distribution of rent earnings among the population by providing goods and services for the community welfare and by acting as the major employer in the country.

Brunei is not an exception. Employment in the government sector entails high incomes and is a major vehicle for redistributing the rents from oil revenues. In 2019, the public sector employed 33.78 per cent of the country's total employed persons. It employs more locals—49.53 per cent of the total locals employed—compared to non-locals who constitute 2.5 per cent of the total non-local employed persons in Brunei. It should be noted that the 66.50 per cent of the total employed persons are locals.[1]

In Brunei's "Integrated Plan of Action on Poverty Eradication", the government's vision has been to build a self-reliant and resilient community by reducing reliance on welfare assistance. This vision is to be achieved by creating capacity for productive employment and entrepreneurship (Ministry of Finance and Economy 2020). Therefore, economic diversification has been a targeted outcome of goal number 3 (Dynamic and Sustainable Economy) of *Wawasan* Brunei 2035 (Ministry of Finance and Economy 2021). The diversification will bring transformation in production and employment, moving toward higher value-added goods and services. However, those with low marketable skills are less likely to benefit from the diversification, which may result in economic inequality. Rising inequality may also be seen among different generations, as they may have different capabilities and opportunities, and therefore different incomes. Poverty in one generation may continue in the next generation as a poverty trap. The government is aware of this challenge and has been working to mitigate it (Prime Minister's Office 2015).

This chapter examines employment as one important source of people's welfare. It also examines other sources of welfare such as from the government, community, and family/relatives. The first section examines sources of financial support for an individual. The remaining sections focus on financial sources from the individuals themselves, particularly from their income. It starts by discussing the working-age population and the labour force—the "source" of working persons. Next is a discussion on unemployed persons, an important social and political phenomenon. It then examines employment, including dependency of non-local employment, followed by an examination on weekly hours worked and monthly income earned. Finally, the chapter presents some recommendations for the aforementioned issues.

SOURCES OF FINANCIAL SUPPORT

There are four main sources of financial support: the state, communities, families/relatives, and the individuals themselves. State support encompasses social safety net which includes various government programmes to help the community. Community support includes the tradition of *gotong-royong* (mutual and reciprocal assistance), philanthropy acts, and volunteerism. Family support includes contributions from spouses, parents (and grandparents), siblings, children (and grandchildren)—the extended family system. The support can be in monetary form and/or in kinds/non-monetary. Types of living arrangements in a household may also provide a means of financial support for an individual in the household. The individual source includes income and wealth (accumulated saving). Income includes earning/wage/salary (people have to "sweat" to earn money), interest, rent, and profit/dividend. The last three items are often called passive income.

State Support

In the political economy domain, Blomqvist (1998) classified Brunei as a benevolent state whereby the welfare of the people is the main concern. To support the rentier system, the state's distribution of resources must guarantee the welfare of its citizens (Asato 2019). Sainah (2010) described that the government of Brunei Darussalam has taken various measures to ensure the welfare of its citizens and residents. The public sector contributes the most in providing social protection to the people.

Moreover, the government attaches great importance to education with the provision of free education for all children at primary and secondary levels, and full scholarships offered to children at the highest level of attainment. Expenditure on universal education in the country constitutes a major proportion of social expenditure. Health and medical services, on the other hand, are provided for all citizens and permanent residents at a highly subsidized minimal rate of B$1 registration fee and B$5 for foreigners.

Brunei housing is heavily subsidized by the government mainly through the Housing Development Department (HDD) that was set up in 1984 to provide housing for Bruneians (Hassan 2017). The locals should fulfil the following criteria: be 18 years of age or older at the date of application, not own land or residential property, earn between B$445.00 to B$3,030.00, and have not disposed of any private land or residential property. They are then eligible to apply for the two different National Housing Schemes. First is the National Housing Programme or better known as the *Rancangan Perumahan Negara* (RPN), accessible to all Bruneians regardless of race. Second is the Landless Indigenous Citizen Scheme or *Skim Tanah Kurnia Rakyat Jati* (STKRJ) exclusively for the indigenous Brunei Malays (Hassan 2017).

Brunei has several retirement schemes for its citizens and permanent residents. Those who started working before 1993 follow the Government Pension System (GPS). It is a defined benefit programme for all employees, where employees do not have to contribute to the system. These employees retire at age 55. Those who started working in 1993 participate in TAP (*Tabungan Amanah Pekerja*—Employee Trust Fund), a defined contribution system, where employees contribute 5 per cent of their salaries, supplemented with the same percentage by the employers, for their own pension. Under TAP, employees retire at age 60. TAP is also supposed to encourage employment in the private sector.

Brunei introduced the Supplementary Contributing Pension (SCP), another defined contribution system, in 2010 to increase the benefit during old age. In addition to the defined contribution system, Brunei also provides a defined benefit system for all citizens and permanent residents aged 60 years old and over, the so-called Old Age Pension (OAP), providing B$250 monthly for all.

Other pensions distributed by the government are administered by the Ministry of Culture, Youths and Sports (MCYS). Among them is the

Monthly Welfare Assistance (MWA) provided through the MCYS via *Jabatan Pembangunan Masyarakat* (JAPEM) or Community Development Department. It is designed to act as an income supplement to protect the underprivileged from poverty, and ease their hardship until they receive a sufficient source of income and become economically independent (Ministry of Finance and Economy 2020).

In December 2019, the total number of MWA recipients was 5,812 heads of households. From April 2019 to March 2020, B$13,049,685.00 of funds were disbursed. The eligibility criteria for this assistance are based on the Minimum Cost of Basic Needs. The Minimum Cost of Basic Needs method is based on the estimated cost of the bundle of goods enough to ensure basic needs are met. In Brunei, this method is adjusted for inflation and takes into account a typical Bruneian household's expenditure (Ministry of Finance and Economy 2021).

Another form of monthly assistance is zakat. In Brunei, giving zakat is a religious obligation, where Muslims whose wealth is above the minimum threshold are obligated to pay 2.5 per cent of their collective assets. Zakat is collected by the Zakat Collection and Distribution Section under the *Majlis Ugama Islam Brunei* (MUIB) or Brunei Darussalam Islamic Religious Council and distributed as assistance to those who are not able to fend for themselves and their families. Zakat is also used to fund enrichment programmes aimed at empowering zakat recipients. In 2018, zakat amounting to B$5.2 million was distributed to 3,669 recipients. This includes the purchasing of medical supplies and equipment that are needed by those incapable of work due to health problems (Ministry of Finance and Economy 2020).

As a rentier state, the welfare of the nation remains as the government's best interest but it needs to be done in a sustainable manner to ensure that it continues in the long term and benefits future generations. To achieve this, the people must seek aspirations and efforts to achieve financial freedom and independence as well as reduce reliance on assistance from the government.

As mentioned by the Ministry of Finance and Economy (2020), the National Council on Social Issues (NCSI) has drafted a poverty eradication plan to create more jobs and entrepreneurship opportunities in order to reduce reliance on welfare assistance. The Plan of Action on Poverty Eradication focuses on empowerment tools to break the poverty cycle and to ensure sustainable income. The government issued the National Welfare System or the *"Sistem Kebajikan Negara"*, a comprehensive and centralized national system is to ensure that nobody is left behind.

Family and Community Support

The Malay culture is termed "collectivist". First, they define [themselves] in groups due to the need to belong and fit into the larger society. Second, communal responsibilities are considered to be more important than individual ones. Third, people share resources, emphasize harmony, define themselves by group membership, and subordinate personal goals to those of the group. The aim of the Brunei Malay culture is to ensure that harmony prevails by avoiding conflict, adhering to proper behaviour, respecting rank and status and complying with those of higher status (Black 2001).

The foundation of the Malay family revolves around Islamic teachings and Malay cultural values. These values are so strong that it has become the way of life in Brunei. The family institution is the dominant aspect of its culture. The concept of the large extended family had long been established and it constitutes the social safety net. Traditionally, an extended family was one where grandparents, parents, aunts and uncles lived under one roof. However, due to modernization and urbanization, having an extended family living in the same household is not practical anymore but families still live close to one another. For example, when the government carried out the resettlement scheme of moving families from the water village to land, family members were settled in one area to preserve this extended family system (Abdul Latif 1996).

Celebrations of auspicious events such as marriage, new birth and thanksgiving ceremonies are family affairs where most extended families are invited and attendance is considered compulsory. Moreover, mournful events such as funerals are considered social and communal gatherings that strengthen familial relations. Such gatherings are filled with communal *gotong-royong* (mutual and reciprocal assistance) that reflects one's responsibility and obligation towards family and community (Asiyah az-Zahra, Siti Norkhalbi and Noor Azam 2017).

Members of a community are commonly defined within the territorial framework of villages and districts and are usually related through kinship and/or ethnic ties with one another. The communities take on important roles like offering assistance and emotional supports to their members. Community leaders in Brunei are the ears and eyes of the government and are responsible for ensuring the well-being of the populace, especially the less fortunate and the needy in their village. The development of the Village Consultative Council and the Neighbourhood Watch has intensified the sense of community and encouraged communal cooperation in ensuring peace, security and harmony of the village and its surrounding neighbourhood (Asiyah az-Zahra, Siti Norkhalbi and Noor Azam 2017).

In addition, there has been a growing number of non-governmental organizations (NGOs) in Brunei that are committed to providing voluntary assistance to communities in the form of moral support, entrepreneurship and education. For instance, the Society for Community Outreach and Training (SCOT) is a registered NGO under the Registrar of Society (ROS) Brunei Darussalam with its mission of being a catalyst for sustainable poverty alleviation in Brunei. SCOT acts as a bridge on coming up with more sustaining ways and strategies to help the underprivileged by providing them with assistance in the form of resources, basic skills and support to help them move out of the vicious cycle of poverty through ongoing sustainable projects (Siti Fatimahwati and Siti Rozaidah 2019).

There are also some state-led community activities. One example is the 1K1P (*Satu Kampung Satu Produk*—One Village One Product) programme, founded in 1993, under the purview of the Ministry of Home Affairs. The objectives include raising village welfare and promoting entrepreneurship as well as competitiveness, to create a social cohesion of integrated village activities. The programme aims to increase production and widen the market for local products. The implementation of this programme is supervised by the village consultative councils.

Another example is the 1K1K (*Satu Kampung Satu Keluarga*—One Village One Family) programme that started in 2017 and became fully operational in 2019, under the responsibility of the Welfare and Well-being Unit of the Brunei-Muara District Department. This programme deals with social issues in each village, handled by the Village Consultative Council or the *Majlis Perundingan Kampong* (MPK). It is not only concerned with financial matters, but also other needed matters such as transportation to school. The long-run objective is, however, to create self-dependency among the people, rather than relying on assistance from the Islamic Religious Council and MCYS.

Individual Support

The decision for one to join the labour force depends on the wage (and its fringe benefit) offered and reservation wage. Reservation wage is the minimum wage that may induce a person to work. When the wage offered is below the reservation wage, a person will choose not to work. In contrast, if the wage offered is higher than the reservation wage, then the person may decide to work. If the person decides to work, the difference between the wage offered and the reservation wage will determine how much effort the person will put into the work.

The reservation wage may be influenced by several factors. First, is the person's wealth. The wealthier the person, the higher the reservation wage as they can afford "not to work". Thus, the wealthier the person, the less likely they are to work. Second, is the availability of financial support from relatives/communities/state. The more support rendered for those persons, the higher their reservation wage, the less likely they are to work. Third, is the attitude towards work. If they love to work, their reservation wage will be lower and they are more likely to work. Attitude may be influenced by the persons' surroundings.

The remaining sections discuss individual support through employment. Otherwise mentioned, all statistics are compiled and/or calculated from the Labour Force Survey 2014 and 2019 conducted by the Department of Statistics, Department of Economic Planning and Statistics (DEPS), Ministry of Finance and Economy (MoFE), Brunei Darussalam.

WORKING-AGE POPULATION AND LABOUR FORCE

In 2019, there were 369,837 persons in the working-age population. Working-age population refers to the part of population that are able to work. The government of Brunei measures working-age population as population aged 15 years old and over (Department of Economic Planning and Statistics 2020b). This definition allows older persons, 65 years and over, to work, in contrast to the measurement of working-age population as 15–64 years old used by the United Nations. The

Brunei government recognizes that older persons may still be able, and willing, to work. This can be a major support to the economy given the declining fertility and rising life expectancy in Brunei.[2]

Furthermore, 237,944 persons of the working-age population have joined the labour force, meaning that the labour force participation rate is 64.3 per cent. The labour force participation rate is higher among males (72.48 per cent) than females (54.83 per cent). The female working-age population may have higher reservation wage because they have an obligation to take care of the family/household. They may also have support from their husbands (see Table 12.1).

The labour force participation in 2019 shows a slight decline from the percentage in 2014 (65.59 per cent). The decline is attributed to the decline in female labour force participation rate from 58.32 per cent in 2014. The rates for the male working-age population remained the same, 72.44 per cent in 2014 and 72.48 per cent in 2019. The decline in female labour force participation may indicate that the female working-age population is more likely to have other financial supports, such as spouses or other relatives. On the other hand, the labour force participation rate for the male working-age population is higher than the female rate, indicating a higher necessity to work among male working-age population than their female counterpart. Societal norms may have pressured men to work, whatever the job.

The labour force participation for locals is lower, only 57.71 per cent, than the rate for the whole working-age population. This rate in 2019 is even lower than 60.44 per cent in 2014. On the other hand, the labour force participation rate for non-locals is very high, almost no change, at 86.73 per cent in 2014 and 86.07 per cent in 2019. In other words, the decline in the overall labour force participation rate is partly because of the decline in the rate among the locals. The non-locals have a greater necessity to work than the locals and have less ability to choose whether to work or not.

The working-age population who are not in the labour force are called the "Outside Labour Force", consisting of population who are neither working nor looking for jobs. There were 131,892 persons (35.66 per cent) of the working-age population who were outside the labour force in 2019. The outside labour force consists of youth who are in school, the female population who take care of the household and family, older persons who retire and do not work for money/in

TABLE 12.1
Labour Force and Unemployment

	Labour Force and Unemployment					
	2014			2019		
	Male	Female	Total	Male	Female	Total
Labour Force Participation Rate	72.44	58.32	65.59	72.48	54.83	64.34
	Local	Non Local	Total	Local	Non Local	Total
	60.44	86.73	65.59	57.71	86.07	64.34
Unemployment Rate	Male	Female	Total	Male	Female	Total
	6.22	7.82	6.91	5.92	8.22	6.82
By Age						
15-24	23.51	27.80	25.28	18.86	25.74	21.30
25-64	3.54	4.96	4.16	3.95	6.04	4.79
65 and +	0.72	1.21	0.88	0	0	0
By education						
Primary and below	3.77	4.56	4.16	3.97	5.70	4.47
Secondary	7.07	9.76	8.17	6.07	9.10	7.19
Technical/ Vocational	6.34	6.59	6.44	7.91	6.73	7.45
Tertiary	4.59	5.67	5.11	5.14	8.24	6.67
	Local	Non Local	Total	Local	Non Local	Total
	8.98	0.98	6.91	9.83	0.21	6.82
By Age						
15-24	29.90	1.61	25.28	29.15	0	21.30
25-64	5.39	0.93	4.16	6.97	0.24	4.79
65 and +	0.93	0	0.88	0	0	0
By education						
Primary and below	7.37	0.78	4.16	10.71	0	4.48
Secondary	10.36	0.52	8.17	10.53	0.39	7.19
Technical/ Vocational	7.82	1.10	6.44	9.40	0	7.45
Tertiary	6.20	2.27	5.11	8.54	0	6.66

kind, and those whose health and skill do not permit them to join the labour market. They may have been supported by the state and/ or communities/families.

However, among those outside the labour force, 12,472 persons (9.46 per cent) are actually "potential labour force"—they may be looking for jobs but are not available currently; or they may be currently able to work but are not currently looking for jobs. They will work if suitable jobs are available.

UNEMPLOYMENT

The labour force consists of those who are working and those who are unemployed. People are said to be working if they have been working one week before the interview. The unemployed are those who are not working but are currently available to work and looking for jobs. It should be noted that the statistics on employment do not include those who work for their own consumption, such as in their own family farms.

There were 221,711 persons (93.18 per cent) of the labour force who were employed and 16,234 persons (6.82 per cent) not employed in 2019. The unemployment rate in 2019 is a slight decline from 6.91 per cent in 2014. The decline in unemployment rate indicates a lower reservation wage in 2019 than in 2014 and/or there have been better employment opportunities in 2019. There are at least four possible statistical contributions to the decline in overall unemployment rate: from male, non-locals, secondary education, and youth (aged 15–24).

Table 12.1 shows the decline in male unemployment rate during 2014–19. On the other hand, female unemployment rate rose from 7.82 per cent in 2014 to 8.22 per cent in 2019. The rise of female unemployment rate is consistent with the declining female labour force participation rate.[3] The table also indicates the declining unemployment rate among non-locals. The very low unemployment rate among non-locals may indicate that they cannot afford to be unemployed and they have to work at whatever the wages. The local unemployment rate rose from 8.98 per cent in 2014 to 9.83 per cent in 2019.

As seen from educational attainment, the highest unemployment rate is among the labour force with technical and vocational education (7.45 per cent), followed by those with secondary education (7.19 per cent), and tertiary education (6.66 per cent). The lowest rate is among those with primary education or below (4.48 per cent). The pattern is different from 2014, when the highest rate was among secondary education (8.17 per cent), followed by technical and vocational education. The third and fourth (lowest) are the same as in 2014. However, over time, during 2014–19, the unemployment rate rose in each educational level, except among those with secondary education. In other words, secondary education contributes to the decline in overall decline in unemployment rate.

The lowest unemployment rates are always found among those with the lowest educational level, primary education and below. This group may also have the lowest socio-economic status, having high necessity to work, and therefore lowering the reservation wage and raising the probability to work. The highest unemployment rate among those with technical and vocation education in 2019 may indicate that technical and vocational education did not necessarily provide better employment prospects. Perhaps, there is a smaller demand for their qualification and/or the wage is under their expectation. The decline in oil prices may have resulted in smaller demand for people with these skills.[4]

Moreover, unemployment rate varies by age. Table 12.1 shows that in 2019, the highest unemployment rate (21.30 per cent) was among the youth (aged 15–24), much higher than 4.79 per cent among the labour force aged 25–64. Nevertheless, the unemployment rate of the youth declined a lot from 25.28 per cent in 2014, and this decline has partly contributed to the overall decline in unemployment rate. Alternatively, the rise of the rate among aged 25–64 could have slowed the decline.

Though very small, the older persons (aged 65 and over) also contribute to the overall decline in unemployment rate. In 2019, there was no unemployment among older persons (65 years and over), which indicates that the older persons may be still working or they do not want to work at prevailing market wages and therefore go to the outside labour force. If they work, it is not clear whether they work for economic necessities or just for fun. This is different from 2014, when some older persons were unemployed, though the unemployment rate was only 0.88 per cent.

While declining, the high level of youth unemployment is the first pressing issue in the Brunei labour market, as it may breed social problems if there is an insufficient number of jobs to maintain current living standards. The reasons for youth unemployment could be varied. The youth may have high reservation wages. They may not take just any job that comes along and are willing to wait until the expected jobs are offered; this means there is no sense of urgency. There can be a mismatch between the occupational aspirations of the youths and the expectations of the employers. Siti Fatimahwati and Siti Rozaidah (2020) concluded that the majority of young people in Brunei aspire towards prestigious jobs with high income and job security such as in the public sector, and there seems to be a lack of risk-taking and entrepreneurship spirit among the youths. They seek jobs in professional, managerial or technical sectors, and they have less preference for manual jobs.

Conversely, from the employers' perspective, the youth lack problem-solving and practical skills, self-awareness and the passion towards improving their leadership capacity (Siti Fatimahwati and Siti Rozaidah 2020). Self-awareness involves an understanding of one's strengths, weaknesses and limitations of how they gather and process information, of how they handle uncertain and stressful situations, and of how they are perceived by and interact with others.

A majority of employers identify the lack of drive and awareness of the importance of leadership from an early age as an inhibiting factor for employability. The perception among some companies towards local jobseekers is that the youth are not sufficiently prepared and are riddled with issues such as quitting without notice, absenteeism and other disciplinary problems. They further add that the least employable youth are risk-averse and lack entrepreneurial spirit.

This is a characteristic of social and cultural norms in a rentier state. The youth seem to be able to afford being unemployed, waiting for the expected jobs. This behaviour reflects a high reservation wage and the lack of urgency to work. This attitude may be attributed to three things. First, they still have parents who can support their daily needs. Second, they may not have any family obligations as they are still young and unmarried. Third, they may perceive that the state will help them. Nevertheless, the drop in youth unemployment rate could indicate the declining support to be unemployed. Perhaps, as discussed later, this decline is related to the decrease in monthly income of individuals (and therefore family/relatives and friends) during 2014–19.

The issue of preferring safe government jobs was already highlighted by the Monarch, recognizing that the job market was already saturated and that there was a need to inculcate a culture of independence and entrepreneurship among the youth: "Whether seeking employment in the private sector, or setting up businesses such as farming or fishing, if it is done with patience and perseverance the blessings will be great" (Rasidah 2018). His Majesty also urged the youth to be more open to working in the private sector, which will be the main driver of economic growth.

That said, the declining percentage of locals working in public sectors, discussed later in this chapter, could provide some hope. Furthermore, some personal observations revealed more promising signs of rising entrepreneurship, though at small scales, such as small-scale online sellers and pop-up retails appearing once a month or whenever there is an event.

EMPLOYMENT

Non-locals

The presence of non-locals is the second pressing issue of the labour market in Brunei. This level of dependence on non-locals has become controversial as the government seeks to nationalize its employment to reduce unemployment among the locals.

In many countries where non-locals are needed for the labour market, non-locals experience a dilemma. On the one hand, they promote economic growth in the regions of destinations. On the other hand, their presence may create unhappiness among the locals in the regions of destinations. Siddiqui et al. (2012) showed that this dilemma is typical in rentier economies whereby the locals do not constitute large percentages of total employed persons, resulting in non-local dependency.

Brunei is not an exception. In 2019, the non-locals constituted 33.5 per cent of total employed persons in Brunei. The non-local dependency does not vary by age. It was 34.21 per cent among the youth (15–24) and 33.96 per cent among those aged 25–64.

However, this dependency varies by characteristics of the employed persons and where they work. Seen from the educational attainment viewpoint, non-locals formed 60.90 per cent of employed persons with education at primary school or below, followed by those who had attained secondary level education (35.28 per cent). Furthermore, there is a contrast in the dependency among private and public sectors. Almost half (49.31 per cent) of the employed persons in private sectors were non-locals. Conversely, non-locals only formed 2.49 per cent of the employed persons in public sectors.

The high dependency on non-locals is especially observed in three sectors. The first, almost all (99.58 per cent) of those working in "activities of households as employers of domestic personnel" were non-locals. The second and third highest were found in construction (78.13 per cent), accommodation and food services activities (66.17 per cent). This indicates a labour market structure that requires non-locals to shoulder the bulk of low-paid manual work (Asato 2019). Remittances make up a large proportion of the migrants' spending. If this money could be spent in the local economy, it would generate economic growth and business. However, sending remittances back home may have been the primary motivation of non-locals to come to Brunei.

The locals, on the other hand, mostly worked in service and sales (23.36 per cent), or as professionals (22.34 per cent), and technicians and associate professionals (14.89 per cent). These occupations contributed to 60.59 per cent of all local employed persons. In contrast, the non-locals worked mostly in elementary occupation (34.14 per cent), craft and related trade (21.85 per cent), and service and sales (14.02 per cent). They constituted 70.01 per cent of all non-local employed persons in 2019.

The above pattern is the same as that in 2014. However, among the locals, there has been an increase in the percentages of service and sales, and professionals, but a decrease in technicians and associate professionals. The overall contribution of these three occupations rose from 58.62 per cent in 2014. Among the non-locals, there has been an increase in the percentages of those working in elementary occupation and craft and related trade, but a decline in service and sales. The total contribution of the three occupations rose from 66.58 per cent in 2014. Therefore, compared to the pattern in 2014, there may have been less intense competition among locals and non-locals, as their segmentation of occupation became sharper.

To reduce the reliance on non-locals, policies have been implemented to prioritize the locals by re-examining immigration policies. This includes replacing non-locals for positions at PMETs (professional, managerial, executive and technical) by license screening the non-locals as well as building capacity for PMETs among the locals (Rasidah 2018). Another policy introduced in 2018 is the Local and Foreign Workforce Ratio, which imposes limits on the number of foreign workers employed and prioritizes Bruneian jobseekers to fill vacancies in eight industries namely Construction, Retail and Wholesale, Education, Transportation and Storage, Accommodation and Food Services, Manufacturing, Professional, Scientific and Technical Services, and Administration (Wasil 2019).

The Annual Census of Enterprises 2019 showed Brunei's private sector hired more locals than foreign workers for the first time in years whereby there was a 2.2 per cent decrease in foreign workers joining the private sector in 2018. The census also found that the number of Bruneians joining the private sector grew 5.6 per cent whereas the number of businesses grew by 1.3 per cent (Han 2020).

However, the main question is why Bruneians have not been willing to take over the jobs done by the non-locals. The number/percentage of non-locals may simply be a symptom and therefore rigid immigration policies may not be sufficient (Pennington 2017).

One of the ways to tackle this is through reskilling and ensuring that the skills acquired in schools are relevant to the needs of the economy. One particular initiative is the Training and Employment Scheme (*Skim Latihan Perkhidmatan*, SLP) introduced in 2011 by the Local Employment and Workforce Development Agency (*Agensi Pekerjaan Tempatan dan Pembangunan Tenaga Kerja*, APTK), Ministry of Home Affairs (MoHA) (UNESCO 2015). The scheme conducts short courses such as book-keeping, motivation, English language proficiency and customer service for job-seekers to upgrade their skills for better employment prospects. It provides locals with suitable job skills and experiences to make them more employable and interested to work for the private sector. Furthermore, it aims for employers to be less reliant on foreign workers.

Employment Status

There are four employment statuses in the statistics of the Department of Economic Planning and Statistics: employers, employees, own-account workers, and contributing family members. In 2019, most employed persons worked as employees (90.7 per cent), with a higher percentage among males (92.2 per cent) than females (89.2 per cent). The high percentage of persons working as employees partly reflects the fact that the non-locals worked mostly (96.6 per cent) as employees. The percentage among locals is only 88.2 per cent. These percentages did not change much during 2014–19, though there was a slight decrease in the percentage of employees among the locals.

There has been a decrease in the percentage of people working as employers[5] among both locals and non-locals. On the other hand, there has been an increase among those working as "own-account workers" and "contributing family members". It should be noted that "contributing family members" constitutes a tiny percentage of both locals and non-locals.

Among the locals, the second highest percentage in 2019 was "own-account workers", followed by "employers". During 2014–19, the percentage of "own-account workers" rose from 5.3 per cent to 7.7 per cent while "contributing family members" increased from a tiny 0.71 per cent to 1.1 per cent. Conversely, there has been a decline in the percentage of those working as employers, from 4.1 per cent in 2014 to 3.0 per cent in 2019. There may have been a shift from "employees" and "employers" to "own-account workers" and "contributing family members" among the locals.

In 2019, the majority (66.2 per cent) of the employed persons—half (50.5 per cent) of the local employed persons and almost all (97.5 per cent) of the non-local employed persons—worked in the private sector. This was an increase from 53.21 per cent in 2014. Moreover, the percentage of males working in the private sector was higher than that of females. In contrast, the percentage of people working in the public sector declined from 46.79 per cent in 2014 to 33.8 per cent in 2019. The percentage of locals alone working in the public sector declined from 60.7 per cent in 2014 to 49.5 per cent in 2019. This trend signals a positive trend in economic diversification by reducing the over-reliance on the public sector for employment opportunities.

Employment status is also distinguished between informal/formal employment and informal/formal sector. In 2019, about 41.7 per cent (or 92,559 persons) of total (221,711) employed persons worked under informal employment. An informal employment is one when the person working does not have social security coverage, paid sick leave and paid annual leave. Furthermore, most of these persons work in informal sectors.

In Brunei, the concept of informal sector refers to the production unit, not to jobs as in informal employment. The informal sectors consist of all unregistered private business enterprises with no records of accounts, domestic workers in the households, and other activities such as small businesses from home (Department of Economic Planning and Statistics 2020a). In 2019, there were 17,900 persons, constituting 8.1 per cent of all employed persons, who worked in informal sectors. The majority (53.2 per cent) of the informal sectors deal with households that hire domestic workers. The other informal sectors may deal with home activities such as selling traditional foods.

Hours Worked and Monthly Income

Some employed persons do not work full-time. Some work part-time (less than 40 hours in a week) while others still want to have more work. The Department of Economic Planning and Statistics (2020b) called these persons "in time-related underemployment". Along with the number of potential labour force[6] and the number of unemployed persons, the number of persons with time-related employment can be seen as part of the "labour under-utilization".

In 2019, there were 16,955 persons with time-related underemployment, 7.32 per cent of the total employment. That means that 7.32 per cent is a potential to increase in total production of the economy, assuming they have the necessary human capital.[7] Therefore, there are 45,661 under-utilized persons, where the unemployed constitute 35.55 per cent; time-related underemployment 37.13 per cent; and potential labour force 27.31 per cent. The labour under-utilization rate is the percentage of labour under-utilization with respect to the sum of labour force and potential labour force. It was 18.2 per cent in 2019, much higher than the unemployment rate. This rate indicates the extent of mismatch between what the economy wants to hire and what the labour wants to work at the prevailing wage.

Moreover, almost all employed persons work only in their main jobs. In 2019, they spent on average 47.2 hours a week, consisting of 46.8 hours weekly in their main jobs and only 0.3 hour in the secondary jobs. Females worked less than males in main jobs. However, on average, either male or female employed person worked longer than

40 hours a week, the threshold of full employment. This may denote the over-utilization of labour.

The employed persons worked longer than the threshold and earned on average B$1,626 monthly. The male earned more (B$1,743) than the female (B$1,440). Though they only spent little time in their secondary jobs, they earned proportionally higher income from the secondary jobs. The male spent only 0.3 hours a week, but they earned B$724 a month, 41.85 per cent of the income from their main jobs. Likewise, the female only spent 0.4 hours, but they received B$375 a month, 26.22 per cent of their main job income. The male workers contributed relatively more from the secondary jobs. This may be due to very high productivity in the secondary jobs or they may use the time during their main jobs to do things related to their secondary jobs. Further studies need to be done on this issue.

However, the relatively high number of hours employed per week (over-utilization of labour) partly reflects the very high number of hours spent working by non-locals. The non-locals spent more time working (55.8 hours a week), much higher than 42.4 hours a week among the locals. The locals spent 0.5 hour a week in secondary jobs. On the other hand, non-locals did not do any secondary job. On average, the locals earned more (B$1,812) than the non-locals (B$1,261).

Furthermore, over time, during 2014–19, the monthly income has been declining among all employed persons regardless of the residential status and districts. The monthly income of locals declined by 10.5 per cent from B$2,003 in 2014 to B$1,793 in 2019; with the decline in male income only 6.8 per cent, but in female income 15.19 per cent. In other words, the decline in monthly income of the locals is contributed more by the decline in female income.

The decline in income among non-locals was 7.69 per cent. It was 13.92 per cent among males and 7.27 per cent among females. In this case, the males have contributed more to the monthly income decline.

A huge decline in monthly income was observed in Temburong (38.02 per cent), declining from B$1,252 in 2014 to only B$776 in 2019. The smallest decline (7.28 per cent) was in Belait, followed by Tutong (10.95 per cent), and Brunei-Muara (12.31 per cent) (Department of Economic Planning and Statistics n.d.).

In other words, the overall decline in monthly income was contributed more by the decline in monthly income among three groups of population: female locals, male non-locals, and persons in Temburong.[8]

CONCLUSION AND POLICY RECOMMENDATIONS

Diversification

In a small domestic economy, the impact of economic diversification may be more on export than employment (Alsharif, Bhattacharya and Intartaglia 2017). In Brunei, economic diversification can also be seen in the contribution of public sector in total employment, as the public sector is mostly funded by oil and gas revenue. This chapter has shown that there has been a shift toward employment in the private sector. However, more incentives to work in private sectors are still needed to accelerate the diversification from heavy reliance on public sector employment.

> The civil service needs a change of mindset to be able to give quality services that satisfy all sectors of the society. The private sector on the other hand, as an engine of growth, needs to focus its attention on the economic agenda of the country particularly its economic diversification programme. (Prime Minister's Office 2015, p. 8)

Youth Unemployment

The reservation wage of the youth may be relatively high because of expectations to have high-earning and prestigious jobs. This high aspiration of the youth and/or their family/society may not match the employers' expectations at the prevailing wage. It is also possible that there are no available jobs, whatever the jobs are. The youth can afford being unemployed because they may still obtain financial support from families, communities, or the state, as well as still being single and young. Therefore, programmes such as TEKAD (*Teguhkan Ekonomi Keluarga Asas berDikari*), which provides skills to welfare recipients, need to be promoted more intensively. Assistance is given only when people are employed, regardless of the earnings from the jobs, to avoid a dependency attitude.

Furthermore, young people need to be exposed to the causal link between work and reward through performance so that they have realistic expectations.[9] Monetary rewards and privileges need to be more closely aligned to work performance across all sectors. This would reduce expectations of high incomes and prestigious jobs, and increase the appreciation of earned hard work for the development of their career (Siti Fatimahwati and Khairul Hidayatullah 2019).

To rectify this issue, higher learning institutions in Brunei have introduced internship programmes in different workplaces as part of the curriculum in schools and universities. This can expose young people to a variety of work experiences and create awareness about the diversity and nature of work involved. This also broadens their choices of occupations and instead of being limited to public sector jobs. There are also more innovative courses involving experiential learning introduced in higher institutions, for example, entrepreneurship and creative arts modules.

Non-locals

The locals may not be able to do jobs the non-locals do or the locals may not be able to compete with the non-locals.[10] There can be two programmes to reduce over-reliance on non-locals. First, is to raise the human capital (health, skill including up-skilling and re-skilling, and ability to move) and attitude of the locals toward employability. Second, is to introduce more mechanization and use of digital technology, including robotization. However, policies are also needed to minimize the negative impact of these two programmes on the cost of living because of rising wages and production costs.

The above programmes should be accompanied by inviting more labour-intensive foreign direct investment (FDI) and domestic investment. Tax subsidy can be provided for such investments. Investment in the newly connected Temburong district can be prioritized to those with labour-intensive projects, enriched with information and communications technology (ICT). Furthermore, small-scale retail entrepreneurship, such as the emergence of pop-up retails and small-scale online businesses, should be promoted. The opening of the new Temburong bridge has witnessed the emergence of these small-scale retails. The government can help to promote these small businesses with the use of digital technology.

Older Persons

The topic of older persons has not been much discussed in terms of older persons' possible contribution to the economy. Brunei's statistics on working-age population does not have any upper limit on age. Everybody aged 15 years old and over can work if they are able and want to. As people live longer, there is a need to consider policies to promote older persons' intensive employment opportunities. The digital technology can be introduced to the older persons so that physical limitation does not restrict them from being employed.

Issues on older persons' employment are not only relevant to the current older persons. It is much more relevant for the future older persons, who are the current younger generation. Life-course approach, including life-long education, should be introduced to the younger generation so that they can be employable and enjoy a healthy and with happy life in their old ages.

NOTES

1. Calculated from the Department of Economic Planning and Statistics (2020b).
2. See Chapter 7 in this book for a discussion on declining fertility and rising life expectancy in Brunei.
3. Further studies need to be done on this issue as the female population has relatively high education.
4. See more discussions on technical and vocational education in Chapter 8 of this book.
5. Employer (*majikan* in Brunei Malay) is not necessarily a professional manager. As long as the person has at least one employee working continuously with them, he/she is an employer.
6. See discussion under the section "Working-Age Population" in this chapter.
7. It should be mentioned here that part-time work is uncommon in the public sector.
8. It is beyond the scope of this chapter to find the determinants of the change in income.
9. It should be noted that Brunei's public sector employment has not been truly based on KPIs (performance-based) yet.
10. Further studies should be conducted to explain this result.

REFERENCES

Abdul Latif bin Haji Ibrahim. 1996. "Cultural and Counter-cultural Forces in Contemporary Brunei Darussalam". In *Cultures in ASEAN and the 21st Century*, edited by Edwin Thumboo. Singapore: University of Singapore Press.

Alsharif, Nouf, Sambit Bhattacharya, and Maurisio Intartaglia. 2017. "Economic Diversification in Resource Rich Countries: History, State of the Knowledge and Research Agenda". *Resource Policy* 52: 154–64.

Asato, Wako. 2019. "Brunei Darussalam: Female Labour Force Participation and Foreign Domestic Workers". In *International Labour Migration in the Middle*

East and Asia. Issues of Inclusion and Exclusion, edited by Lian Kwen Lee, Naomi Hosoda, and Masako Ishii, pp. 115–41. Singapore: Springer.

Asiyah az-Zahra Ahmad Kumpoh, Siti Norkhalbi Haji Wahsalfelah, and Noor Azam Hj-Othman. 2017. "Socio-Cultural Dynamics in Bruneian Society". In *Comparative Studies in ASEAN Cultures and Societies,* edited by ASEAN and Asia Studies Centre, pp. 1–44. Bangkok: Semadhma Publishing House.

Beblawi, Hazem. 1987. "The Rentier State in the Arab World". In *The Rentier State,* edited by Hazem Beblawi, and Giacomo Luciani, pp. 49–62. London: Croom Helm.

Benli, Altunisik Meliha. 2014. "Rentier State Theory and the Arab Uprisings: An Appraisal". *International Relations* 11, no. 42: 75–91.

Black, Ann. 2001. "Alternative Dispute Resolution in Brunei Darussalam: The Blending of Imported and Traditional Processes". *Bond Law Review* 13, no. 2: 1–6.

Blomqvist, Hans. 1998. "The Endogenous State of Brunei Darussalam: The Traditional Society Versus Economic Development". *The Pacific Review* 11, no. 4: 541–59.

Department of Economic Planning and Statistics. 2020a. *Brunei Darussalam Key Economic Developments. Quarter 2 2020.* http://www.deps.gov.bn/DEPD%20Documents%20Library/NDP/Planning/BKED_DevQ2_2020.pdf (accessed 14 December 2020).

———. 2020b. *Report of the Labour Force Survey 2019.* Brunei Darussalam: Department of Statistics, Department of Economic Planning and Statistics, Ministry of Finance and Economy.

———. N.d. "Wages and Compensation Costs". https://deps.mofe.gov.bn/SitePages/Wages%20and%20compensation%20costs.aspx. Brunei Darussalam: Department of Economic Planning and Statistics, Ministry of Finance and Economy.

Han, Shareen. 2020. "Bruneians Outnumber Foreign Workers in Private Sector, Enterprise Census Shows". *The Scoop,* 7 December 2020. https://thescoop.co/2020/12/07/bruneians-outnumber-foreign-workers-in-private-sector-enterprise-census-shows/ (accessed 14 December 2020).

Hassan, Noor Hasharina. 2017. "Housing Matters: The Value of Home Ownership in Brunei Darussalam". *Working Paper,* no. 36. Brunei: Institute of Asian Studies, Universiti Brunei Darussalam.

Mahdavy, Hossein. 1970. "Patterns and Problems of Economic Development in Rentier States: The Case of Iran". In *Studies in Economic History of the Middle East from the Rise of Islam to the Present Day,* edited by M.A. Cook, pp. 428–67. Oxford: Oxford University.

Ministry of Finance and Economy. 2020. *United Nations High Level Political Forum on Sustainable Development Voluntary National Review Report of*

Brunei Darussalam. https://sustainabledevelopment.un.org/content/
documents/26410VNR_2020_Brunei_Report.pdf (accessed 22 December 2020).
———. 2021. *Towards a Dynamic and Sustainable Economy: Economic Blueprint for Brunei Darussalam.* Bandar Seri Begawan: Ministry of Finance and Economy.
Pennington, John. 2017. "Life after Foreign Labour: Why Brunei Needs to Get to Work". *ASEAN Today,* 4 April 2017. https://www.aseantoday.com/2017/04/life-after-foreign-labour-why-brunei-needs-to-get-to-work/ (accessed 14 December 2020).
Prime Minister's Office. 2015. *Brunei Darussalam Millennium Development Goals and Beyond. Towards the Post-2015 Development Agenda.* Bandar Seri Begawan: Department of Economics Planning and Development, Prime Minister's Office, Government of Brunei Darussalam.
Rasidah Hj Abu Bakar. 2018. "HM Urges Jobseekers to Start Businesses, Be Open to Private Sector Jobs". *The Scoop,* 5 July 2018. https://thescoop.co/2018/07/05/hm-reiterated-jobseekers-seek-employment-privatesector-engage-entrepreneurship (accessed 14 December 2020).
Sainah binti Haji Saim, Hajah. 2010. "Social Protection in Brunei Darussalam: Current State and Challenges". In *Social Protection in East Asia: Current State and Challenges,* edited by M.G.S. Asher, and F. Parulian, pp. 124–56. ERIA Research Project Report 2009-9. Jakarta: ERIA.
Siddiqui, Shamim Ahmad, Alaa Aldin Abdul Rahim Athmay, and Hamdan Mohammed. 2012. "Development and Growth through Economic Diversification: Are there Solutions for Continued Challenges Faced by Brunei Darussalam?" *Journal of Economics and Behavioural Studies* 4, no. 7: 397–413.
Siti Fatimahwati Pehin Dato Musa, and Khairul Hidayatullah Basir. 2019. "Youth Unemployment and the Rentier Economy in Brunei: Lessons from Norway". *Al Abqari Journal,* Special Issue 20, no. 2: 1–22.
Siti Fatimahwati Pehin Dato Musa, and Siti Rozaidah Idris, Dk. 2019. "Society for Community Outreach and Training (SCOT)'s Green Xchange Project". In *Green Behavior and Corporate Social Responsibility in Asia,* edited by Farzana Quoquab, and Jihad Mohammad, pp. 155–61. Bingley, UK: Emerald Publishing.
———. 2020. "Addressing Issues of Unemployment in Brunei: The Mismatch between Employers Expectations and Employees Aspirations". *International Journal of Asian Business and Information Management* 11, no. 2: 88–101.
United Nations Educational, Scientific and Cultural Organization (UNESCO). 2015. *Education for All 2015 National Review Report: Brunei Darussalam.* https://unesdoc.unesco.org/ark:/48223/pf0000230503 (accessed 22 December 2020).
Wasil, Wardi. 2019. "MoHA to Introduce New Limits on Number of Foreign Workers". *The Scoop,* 13 March 2019. https://thescoop.co/2019/03/13/moha-new-workforce-ratio-to-free-up-more-jobs-for-locals/ (accessed 22 December 2020).

INDEX

Page references followed by n indicate an endnote.

geographical population distribution,
163–68
GHG emissions. *See* greenhouse gas
(GHG) emissions
Global Islamic Economy Indicator
Score, 43
global warming, 103. *See also* climate
change
governance quality (GQ), 300n7
government, digital transformation
in, 141–43
government assistance, 307–10
Government Pension System (GPS),
308
GQ (governance quality), 300n7
green and blue economy, 53
green corridors, 62, 63
green lungs of urban ecosystems, 62
Green Protocol, 105
greenhouse gas (GHG) emissions
commitment to reducing, 85–87,
103–4, 113
and oil and gas production, 114
strategies for reducing, 117–21,
129–31
See also carbon emissions
greenfield FDI, 279, 288. *See also*
foreign direct investment (FDI)
greying population, 20, 181–82,
233–35
Guangxi Beibu Gulf Group, 40

H
halal industry, 43, 150, 257
Hassanal Bolkiah, 35–37, 53
haze, 65. *See also* environment
HDD (Housing Development
Department), 308
health, 29, 175–76, 179, 181, 186,
221–27, 235–39
Health Promotion Blueprint 2011–
2015, 236, 237

healthcare
digital transformation in, 143–44,
228, 235
ecosystems in, 18–19, 235–39
Heart of Borneo region (HoB), 63
heath forests, 57–58
Hengyi Industries, 40, 98–99, 127,
258, 275
Higher National Technical Education
Certificate (HNTec), 207
HoB (Heart of Borneo region), 63
housing, subsidized, 308
Housing Development Department
(HDD), 308
human-ecosystem dependency, 53–54
human resource development, 18,
201–4, 212, 214–17
hydrocarbons, 90, 98–102. *See also*
climate change; energy; fossil
fuels; oil and gas
hydropower production, 89, 91–92
hypertension, prevalence of, 225

I
I-Usahawan initiative, 258
IBTE (Institute of Brunei Technical
Education), 202, 203, 208, 209
iCentre, 257
ICT integration (Information and
Communication Technology
integration), 137, 140, 141–52,
263
IEA (International Energy Agency),
87–91
immunizations, 223–24
import concentration, 286–87
Important Bird Area, 57
IMR (Infant Mortality Rate), 223
inclusive learning. *See* lifelong
learning
income from employment, 322–23
independence of Brunei, 35–37